CHEVROLET PICKUP
PARTS INTERCHANGE MANUAL
1967–1978

Paul Herd

MBI Publishing Company

First published in 1999 by MBI Publishing Company, 729 Prospect Avenue, PO Box 1, Osceola, WI 54020-0001 USA

The information in this book is true and complete to the best of our knowledge. All recommendations are made without any guarantee on the part of the author or Publisher, who also disclaim any liability incurred in connection with the use of this data or specific details.

We recognize that some words, model names and designations, for example, mentioned herein are the property of the trademark holder. We use them for identification purposes only. This is not an official publication.

All drawings and illustrations in this book are the copyrighted property of General Motors Corporation and they are reproduced under license from General Motors Corporation.

MBI Publishing Company books are also available at discounts in bulk quantity for industrial or sales-promotional use. For details write to Special Sales Manager at Motorbooks International Wholesalers & Distributors, 729 Prospect Avenue, PO Box 1, Osceola, WI 54020-0001 USA.

Library of Congress Cataloging-in-Publication Data
Herd, Paul.
    Chevrolet pickup parts interchange manual, 1967–1978/
    Paul Herd.
      p. cm.
    Includes index.
    ISBN 0-7603-0680-X (pbk.: alk. paper)
    1. Chevrolet trucks—Parts Catalogs. 2. Pickup trucks—parts
Catalogs. I. Title.
TL230.5.C45H47   1999
629.2—dc21   99-39198

On the front cover: The clean lines of a classic 1970 model are readily apparent in this beauty belonging to Larry Bailey, of Cleveland, Georgia. *Mike Mueller*

On the back cover: Top: This fine example of a 1972 Cheyenne belongs to Rob Granger, of Eustis, Florida. *Mike Mueller*
Bottom: A typical 1967-70 speedometer as it appears when removed from the vehicle.

Designed by Bruce Leckie

Printed in the United States of America

Contents

Preface

Acknowledgments

Tough and dependable: Two words that easily describe the Chevrolet pickup. Chevrolet had been running a hard race against the Ford trucks and coming up in second place. With an all-new design that was introduced in 1967, Chevrolet raced to the head of the class. The all-new pickup was still just as tough and dependable as the earlier models, but now it had beauty. Its lines were smooth and sporty, and it offered something for everyone.

The basic truck was aimed at the buyer who wanted a "workhorse," while packages like the CST (Custom Sport Truck) and Cheyenne added grace and sports car–like equipment, such as bucket seats. When the 396-ci big-block was added between the frame rails, the truck had muscle.

In the mid-sixties the designers at the truck division presented another concept—a bobtail pickup, a concept that was quickly voted down. But designers added a four-wheel-drive chassis and removed the roof, replacing it with a removable fiberglass shell that extended over the bed, and the Blazer was born, adding a convertible truck to Chevy's line-up in 1969.

For 1973, the Chevrolet pickup lost it sporty lines, but it developed a no-nonsense attitude and look—a look that would last until more aerodynamic styling was introduced in 1988.

Today, no other truck has the status and collectibility that the Chevrolet has. It has grown from a workhorse to a classic. Whereas it used to sit next to a barn, with golden straws of hay being blown about in the bed, it now is gleaming with bright new paint and trim sitting next to Chevelles and Camaros at car shows. Yet for some of these great trucks there is no rest; decades later some are still on the road plugging away, working as hard as on the first day they came off the assembly line. For a truck, that is the greatest honor there is.

This book would have not been possible without the tireless efforts of Ed Witte, owner and operator of CST Truck Parts in Aurora, Missouri. Ed graciously pulled parts and cleaned them up so that they could be photographed for this book. He was an invaluable source on the 1967–1972 trucks. (CST Truck Parts can be contacted at: P.O. Box 294, Aurora, MO 65605, phone: (417) 678-6994 FAX: (417) 678-7305) Also a thanks to his wife, Kris, who put up with our late-night photo sessions. Thank you Dan Dryke and the GM Technology Department for allowing me to use the illustrations that are part of this guide. A special thank you to my church family at Emmanuel; it is with your love and help that I am able to grow in Christ daily. And to my cousin Becky and her family: Thanks for all the help each and every day. I dedicate this book to you.

—Paul Herd

Ed Witte, owner of CST Truck Parts, poses in front of an antique gas station that is part of the property at his business in Aurora, Missouri. He has a huge selection of reproduction, NOS, and used parts for 1967–1972 Chevrolet pickup trucks. He can be reached by phone at 417-678-6994.

Introduction

Chevy pickups were made in 1/2-, 3/4-, and 1-ton models, but you would be surprised by the number of parts that will interchange between these trucks and with other Chevrolet cars. In fact, money can be saved by using a part from an Impala instead of the one from a pickup, even though they are the same exact part.

Even those special pickup parts can be found on more than one model year. Thus, it opens a wider range for parts. You will find most 1967–1972 parts will interchange with each other, as will the 1973–1978 parts.

This is the purpose of this book, to cross-reference all matching part numbers for the 1967–1978 Chevrolet pickup and Blazer models. You may be surprised by how many parts your truck shares with other Chevrolets and other GM models.

Part numbers used in this book were drawn from original part books. Sometimes as parts got older they were grouped together under one part number. This may not necessarily be the correct part number that was installed on the car originally but will have the same look and fit as the original unit. Whenever possible, only original part numbers are used as the interchange basis for this guide.

How to Use This Guide

This book is divided into 11 sections, each of which is further divided into individual subdivisions that make up the entire section. For example, chapter 1 is divided by components such as cylinder block, short block, crankshaft, connecting rods, and so on.

At the beginning of each of these subdivisions is an interchange listing of the models, along with other necessary data to allow you to find the part you're looking for. It will look similar to this:

Hood
Model Identification
1971	Interchange Number
Blazer	1
C-10	5
C-20	5
C-30	5

By finding your model year and model in the chart, you will be able to find the interchange number that will list the models and model years that the particular part can be found on. Then, trace through the interchange to find the interchange number you are looking for. The interchange is listed in numerical order. For example, if you were looking for a hood for your 1971 C-10 pickup you would look for Interchange Number 5, where you will find a section like this:

Interchanges
Interchange Number: 5
Part Number(s): 3990702
Usage: 1970–1972 C-10, C-20, and C-30 Chevrolet; 1500 to 3500 GMC truck; Blazer and Jimmy

Part numbers—if listed—are either the original or original replacement part numbers. Usage lists the models and model years that this part was used on. Note(s) lists things to watch for during your interchange, such as body style or options restrictions. It may also list modifications that can be done to make other parts fit or give you a cross-reference to another interchange that will also fit.

Decoding VIN Data Tags
1967–1969

A combination gross vehicle weight (GVW) and vehicle identification number (VIN) tag was fitted to all 1967–1969 Chevrolet trucks. It is attached to the upper driver's-side door pillar of all cab-style models. Stamped into the stainless plate will be the words Maximum GVW Rating. Below this will be a number that signifies the GVW. Below the GVW rating is the VIN.

It will begin with a single letter that indicates the chassis type. The letter C indicates two-wheel-drive models and the letter K is placed on four-wheel-drive models. The second letter in the VIN represents the engine type but not engine size. Two codes were used for the models listed in this guide: S is for six-cylinders and E is for V-8 gasoline engines. Following this letter is a single-digit code that indicates the GVW range: 1 is for 3,900–5,800 pounds, 2 is for 5,200–7,500 pounds, and 3

Shown is a 1968 Maximum GVW and vehicle identification plate from a C-20 model.

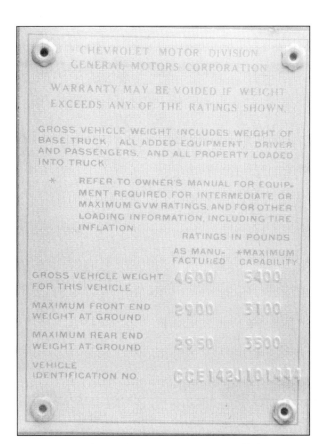

This vehicle identification number plate was changed in 1971 and is typical for 1972 models.

is for 6,600–14,000 pounds. Next is a single digit for model code: 4 is for pickup, 5 is for panel, 3 is for cab, 9 is for stake, and 6 is for carry all (Suburban). Following this code is a last digit of the model year (7 for 1967, 8 for 1968, or 9 for 1969). Next is a letter code that indicates the factory at which the truck was built, which has little effect on the interchange. This is followed by the vehicle number; each year's production begins with 100001.

1970–1972

A combination GVW and VIN tag was fitted to all 1970–1972 Chevrolet trucks. It is attached to the lower driver's-side door jamb. It is larger than the previous style used in earlier models. It breaks the gross weight down by front and rear of the truck; however, the only real importance is the block marked "Vehicle Identification Number." First letter in the VIN is the letter C, which stands for Chevrolet Division. The following code breaks down the same as the 1967–1969 method above, except the model year codes are 0 for 1970, 1 for 1971, or 2 for 1972.

1973–1978

The plate was again restyled for 1973 models and the tag was placed sideways on the lower driver's door jamb. The VIN number is positioned in the center of the plate. More information was coded into the 1973–1978

VIN than in previous years. The first letter is the letter C, which represents the Chevrolet line. The second is either the letter C, for two-wheel drive, or the letter K, for four-wheel drive.

The third letter in the VIN represents the original engine; see charts for codes.

Next is a single digit that depicts the series: 1 for C-10, 2 for C-20, or 3 for C-30. Following this is a single digit that denotes the body style: 3 for chassis/cab, 4 for pickup, 6 for Suburban, or 8 for Blazer. In the sixth position of the VIN is the last digit of the model year (3 for 1973, 4 for 1974, 5 for 1975, 6 for 1976, 7 for 1977, or 8 for 1978). Next is a letter code for the assembly plant. The last digits are the serial number, and all models in these years begin each year's production at 100000, except some Flint-built four-wheel drives begin at 300000.

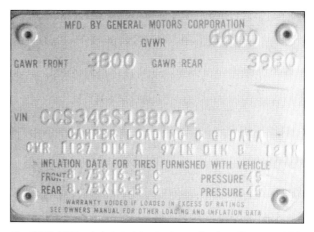

The 1975–1978 style included the tire size on the plate. Shown is a 1976 model with 16 1/2-inch wheels.

1973–1978 VIN Engine Codes

Engine Size	VIN Code	Years Used
250-ci six-cylinder	Q	1973–1975
292-ci six-cylinder	T	1973–1978
307-ci V-8	X	1973–1975
305-ci V-8	Q	1976
305-ci V-8	U	1977–1978
350-ci, two-barrel V-8	V	1973–1976
350-ci, four-barrel V-8	Y	1973–1975
350-ci, four-barrel V-8	L	1976–1978
400-ci V-8	M	1973–1975
400-ci V-8	U	1976
400-ci V-8	R	1977–1978
454-ci V-8 C-10 ton	Z	1973–1975
454-ci V-8 C-20 or C-3	L	1973–1975
454-ci V-8 C-20 ton	S	1976
454-ci V-8 C-20 or C-30 ton	Y	1976
454-ci V-8 C-10, C-20, C30	S	1977–1978

1 Engines

As explained in the introductory pages of this guide, this chapter is divided into sections of parts that make up the engine as a whole. As a complete unit, engines are pretty much interchangeable. You will also find that powerplants from automobiles can fit your truck, including big-blocks. For example, your 1972 pickup came with a 350-ci V-8: It is possible that a 454-ci big-block can be fitted in to your pickup. Note that items such as motor mounts, radiator, and in some cases even the suspension may have to be changed to accommodate a complete engine swap. Note that swapping larger engines into a van is not as simple as swapping the same unit into a pickup. This is due to the limited space the van's design allows for the engine compartment.

Cylinder Blocks

Cylinder blocks are identified by their casting number. On small-blocks, this number is located at the back of the block on the passenger's side of the flywheel flange. On big-blocks it is located on a boss near the top of the bell housing on the driver's side. (Note this interchange is limited to the bare block only. Short-blocks can use the same block on a low-powered truck engine and on a special high-performance car, like the Camaro.)

Model Identification

1967	Interchange Number
283-ci V-8	2
327-ci V-8	1
1968	
307-ci V-8	3
327-ci V-8	4
396-ci V-8	5
1969	
307-ci V-8	3
350-ci V-8	6
396-ci V-8	5
1970	
307-ci V-8	9
350-ci V-8	6
396-ci V-8	13
1971	
307-ci V-8	9
350-ci V-8	7
402-ci V-8	8

1972	
307-ci V-8	9
350-ci V-8	7
402-ci V-8	8
1973	
307-ci V-8	
C-10	14
C-20, except Suburban	9
C-20, Suburban	14
350-ci V-8	
C-10	11
C-20, except Suburban	7
C-20, Suburban	11
C-30	7
454-ci V-8	10
1974–1978	
350-ci V-8	
C-10, with EGR	11
C-10, without EGR	7
C-20, except Suburban	7
C-20, Suburban	11
C-20, without EGR	7
C-30	7
454-ci V-8	12

Interchanges

Interchange Number: 1
Casting Number(s): 3892657, 3782870, or 3858174
Usage: 1964–1967 Chevrolet C-10 to C-30 with 327-ci V-8; 1964–1967 Chevelle and full-size Chevrolet with 327-ci V-8; 1967 Camaro with 327-ci V-8
Note(s): Small journal

Interchange Number: 2
Casting Number(s): 3849852 or 3896948
Usage: 1958–1967 Chevrolet C-10 to C-30 with 283-ci V-8; 1964–1967 Chevelle and full-size Chevrolet with 283-ci V-8; 1964–1967 GMC pickup with 283-ci V-8

Interchange Number: 3
Casting Number(s): 3932371 or 3941174
Usage: 1968–1969 Chevrolet C-10 to C-30 with 307-ci V-8; 1969 Blazer with 307-ci V-8; 1968–1969 Chevelle, full-size Chevrolet, and Nova with 307-ci V-8; 1968–1969 GMC pickup with 307-ci V-8

The casting number for a big block is found at the rear of the block on the left-hand side.

Interchange Number: 4

Usage: 1968 Chevrolet C-10 to C-30 with 327-ci V-8; 1968 GMC pickup with 327-ci V-8

Interchange Number: 5

Usage: 1968–1969 Chevrolet C-10 to C-30 with 396-ci V-8; early-1969 Camaro, Chevelle, Impala, and Nova with 396-ci V-8 (except 375-horsepower versions)

Interchange Number: 6

Usage: 1969–1970 Chevrolet C-10 to C-30 with 350-ci V-8; 1969–1970 Blazer with 350-ci V-8; 1970 GMC Jimmy with 350-ci V-8; 1968–1969 Camaro, Chevelle, Impala, and Corvette with 350-ci V-8 (except LT-1 and Z-28 models); 1969 to early-1971 Chevrolet and GMC van

Interchange Number: 7

Usage: 1971–1972 Chevrolet C-10 to C-30 with 350-ci V-8; 1971–1972 Camaro, Chevelle, Impala, Monte Carlo, Nova, and Corvette with 350-ci V-8 (except LT-1 and Z-28 models); late 1971 to 1972 Chevrolet and GMC van with 350-ci V-8; 1973 C-20 (except Suburban) with 350-ci V-8; 1973 Chevrolet C-30 pickup and 1973 GMC 2500 and 3500 series (except Suburban and bus) with 350-ci V-8; 1974–1978 Chevrolet C-10 to C-30 truck and GMC 1500 to 3500 series with 350-ci V-8 without EGR

Interchange Number: 8

Usage: 1971–1972 Chevrolet C-10 to C-30 with 402-ci V-8; late-1969 to 1971 Camaro, Chevelle, Impala, and Nova with 402-ci V-8 (except 375-horsepower versions); 1971–1972 GMC pickup with 396-ci V-8

Interchange Number: 9

Usage: 1970–1972 Chevrolet C-10 to C-30 with 307-ci V-8; 1970–1972 Chevelle, Camaro, Nova, GMC Sprint, GMC pickup, Jimmy, and Ventura II with 307-ci V-8; 1973 C-20 and C-30 Chevrolet and GMC 2500 and 3500 series with 307-ci (except Suburban)

Interchange Number: 10

Usage: 1973 Chevrolet C-10 to C-30 and GMC 1500 to 3500 series; 1971–1973 Chevelle, Corvette, Impala, Monte Carlo, and Sprint with 454-ci V-8 (except with LS6 option)

Interchange Number: 11

Usage: 1973–1978 Chevrolet C-10 pickup, van, Suburban, Camaro, Chevelle, Corvette, Impala, Monte Carlo, Nova, GMC Sprint, Blazer, Jimmy, and GMC 1500-series pickup and van with 350-ci V-8 (except L-82 and Z-28 models); 1978–1979 Century, Firebird, Cutlass, Omega, and Skylark with Chevrolet 350-ci V-8

Note(s): 1978–1979 engines for non-Chevrolet models have L VIN engine code; 1975–1978 models have EGR valve

Interchange Number: 12

Usage: 1974–1978 Chevrolet C-10 to C-30 with 454-ci V-8; 1974–1976 Chevelle, Monte Carlo, and Impala with 454-ci V-8; 1974 Corvette with 454-ci V-8; 1974–1975 GMC Sprint with 454-ci V-8; 1974–1978 GMC pickup, Jimmy, and Suburban with 454-ci V-8

Interchange Number: 13

Usage: 1970 Chevrolet C-10 to C-30 with 402-ci V-8; 1970 Chevelle and Nova with 402-ci V-8; 1970 GMC pickup with 402-ci V-8

Interchange Number: 14

Usage: 1973 Chevrolet C-10 and C-20 Suburban, GMC 1500 and 2500 Suburban, Chevelle, Camaro, Nova, Jimmy, Blazer, and Sprint with 307-ci V-8

Short-Blocks

A short-block is a complete engine without the induction system, cylinder heads, exhaust system, or oil pan. To be interchangeable the block must have the same inner components.

A series of letters and numbers is used to identify short-blocks. The identification number will indicate where the engine was built, the date it was built, the models it will fit, and the horsepower it will generate. The casting code can be found on the passenger's side just below the cylinder head. A typical code will look like this: T 11 30 69. This particular engine was manufactured at the Tondawanda engine plant (T) on November 30 (11 30), and the 69 code indicates that it was originally installed in a 1970 Chevrolet pickup.

Model Identification

1967   Interchange Number
283-ci V-8

manual transmission 1
automatic transmission 1

327-ci V-8

manual transmission 2
automatic transmission 2

1968
307-ci V-8 3
327-ci V-8 2
396-ci V-8 4

1969
307-ci V-8 3
350-ci V-8 5
396-ci V-8 4

1970
307-ci V-8 6
350-ci V-8 5
396-ci V-8 7

1971–1972
307-ci V-8 6
350-ci V-8

Except LPG 8
LPG 9

396-ci V-8 10

1973
350-ci V-8

Except LPG 11
LPG 18

454-ci V-8 12

1974
350-ci V-8

Except LPG 11
LPG 18

454-ci V-8 14

1975
350-ci V-8 11
400-ci V-8 16
454-ci V-8 15

1976–1978
305-ci V-8 (1977 only) 19
305-ci V-8 (1978 only) 20
350-ci V-8 11
400-ci V-8 16
454-ci V-8 17

Interchanges

Interchange Number: 1

Horsepower: 175
Carburetor: Two-barrel
Usage: 1964–1967 Chevrolet pickup and Chevelle with 283-ci V-8; 1962–1967 Impala with 283-ci V-8
Engine ID Codes:

Manual

Pickup: WA or WF (with AIR)
Four-wheel drive: WI or WB (with AIR)
Van: WD or WL (with AIR)
Chevelle: J (three-speed) or JA (four-speed)
Impala: C

Automatic

Pickup: WE (Powerglide), WH (Powerglide with AIR), or WR (Turbo-Hydra-Matic)

Four-wheel drive: N/A

Van: WM (Powerglide) or WW (Powerglide with AIR)

Chevelle: JD

Impala: D

Interchange Number: 2

Horsepower: 220

Carburetor: Four-barrel

Usage: 1966–1968 Chevrolet and GMC pickup with 327-ci V-8

Engine ID Codes:

Manual

Pickup: YS (1966–1968) or YC (with AIR, 1967–1968)

Four-wheel drive: YM or YX (with AIR, 1967–1968 only)

Automatic

Pickup with Powerglide: YR (1966–1968) or YD (with AIR, 1967–1968 only)

Pickup with Turbo-Hydra-Matic: YH (1966–1968) or YJ (with AIR, 1967 only)

Interchange Number: 3

Horsepower: 200

Carburetor: Two-barrel

Usage: 1968–1969 Chevrolet pickup, Chevelle, and Nova with 307-ci V-8; 1969 Blazer and Camaro with 307-ci V-8

Engine ID Codes:

Manual

Pickup: WA, WB (1968), or UA

Four-wheel drive: WI or WB (with AIR)

Chevelle: J (three-speed) or JA (four-speed)

Impala: C

Automatic

Pickup: WE (Powerglide), WH (Powerglide with AIR), WR (Turbo-Hydra-Matic, 1968), UC, UM (Turbo-Hydra-Matic 350), UE (Turbo-Hydra-Matic 400, C-20 only), or UN (Turbo-Hydra-Matic 400, C-10 models)

Four-wheel drive: UF (Turbo-Hydra-Matic 400, K20 model only)

Van: WM (Powerglide) or WW (Powerglide with AIR)

Chevelle: JD

Impala: D

Interchange Number: 4

Horsepower: 310

Carburetor: Four-barrel

Usage: 1968–1969 Chevrolet C-10 to C-30 truck and GMC pickup; 1966–1969 Impala and Chevelle; 1967–1969 Camaro; 1968–1969 Nova—all with 396-ci V-8 (except 375-horsepower versions)

Engine ID Codes:

Manual

Pickup: XF or XE* (1968); YR (1969)

Four-wheel drive: N/A

Camaro: MQ or MR* (1967–1968); MT (1968); LH, KC, or JJ (1969)

Chevelle: EG or EX* (1967); KD, KG, or KI (1968–1969)

Nova: MQ (1968); JH or KC (1969)

Automatic

Pickup: XH or XG* (1968); YP (1969)

Camaro/Nova: JL

Chevelle: KF

Note(s): *With AIR emissions

Interchange Number: 5

Horsepower: 255

Carburetor: Four-barrel

Usage: 1969–1970 Chevrolet and GMC pickup (light duty); 1969–1970 Camaro, Chevelle, Impala, and Nova; 1970 Monte Carlo—all with 350-ci V-8 (except 1970 Z-28)

Engine ID Codes:

Manual

Pickup: XA (1969)

Four-wheel drive: XW

Camaro: HA (1969); CNJ (1970)

Chevelle: HA or HD* (1969); CNQ (1970)

Corvette: HY (1969); CTL (1970)

Impala: HG or HD* (1969); CNJ (1970)

Nova: HA or HP* (1969); CNJ (1970)

Powerglide Automatic

Camaro/Chevelle/Nova: HE (1969); CNK (1970)

Impala: HK (1969); CNS (1970)

Turbo-Hydra-Matic 350 Automatic

Camaro/Chevelle/Nova: HB (1969); CNE (1970)

Impala: HN (1969); CNR or CNT Police (1970)

Note(s): *With heavy-duty clutch; for light-duty truck only

Interchange Number: 6

Horsepower: 200

Carburetor: Two-barrel

Usage: 1970–1972 C-10 to C-30 Chevrolet and 1500 to 3500 GMC truck; 1970–1972 Camaro, Chevelle, Blazer, Jimmy, Nova, and Monte Carlo; 1971–1972 Ventura II

Engine ID Codes:

Manual

Pickup: TAN, TAS, or TAT for 1970; TDA, TDB, TRA*, TAD*, TJR, or TJT for 1971–1972

Camaro/Chevelle/Nova: CNC or CND for 1970; CCA for 1971; GKG or CAY* for 1972

Powerglide Automatic

Pickup: TAI or TAJ for 1970

Camaro/Chevelle/Nova: CNE for 1970; CCC for 1971

Turbo-Hydra-Matic Automatic
Pickup with T.H. 350: TAH, TAK, TAO, or TAP for 1970; TDL, TDP, TAH*, TAJ* TJP, or TJS for 1971–1972

Pickup with T.H. 400: TAL for 1970; TRJ for 1971–1972

Camaro/Chevelle/Nova: CNF for 1970; CTK or CMA* for 1971–1972

Note(s): *With NB2 emissions

Interchange Number: 7
Horsepower: 310

Carburetor: Four-barrel

Usage: 1970 C-10 to C-30 Chevrolet and 1500 to 3500 GMC truck, Camaro, Chevelle, and Monte Carlo with 396-ci (except 375-horsepower version)

Engine ID Codes:

Manual
Pickup: TBH

Camaro/Chevelle/Nova: CTX

Automatic
Pickup: TBG

Camaro/Chevelle/Nova: CTW

Interchange Number: 8
Horsepower: 245/270

Carburetor: All

Usage: 1971–1972 C-10 to C-30 Chevrolet and 1500 to 3500 GMC truck, Camaro, Chevelle, Monte Carlo, and Nova with 350-ci V-8 (except Z-28 and LPG models)

Engine ID Codes:

Manual
Pickup: TBL*, TFH, TDD, TDG, TRK, or TRH for 1971–1972

Camaro/Chevelle/Nova: CKK, CKA, CDA*, or CDG* for 1971–1972

Automatic
Pickup with TH 350: TFD*, TFJ*, TDJ, TDR, TRL, or TRJ for 1971–1972

Pickup with TH 400: TRJ for 1971–1972

Camaro/Chevelle/Nova: CGL or CJD for 1971; CTL, CKD, CSH, CMD*, CDD*, or CAR* for 1972

Note(s): *With NB2 emissions

Interchange Number: 9
Horsepower: 270

Carburetor: N/A

Usage: 1971–1972 C-10 to C-30 Chevrolet and 1500 to 3500 GMC truck with LPG engine

Engine ID Codes:

Manual
Pickup: TDH

Automatic
Pickup with TH 350/400: TDK for 1971–1972

Interchange Number: 10
Horsepower: 350

Carburetor: Four-barrel

Usage: 1971 C-10 to C-30 Chevrolet and 1500 to 3500 GMC truck; 1971–1972 Camaro, Chevelle, Monte Carlo, Nova, and Sprint—all with 396/402-ci V-8 (except with LS6 options)

Engine ID Codes:

Manual
Pickup: TKA, TKW, or TKM*

Camaro/Chevelle/Nova: CLC

Automatic
Pickup: TKB, TKX, or TLM*

Camaro/Chevelle/Nova: CLD

Note(s): *With AIR emissions

Interchange Number: 11
Horsepower: 155

Carburetor: Four-barrel

Usage: 1973–1974 C-10 Chevrolet and 1500 GMC truck, Blazer, and Jimmy; 1975–1977 C-10 to C-30 Chevrolet and 1500 to 3500 GMC truck, Blazer, and Jimmy; 1973–1979 G-20 to G-30 Chevrolet and 2500 to 3500 GMC van; 1973–1979 Camaro, Chevelle, Impala, Monte Carlo, Nova, and Sprint; 1978–1979 Firebird, LeMans, Omega, Phoenix, Skylark, and Century with 350-ci V-8.

Engine ID Codes:

Manual
Pickup: TJB, TJC, TDY*, and TJH for 1973; TJA, TJB, TJC, TJD*, or TMR for 1974; TXC*, TXD, TYC, TYD, TYW*, TYX, TYN#, TZC, or TZJ*# for 1975; TYC, TWJ, TKA, TKB, TKH, TYX, TYW* TXD, TXC* for 1976; TWJ*, TWD, TWF, TYX, TYW*, TXD, or TXC* for 1977

Camaro/Chevelle/Nova: CKB, CKH*, CKA, or CKC* for 1973; CKH or CMC for 1974

Automatic
Pickup: TJA, TJZ, TJY*, or TJX for 1973; TJY*, TKT, TKU, TKY, TWS*, or TMM for 1974; TXA*, TYX, TYY*, TYZ, TME*, TJG#, TZA, TZD#, or TZK*# for 1975; TKF, TJK, TKB, TYZ, TYY*, TXB, or TXA* for 1976–1977

Camaro/Chevelle/Impala/Nova: CKD*, CKJ, CKK*, CKL, CKS, CLT*, CLU, CLW, or CLX for 1973; CKD*, CMA, CMD, CMH, CMJ, CMK*, or CMR for 1974

Note(s): *With NB2 emissions; #With CC AIR emissions

Interchange Number: 12
Horsepower: 250

Carburetor: Four-barrel

Usage: 1973 C-10 to C-30 Chevrolet and 1500 to 3500 GMC truck; 1971–1973 Chevelle, Impala, Monte Carlo, and Sprint—all with 454-ci V-8 (except with LS6 option)

A typical engine ID number.

Engine ID Codes:
Manual
    Pickup: TRA* or TRJ
    Chevelle/Monte Carlo: CPA or CRX# for 1971–1972; CWA or CWC* for 1973
Automatic
    Pickup: TRL*, TRB*, TRH, or TRK
    Chevelle/Monte Carlo: CPD or CRW* for 1971–1972; CWB or CWD* for 1973
    Impala: CWD*, CWJ*, CWK, or CWL for 1973
    Note(s): *With NB2 emissions, #With CC AIR emissions
Interchange Number: 14
    Horsepower: 230
    Carburetor: Four-barrel
    Usage: 1974 C-10 to C-30 Chevrolet and 1500 to 3500 GMC truck; 1974 Chevelle, Impala, Monte Carlo, and Sprint—all with 454-ci V-8
    Engine ID Codes:
Manual
    Pickup: TRJ
    Chevelle/Monte Carlo: CWA or CXM
Automatic
    Pickup: TRW, TRT, TRU*, TRH, or TRL*
    Chevelle/Monte Carlo: CWD*, CWX, CXR, or CXS
    Impala: CWU, CWW*, CWY*, CXA*, CXB*, CXC*, CXT, or CXU
    Note(s): *With NB2 emissions
Interchange Number: 15
    Horsepower: 215
    Carburetor: 461
    Usage: 1975 C-10 to C-30 Chevrolet and 1500 to 3500 GMC truck; 1975 Chevelle, Impala, Monte Carlo, and Sprint—all with 454-ci V-8

Engine ID Codes:
Manual
    Pickup: TRZ, TSC, or TSJ#
Automatic
    Pickup: TSA*, TSD, TSM#, TSK, or TSL*
    Chevelle/Monte Carlo: CXW
    Note(s): *With NB2 emissions, #With CC AIR emissions
Interchange Number: 16
    Horsepower: 175
    Carburetor: Four-barrel
    Usage: 1975–1978 C-10 to C-20 Chevrolet and 1500 to 2500 GMC truck, Blazer, and Jimmy with four-wheel drive
    Engine ID Codes:
Automatic
    Pickup: TLL*, TLM, TLR*, or TLS
    Note(s): *With NB2 emissions
Interchange Number: 17
    Horsepower: 205
    Carburetor: Four-barrel
    Usage: 1976–1979 C-10 to C-30 Chevrolet and 1500 to 3500 GMC truck with 454-ci V-8
    Engine ID Codes:
Manual
    Pickup: TRZ* or TSC for 1976–1977
Automatic
    Pickup: TSA*, TSD, TSM#, TSK, or TSL for 1976–1977
    Note(s): *With NB2 emissions, #With CC AIR emissions
Interchange Number: 18
    Usage: 1973–1974 C-10 to C-30 Chevrolet and 1500 to 3500 GMC truck with LPG 350-ci V-8
    Engine ID Codes:
Manual
    Pickup: TMJ
Automatic
    Pickup: TMH
Interchange Number: 19
    Horsepower: 140
    Carburetor: Two-barrel
    Usage: 1977 C-10 to C-30 Chevrolet and 1500 to 3500 GMC truck, Blazer, Jimmy, Impala, Omega, Phoenix, Starfire, Ventura II, Firebird, LeMans, Century; 1976–1977 Camaro, Nova, Monza, Monte Carlo with 305-ci V-8
    Engine ID Codes:
Manual
    Pickup: UTA or UTF
    Cars: CPC, CPB, CPA
Automatic
    Pickup: UTB or UTH

Interchange Number: 20
    Horsepower: 140
    Carburetor: Two-barrel
    Usage: 1978 C-10 to C-30 Chevrolet and 1500 to
        3500 GMC truck, Blazer, Jimmy, Impala, Omega,
        Phoenix, Starfire, Ventura II, Firebird, LeMans,
        and Century; 1977–1978 Camaro, Nova,
        Monza, and Monte Carlo—all with 305-ci V-8
    Engine ID Codes:
Manual
    Pickup: UTA or UTF
    Chevelle/Monte Carlo: CER, CEM
Automatic
    Pickup: UTB or UTH

Crankshafts

Chevrolet truck engines were built to last, and thus some used a forged crankshaft. A forged crankshaft can replace a cast-iron crankshaft, but a cast crank should never take the place of a forged unit. A quick method of determining whether a crank is forged is to lightly tap one of the counterweights with a wrench. A ringing sound should be heard. A dull sound indicates a cast-iron crankshaft.

    Crankshafts are largely interchangeable between transmissions. The clutch pilot bushing must be removed when swapping from a vehicle that was originally installed with a manual transmission to a truck with an automatic transmission.

Model Identification

Interchanges

Interchange Number: 1
    Part Number(s): 3889303
    Forging Number(s): 3735236, 3815822, or 3836236
    Usage: 1957–1967 Chevrolet and GMC truck and
        full-size Chevrolet with 283-ci V-8; 1955–1957
        Chevrolet and GMC truck and full-size
        Chevrolet with 265-ci V-8; 1963–1967 Chevy II
        and 1964–1967 Chevelle with 283-ci V-8

Interchange Number: 2
    Part Number(s): 3889305
    Forging Number(s): 3782690
    Usage: 1962–1967 Chevrolet and GMC truck with
        327-ci V-8

Interchange Number: 3
    Part Number(s): 3930809
    Usage: 1968 C-10 to C-30 Chevrolet and 1500 to
        3500 GMC truck, Camaro, Chevelle, Impala,
        and Nova with 307-ci V-8; 1968 Camaro,
        Chevelle, Impala, and Nova with 327-ci V-8
        (250- or 275-horsepower versions only)

Interchange Number: 4
    Part Number(s): 3914682
    Usage: 1968 C-10 to C-30 Chevrolet and 1500 to
        3500 GMC truck with 327-ci V-8

Interchange Number: 5
    Part Number(s): 3882841
    Forging Number(s): 6223
    Usage: 1968–1972 C-10 to C-30 Chevrolet and
        1500 to 3500 GMC truck; 1967–1972 Camaro,
        Chevelle, Impala, and Nova—all with 396/402-
        ci 375-horsepower V-8

Interchange Number: 6
    Part Number(s): 3941172
    Usage: 1969–1973 C-10 to C-30 Chevrolet and
        1500 to 3500 GMC truck, Camaro, Chevelle,
        Impala, and Nova with 307-ci V-8; 1971–1972
        Ventura with 307-ci V-8

Interchange Number: 7
    Part Number(s): 3932444
    Usage: 1969–1978 C-10 to C-30 Chevrolet and
        1500 to 3500 GMC truck, Camaro, Chevelle,
        Impala, and Nova; 1970–1974 Monte Carlo—all
        with 350-ci V-8 (except Z-28 models)

Interchange Number: 8

Part Number(s): 336782

Usage: 1973–1978 C-10 Chevrolet and 1500 GMC truck (all transmissions); 1973–1974 C-20 Suburban; 1973–1974 C-20 to C-30 Chevrolet and 2500 to 3500 GMC truck with manual transmission; 1973–1978 Chevrolet motorhome; 1973–1974 Chevelle and Monte Carlo; 1975–1978 C-20 to C-30 Chevrolet and 2500 to 3500 GMC truck with 454-ci V-8 all models, all transmissions.

Interchange Number: 9

Part Number(s): 3967463

Usage: 1973–1974 C-20 to C-30 Chevrolet and 2500 to 3500 GMC truck with automatic transmissions; 1970 Chevelle, Impala, and Monte Carlo—all with 454-ci V-8 (except LS6 models)

Note(s): Salvage-yard dealers say Interchange Number 8 will fit

Interchange Number: 10

Part Number(s): 361982

Usage: 1977–1981 C-10 to C-30 Chevrolet and 1500 to 3500 GMC truck, Blazer, and Jimmy; 1976–1981 Camaro, Impala, Malibu, Monte Carlo, and Nova; 1977–1978 LeMans, Cutlass, and Grand Prix; 1977–1981 Firebird; 1980 Corvette—all with 305-ci V-8

Connecting Rods
Model Identification

1967	Interchange Number
283-ci V-8	1
327-ci V-8	1
1968	
307-ci V-8	3
327-ci V-8	3
396-ci V-8	4
1969–1972	
307-ci V-8	3
350-ci	3
396-ci V-8	4
1973	
307-ci V-8	3
350-ci	3
454-ci V-8	4
1974	
350-ci	3
454-ci V-8	4
1975–1976	
350-ci	3
400-ci V-8 (1976 only)	5
454-ci V-8	4
1977–1978	
305-ci V-8	3
350-ci	3
400-ci V-8	5
454-ci V-8	4

Interchanges

Interchange Number: 1

Part Number(s): 3864881

Usage: 1962–1967 Chevrolet and GMC truck and Impala and 1964–1967 Chevelle with 283- or 327-ci V-8; 1967 Camaro with 302- or 327-ci V-8

Interchange Number: 2

Part Number(s): 3864881

Usage: 1962–1967 Chevrolet and GMC truck and Impala and 1964–1967 Chevelle with 283- or 327-ci V-8; 1967 Camaro with 302- or 327-ci V-8

Interchange Number: 3

Part Number(s): 14031310

Usage: 1968–1980 Chevrolet C-10 to C-30, 1500 to 3500 GMC truck or van, Blazer, Jimmy, Camaro, Chevelle, Impala, and Nova with 307-ci or 350-ci V-8 (except Z-28 models); 1967 Camaro with 350-ci V-8; 1977–1978 C-10 to C-30 Chevrolet and 1500 to 3500 GMC truck, Blazer, Jimmy, Camaro, Chevelle, Impala, Monte Carlo, Nova, Firebird, Omega, Phoenix, LeMans, Grand Prix, and Cutlass with 305- or 307-ci V-8; 1980 Corvette with 305-ci V-8

Interchange Number: 4

Part Number(s): 147075624

Usage: 1968–1972 C-10 to C-30 Chevrolet and 1500 to 3500 GMC truck; 1965–1972 Impala; 1967–1972 Chevelle and Camaro; 1968–1972 Nova; 1970–1972 Monte Carlo all with 396/402-ci V-8 (except with L78 option); 1973–1978 C-10 to C-30 Chevrolet and 1500 to 3500 GMC truck; 1970–1975 Chevelle, Impala, Monte Carlo, Sprint all with 454-ci V-8, except LS6 option; 1966–1969 Impala with 427-ci V-8 (except 425-horsepower)

Interchange Number: 5

Part Number(s): 361933

Usage: 1976–1978 C-10 to C-30 Chevrolet and 1500 to 3500 GMC truck, Blazer, and Jimmy with four-wheel drive; 1970–1976 Impala; 1974–1976 Chevelle and Sprint—all with 400-ci small-block V-8

Pistons

Piston size—if given—is diameter by height.

Model Identification

1967	Interchange Number
283-ci V-8	1
327-ci V-8	2

350-ci	3
400-ci V-8	5
454-ci V-8	4

1968

307-ci V-8 3
327-ci V-8 2
396-ci V-8 4

1969

307-ci V-8 3
350-ci V-8 5
396-ci V-8

    early 4
    late 6

1970

307-ci V-8 3
350-ci V-8 5
396-ci V-8 6

1971–1972

307-ci V-8 3
350-ci V-8 7
402-ci V-8 8

1973–1974

307-ci V-8 (1973 only) 3
350-ci V-8

    C-10 9
    C-20
        except Suburban 7
        Suburban 9
    C-30 7

454-ci V-8

    1973 10

1974

C-10 11
C-20, except Suburban 12
C-20 Suburban 11

1975

350-ci V-8

    C-10 9
    C-20, except Suburban 7
    C-20 Suburban 9
    C-30 7

454-ci V-8

    C-10
        without heavy-duty chassis 11
        with heavy-duty chassis 10
    C-20
        except Suburban 12
        Suburban 10

1976

305-ci V-8 13
350-ci V-8

    C-10 9
    C-20
        except Suburban 7
        Suburban 9
    C-30 7

454-ci V-8

    C-10
        without heavy-duty chassis 11
        with heavy-duty chassis 10
    C-20
        except Suburban 12
        Suburban 10

1977–1978

305-ci V-8 13
350-ci V-8

    C-10 9
    C-20
        except Suburban 7
        Suburban 9
    C-30 7

400-ci V-8 14
454-ci V-8

    C-10
        without heavy-duty chassis 11
        with heavy-duty chassis 10
    C-20
        except Suburban 12
        Suburban 10

Interchanges

Interchange Number: 1

    Part Number(s): 3860407
    Size: 3 7/8x3 51/64
    Usage: 1962–1967 all Chevrolet and GMC models with a 283-ci V-8; 1962–1970 Chevy II/Nova with 153-ci four-cylinder; 1964–1969 Chevelle, Impala, and Chevy II/Nova; and 1967–1969 Camaro—all with 230-ci six-cylinder

Interchange Number: 2

    Part Number(s): 3816974
    Size: 4x3 17/32
    Usage: 1962–1968 C-10 to C-30 Chevrolet and 1500 to 3500 GMC truck and van

Interchange Number: 3

    Part Number(s): 3923294
    Usage: 1968–1973 all Chevrolet and GMC models with 307-ci V-8; 1971–1972 Ventura II with 307-ci V-8

Interchange Number: 4

    Part Number(s): 3878227 (left bank) and 3878228 (right bank)
    Usage: 1968 to early-1969 C-10 to C-30 Chevrolet and 1500 to 3500 GMC truck; 1966 to early-1969 Chevelle and Impala; 1967 to early-1969 Camaro; 1968 to early-1969 Nova—all with 396-ci V-8 (cars are equipped with the 375-horsepower L78 option)

Interchange Number: 5

    Part Number(s): 3911020
    Usage: 1969–1970 all Chevrolet and GMC models with 350-ci V-8 (except with Z-28 or LT-1 options)

Interchange Number: 6
  Part Number(s): 3969981 (left bank) and 3969982 (right bank)
  Usage: Late-1969 to 1970 C-10 to C-30 Chevrolet and 1500 to 3500 GMC truck, Camaro, Chevelle, Impala, and Nova; 1970 Monte Carlo—all with 402-ci (396) V-8 (except with L78 375-horsepower version in cars)

Interchange Number: 7
  Part Number(s): 3911020
  Usage: 1971–1972 all Chevrolet and GMC models with 350-ci V-8 (except with Z-28 or LT-1 options); 1973–1974 C-20 to C-30 Chevrolet and 2500 to 3500 GMC truck; 1973–1974 G-30 1-ton van Chevrolet and 3500 GMC van; 1974–1978 C-10 Chevrolet and 1500 GMC truck with 350-ci V-8, with EGR

Interchange Number: 8
  Part Number(s): 3993861 (left bank) and 399382 (right bank)
  Usage: 1971–1972 C-10 to C-30 Chevrolet and 1500 to 3500 GMC truck, Camaro, Chevelle, Impala, Monte Carlo, and Nova—all with 402-ci (396) V-8

Interchange Number: 9
  Part Number(s): 6271097
  Usage: 1973–1981 C-10 Chevrolet and 1500 GMC truck; 1973–1974 G-20 Chevrolet and 2500 GMC van, Camaro, Chevelle, Corvette, Impala, Monte Carlo, Nova, Blazer, Jimmy, C-20 and 2500 Suburban, and Sprint; 1978–1979 Cutlass, Firebird, Century, LeMans, Skylark, Phoenix, Omega, and full-size Oldsmobile—all with 350-ci V-8 (except Z-28 or L-88 models)
  Note(s): No Chevrolet models have L code in VIN

Interchange Number: 10
  Part Number(s): 33058
  Usage: 1973 C-10 to C-30 Chevrolet and 1500 to 3500 GMC truck; 1971–1976 Chevelle, Corvette, Impala, Monte Carlo, and Sprint; 1975–1978 Suburban; 1975 C-10 with heavy-duty chassis—all with 454-ci V-8 (except LS6 models)

Interchange Number: 11
  Part Number(s): 340206
  Usage: 1974 C-10 Chevrolet and 1500 GMC truck; Chevelle, Corvette, Impala, Monte Carlo, and Sprint; C-20 and 2500 Suburban; 1975 C-10 without heavy-duty chassis—all with 454-ci V-8
  Note(s): Will not fit C-20 or C-30 models

Interchange Number: 12
  Part Number(s): 340209
  Usage: 1974–1979 C-20 to C-30 Chevrolet and 2500 to 3500 GMC truck (except C-20 and 2500 Suburban) with 454-ci V-8
  Note(s): Will not fit C-10 models

Interchange Number: 13
  Part Number(s): 364702
  Usage: 1977–1981 C-10 to C-30 Chevrolet and 1500 to 3500 GMC truck, Blazer, Jimmy, and Firebird; 1976–1981 Camaro, Chevelle/Malibu, Impala, Nova, Monte Carlo, and Monza; 1977–1980 Cutlass; 1977–1979 Omega, Starfire, and Phoenix; 1980 Corvette—all with 305-ci V-8

Interchange Number: 14
  Part Number(s): 3991457
  Usage: 1976–1979 C-10 to C-30 Chevrolet and 1500 to 3500 GMC truck, Blazer, and Jimmy four-wheel drive; 1971–1979 Impala—all with 400-ci small-block V-8

Camshafts
Model Identification

1967	Interchange Number
283-ci V-8	1
327-ci V-8	1
1968–1970	
307-ci V-8	1
350-ci V-8	1
396-ci V-8	2
1971–1972	
307-ci V-8	1
350-ci V-8	1
396-ci V-8	3
1973	
307-ci V-8	1
350-ci V-8	1
454-ci V-8	4
1974	
350-ci V-8	
two-barrel	1
four-barrel	
without California emissions	1
with California emissions	5
454-ci V-8	4
1975	
350-ci V-8	1
454-ci V-8	4
1976–1978	
350-ci V-8	1
400-ci V-8	1
454-ci V-8	4

Interchanges
Interchange Number: 1
  Part Number(s): 3896929
  Type: Hydraulic
  Usage: 1959–1967 283-ci V-8; 1962–1969 327-ci V-8 (all but special high-performance models); 1967–1979 350-ci V-8 (all but 1970 Z-28

models and 1974 with California emissions); 1968–1973 307-ci V-8; 1970–1978 400-ci, two-barrel, small-block V-8.

Note(s): Gasoline engines only

Interchange Number: 2

Part Number(s): 3874872

ID Number(s): 3874874

Usage: 1965–1970 396-ci, except 350- or 375-horsepower versions

Interchange Number: 3

Part Number(s): 3963544

ID Number(s): 3963445

Usage: 1971–1972 C-10 to C-30 Chevrolet and 1500 to 3500 GMC truck, Camaro, Chevelle, Impala, Monte Carlo, Nova, and Sprint all with 396-ci V-8; 1970 Camaro, Chevelle, Monte Carlo, and Nova all with 396-ci/402-ci 350-horsepower or 454-ci V-8 (except LS6 models); 1976 Impala; 1976–1981 C-10 to C-30 Chevrolet and 1500 to 3500 GMC truck all with 454-ci V-8

Interchange Number: 4

Part Number(s): 353040

Usage: 1973–1975 C-10 to C-30 Chevrolet and 1500 to 3500 GMC truck, Chevelle, Corvette, Impala, Monte Carlo, and Sprint with 454-ci V-8

Interchange Number: 5

Part Number(s): 3998962

Usage: 1974 C-10 to C-30 Chevrolet and 1500 GMC truck, van, Blazer, and Jimmy, with 350-ci, four-barrel V-8, with California emissions; 1972 Camaro, Chevelle, Impala, Monte Carlo, Nova, and Sprint with 350-ci V-8, with NOX emissions; 1974 Camaro, Chevelle, Impala, Monte Carlo, and Nova with 400-ci small-block and California emissions

Timing Chains and Sprockets

Small-blocks used two different chains, and both were the early link type. The 1967 models in this guide used part number 3704150; it housed an 18-tooth steel sprocket, part number 3599980, and an iron sprocket, part number 3865964, that was stamped with the number 3704214.

Beginning in 1968 the chain was listed as part number 3896961. It used an 18-tooth steel sprocket, listed as part number 3896959, and 36-tooth cam sprocket, listed as part number 340235. It was used in all small-block applications, except the 400-ci small-block.

The 400-ci small-block used chain part number 3735411 and a steel crankshaft sprocket with 22-teeth, part number 3735413. The camshaft sprocket was listed as part number 3735412 and had 44 teeth.

Chevrolet trucks used the non-high-performance set-up, which included chain part number 3902428, a 19-tooth steel crankshaft sprocket (part number 3902426), and a 38-tooth camshaft sprocket (part number 330814), which was made of aluminum. If hopping up your pickup is in your plans, then you should switch to the high-performance chain and the crankshaft sprocket listed as part number 3860035, which is 3.5 inches in diameter. This switch, along with the later-style L78 cam, could add horses to your truck's big-block.

Main Bearing Caps

The change in main bearing caps for small-blocks is the difference in journal size. All 283-ci and those 327-ci V-8s made in or before 1967 used small journals, while those after used larger journals. All small-blocks used the same cap in all locations, except the 350-ci V-8, which used a different cap in the number one position. It used the same cap that the 305- and 307-ci V-8 used, however, for positions 2, 3, and 4. The specialty block 400-ci used a unique set of main caps that will not interchange with other small-blocks. Note that most truck blocks used four-bolt mains.

All big-blocks used the same two-bolt mains for all years; thus those from a 454-ci V-8 will fit your 1968 396-ci powerplant. While main caps will swap locations, due to wear, their location should be noted during an engine rebuild and replaced in the same location.

Cylinder Heads
Model Identification

1967	Interchange Number
283-ci V-8	1
327-ci V-8	2
1968	
307-ci V-8	3
327-ci V-8	3
396-ci V-8	13
1969	
307-ci V-8	4
350-ci V-8	
driver's side	7
passenger's side	6
396-ci V-8	13
1970	
307-ci V-8	4
350-ci V-8	8
396-ci V-8	14
1971	
307-ci V-8	5
350-ci V-8	9
396-ci V-8	15
1972	
307-ci V-8	5
350-ci V-8	
C-10	9
C-20	5

Cylinder head casting numbers are located on the runners.

Interchanges

Interchange Number: 1

Part Number(s): 3817680

Casting Number(s): 3795896 or 3836842

Usage: 1964–1967 C-10 to C-30 Chevrolet and 1500 to 3500 GMC truck and van, Chevelle, Impala, and Chevy II with 283-ci V-8

Interchange Number: 2

Part Number(s): 3958602

Casting Number(s): 3814480

Usage: 1966–1967 C-10 to C-30 Chevrolet and 1500 to 3500 GMC truck and van with 327-ci V-8; 1963–1966 C-50 Chevrolet and 5500 GMC truck with 283-ci V-8

Interchange Number: 3

Casting Number(s): 3911032

Usage: 1968 C-10 to C-30 Chevrolet and 1500 to 3500 GMC truck and van, Camaro, Chevelle, Impala, Nova, Blazer, and Jimmy with 307-ci V-8; 1968 C-10 to C-30 Chevrolet and 1500 to 3500 GMC truck and van with 327-ci V-8

Note(s): Will fit Interchange Number 2

Interchange Number: 4

Part Number(s): 3958602

Casting Number(s): 3927185

Usage: 1969–1970 C-10 to C-30 Chevrolet and 1500 to 3500 GMC truck, Camaro, Chevelle, Impala, Nova, Blazer, and Jimmy with 307-ci V-8; 1969 to early-1971 G-10 to G-30 Chevrolet and 1500 to 3500 GMC van with 307-ci V-8

Interchange Number: 5

Part Number(s): 6272069

Casting Number(s): 3795896

Usage: 1971–1972 C-10 to C-30 Chevrolet and 1500 to 3500 GMC truck, Camaro, Chevelle, Impala, Nova, Blazer, and Jimmy with 307-ci V-8; late-1971 G-10 to G-30 Chevrolet and 1500 to 3500 GMC van with 307-ci V-8; 1972–1973 C-20 to C-30 Chevrolet and 2500 to 3500 GMC truck (except Suburban models); 1972–1973 C-10 Chevrolet and 1500 GMC truck with heavy-duty chassis 307-ci V-8

Interchange Number: 6

Part Number(s): 3946813

Casting Number(s): 3946813

Usage: 1969 C-10 to C-30 Chevrolet and 1500 to 3500 GMC truck; 1969–1970 C-40 to C-50 Chevrolet and 4500 to 5500 GMC truck—all with 350-ci V-8 (except with LPG), right-hand side only

Interchange Number: 7

Part Number(s): 3958605

Casting Number(s): 3932454

Usage: 1969 C-10 to C-30 Chevrolet and 1500 to 3500 GMC truck; 1969–1970 C-40 to C-50 Chevrolet and 4500 to 5500 GMC truck—all with 350-ci V-8 (except trucks with LPG), left-hand side only

Interchange Number: 8

Part Number(s): 3958606

Casting Number(s): 3932441

Usage: 1970 C-10 to C-30 Chevrolet and 1500 to 3500 GMC truck, Blazer, and Jimmy with 350-ci V-8 (except truck models with LPG); 1969–1970 Camaro, Chevelle, Impala, Nova with 350-ci V-8 (except Z-28 models); 1970 Monte Carlo with 350-ci V-8; 1970 to early-1971 G-10 to G-30 Chevrolet and 1500 to 3500 GMC van with 350-ci V-8

Interchange Number: 9

Part Number(s): 6260856

Casting Number(s): 3973487

Usage: 1971 C-10 to C-30 Chevrolet and 1500 to 3500 GMC truck, Blazer, and Jimmy with 350-ci V-8; 1972–1979 C-10 Chevrolet and 1500 GMC truck with 350-ci V-8 (except four-wheel drive or with heavy-duty chassis); 1972–1979 C-20 and 2500 Suburban with 350-ci V-8; 1971–1977 Camaro, Chevelle, Corvette, Impala, Monte Carlo, Nova, and Sprint with 350-ci V-8 (except Z-28, LT-1, and L-88 models). Or truck models with LP gas: late-1971 to 1979 G-10 to G-30 Chevrolet and 1500 to 3500 GMC van with 350-ci V-8; 1973 C-10 to C-30 Chevrolet and 1500 to 3500 GMC truck, van, Blazer, Jimmy, Camaro, Chevelle, Impala, and Nova with 307-ci V-8; 1977 full-size Oldsmobile, Omega, Phoenix Ventura II, and Skylark with 350-ci V-8; 1978–1979 Corvette with 350-ci V-8 (except L-88)

Interchange Number: 10
Part Number(s): 464033
Casting Number(s): N/A
Usage: 1974–1980 C-20 to C-30 Chevrolet and 2500 to 3500 GMC truck; 1975–1978 C-10 Chevrolet and 1500 GMC truck, Blazer, and Jimmy with four-wheel drive; 1978 G-30 Chevrolet and 3500 GMC van (except California); 1973–1978 C-10 Chevrolet and 1500 GMC truck with heavy-duty chassis, two-wheel-drive, 350-ci V-8

Interchange Number: 11
Part Number(s): 463374
Casting Number(s): N/A
Usage: 1977–1978 C-10 to C-20 Chevrolet and 1500 to 2500 GMC truck, Blazer, and Jimmy with 305-ci V-8

Interchange Number: 11a
Part Number(s): 359945
Casting Number(s): 3932882
Usage: 1975–1976 C-10 Chevrolet and 1500 GMC truck, Blazer, and Jimmy four-wheel drive; C-20 and 2500 Suburban; G-20 to G-30 Chevrolet and 2500 to 3500 GMC van—all with 400-ci V-8

Interchange Number: 12
Part Number(s): 464035
Casting Number(s): N/A
Usage: 1977–1978 C-20 Chevrolet and 2500 GMC truck; 1977–1978 Blazer and Jimmy four-wheel drive; 1977–1978 C-10 Chevrolet and 1500 GMC truck—all with 400-ci V-8.

Interchange Number: 13
Part Number(s): 3933146
Casting Number(s): 3933148
Usage: 1968–1969 C-10 to C-30 Chevrolet and 1500 to 3500 GMC truck with 396-ci V-8; 1969 Impala all with 396-ci V-8.

Interchange Number: 14
Part Number(s): 3973195
Casting Number(s): 3975950
Usage: 1970 C-10 to C-30 Chevrolet and 1500 to 3500 GMC truck with 396/402-ci V-8

Interchange Number: 15
Part Number(s): 3993818
Casting Number(s): 3993820
Usage: 1971–1972 C-10 to C-30 Chevrolet and 1500 to 3500 GMC truck, Camaro, Chevelle, Impala, Monte Carlo, Nova, and Sprint with

396/402-ci V-8 (without AIR on 1972 models); 1971 Chevelle, Impala, Monte Carlo, and Sprint with 454-ci V-8 (except LS6 models)

Interchange Number: 16
Part Number(s): 6272290
Casting Number(s): N/A
Usage: 1972 C-10 to C-30 Chevrolet and 1500 to 3500 GMC truck with 396/402-ci V-8, with AIR emissions

Interchange Number: 17
Part Number(s): 353047
Casting Number(s): N/A
Usage: 1973 C-10 to C-30 Chevrolet and 1500 to 3500 GMC truck, Chevelle, Corvette, Impala, Monte Carlo, and Sprint with 454-ci V-8

Interchange Number: 18
Part Number(s): 336780
Casting Number(s): N/A
Usage: 1974–1978 C-10 to C-30 Chevrolet and 1500 to 3500 GMC truck with 454-ci V-8 (except with California emissions); 1974 Chevelle, Corvette, Impala, Monte Carlo, and Sprint with 454-ci V-8

Interchange Number: 19
Part Number(s): 343783
Casting Number(s): N/A
Usage: 1975–1978 C-10 to C-30 Chevrolet and 1500 to 3500 GMC truck with 454-ci V-8, with California emissions; 1975 Chevelle, Corvette, Impala, Monte Carlo, and Sprint with 454-ci V-8

Valve Covers
Model Identification

1967	Interchange Number
283-ci V-8	14
327-ci V-8	14
1968–1972	
307-ci V-8	12
327-ci V-8	12
396-ci V-8	
driver's side	6
passenger's side	7
1973	
307-ci V-8	
driver's side	1
passenger's side	3
350-ci V-8	
driver's side	1
passenger's side	4
454-ci V-8	
driver's side	6
passenger's side	7

1974

350-ci V-8
   driver's side 1
   passenger's side 2
454-ci V-8
   driver's side 6
   passenger's side 7

1975–1976

350-ci V-8
   driver's side 1
   passenger's side 2
454-ci V-8
   driver's side 8
   passenger's side 9

1977–1978

305-ci V-8
   driver's side 1
   passenger's side 2
350-ci V-8
   except diesel
      driver's side 1
      passenger's side 2
   diesel 5
400-ci V-8
   driver's side 1
   passenger's side 2
454-ci V-8
   driver's side 10
   passenger's side 11

Interchanges

Interchange Number: 1

   Part Number(s): 14025551
   Position: Driver's side
   Usage: 1977–1980 C-10 to C-30 Chevrolet and
      1500 to 3500 GMC truck, Blazer, G-10 to G-30
      Chevrolet and 1500 to 3500 GMC van,
      Camaro, Chevelle, Impala, Monte Carlo, Nova,
      Phoenix, Omega, Apollo, and full-size
      Oldsmobile with 305-ci V-8; 1978–1979 Sunbird
      with 305-ci V-8; 1977 full-size Pontiac, Firebird,
      and Century with 305-ci V-8; 1978 full-size
      Buick, Cutlass, Firebird, and Grand Prix with
      305-ci V-8; 1973 C-10 to C-30 Chevrolet and
      1500 to 3500 GMC truck, Blazer, and Jimmy
      with 307-ci V-8; 1973–1980 C-10 to C-30
      Chevrolet and 1500 to 3500 GMC truck,
      Blazer, and Jimmy with 350-ci V-8 (except
      diesel); 1975–1979 C-10 to C-30 Chevrolet
      and 1500 to 3500 GMC truck, Blazer, Jimmy,
      and Impala with 400-ci V-8

Interchange Number: 2

   Part Number(s): 14025552
   Position: Passenger's side
   Usage: 1977–1980 C-10 to C-30 Chevrolet and
      1500 to 3500 GMC truck, Blazer, Camaro,
      Chevelle, Impala, Monte Carlo, Nova, Phoenix,
      Omega, Apollo, and full-size Oldsmobile with
      305-ci V-8; 1978–1979 Sunbird with 305-ci V-8;
      1977 full-size Pontiac, Firebird, and Century
      with 305-ci V-8; 1978 full-size Buick, Cutlass,
      Firebird, and Grand Prix with 305-ci V-8;
      1978–1979 Camaro, Impala, Cutlass, Firebird,
      LeMans, Monte Carlo, Nova, Omega, Phoenix,
      Skylark, Sprint, and Century with 350-ci
      (Chevrolet-built) V-8; 1974–1980 C-10 to C-30
      Chevrolet and 1500 to 3500 GMC truck,
      Blazer, and Jimmy with 350-ci V-8 (except
      diesel); 1975–1979 C-10 to C-30 Chevrolet
      and 1500 to 3500 GMC truck, Blazer, Jimmy,
      and Impala with 400-ci V-8

Interchange Number: 3

   Part Number(s): 340269
   Position: Passenger's side
   Usage: 1973 C-10 to C-30 Chevrolet and 1500
      to 3500 GMC truck, Blazer, and Jimmy with
      307-ci V-8

Interchange Number: 4

   Part Number(s): 333866
   Position: Passenger's side
   Usage: 1973 C-10 to C-30 Chevrolet and 1500
      to 3500 GMC truck, Blazer, and Jimmy with
      350-ci V-8

Interchange Number: 5

   Part Number(s): 556263
   Position: Either side
   Usage: 1978 C-10 to C-30 Chevrolet and 1500 to
      3500 GMC truck with 350-ci diesel V-8

Interchange Number: 6

   Part Number(s): 338261
   Position: Driver's side
   Usage: 1968–1972 C-10 to C-30 Chevrolet and
      1500 to 3500 GMC with 396/402-ci V-8;
      1973–1974 C-10 to C-30 Chevrolet and 1500
      to 3500 GMC truck with 454-ci V-8; 1965–1969
      Impala with 396- or 427-ci V-8 (except Impala
      SS models)

Interchange Number: 7

   Part Number(s): 338262
   Position: Passenger's side
   Usage: 1968–1972 C-10 to C-30 Chevrolet and
      1500 to 3500 GMC with 396/402-ci V-8;
      1973–1974 C-10 to C-30 Chevrolet and 1500
      to 3500 GMC truck with 454-ci V-8; 1965–1969
      Impala with 396- or 427-ci V-8 (except Impala
      SS models); 1970 Chevelle with 396/402-ci V-8

Interchange Number: 8

   Part Number(s): 14082481
   Position: Driver's side
   Usage: 1975–1976 C-10 to C-30 Chevrolet and
      1500 to 3500 GMC truck with 454-ci V-8

Interchange Number: 9
    Part Number(s): 346286
    Position: Passenger's side
    Usage: 1975–1976 C-10 to C-30 Chevrolet and
        1500 to 3500 GMC truck with 454-ci V-8
Interchange Number: 10
    Part Number(s): 14075619
    Position: Driver's side
    Usage: 1977–1978 C-10 to C-30 Chevrolet and
        1500 to 3500 GMC truck with 454-ci V-8
Interchange Number: 11
    Part Number(s): 14075620
    Position: Passenger's side
    Usage: 1977–1978 C-10 to C-30 Chevrolet and
        1500 to 3500 GMC truck with 454-ci V-8
Interchange Number: 12
    Part Number(s): 6272227
    Position: Either side

Usage: 1969–1972 C-10 to C-30 Chevrolet and
    1500 to 3500 GMC truck, Blazer, Jimmy,
    Camaro, Chevelle, Impala, and Nova 307-ci V-8;
    1970–1972 Monte Carlo with 350-ci V-8;
    1968–1969 C-10 to C-30 Chevrolet and 1500
    to 3500 GMC truck and van, Camaro, Chevelle,
    Impala, and Nova with 327-ci V-8; 1968–1972
    C-10 to C-30 Chevrolet and 1500 to 3500
    GMC truck, Blazer, Jimmy, Camaro, Chevelle,
    Impala, and Nova with 307-ci V-8
Interchange Number: 14
    Part Number(s): 3910298
    Position: Either side
    Usage: 1965–1967 C-10 to C-30 Chevrolet and
        1500 to 3500 GMC truck and van and full-size
        Chevrolet with 283- or 327-ci V-8 (except spe-
        cial high-performance models)

2 Fuel Systems

Fuel Tanks

Model Identification

1967–1969	***Interchange Number***
C-10 to C-30	
all cab models	1
Blazer (1969 only)	2
Suburban	3
1970	
C-10	
all cab models	
without EEC	1
with EEC	4
C-20 and C-30	
all cab models	1
Blazer	
without EEC	2
with EEC	5
Suburban	
without EEC	3
with EEC	6
1971–1972	
C-10	
all cab models	4
C-20 and C-30	1
Blazer	7
Suburban	8
1973–1974	
C-10	
all cab models	
except 117.5-inch wheelbase	12
117.5-inch wheelbase	11
C-20	
except 117.5-inch wheelbase	12
117.5-inch wheelbase	11
C-30	11
Blazer	
except 30-gallon.	10
30-gallon	9
Suburban	
25-gallon.	13
30-gallon.	9
40-gallon.	10
1975–1976	
C-10	
all cab models	
except 117.5-inch wheelbase	12
117.5-inch wheelbase	14
C-20	
except 117.5-inch wheelbase	
front	14
rear	13
117.5-inch wheelbase	11
C-30	
front	14
rear	13
Blazer	
except 30-gallon.	10
30-gallon	9
Suburban	
25-gallon.	13
30-gallon.	9
40-gallon.	10

Interchanges

Interchange Number: 1

Part Number(s): 6272125
Capacity: 21 gallons
Usage: 1967–1969 C-10 to C-40 Chevrolet cab models; 1970 C-10 Chevrolet and 1500 GMC truck cab models without EEC emissions; 1970–1972 C-20 to C-40 Chevrolet and 2500 to 3500 GMC cab models

Interchange Number: 2

Part Number(s): 6263057
Capacity: 23.5 gallons
Usage: 1969 Blazer; 1970 Blazer and Jimmy without EEC emissions

Interchange Number: 3

Part Number(s): 3977674
Capacity: 23.5 gallons
Usage: 1967–1970 Suburban without EEC emissions

Interchange Number: 4

Part Number(s): 6272124
Capacity: 20 gallons
Usage: 1970–1972 C-10 with EEC emissions

Interchange Number: 5

Part Number(s): 3995715
Capacity: 23.5 gallons
Usage: 1970 Blazer and Jimmy with EEC emissions

Intake manifolds can be identified by casting numbers.

Interchange Number: 6
    Part Number(s): 3995716
    Capacity: 23.5 gallons
    Usage: 1970 Suburban with EEC emissions

Interchange Number: 7
    Part Number(s): 3995793
    Capacity: 21 gallons
    Usage: 1971–1972 Blazer and Jimmy

Interchange Number: 8
    Part Number(s): 3995794
    Capacity: 20 gallons
    Usage: 1971–1972 Suburban

Interchange Number: 9
    Part Number(s): 6259406
    Capacity: 30 gallons
    Usage: 1973–1974 Blazer, Jimmy, and Suburban with
        30-gallon fuel tank

Interchange Number: 10
    Part Number(s): 6259406
    Capacity: 40 gallons
    Usage: 1973–1974 Blazer, Jimmy, and Suburban with
        40-gallon fuel tank

Interchange Number: 11
    Part Number(s): 6263897
    Usage: 1973–1974 C-10 to C-20 Chevrolet and
        1500 to 2500 GMC truck with 117-inch wheel-
        base

Interchange Number: 12
    Part Number(s): 6263865
    Usage: 1973–1974 C-10 to C-30 Chevrolet and
        1500 to 2500 GMC truck (except with 117.5-
        inch wheelbase)

Interchange Number: 13
    Part Number(s): 475428
    Capacity: 25 gallons
    Usage: 1973–1981 Blazer, Jimmy, and Suburban with
        25-gallon fuel tank; 1975–1981 C-20 to C-30
        Chevrolet and 2500 to 3500 GMC truck-cab
        models with rear tank

Interchange Number: 14
    Part Number(s): 471687
    Capacity: 20 gallons
    Usage: 1975–1981 C-10 to C-30 Chevrolet and 1500
        to 3500 GMC truck with 131.5-inch wheelbase
        (front tank for C-20 and C-30 models)
    Note: Interchange Number 12 will fit

Fuel Caps
Model Identification

1967	*Interchange Number*

C-10 to C-30
all cab models 5

1968–1969
Blazer (1969 only)
    without body side moldings 5
    with body side moldings 4
C-10
    without body side moldings 5
    with body side moldings 4
C-20
    without body side moldings 5
    with body side moldings 4
C-30
    without body side moldings 5
    with body side moldings 4
Suburban
    without body side moldings 5
    with body side moldings 4

1970
Blazer
    without body side moldings 5
    with body side moldings 4
    with EEC emissions 3
C-10
    without EEC emissions
        without body side moldings 5
        with body side moldings 4
    with EEC emissions 3
C-20 and C-30
    without body side moldings 5
    with body side moldings 4

1971
Blazer
    chrome cap 1
C-10
    standard cap 3
    Fleetside with auxiliary fuel tank 2
C-20
    without body side moldings 5
    with body side moldings 4
    Fleetside with auxiliary fuel tank 2

C-30

    without body side moldings 5

    with body side moldings 4

    Fleetside with auxiliary fuel tank 2

1972

Blazer, chrome cap 1

C-10, chrome cap 1

C-20

    except Suburban

        Fleetside with auxiliary fuel tank 1

        all without body side moldings 5

        all with body side moldings 4

    Suburban, chrome cap 1

C-30

    except Suburban

        Fleetside with auxiliary fuel tank 1

        Fleetside with chrome cap 1

        all without body side moldings 5

        all with body side moldings 4

1973–1978

Blazer

    without woodgrain exterior 6, 12

    with woodgrain exterior

        1973–1975 8

        1976–1977 13

        1978 14

C-10

    Fleetside without woodgrain exterior 6, 12

    Fleetside with woodgrain exterior

        1973–1975. 8

        1976–1977 13

        1978 14

    Stepside

        without EEC 11

        with EEC

            painted cap 7

            chrome cap 10

C-20

    Fleetside without woodgrain exterior 6, 12

    Fleetside with woodgrain exterior

        1973–1975 8

        1976–1977 13

        1978 14

    Stepside

        without EEC 11

        with EEC

            painted cap 7

            chrome cap 10

C-30

    Fleetside without woodgrain exterior 6, 12

    Fleetside with woodgrain exterior

        1973–1975 8

        1976–1977 13

        1978 14

Stepside

    without EEC 11

    with EEC

        painted cap 7

        chrome cap 10

Suburban

    without woodgrain exterior 6, 12

        1976–1977 13

        1978 14

Interchanges

Interchange Number: 1

    Part Number(s): 6263474

    Usage: 1972 C-10 Chevrolet and 1500 GMC truck, Blazer, Jimmy, and C-20 Suburban or Fleetside with auxiliary fuel tank

    Note(s): Chrome cap

Interchange Number: 2

    Part Number(s): 3994191

    Usage: 1970–1971 C-10 to C-30 Chevrolet and 1500 to 3500 GMC Fleetside truck with auxiliary fuel tank

Interchange Number: 3

    Part Number(s): 3975177

    Usage: 1970–1971 C-10 Chevrolet and 1500 GMC truck; G-10 Chevrolet and 1500 GMC van with EEC emissions

Interchange Number: 4

    Part Number(s): 3927086

    Usage: 1968–1970 C-10 Chevrolet pickup and Blazer; 1968–1972 C-20 to C-30 Chevrolet pickup and Suburban—all with body side moldings and except 1970 models with EEC emissions

Interchange Number: 5

    Part Number(s): 3914958

    Usage: 1967–1970 C-10 Chevrolet pickup; 1969–1970 Blazer; 1967–1972 C-20 to C-30 Chevrolet and cab models; 1970 G-10 to G-20 Chevrolet; 1967–1970 Suburban—all except with body side moldings or EEC emissions

Interchange Number: 6

    Part Number(s): 14002255

    Usage: 1973–1978 C-10 to C-30 Chevrolet Fleetside only, Blazer, Jimmy, and Suburban (without woodgrain exterior; 1976–1978 1500 to 3500 GMC Wideside (Fleetside) truck

Interchange Number: 7

    Part Number(s): 366668

    Usage: 1973–1976 C-10 to C-30 Chevrolet and 1500 to 3500 Stepside only; 1974–1978 G-10 to G-30 Chevrolet and 1500 to 3500 GMC van; P10 to P30 Chevrolet service van—all without woodgrain exterior

Interchange Number: 8
    Part Number(s): 334595
    Usage: 1973–1975 C-10 to C-30 Chevrolet and 1500 to 3500 GMC truck, Blazer, and Jimmy—all with woodgrain exterior, Fleetside models only

Interchange Number: 9
    Part Number(s): 3914958
    Usage: 1973 C-10 Chevrolet and 1500 GMC cab models with LPG and woodgrain exterior; 1976–1978 P20 to P30 Chevrolet service van with 30-gallon tank

Interchange Number: 10
    Part Number(s): 6263474
    Usage: 1973 C-10 to C-30 Chevrolet and 1500 to 3500 GMC Stepside with EEC

Interchange Number: 11
    Part Number(s): 343171
    Usage: 1973–1975 C-10 to C-30 Chevrolet and 1500 to 3500 GMC Stepside without EEC

Interchange Number: 12
    Part Number(s): 343172
    Usage: 1973–1975 C-10 to C-30 Chevrolet and 1500 to 3500 GMC Fleetside, Blazer, Jimmy, and Suburban without woodgrain trim
    Note(s): Chrome with black handle

Interchange Number: 13
    Part Number(s): 3431616
    Usage: 1976–1977 C-10 to C-30 Chevrolet and 1500 to 3500 GMC Fleetside, Blazer, Jimmy, and Suburban with woodgrain

Interchange Number: 14
    Part Number(s): 471674
    Usage: 1978–1979 C-10 to C-30 Chevrolet and 1500 to 3500 GMC Fleetside, Blazer, Jimmy, and Suburban with woodgrain

Fuel Pumps
Model Identification

1967	Interchange Number
283-ci V-8	1
327-ci V-8	
early	1
late	2
1968	
307-ci V-8	1
327-ci V-8	2
396-ci V-8	7
1969	
307-ci V-8	1
350-ci V-8	3
396-ci V-8	8
1970–1971	
307-ci V-8	1
350-ci V-8	4
396/402-ci	8
1972	
307-ci V-8	1
350-ci V-8	
with manual transmission	4
with automatic transmission	5
396-ci V-8	8
1973	
307-ci V-8	9
350-ci V-8	
with manual transmission	4
with automatic transmission	5
454-ci V-8	10
1974	
350-ci V-8	
with manual transmission	4
with automatic transmission	5
454-ci V-8	10
1975	
350-ci V-8	
with manual transmission	4
with automatic transmission	5
454-ci V-8	10
1976	
350-ci V-8	
with manual transmission	4
with automatic transmission	5
400-ci V-8	5
454-ci V-8	10
1977	
305-ci V-8	4
350-ci V-8	
with manual transmission	4
with automatic transmission	5
400-ci V-8	5
454-ci	10
1978	
305-ci V-8	4
350-ci V-8	
two-wheel drive	
with manual transmission	4
with automatic transmission	5
four-wheel drive	
manual transmission	11
automatic transmission	12
400-ci V-8	5
454-ci V-8	10

Interchanges
Interchange Number: 1
    Part Number(s): 6416712
    Stamped: 40503 or 40433
    Usage: 1967 C-10 to C-30 Chevrolet and 1500 to

3500 GMC truck, van, Chevelle, Chevy II, and Impala with 283-ci V-8; early-1967 C-10 to C-30 Chevrolet and 1500 to 3500 GMC truck and van, Camaro, Chevelle, Chevy II, and Impala with 327-ci V-8 (except special high-performance); 1968–1972 C-10 to C-30 Chevrolet and 1500 to 3500 GMC truck and van, Blazer, Jimmy, Camaro, Chevelle, Impala, and Nova with 307-ci V-8

Interchange Number: 2
Part Number(s): 64170422
Stamped: 40524 or 40525
Usage: Late-1967 to 1968 C-10 to C-30 Chevrolet and 1500 to 3500 GMC truck, van, Chevelle, Chevy II/Nova, and Impala with 327-ci V-8; 1967–1968 Camaro Z-28 with 302-ci V-8; 1967–1968 Camaro with 350-ci V-8

Interchange Number: 3
Part Number(s): 6470779
Stamped: 40669
Usage: 1969 C-10 to C-30 Chevrolet and 1500 to 3500 GMC truck, van, Camaro, Chevelle, Impala, and Nova with 350-ci V-8; 1969 Camaro Z-28 with 302-ci V-8

Interchange Number: 4
Part Number(s): 6470779
Stamped: 40726
Usage: 1969–1971 C-10 to C-30 Chevrolet and 1500 to 3500 GMC truck, Blazer, and Jimmy 350 ci; 1970–1974 Camaro, Chevelle, Impala, Monte Carlo, Nova, Sprint with 350-ci, two-barrel V-8; 1972–1978 C-10 to C-30 Chevrolet and 1500 to 3500 GMC truck, Blazer, and Jimmy with manual transmission (except 1978 four-wheel-drive models) 350 ci; 1977–1980 C-10 to C-30 Chevrolet and 1500 to 3500 GMC truck, Blazer, Jimmy, Camaro, Chevelle, Impala, Monte Carlo, Nova, and Sprint; Firebird; Cutlass, Century, LeMans, Omega, Skylark, and Phoenix, all with 305-ci V-8

Interchange Number: 5
Part Number(s): 6470777
Stamped: 41216
Usage: 1972–1978 C-10 to C-30 Chevrolet and 1500 to 3500 GMC truck, Blazer, and Jimmy with 350-ci V-8 and automatic transmission (except 1978 four-wheel-drive models); 1973–1974 Chevelle, Monte Carlo, and Sprint with 350-ci, four-barrel or 400-ci, two-barrel V-8 and air conditioning; 1975–1977 C-10 to C-30 Chevrolet and 1500 to 3500 GMC truck, Blazer, and Jimmy with 400-ci V-8

Interchange Number: 6
Part Number(s): 6470777
Stamped: 41216
Usage: 1972–1978 C-10 to C-30 Chevrolet and 1500 to 3500 GMC truck, Blazer, and Jimmy 350-ci

Interchange Number: 7
Part Number(s):
Stamped: 40468
Usage: 1968 C-10 to C-30 Chevrolet and 1500 to 3500 GMC truck with 396-ci; 1967–1968 Camaro, Chevelle, Impala, and Nova with 396- or 427-ci V-8

Interchange Number: 8
Part Number(s):
Stamped: 40470 or 40727
Usage: 1969–1972 C-10 to C-30 Chevrolet and 1500 to 3500 GMC truck, Camaro, Chevelle, Impala, and Nova with 396/402-ci V-8; 1971–1972 Sprint with 402-ci V-8

Interchange Number: 9
Part Number(s): 6470778
Stamped: 40988
Usage: 1973 C-10 to C-30 Chevrolet and 1500 to 3500 GMC truck, Blazer, and Jimmy with 307-ci V-8

Interchange Number: 10
Part Number(s): 6470761
Stamped: 41001
Usage: 1973–1980 C-10 to C-30 Chevrolet and 1500 to 3500 GMC truck with 454-ci V-8; 1974–1975 Chevelle, Impala, Monte Carlo, and Sprint with 454-ci V-8

Interchange Number: 11
Part Number(s): 6471492
Stamped: : N/A
Usage: 1978–1980 C-10 to C-30 Chevrolet and 1500 to 3500 GMC truck, Blazer, and Jimmy four-wheel drive with manual transmission

Interchange Number: 12
Part Number(s): 6471493
Stamped: N/A
Usage: 1978–1980 C-10 to C-30 Chevrolet and 1500 to 3500 GMC truck, Blazer, and Jimmy four-wheel drive with automatic transmission

Intake Manifolds
Model Identification

1967	*Interchange Number*
283-ci V-8 1	
327-ci, four-barrel V-8 2	
1968	
307-ci V-8 3	

Interchanges

Interchange Number: 1
   Casting Number(s): 3877652
   Type: Cast iron
   Usage: 1966–1967 C-10 to C-30 Chevrolet and 1500 to 3500 GMC truck and van, Chevelle, and Impala with 283- or 327-ci, two-barrel V-8

Interchange Number: 2
   Casting Number(s): 3872783
   Type: Cast iron
   Usage: 1966–1967 C-10 to C-30 Chevrolet and 1500 to 3500 GMC truck and van with 327-ci, four-barrel V-8; 1966 Chevelle, Chevy II, and Impala with 283-ci, four-barrel or 327-ci, four-barrel V-8 (except special high-performance applications)

Interchange Number: 3
   Casting Number(s): 3919801
   Type: Cast iron
   Usage: 1968 C-10 to C-30 Chevrolet and 1500 to 3500 GMC truck and van, Camaro, Chevelle, Impala, and Nova with 307-ci or 327-ci, two-barrel V-8

Interchange Number: 4

Casting Number(s): 3872783

Type: Cast iron

Usage: 1968 C-10 to C-30 Chevrolet and 1500 to 3500 GMC truck and van, 327-ci; 1967–1968 Camaro, Chevelle, Impala, and Nova with 327-ci, four-barrel V-8

Interchange Number: 5

Casting Number(s): N/A

Type: Cast iron

Usage: 1969–1970 C-10 to C-30 Chevrolet and 1500 to 3500 GMC truck and van, 307-ci; 1967–1968 Camaro, Chevelle, Impala, and Nova with 307-ci V-8; early-1971 G-10 to G-30 Chevrolet and 1500 to 3500 GMC van with 307-ci V-8

Interchange Number: 6

Casting Number(s): 3965577

Type: Cast iron

Usage: 1969–1970 C-10 to C-30 Chevrolet and 1500 to 3500 GMC truck and van, 350-ci 4661; 1967–1968 Blazer, Camaro, Chevelle, Impala, Nova with 350-ci, four-barrel V-8; 1970 Monte Carlo and Jimmy with 350-ci, four-barrel V-8; early-1971 G-10 to G-30 Chevrolet and 1500 to 3500 GMC van with 350-ci, four-barrel V-8

Interchange Number: 7

Casting Number(s): N/A

Type: Cast iron

Usage: 1971 C-10 Chevrolet and 1500 GMC truck, Blazer, Jimmy, Camaro, Chevelle, Impala, Nova, and Ventura II with 307-ci V-8; late-1971 G-10 to G-30 Chevrolet and 1500 to 3500 GMC van with 307-ci V-8

Interchange Number: 8

Casting Number(s): 3973465

Type: Cast iron

Usage: 1971 C-20 to C-30 Chevrolet and 2500 to 3500 GMC truck with 307-ci V-8; 1971 Camaro, Chevelle, Impala, Nova, Sprint, and Ventura II with 350-ci, two-barrel V-8; 1971 C-40 Chevrolet and 4500 GMC truck with 350-ci V-8

Interchange Number: 9

Casting Number(s): 3973469

Type: Cast iron

Usage: 1971–1972 C-10 to C-30 Chevrolet and 1500 to 3500 GMC truck, Blazer, Jimmy, Chevelle, Corvette, Impala, Monte Carlo, and Nova with 350-ci, four-barrel V-8; 1973 C-20 to C-30 Chevrolet and 2500 to 3500 GMC truck (except Suburban) with 350-ci, four-barrel V-8; 1975–1978 C-10 to C-30 Chevrolet and 1500 to 3500 GMC truck and van, Blazer, and Jimmy 350-ci 4661 without EGR

Interchange Number: 10

Part Number(s): 3998149

Type: Cast iron

Usage: 1972 C-10 Chevrolet and 1500 GMC truck, Blazer, Jimmy, C-20 Suburban, Camaro, Chevelle, Impala, Monte Carlo, Nova, and Ventura II with 307-ci V-8

Interchange Number: 11

Part Number(s): 6262930

Type: Cast iron

Usage: 1972 C-20 to C-30 Chevrolet and 2500 to 3500 GMC truck (except Suburban) with 307-ci V-8; 1972 Camaro, Chevelle, Impala, Monte Carlo, Nova, and Ventura II with 350-ci, two-barrel V-8; 1972–1973 C-40 to C-50 Chevrolet and 4500 to 5500 GMC truck, without air brakes, 350-ci

Interchange Number: 12

Part Number(s): 6271060

Type: Cast iron

Usage: 1973 C-10 Chevrolet and 1500 GMC truck, Blazer, Jimmy, C-20 Suburban, Camaro, Chevelle, Impala, Monte Carlo, Nova, and Ventura II with 307-ci V-8

Interchange Number: 13

Part Number(s): 3997772

Type: Cast iron

Usage: 1973 C-20 to C-30 Chevrolet and 2500 to 3500 GMC truck (except Suburban) with 307-ci V-8; 1973 Camaro, Chevelle, Impala, Monte Carlo, Nova, and Ventura II with 350-ci, two-barrel V-8

Interchange Number: 14

Part Number(s): 3997770

Type: Cast iron

Usage: 1973 C-10 Chevrolet and 1500 GMC truck, Blazer, Jimmy, C-20 Suburban, Camaro, Chevelle, Corvette, Impala, Monte Carlo, and Nova with 350-ci V-8 (except LT-1 and Z-28 models)

Interchange Number: 15

Part Number(s): 340265

Type: Cast iron

Usage: 1974 C-10 Chevrolet and 1500 GMC truck, Blazer, Jimmy, C-20 Suburban, Camaro, Chevelle, Impala, Monte Carlo, and Nova with 350-ci, two-barrel V-8

Interchange Number: 16

Part Number(s): 340260

Type: Cast iron

Usage: 1974 C-10 to C-30 Chevrolet and 1500 to 3500 GMC truck, Blazer, Jimmy, C-20 Suburban, Camaro, Chevelle, Corvette, Impala, Monte Carlo, and Nova with 350-ci, four-barrel V-8

Interchange Number: 17

Part Number(s): 343755

Type: Cast iron

Usage: 1975–1976 C-10 Chevrolet and 1500 GMC truck, Blazer, Jimmy, C-20 Suburban, Camaro Chevelle, Impala, Monte Carlo, and Nova with 350-ci, two-barrel V-8; 1977–1978 C-10 to C-30 Chevrolet and 1500 to 3500 GMC truck and van, Blazer, Jimmy, Camaro, Chevelle, Impala, Monte Carlo, Nova, Firebird, Cutlass, Sunbird, Monza, Sprint, LeMans, Century, Omega, and Starfire with 305-ci V-8

Interchange Number: 18

Part Number(s): 14014499

Type: Cast iron

Usage: 1975–1980 C-10 to C-30 Chevrolet and 1500 to 3500 GMC truck, Blazer, Jimmy, Camaro Chevelle, Corvette, Impala, Monte Carlo, and Nova 350-ci 4661; 1978–1979 Cutlass, Omega, Phoenix, Century, LeMans, Sprint, Skylark, and Grand Prix with 350-ci, four-barrel or 400-ci, four-barrel V-8 with EGR

Interchange Number: 19

Part Number(s): 22500203

Type: Cast iron

Usage: 1978 C-10 to C-30 Chevrolet and 1500 to 3500 GMC truck and full-size Oldsmobile and Seville with diesel engine

Interchange Number: 20

Part Number(s): 3957996

Type: Cast iron

Usage: 1968–1969 C-10 to C-30 Chevrolet and 1500 to 3500 GMC truck with 396-ci; 1966–1969 Chevelle and Impala; 1967–1969 Camaro; 1968–1969 Nova all with 396-ci V-8 (except 350- or 375-horsepower versions); 1966–1968 Impala 427-ci, 390-horsepower V-8

Interchange Number: 21

Part Number(s): 3977608

Type: Cast iron

Usage: 1970–1971 C-10 to C-30 Chevrolet and 1500 to 3500 GMC truck, Camaro, Chevelle, Impala, Monte Carlo, and Nova with 396-ci V-8 (except 350- or 375-horsepower versions); 1970–1971 Chevelle, Corvette, Impala, Monte Carlo, and Sprint with 454-ci V-8 (except LS6 models)

Interchange Number: 22

Part Number(s): 3977608

Type: Cast iron

Usage: 1972 C-10 to C-30 Chevrolet and 1500 to 3500 GMC truck, Camaro, Chevelle, Impala, Monte Carlo, and Nova with 402-ci V-8 (except 350- or 375-horsepower versions); 1972 Chevelle, Corvette, Impala, Monte Carlo, and Sprint with 454-ci V-8

Interchange Number: 23

Part Number(s): 353068

Type: Cast iron

Usage: 1973 C-10 Chevrolet and 1500 GMC truck, C-20 Suburban, Chevelle, Corvette, Impala, Monte Carlo, and Sprint with 454-ci V-8 without NOX emissions

Interchange Number: 24

Part Number(s): 333839

Type: Cast iron

Usage: 1973 C-20 to C-30 Chevrolet and 2500 to 3500 GMC truck (except Suburban) with 454-ci V-8 without NOX emissions

Interchange Number: 25

Part Number(s): 330841

Type: Cast iron

Usage: 1973 C-20 to C-30 Chevrolet and 2500 to 3500 GMC truck (except Suburban) with 454-ci V-8 with NOX emissions

Interchange Number: 26

Part Number(s): 336788

Type: Cast iron

Usage: 1974 C-10 Chevrolet and 1500 GMC truck, C-20 Suburban, Chevelle, Corvette, Impala, Monte Carlo, and Sprint with 454-ci V-8

Interchange Number: 27

Part Number(s): 340217

Type: Cast iron

Usage: 1974 C-20 to C-30 Chevrolet and 2500 to 3500 GMC truck (except Suburban) with 454-ci V-8; 1975 C-10 to C-30 Chevrolet and 1500 to 3500 GMC truck with 454-ci V-8, without EGR

Interchange Number: 28

Part Number(s): 346241

Type: Cast iron

Usage: 1975 C-10 to C-30 Chevrolet and 1500 to 3500 GMC truck, Chevelle, Corvette, Impala, Monte Carlo, and Sprint with 454-ci V-8 with EGR

Interchange Number: 29

Part Number(s): 364764

Type: Cast iron

Usage: 1976–1978 C-10 to C-30 Chevrolet and 1500 to 3500 GMC truck, Chevelle, Impala, Monte Carlo, and Sprint with 454-ci V-8 with EGR

Interchange Number: 30

Part Number(s): 340217

Type: Cast iron

Usage: 1976–1978 C-10 to C-30 Chevrolet and 1500 to 3500 GMC truck with 454-ci V-8 without EGR

Carburetors

Carburetors used on the trucks covered in this manual differ in a number of ways, based on engine size, type of transmission, emission controls, and in some cases model and options installed on the truck. Only Rochester carburetors were used on Chevrolet models in the guide.

Typically, the Rochester ID number is found stamped on a metal tag or stamped onto the body itself. There is a drawback to the units with a metal tag. The tag is easily lost, and then the only way to identify the carburetor is to know exactly what the linkage looks like that you are needing, or to identify it by its jets. The latter method requires the use of an expert. Worse yet, jets can be changed, thus eliminating this means of identification. The best method is that you get a written statement from the seller of what it fits. This way if the unit does not fit, you can get your money back. Beware of sellers who won't make this agreement.

Model Identification

An air cleaner for a 1968 307-ci V-8.

Interchanges

Interchange Number: 1
  Usage: 1967 C-10 to C-30 Chevrolet truck and 1500 to 3500 GMC truck with 283-ci V-8, without AIR
  Model: Two-barrel
  ID Number(s): 7027105

Interchange Number: 2
  Usage: 1967 C-10 to C-30 Chevrolet truck and 1500 to 3500 GMC truck with 283-ci V-8, with AIR
  Model: Two-barrel
  ID Number(s): 7037105

Interchange Number: 3
  Usage: 1967 C-10 to C-30 Chevrolet truck and 1500 to 3500 GMC truck with 327-ci V-8, without AIR

Model: Four-barrel
ID Number(s): 7027125

Interchange Number: 4

Usage: 1967 C-10 to C-30 Chevrolet truck and 1500 to 3500 GMC truck with 327-ci V-8, with AIR
Model: Four-barrel
ID Number(s): 7037125

Interchange Number: 5

Usage: 1968 C-10 Chevrolet and 1500 GMC truck and Blazer with 307-ci V-8
Model: Two-barrel
ID Number(s): 7028105 (early) or 7028125 (late)

Interchange Number: 6

Usage: 1968 C-20 to C-30 Chevrolet and 2500 to 3500 GMC truck with 307-ci V-8
Model: Two-barrel
ID Number(s): 7028107 (early) or 7028127 (late)

Interchange Number: 7

Usage: 1968 C-10 to C-30 Chevrolet and 1500 to 3500 GMC truck and Blazer with 327-ci V-8
Model: Four-barrel
ID Number(s): 7028213

Interchange Number: 8

Usage: 1969 C-10 to C-30 Chevrolet and 1500 to 3500 GMC truck and Blazer with 307-ci V-8 without governor
Model: Two-barrel
ID Number(s): 7029105

Interchange Number: 9

Usage: 1969 C-10 to C-30 Chevrolet and 1500 to 3500 GMC truck and Blazer with 307-ci V-8 with governor
Model: Two-barrel
ID Number(s): 7029108

Interchange Number: 10

Usage: 1969 C-10 to C-30 Chevrolet and 1500 to 3500 GMC truck, Blazer, Camaro, Chevelle, Corvette, Impala, and Nova with 350-ci V-8 (except LT-1 models); 1968 Camaro, Chevelle, Corvette, Impala, and Nova with 327-ci V-8—all models with manual transmission
Model: Four-barrel
ID Number(s): 7029223

Interchange Number: 11

Usage: 1969 C-10 to C-30 Chevrolet and 1500 to 3500 GMC truck and Blazer with 350-ci V-8 with automatic transmission
Note(s): Units from cars will not fit due to different linkages
Model: Four-barrel
ID Number(s): 7029224

Interchange Number: 12

Usage: 1970 C-10 to C-30 Chevrolet and 1500 to 3500 GMC truck, Blazer, and Jimmy with 307-ci V-8 and manual transmission
Model: Two-barrel
ID Number(s): 7040105

Interchange Number: 13

Usage: 1970 C-10 Chevrolet and 1500 GMC truck, Blazer, and Jimmy with 307-ci V-8 and automatic transmission
Model: Two-barrel
ID Number(s): 7040125

Interchange Number: 14

Usage: 1970 C-20 to C-30 Chevrolet and 2500 to 3500 GMC truck with 307-ci V-8 and automatic transmission
Model: Two-barrel
ID Number(s): 7040108

Interchange Number: 15

Usage: 1970 C-10 to C-30 Chevrolet and 1500 to 3500 GMC truck, Blazer, and Jimmy with 350-ci V-8, with EEC
Model: Four-barrel
ID Number(s): 7040511

Interchange Number: 16

Usage: 1970 C-10 to C-30 Chevrolet and 1500 to 3500 GMC truck, Blazer, and Jimmy with 350-ci V-8, without EEC
Model: Four-barrel
ID Number(s): 7040208

Interchange Number: 17

Usage: 1970 C-10 to C-30 Chevrolet and 1500 to 3500 GMC truck with 396-ci V-8, without EEC
Model: Four-barrel
ID Number(s): 7040206

Interchange Number: 18

Usage: 1970 C-10 to C-30 Chevrolet and 1500 to 3500 GMC truck with 396-ci V-8, with EEC
Model: Four-barrel
ID Number(s): 7040509

Interchange Number: 19

Usage: 1971 C-10 Chevrolet and 1500 GMC truck, Blazer, and Jimmy with 307-ci V-8 and manual transmission
Model: Two-barrel
ID Number(s): 7041105

Interchange Number: 20

Usage: 1971 C-10 Chevrolet and 1500 GMC truck, Blazer, and Jimmy with 307-ci V-8 and automatic transmission
Model: Two-barrel
ID Number(s): 7041125

Interchange Number: 21

Usage: 1971 C-20 to C-30 Chevrolet and 2500 to 3500 GMC truck 307-ci V-8 and manual transmission
Model: Two-barrel
ID Number(s): 7041139

An air cleaner for a 1970 C-30 with 350-ci V-8.

Interchange Number: 22
Usage: 1971 C-20 to C-30 Chevrolet and 2500 to 3500 GMC truck with 307-ci V-8 and automatic transmission
Model: Two-barrel
ID Number(s): 7041138

Interchange Number: 23
Usage: 1971 C-10 Chevrolet and 1500 GMC truck, Blazer, and Jimmy with 350-ci V-8, all transmissions
Model: Four-barrel
ID Number(s): 7041211

Interchange Number: 24
Usage: 1971 C-10 Chevrolet and 1500 GMC truck, Blazer, and Jimmy with 350-ci V-8, all transmissions
Model: Four-barrel
ID Number(s): 7041208

Interchange Number: 25
Usage: 1971 C-20 to C-30 Chevrolet and 2500 to 3500 GMC truck with 402-ci V-8, all transmissions
Model: Four-barrel
ID Number(s): 7041206

Interchange Number: 26
Usage: 1972 C-10 to C-30 Chevrolet and 1500 to 3500 GMC truck, Blazer, and Jimmy with 307-ci V-8 and automatic transmission
Model: Two-barrel
ID Number(s): 7042104
Note(s): Salvage-yard dealers say 7042102, which is from a 1972 G-10/1500 van with 307-ci V-8 and automatic transmission, will fit

Interchange Number: 27
Usage: 1972 C-10 to C-30 Chevrolet and 1500 to 3500 GMC truck, Blazer, and Jimmy 307-ci V-8 and manual transmission
Model: Two-barrel
ID Number(s): 7042105
Note(s): Salvage-yard dealers say 7042103, which is from a 1972 G-10/1500 van with 307-ci V-8 and manual transmission, will fit

Interchange Number: 28
Usage: 1972 C-10 Chevrolet and 1500 GMC truck, Blazer, and Jimmy with 350-ci V-8, except California, with all transmissions
Model: Four-barrel
ID Number(s): 7042210 or 7042211

Interchange Number: 29
Usage: 1972 C-10 Chevrolet and 1500 GMC truck with 402-ci with manual transmission
Model: Four-barrel
ID Number(s): 7042219

Interchange Number: 30
Usage: 1972 C-10 Chevrolet and 1500 GMC truck with 402-ci with automatic transmission
Model: Four-barrel
ID Number(s): 7042218

Interchange Number: 31
Usage: 1972 C-20 to C-30 Chevrolet and 1500 to 3500 GMC truck with 402-ci with manual transmission
Model: Four-barrel
ID Number(s): 7042207

Interchange Number: 32
Usage: 1972 C-20 to C-30 Chevrolet and 2500 to 3500 GMC truck with 402-ci with automatic transmission
Model: Four-barrel
ID Number(s): 7042208

Interchange Number: 33
Usage: 1973 C-10 Chevrolet and 1500 GMC truck, Blazer, Jimmy, Camaro, Chevelle, and Nova with 307-ci V-8, all transmissions
Model: Two-barrel
ID Number(s): 7043105 or 7043101

Interchange Number: 34
Usage: 1973 C-20 to C-30 Chevrolet and 2500 to 3500 GMC truck with 307-ci V-8, all transmissions
Model: Two-barrel
ID Number(s): 7043108

Interchange Number: 35
Usage: 1973 C-10 to C-30 Chevrolet and 1500 to 3500 GMC truck, Blazer, Jimmy, Camaro, Chevelle, Corvette, Impala, Monte Carlo, Nova, and Sprint with 350 V-8 (except with Z-28, L-88, or with California emissions), all transmissions
Model: Four-barrel
ID Number(s): 7043202 or 7043203

Interchange Number: 36
Usage: 1973 C-10 Chevrolet and 1500 GMC truck with 454-ci V-8 and manual transmission
Model: Four-barrel
ID Number(s): 7043201

Interchange Number: 37
Usage: 1973 C-10 Chevrolet and 1500 GMC truck with 454-ci V-8 and automatic transmission
Model: Four-barrel
ID Number(s): 7043200

Interchange Number: 38
Usage: 1973 C-20 to C-30 Chevrolet and 2500 to 3500 GMC truck, with all transmissions
Model: Four-barrel
ID Number(s): 7043207

Interchange Number: 39
Usage: 1973 C-20 to C-30 Chevrolet and 2500 to 3500 GMC truck with 350-ci V-8, all transmissions
Model: Four-barrel
ID Number(s): 7043208

Interchange Number: 40
Usage: 1974 C-10 Chevrolet and 1500 GMC truck, Blazer, Jimmy, Camaro, Chevelle, Monte Carlo, Nova, and Sprint with 350-ci V-8 and manual transmission
Model: Two-barrel
ID Number(s): 7044113 or 7044111

Interchange Number: 41
Usage: 1974 C-10 Chevrolet and 1500 GMC truck, Blazer, Jimmy, Camaro, Chevelle, Impala, Monte Carlo, Nova, and Sprint with 350-ci V-8 and automatic transmission
Model: Two-barrel
ID Number(s): 7044114 or 7044112

Interchange Number: 42
Usage: 1974 C-10 Chevrolet and 1500 GMC truck, Blazer, Jimmy, Camaro, Chevelle, Impala, Monte Carlo, Nova, and Sprint with 350-ci V-8 and automatic transmission (except Z-28 or with California emissions)
Model: Four-barrel
ID Number(s): 7044202 or 7044206

Interchange Number: 43
Usage: 1974 C-10 Chevrolet and 1500 GMC truck, Blazer, Jimmy, Camaro, Chevelle, Monte Carlo, Nova, and Sprint with 350-ci V-8 and manual transmission (except Z-28 or with California emissions)
Model: Four-barrel
ID Number(s): 7044203 or 7044207

Interchange Number: 44
Usage: 1974 C-20 to C-30 Chevrolet and 2500 to 3500 GMC truck with 350-ci V-8, all transmissions

Model: Four-barrel
ID Number(s): 7044213

Interchange Number: 45
Usage: 1974 C-10 Chevrolet and 1500 GMC truck, Blazer, Jimmy, Camaro, Chevelle, Monte Carlo, Nova, and Sprint with 350-ci V-8 and manual transmission and California emissions (except Z-28)
Model: Four-barrel
ID Number(s): 7044507 or 7044563

Interchange Number: 46
Usage: 1974 C-10 Chevrolet and 1500 GMC truck, Blazer, Jimmy, Camaro, Chevelle, Monte Carlo, Nova, and Sprint with 350-ci V-8 and automatic transmission and California emissions (except Z-28); 1974 Suburban 454-ci V-8
Model: Four-barrel
ID Number(s): 7044502

Interchange Number: 47
Usage: 1974 C-10 Chevrolet and 1500 GMC truck, Chevelle, Corvette, Impala, Monte Carlo, and Sprint with 454-ci V-8, all transmissions (without California emissions)
Model: Four-barrel
ID Number(s): 7044223
Note(s): Automatic transmission only in cars

Interchange Number: 48
Usage: 1974 C-10 Chevrolet and 1500 GMC truck, Chevelle, Corvette, Impala, Monte Carlo, and Sprint with 454-ci V-8, all transmissions, with California emissions
Model: Four-barrel
ID Number(s): 7044500
Note(s): Automatic transmission only in cars

Interchange Number: 49
Usage: 1974 C-20 to C-30 Chevrolet and 2500 to 3500 GMC truck with 454-ci V-8, all transmissions, with California emissions
Model: Four-barrel
ID Number(s): 70445512 or 7044517

Interchange Number: 50
Usage: 1974 C-20/2500 Suburban with 350-ci, four-barrel V-8 or 454-ci, four-barrel V-8 without California emissions
Model: Four-barrel
ID Number(s): 7044227

Interchange Number: 51
Usage: 1974 C-20 to C-30 Chevrolet and 2500 to 3500 GMC (except Suburban) with 454-ci V-8, without California emissions
Model: Four-barrel
ID Number(s): 7044212 or 7044217

Interchange Number: 52
Usage: 1975–1976 C-10 Chevrolet and 1500 GMC truck, Blazer, Camaro, Chevelle, Impala, Nova,

and G-10 Chevrolet and 1500 GMC van with 350-ci V-8

Model: Two-barrel

ID Number(s): 7045114, 7045115, 7045116, 7045123, 7045124, 17056115, 17056116, 17056123, or 17056124

Interchange Number: 53

Usage: 1975 C-10 Chevrolet and 1500 GMC truck with heavy-duty chassis; C-10/1500 Suburban; C-20 to C-30 and 2500 to 3500 GMC truck and service van with 454-ci V-8, without California emissions

Model: Four-barrel

ID Number(s): 7045212 or 7045217

Interchange Number: 54

Usage: 1975–1976 C-10 Chevrolet and 1500 GMC truck with heavy-duty chassis; C-10/1500 Suburban; C-20 to C-30 and 2500 to 3500 GMC truck and service van with 454-ci V-8, with California emissions

Model: Four-barrel

ID Number(s): 7045512, 7045517, 17056512, or 17056517

Interchange Number: 55

Usage: 1975–1976 C-10 Chevrolet and 1500 GMC truck with heavy-duty chassis; C-10/1500 Suburban; C-20 to C-30 and 2500 to 3500 GMC truck, Blazer, and Jimmy all with 350-ci V-8, with California emissions; 1975–1976 C-10 to C-20 Chevrolet and 1500 to 2500 GMC truck, Blazer, and Jimmy four-wheel drive; G-20 to G-30 Chevrolet and 2500 to 3500 GMC van with 400-ci V-8

Model: Four-barrel

ID Number(s): 7045215, 7045585, 7045583, 7045586, 7045225, or 7045588

Interchange Number: 56

Usage: 1975–1976 C-10 Chevrolet and 1500 GMC truck with heavy-duty chassis; C-10/1500 Suburban; C-20 to C-30 and 2500 to 3500 GMC truck, Blazer, and Jimmy—all with 350-ci V-8, without California emissions

Model: Four-barrel

ID Number(s): 7045213 or 7045216

Interchange Number: 57

Usage: 1975 C-10 Chevrolet and 1500 GMC truck without heavy-duty chassis, Blazer, and Jimmy with 350-ci V-8 and automatic transmission, two-wheel drive only

Model: Four-barrel

ID Number(s): 7045202

Interchange Number: 58

Usage: 1975 C-10 Chevrolet and 1500 GMC truck without heavy-duty chassis with 454-ci V-8

Model: Four-barrel

ID Number(s): 7045220

Interchange Number: 59

Usage: 1976–1977 C-10 Chevrolet and 1500 GMC truck with heavy-duty chassis with 454-ci V-8 (without California emissions); C-10/1500 Suburban all powerplants, without California emissions; C-20 to C-30 Chevrolet and 2500 to 3500 GMC truck with 454-ci V-8, without California emissions

Model: Four-barrel

ID Number(s): 17056212 or 17056217

Interchange Number: 60

Usage: 1976 C-10 Chevrolet and 1500 GMC truck without heavy-duty chassis with 350-ci V-8 and manual transmission, without California emissions

Model: Four-barrel

ID Number(s): 17056209

Interchange Number: 61

Usage: 1976 C-10 Chevrolet and 1500 GMC truck without heavy-duty chassis with 350-ci V-8 and automatic transmission, without California emissions

Model: Four-barrel

ID Number(s): 17056208

Interchange Number: 62

Usage: 1976 C-10 Chevrolet and 1500 GMC truck without heavy-duty chassis with 350-ci V-8 and manual transmission, with California emissions

Model: Four-barrel

ID Number(s): 17056509

Interchange Number: 63

Usage: 1976 C-10 Chevrolet and 1500 GMC truck without heavy-duty chassis with 350-ci V-8 and automatic transmission, with California emissions

Model: Four-barrel

ID Number(s): 17056508

Interchange Number: 64

Usage: 1976 C-10 Chevrolet and 1500 GMC truck without heavy-duty chassis with 454-ci V-8

Model: Four-barrel

ID Number(s): 17056221

Interchange Number: 65

Usage: 1977 C-10 to C-30 Chevrolet and 1500 to 3500 GMC truck with 454-ci V-8, with California emissions

Model: Four-barrel

ID Number(s): 17057512 or 17057517

Interchange Number: 66

Usage: 1977 C-10 and 1500 GMC truck with 454-ci V-8, without heavy-duty chassis

Model: Four-barrel

ID Number(s): 17057221

Interchange Number: 67
Usage: 1977 C-10 and 1500 GMC truck with 350-ci V-8 and automatic transmission, without heavy-duty chassis or California emissions
Model: Four-barrel
ID Number(s): 17057202 or 17057204

Interchange Number: 68
Usage: 1977 C-10 and 1500 GMC truck with 350-ci V-8 and automatic transmission, without heavy-duty chassis, with California emissions
Model: Four-barrel
ID Number(s): 17057502 or 17057504

Interchange Number: 69
Usage: 1977 C-10 and 1500 GMC truck with 350-ci V-8, with high-altitude package
Model: Four-barrel
ID Number(s): 17057582 or 17057584

Interchange Number: 70
Usage: 1977 C-10 and 1500 GMC truck with 350-ci V-8 and heavy-duty chassis; C-20 to C-30 Chevrolet and 2500 to 3500 GMC truck; G-20 to G-30 Chevrolet and 2500 to 3500 GMC van—all with 350-ci V-8, without California emissions
Model: Four-barrel
ID Number(s): 17057213

Interchange Number: 71
Usage: 1977 C-10 to C-30 and 1500 to 3500 GMC truck, Blazer, and Jimmy with 400-ci V-8, with California emissions
Model: Four-barrel
ID Number(s): 17057529

Interchange Number: 72
Usage: 1977 C-10 to C-30 Chevrolet and 1500 to 3500 GMC truck, Blazer, and Jimmy with 400-ci V-8, without California emissions
Model: Four-barrel
ID Number(s): 17057229

Interchange Number: 73
Usage: 1977 C-10 Chevrolet and 1500 GMC truck, Blazer, and Jimmy with 350-ci V-8 and manual transmission, without California emissions
Model: Four-barrel
ID Number(s): 17057503

Interchange Number: 74
Usage: 1977 C-10 Chevrolet and 1500 GMC truck with heavy-duty chassis, C-20 to C-30 Chevrolet and 2500 to 3500 GMC truck, Blazer, Jimmy, and Suburban—all with 350-ci V-8, with California emissions
Model: Four-barrel
ID Number(s): 7045215 or 7045585

Interchange Number: 75
Usage: 1977 C-10 Chevrolet and 1500 GMC truck and G-10 Chevrolet and 1500 GMC van with 305-ci V-8 and automatic transmission, with air conditioning
Model: Two-barrel
ID Number(s): 17057110

Interchange Number: 76
Usage: 1977 C-10 Chevrolet and 1500 GMC truck with 305-ci V-8 and automatic transmission, without air conditioning
Model: Two-barrel
ID Number(s): 17057108

Interchange Number: 77
Usage: 1977 C-10 Chevrolet and 1500 GMC truck with 305-ci V-8 and manual transmission, with air conditioning
Model: Two-barrel
ID Number(s): 17057123

Interchange Number: 78
Usage: 1977 C-10 Chevrolet and 1500 GMC truck with 305-ci V-8 and manual transmission, without air conditioning
Model: Two-barrel
ID Number(s): 17057113

Interchange Number: 79
Usage: 1977 C-10 to C-20 and 1500 to 2500 Suburban, Blazer, and Jimmy with 305-ci V-8
Model: Two-barrel
ID Number(s): 17057137

Interchange Number: 80
Usage: 1978 C-10 to C-20 and 1500 to 2500 Suburban, Blazer, and Jimmy with 305-ci V-8, all transmissions
Model: Two-barrel
ID Number(s): 17058127

Interchange Number: 81
Usage: 1978 C-10 Chevrolet and 1500 GMC truck with 350-ci V-8 and manual transmission, without California emissions
Model: Four-barrel
ID Number(s): 17058201

Interchange Number: 82
Usage: 1978 C-10 Chevrolet and 1500 GMC truck with 350-ci V-8 and manual transmission, with California emissions
Model: Four-barrel
ID Number(s): 17058503

Interchange Number: 83
Usage: 1978 C-10 Chevrolet and 1500 GMC truck with 350-ci V-8 and automatic transmission, without California emissions or air conditioning
Model: Four-barrel
ID Number(s): 17058202

Interchange Number: 84
> Usage: 1978 C-10 Chevrolet and 1500 GMC truck with 350-ci V-8 and auto transmission, with air conditioning, without California emissions
> Model: Four-barrel
> ID Number(s): 17058204

Interchange Number: 85
> Usage: 1978 C-10 Chevrolet and 1500 GMC truck with 350-ci V-8 and auto transmission, with California emissions, without air conditioning
> Model: Four-barrel
> ID Number(s): 17058506

Interchange Number: 86
> Usage: 1978 C-10 Chevrolet and 1500 GMC truck with 350-ci V-8 and automatic transmission, with California emissions and air conditioning
> Model: Four-barrel
> ID Number(s): 17058508

Interchange Number: 87
> Usage: 1978 C-20 to C-30 Chevrolet 2500 to 3500 GMC truck and G-20 to G-30 Chevrolet and 2500 to 3500 GMC van with 350-ci V-8 and manual transmission
> Model: Four-barrel
> ID Number(s): 17058213

Interchange Number: 88
> Usage: 1978 C-10 to C-20 Chevrolet and 1500 to 2500 GMC truck, Blazer, and Jimmy with 400-ci V-8, without air conditioning
> Model: Four-barrel
> ID Number(s): 17058527

Interchange Number: 89
> Usage: 1978 C-10 to C-20 Chevrolet and 1500 to 2500 GMC truck, Blazer, and Jimmy with 400-ci V-8, with air conditioning
> Model: Four-barrel
> ID Number(s): 17058528

Interchange Number: 90
> Usage: 1968 C-10 to C-30 Chevrolet and 1500 to 3500 GMC truck and 1968–1969 Camaro, Chevelle, Impala, and Nova with 396-ci V-8 and manual transmission (except 375-horsepower option); 1968–1969 Impala with 427-ci 390-horsepower and manual transmission
> Model: Four-barrel
> ID Number(s): 7028217

Interchange Number: 91
> Usage: 1968 C-10 to C-30 Chevrolet and 1500 to 3500 GMC truck and 1968–1969 Camaro, Chevelle, Impala, and Nova with 396-ci V-8 and automatic transmission (except 375-horse-power option); 1968–1969 Impala with 427-ci 390-horsepower and automatic transmission
> Model: Four-barrel
> ID Number(s): 7028218

Interchange Number: 92
> Usage: 1969 C-10 to C-30 Chevrolet and 1500 to 2500 GMC truck with 396-ci V-8
> Model: Four-barrel
> ID Number(s): 7029214

Air Cleaners
Model Identification

1967	*Interchange Number*
283-ci V-8	
paper	
without PCV	1
with PCV	2
oil bath	3
327-ci V-8	
paper	4
oil bath	5
1968	
307-ci V-8	
paper	
manual transmission	6
automatic	7
oil bath	8
327-ci V-8	
paper	
manual transmission	10
automatic transmission	11
oil bath	9
396-ci V-8	10
1969	
307-ci V-8	
paper	
manual transmission	6
automatic transmission	7
oil bath	8
350-ci, four-barrel V-8	
paper, except LPG	
manual transmission	12
automatic transmission	13
paper, LPG	14
oil bath	
except LPG	16
LPG	15
396-ci V-8	10
1970	
307-ci V-8	
paper	
manual transmission	6
automatic transmission	7
oil bath	18
350-ci, four-barrel V-8	
paper	13
oil bath	18
396-ci V-8	13

Interchanges
Interchange Number: 1
Part Number(s): 6423927
Usage: 1967 C-10 to C-30 Chevrolet and 1500 to 3500 GMC truck with 283-ci, two-barrel V-8, without PCV
Note(s): Paper filter
Interchange Number: 2
Part Number(s): 6484445
Usage: 1967 C-10 to C-30 Chevrolet and 1500 to 3500 GMC truck with 283-ci, two-barrel V-8, with PCV
Note(s): Paper filter
Interchange Number: 3
Part Number(s): 6423060
Usage: 1967 C-10 to C-30 Chevrolet and 1500 to 3500 GMC truck with 283-ci, two-barrel V-8, without PCV
Note(s): Oil-bath filter
Interchange Number: 4
Part Number(s): 6420903

Usage: 1967 C-10 to C-30 Chevrolet and 1500 to 3500 GMC truck with 327-ci, four-barrel V-8

Note(s): Paper filter

Interchange Number: 5

Part Number(s): 6423061

Usage: 1967 C-10 to C-30 Chevrolet and 1500 to 3500 GMC truck with 327-ci, four-barrel V-8

Note(s): Oil-bath filter

Interchange Number: 6

Part Number(s): 6483723

Usage: 1968–1970 C-10 to C-30 Chevrolet and 1500 to 3500 GMC truck with 307-ci, two-barrel V-8 and manual transmission

Note(s): Paper filter

Interchange Number: 7

Part Number(s): 6483700

Usage: 1968–1969 C-10 to C-30 Chevrolet and 1500 to 3500 GMC truck with 307-ci, two-barrel V-8 and automatic transmission; 1970–1971 C-10 to C-30 Chevrolet and 1500 to 3500 GMC truck, Blazer, and Jimmy with 307-ci V-8, all transmissions

Note(s): Paper filter

Interchange Number: 8

Part Number(s): 6484020

Usage: 1968–1969 C-10 to C-30 Chevrolet and 1500 to 3500 GMC truck with 307-ci, two-barrel V-8

Note(s): Oil-bath filter

Interchange Number: 9

Part Number(s): 6483701

Usage: 1968 C-10 to C-30 Chevrolet and 1500 to 3500 GMC truck with 307-ci, two-barrel V-8

Note(s): Oil-bath filter

Interchange Number: 10

Part Number(s): 6483808

Usage: 1968 C-10 to C-30 Chevrolet and 1500 to 3500 GMC truck with 327-ci, four-barrel V-8 and manual transmission; 1968–1969 C-10 to C-30 Chevrolet and 1500 to 3500 GMC truck with 396-ci V-8

Note(s): Paper filter

Interchange Number: 11

Part Number(s): 6484164

Usage: 1968 C-10 to C-30 Chevrolet and 1500 to 3500 GMC truck with 327-ci, four-barrel V-8 and automatic transmission

Note(s): Paper filter

Interchange Number: 12

Part Number(s): 6485381

Usage: 1969 C-10 to C-30 Chevrolet and 1500 to 3500 GMC truck with 350-ci, four-barrel V-8 and manual transmission, except with LPG

Note(s): Paper filter

Interchange Number: 13

Part Number(s): 6485382

Usage: 1969 C-10 to C-30 Chevrolet and 1500 to 3500 GMC truck with 350-ci, four-barrel V-8 and automatic transmission; 1970–1971 C-10 to C-30 Chevrolet and 1500 to 3500 GMC truck, Blazer, and Jimmy with 350-ci, four-barrel V-8 or 396-ci, four-barrel V-8, all transmissions

Note(s): Paper filter

Interchange Number: 14

Part Number(s): 6484667 (manual)

Usage: 1969 C-10 to C-30 Chevrolet and 1500 to 3500 GMC truck with 350-ci, four-barrel V-8 and manual transmission, with LPG

Note(s): Paper filter

Interchange Number: 15

Part Number(s): 6484987

Usage: 1969 C-10 to C-30 Chevrolet and 1500 to 3500 GMC truck with 350-ci, four-barrel V-8 and manual transmission, with LPG

Note(s): Oil-bath filter

Interchange Number: 16

Part Number(s): 6485384

Usage: 1969 C-10 to C-30 Chevrolet and 1500 to 3500 GMC truck with 350-ci, four-barrel V-8 and manual transmission, except with LPG

Note(s): Oil-bath filter

Interchange Number: 17

Part Number(s): 6485384

Usage: 1969 C-10 to C-30 Chevrolet and 1500 to 3500 GMC truck with 350-ci, four-barrel V-8 and manual transmission, except with LPG

Note(s): Oil-bath filter

Interchange Number: 18

Part Number(s): 6486151 (two-wheel drive) or 6485787 (four-wheel drive)

Usage: 1970–1971 C-10 to C-30 Chevrolet and 1500 to 3500 GMC truck, Blazer, and Jimmy with 307-ci, two-barrel or 350-ci, four-barrel V-8

Note(s): Oil-bath filter

Interchange Number: 19

Part Number(s): 6487575

Usage: 1973 C-10 to C-30 Chevrolet and 1500 to 3500 GMC truck and Blazer with 307-ci, two-barrel V-8; 1974 C-10 Chevrolet and 1500 to 3500 GMC truck with 350-ci, two-barrel V-8

Interchange Number: 20

Part Number(s): 8994137

Usage: 1973–1974 C-10 to C-30 Chevrolet and 1500 to 3500 GMC truck and Blazer with 350-ci, four-barrel V-8, all transmissions

Interchange Number: 21

   Part Number(s): 8996407

   Usage: 1973–1974 C-10 to C-30 Chevrolet and 1500 to 3500 GMC truck; 1975–1977 C-10 with heavy-duty chassis and Suburban—all with 454-ci V-8, without California emissions

Interchange Number: 22

   Part Number(s): 8994031

   Usage: 1975 C-10 Chevrolet and 1500 GMC truck, Blazer, and Jimmy with 350-ci, two-barrel V-8; 1976 C-10 Chevrolet and 1500 GMC truck, Blazer, and Jimmy with 305-ci V-8

Interchange Number: 23

   Part Number(s): 8994137

   Usage: 1975–1976 C-10 to C-30 Chevrolet and 1500 to 3500 GMC truck, Blazer, and Jimmy with 350-ci, four-barrel V-8 or 400-ci, four-barrel V-8, without California emissions

Interchange Number: 24

   Part Number(s): 8995069

   Usage: 1975–1976 C-10 to C-30 Chevrolet and 1500 to 3500 GMC truck, Blazer, and Jimmy with 350-ci, four-barrel V-8 or 400-ci, four-barrel V-8, with California emissions

Interchange Number: 25

   Part Number(s): 8994030

   Usage: 1975 C-10 Chevrolet and 1500 GMC truck without heavy-duty chassis

Interchange Number: 26

   Part Number(s): 8994032

   Usage: 1975 C-10 Chevrolet and 1500 GMC truck without heavy-duty chassis, with 350-ci, four-barrel V-8

Interchange Number: 27

   Part Number(s): 8995215

   Usage: 1975 C-10 Chevrolet and 1500 GMC truck without heavy-duty chassis, with 350-ci, four-barrel V-8

Interchange Number: 28

   Part Number(s): 8996430

   Usage: 1975–1978 C-10 Chevrolet and 1500 GMC truck, Blazer, and Jimmy with 305-ci V-8, except 1978 Suburban

Interchange Number: 29

   Part Number(s): 8995523

   Usage: 1977–1978 C-10 to C-20 Chevrolet and 1500 to 3500 GMC truck, Blazer, and Jimmy with 350-ci V-8, without heavy-duty chassis, with California emissions

Interchange Number: 30

   Part Number(s): 8997577

   Usage: 1977–1978 C-10 to C-20 Chevrolet and 1500 to 3500 GMC truck, Blazer, and Jimmy with 350-ci V-8, with heavy-duty chassis, without California emissions

Interchange Number: 31

   Part Number(s): 8994631

   Usage: 1978 C-10 to C-20 Chevrolet and 1500 to 2500 Suburban with 305-ci V-8

Interchange Number: 32

   Part Number(s): 8996030

   Usage: 1978 C-10 to C-20 Chevrolet and 1500 to 2500 Suburban or cab models with California emissions; 1978 C-10 Chevrolet and 1500 GMC truck without heavy-duty chassis—all with 454-ci V-8

Interchange Number: 33

   Part Number(s): 8996407

   Usage: 1978 C-10 to C-30 Chevrolet and 1500 to 3500 GMC truck with 454-ci V-8, without California emissions, with heavy-duty chassis

Interchange Number: 33

   Part Number(s): 8996408

   Usage: 1978 C-30 Chevrolet and 3500 GMC truck with 454-ci V-8, with California emissions

Interchange Number: 34

   Part Number(s): 8996039

   Usage: 1978 C-10 Chevrolet and 1500 GMC truck with diesel engine

3 Oil and Cooling Systems

Oil Pumps
Model Identification

1967	Interchange Number
283-ci V-8	1
327-ci V-8	1
1968	
307-ci V-8	1
327-ci V-8	1
396-ci V-8	3
1969–1972	
307-ci V-8	1
350-ci V-8	1
396-ci V-8	3
1973	
307-ci V-8	1
350-ci V-8	1
454-ci V-8	3
1974–1978	
350-ci V-8	2
454-ci V-8	3

Interchanges

Interchange Number: 1

Part Number(s): 3821979

Usage: 1960–1973 C-10 to C-30 Chevrolet and 1500 to 3500 GMC truck and Impala; 1964–1973 Chevelle and Chevy II/Nova; 1967–1973 Camaro and Corvette; 1970–1973 Monte Carlo and Jimmy; 1969–1973 Blazer; 1971–1972 Ventura II—all with 283-, 307-, 327-, or 350-ci V-8, except Z-28, LT-1, L-88, or models with special high-performance equipment

Interchange Number: 2

Part Number(s): 3764547

Usage: 1974–1981 C-10 to C-30 Chevrolet and 1500 to 3500 GMC truck, Blazer, Jimmy, Camaro, Chevelle, Impala, Monte Carlo, Nova, and Sprint with 350-ci V-8; 1977–1980 Century, LeMans, Firebird, Starfire, Omega, Sunbird, Skylark, and Grand Prix with 305- or 350-ci V-8; 1975–1980 C-10 to C-30 Chevrolet and 1500 to 3500 GMC truck, Blazer, Jimmy, Impala, and Monte Carlo with 400-ci V-8; 1973 C-10 to C-30 Chevrolet and 1500 to 3500 GMC truck, Blazer, Jimmy, Camaro, Chevelle, and Nova with 307-ci V-8

Interchange Number: 3

Part Number(s): 475906

Usage: 1968–1972 C-10 to C-30 Chevrolet and 1500 to 3500 GMC truck, Camaro, Chevelle, Impala, and Nova with 396/402-ci V-8 (except 375-horsepower option); 1966–1969 Impala, Corvette with 427-ci V-8 (except special high horsepower); 1970–1979 C-10 to C-30 Chevrolet and 1500 to 3500 GMC truck and 1970–1976 Chevelle, Impala, Monte Carlo, Sprint with 454-ci V-8

Oil Pans
Model Identification

1967	Interchange Number
283-ci V-8	1
327-ci V-8	1
1968	
307-ci V-8	1
327-ci V-8	1
396-ci V-8	3
1969–1970	
307-ci V-8	1
350-ci V-8	1
396-ci V-8	
1969	3
1970	4
1971–1972	
307-ci V-8	2
350-ci V-8	2
396-ci V-8	4
1973–1974	
307-ci V-8 (1973 only)	2
350-ci V-8	2
454-ci V-8	4
1975–1976	
350-ci V-8	2
400-ci V-8	2
454-ci V-8	5
1977–1978	
305-ci V-8	2
350-ci V-8	2

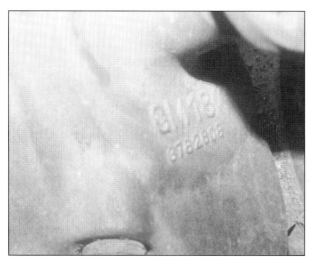

A water pump casting number.

Interchanges

Interchange Number: 1

Part Number(s): 359939

Usage: 1958–1970 C-10 to C-30 Chevrolet and 1500 to 3500 GMC truck; 1969–1970 Blazer; 1970 Jimmy; 1958–1964 Impala; 1964–1967 Chevelle—all with 283-, 307-, 327-, or 350-ci V-8

Interchange Number: 2

Part Number(s): 465221

Usage: 1970–1979 C-10 to C-30 Chevrolet and 1500 to 3500 GMC truck, Blazer, Jimmy, Camaro, Chevelle, Impala, Monte Carlo, and Nova with 307- or 350-ci V-8; 1971–1972 Ventura II with 307- or 350-ci V-8; 1977–1979 C-10 to C-30 Chevrolet and 1500 to 3500 GMC, Blazer, Jimmy, Camaro, Impala, Malibu, Monte Carlo, Nova, Omega, Sprint, Firebird, and LeMans with 305-ci V-8; 1976–1979 C-10 to C-30 Chevrolet and 1500 to 3500 GMC truck, Blazer, Jimmy, Monte Carlo, Impala, and Sprint with 400-ci V-8

Interchange Number: 3

Part Number(s): 3974328

Usage: 1968–1969 C-10 to C-30 Chevrolet and 1500 to 3500 GMC truck; 1967–1969 Impala with 396-ci V-8; 1970 Chevelle, Impala, Monte Carlo with 454-ci V-8

Interchange Number: 4

Part Number(s): 3985999

Usage: 1970–1972 C-10 to C-30 Chevrolet and 1500 to 3500 GMC truck with 396-ci V-8; 1965–1974 Chevelle, 1968–1972 Nova, 1970–1972 Monte Carlo—all with 396/402-ci V-8. 1971–1974 Chevelle, Impala, and Monte Carlo; 1973–1974 C-10 to C-30 Chevrolet and 1500 to 3500 GMC truck—all with 454-ci V-8

Interchange Number: 5

Part Number(s): 346232

Usage: 1975–1976 C-10 to C-30 Chevrolet and 1500 to 3500 GMC truck, Impala, Monte Carlo, Sprint, and Chevelle; 1977–1981 P10 to P30 Chevrolet service van—all with 454-ci V-8

Interchange Number: 6

Part Number(s): 14081031

Usage: 1977–1979 C-10 to C-30 Chevrolet and 1500 to 3500 GMC truck and motorhome with 454-ci V-8

Radiators
Model Identification

1967	Interchange Number
283-ci V-8 1	
327-ci V-8	
without air conditioning 1	
with air conditioning .2	
1968	
307-ci V-8	
manual transmission	
without heavy-duty cooling or air conditioning . .3	
with heavy-duty cooling 1	
automatic transmission 1	
327-ci V-8	
without air conditioning 1	
with air conditioning .2	
396-ci V-8	
without air conditioning or heavy-duty cooling .1	
with air conditioning or heavy-duty cooling 2	
1969–1972	
307-ci V-8	
manual transmission	
without heavy-duty cooling or air conditioning . .3	
with heavy-duty cooling 1	
automatic transmission 1	
350-ci V-8	
without air conditioning 1	
with air conditioning .2	
396/402-ci V-8	
without air conditioning or heavy-duty cooling .1	
with air conditioning or heavy-duty cooling 2	
1973	
307-ci V-8	
manual transmission	
without heavy-duty cooling or air conditioning 4	
with heavy-duty cooling or air conditioning . .5	
automatic transmission 6	

350-ci V-8

 manual transmission

  without heavy-duty cooling or air conditioning .4

  with heavy-duty cooling or air conditioning . .5

 automatic transmission .6

454-ci V-8 with manual transmission

 without air conditioning or heavy-duty cooling .9

 with air conditioning

  except 4.10 gears .7

  4.10 gears 10

454-ci V-8 with automatic transmission

 without air conditioning 8

 with air conditioning .7

1974

350-ci V-8

 manual transmission

  without heavy-duty cooling or air conditioning .4

  with heavy-duty cooling or air conditioning . .5

 automatic transmission .6

454-ci V-8 with manual transmission

 without air conditioning or heavy-duty cooling .9

 with air conditioning

  except 4.10 gears .7

  4.10 gears 10

454-ci V-8 with automatic transmission

 without air conditioning 8

 with air conditioning .7

1975–1976

350/400-ci

 manual transmission

  without heavy-duty cooling or air conditioning .4

  with heavy-duty cooling or air conditioning . .5

 automatic transmission .6

454-ci V-8 with manual transmission

 without air conditioning or heavy-duty cooling .9

 with air conditioning

  except 4.10 gears .7

  4.10 gears 10

454-ci V-8 with automatic transmission

 without air conditioning 8

 with air conditioning .7

1977–1978

350- or 400-ci V-8

 manual transmission

  without heavy-duty cooling or air conditioning .4

  with heavy-duty cooling or air conditioning . .5

 automatic transmission

  without air conditioning 4, 5

  with air conditioning 5

454-ci V-8 with manual transmission

 without air conditioning or heavy-duty cooling .9

 with air conditioning

  except 4.10 gears .7

  4.10 gears 10

454-ci V-8 with automatic transmission

 without air conditioning 8

 with air conditioning .7

Interchanges

Interchange Number: 1

Part Number(s): 3023706

Dimensions: 17x28 3/8x2 inches

Type: Modine #366

Usage: 1967 C-10 to C-30 Chevrolet and 1500 to 3500 GMC truck with 283-ci V-8; 1968–1971 C-10 to C-30 with 307-ci V-8 and automatic transmission or heavy-duty cooling or air conditioning; 1972 C-10 to C-30 Chevrolet and 1500 to 3500 GMC, Blazer, and Jimmy with 307-ci V-8 and automatic transmission or heavy-duty cooling; 1969–1972 C-10 to C-30 Chevrolet and 1500 to 3500 GMC, Blazer, and Jimmy with 350-ci, 396-ci, or 402-ci V-8, without heavy-duty cooling or air conditioning or automatic transmission; 1971–1972 G-10 to G-30 Chevrolet and 1500 to 3500 GMC van, all powerplants with air conditioning or heavy-duty cooling

Interchange Number: 2

Part Number(s): N/A

Dimensions: 17x28 3/8x2 5/8 inches

Type: Modine #369

Usage: 1967–1968 C-10 to C-30 Chevrolet and 1500 to 3500 GMC truck with 327-ci V-8, with air conditioning; 1968–1972 C-10 to C-30 Chevrolet and 1500 to 3500 GMC truck, Blazer, and Jimmy with 350-ci or 396/402-ci V-8, with air conditioning or heavy-duty cooling or manual transmission

Interchange Number: 3

Part Number(s): N/A

Dimensions: 17x28 3/8x 1 1/4 inches

Type: Modine N/A

Usage: 1968–1972 C-10 to C-30 Chevrolet and 1500 to 3500 GMC truck, Blazer, and Jimmy with 307- or 350-ci V-8 and manual transmission, without heavy-duty cooling

Interchange Number: 4

Part Number(s): 3030100

Dimensions: 17x28 3/8x 1 1/4 inches

Type: Modine #360

ID codes: CD, CE, CH, CI, CK, CM, CN, CR, CU, CW, CX, CY, CZ, OA, OE, OF, OG, OJ, OR, OW, or OY

Usage: 1973–1976 C-10 to C-30 Chevrolet and 1500 to 3500 GMC truck, Blazer, and Jimmy with 305-, 307-, or 350-ci V-8; 1977–1979 C-10 to C-30 Chevrolet and 1500 to 3500 GMC with 305- or 350-ci V-8 and manual transmission;

1978–1979 C-10 to C-30 Chevrolet and 1500 to 3500 GMC truck with 305- or 350-ci V-8 and automatic transmission, without air conditioning, with 1 1/4-inch core; 1973–1977 Chevelle, Monte Carlo, and Sprint with 350- or 400-ci V-8; 1973–1976 Impala with 350- or 400-ci V-8; 1973–1977 Cutlass with 350- or 455-ci V-8; 1974–1977 Grand Prix and LeMans with 350-, 400-, or 455-ci V-8; 1973–1977 Century with 350-ci V-8; 1972–1975 LeSabre with 350-ci V-8; 1972–1978 G-10 to G-30 Chevrolet and 1500 to 3500 GMC van with 350-ci V-8—all without heavy-duty cooling or air conditioning

Note(s): When interchanging cores from a model with automatic transmission to a model with manual transmission, or vice versa, it may be necessary to add or plug lines for transmission cooler lines. To use all cores it may be necessary to use a larger (1 3/4-inch) bottom hose.

Interchange Number: 5
Part Number(s): 3031446
Dimensions: 17x28 3/8x 2 inches
ID Codes: CV, OK, or PS
Type: Modine #361
Usage: 1973–1976 C-10 to C-30 Chevrolet and 1500 to 3500 GMC truck, Blazer, and Jimmy with 305-, 307-, or 350-ci V-8; 1977–1979 C-10 to C-30 Chevrolet and 1500 to 3500 GMC with 305- or 350-ci V-8 and manual transmission; 1978–1979 C-10 to C-30 Chevrolet and 1500 to 3500 GMC truck with 305- or 350-ci V-8 and automatic transmission, without air conditioning, with 2-inch core; 1973–1977 Chevelle, Monte Carlo, or Sprint with 350- or 400-ci V-8; 1973–1976 Impala with 350- or 400-ci V-8; 1973–1977 Cutlass with 350- or 455-ci V-8; 1974–1977 Grand Prix or LeMans with 350-, 400-, or 455-ci V-8; 1973–1977 Century with 350-ci V-8; 1972–1975 LeSabre 350-ci V-8—all models are with heavy-duty cooling or air conditioning

Note(s): When interchanging cores from a model with automatic transmission to a model with manual transmission, or vice versa, it may be necessary to add or plug lines for transmission cooler lines. To use all cores it may be necessary to use a larger (1 3/4-inch) bottom hose.

Interchange Number: 6
Part Number(s): N/A
Dimensions: 17x28 3/8x2 inches
Type: Modine #362
Usage: 1973–1977 C-10 to C-30 Chevrolet and 1500 to 3500 GMC truck, Blazer, and Jimmy with 305-, 307-, or 350-ci V-8 and automatic

transmission; 1972–1977 G-10 to G-30 Chevrolet and 1500 to 3500 GMC van all with V-8 and automatic transmission; 1970–1974 Cadillac without air conditioning; 1975 Delta 88 with 350-ci V-8, with air conditioning, with cool probe

Note(s): When interchanging cores from a model with automatic transmission to a model with manual transmission, or vice versa, it may be necessary to add or plug lines for transmission cooler lines. To use all cores it may be necessary to use a larger (1 3/4-inch) bottom hose.

Interchange Number: 7
Part Number(s): 3030223
ID Codes: XF, XN, XO, or XQ
Usage: 1973–1979 C-10 to C-30 Chevrolet and 1500 to 3500 GMC truck with 454-ci V-8, with air conditioning and automatic transmission, or with manual transmission with 3.73 rear-axle gears and air conditioning

Interchange Number: 8
Part Number(s): 3039115
Usage: 1973–1979 C-10 to C-30 Chevrolet and 1500 to 3500 GMC truck with 454-ci V-8 and automatic transmission, without air conditioning or heavy-duty cooling

Interchange Number: 9
Part Number(s): 3039117
Usage: 1973–1979 C-10 to C-30 Chevrolet and 1500 to 3500 GMC truck with 454-ci V-8 and manual transmission, without air conditioning

Interchange Number: 10
Part Number(s): 3036739
Usage: 1973–1979 C-10 to C-30 Chevrolet and 1500 to 3500 GMC truck with 454-ci V-8 and manual transmission, with air conditioning and 4.10 rear-axle gears

Fan Blades

Fan blades are identified by their diameter and number of blades, along with the type of drive that was used. Interchange involves the bare fan assembly, without the driver or spacers. The interchange rule for fans is more blades are okay, but fewer are not. For example, you can replace your four-blade fan with a seven-blade unit, but you would never replace a seven-blade unit with a four-blade unit.

Model Identification

Interchanges

Interchange Number: 1

    Part Number(s): 343362
    Number of blades: Five
    Diameter: 18.5 inches
    Usage: 1973–1976 C-10 to C-30 Chevrolet and 1500 to 3500 GMC truck, Blazer, and Jimmy with six-cylinder or 307- or 350-ci V-8 and manual transmission

Interchange Number: 2

    Part Number(s): 6272734
    Number of blades: Five
    Diameter: 19.5 inches
    Usage: 1973–1977 C-10 to C-30 Chevrolet and 1500 to 3500 GMC truck, Blazer, and Jimmy with 305-, 307-, or 350-ci V-8 and automatic transmission

Interchange Number: 3

    Part Number(s): 336032
    Number of blades: Seven
    Diameter: 18 3/4 inches
    Usage: 1973–1979 C-10 to C-30 Chevrolet and 1500 to 3500 GMC truck, Blazer, and Jimmy with 305-, 307-, or 350-ci V-8

Interchange Number: 4

    Part Number(s): 3991431
    Number of blades: Seven
    Diameter: 19.5 inches
    Usage: 1973–1978 C-10 to C-30 Chevrolet and 1500 to 3500 GMC truck, Blazer, and Jimmy with 305-, 307-, or 350-ci V-8, with air conditioning; 1973–1976 Chevelle, Impala, LeMans, Monte Carlo, Nova, Grand Prix, Ventura II, and Sprint 307-ci V-8 with air conditioning; 1967–1971 Firebird 307-ci V-8 with air conditioning; 1977–1979 Phoenix 307-ci V-8 with air conditioning; 1967–1976 full-size Pontiac 307-ci V-8 with air conditioning; 1977 Century 307-ci V-8 with air conditioning; 1973–1978 C-10 to C-30 Chevrolet and 1500 to 3500 GMC truck with 454-ci V-8, without air conditioning; 1973–1974 C-10 to C-30 Chevrolet and 1500 to 3500 GMC truck 454-ci V-8 and manual transmission, without air conditioning; 1975–1978 C-10 to C-30 Chevrolet and 1500 to 3500 GMC truck with 454-ci V-8, all applications without air conditioning

Interchange Number: 6

    Part Number(s): 336006
    Number of blades: Six
    Diameter: 19.5 inches
    Usage: 1973–1978 C-10 to C-30 Chevrolet and 1500 to 3500 GMC truck with 454-ci V-8, with air conditioning or automatic transmission; 1973–1974 C-20 and 2500 Suburban with 454-ci V-8; 1975–1976 C-10 to C-30 Chevrolet and 1500 to 3500 GMC truck, Blazer, and Jimmy with 400-ci V-8

Interchange Number: 7

    Part Number(s): 461317
    Number of blades: Four
    Diameter: 19.5 inches
    Usage: 1977–1979 C-10 to C-30 Chevrolet and 1500 to 3500 GMC truck, Blazer, and Jimmy without air conditioning (except V-8 models with automatic transmission)

Interchange Number: 8

    Part Number(s): 627201
    Number of blades: Seven
    Diameter: 18 inches
    Usage: 1972 C-10 to C-30 Chevrolet and 1500 to 3500 GMC truck, Blazer, and Jimmy with 307- or 350-ci V-8 and automatic transmission, without air conditioning

Interchange Number: 9

    Part Number(s): 3993318
    Number of blades: N/A
    Diameter: N/A
    Usage: 1971–1972 C-10 to C-30 Chevrolet and 1500 to 3500 GMC truck with 396/402-ci V-8

Interchange Number: 10

    Part Number(s): 6270076
    Number of blades: Four
    Diameter: 18 inches
    Usage: 1969–1972 C-10 to C-30 Chevrolet and 1500 to 3500 GMC truck, Blazer, and Jimmy with 307- or 350-ci V-8 and manual transmission, without air conditioning or heavy-duty cooling

Interchange Number: 11

    Part Number(s): 3991431
    Number of blades: Six
    Diameter: 19 inches
    Usage: 1968–1972 C-10 to C-30 Chevrolet and 1500 to 3500 GMC truck with 396/402-ci V-8 and air conditioning

Interchange Number: 12

    Part Number(s): 393996
    Number of blades: Seven
    Diameter: 18 inches
    Usage: 1966–1972 C-10 to C-30 Chevrolet and 1500 to 3500 GMC truck with all V-8 powerplants (except 396/402-ci), with air conditioning; 1969–1970 Camaro Z-28; 1969 Impala 427-ci 425-horsepower V-8; 1969 Chevelle V-8, with air conditioning; 1969–1970 Camaro, Chevelle, and Nova with 396-ci 375-horsepower V-8; 1970–1972 Camaro, Chevelle, Impala, Monte Carlo, and Nova with V-8 engine and air conditioning

Interchange Number: 13
Part Number(s): N/A
Number of blades: N/A
Diameter: 18
Usage: 1967 C-10 to C-30 Chevrolet and 1500 to 3500 GMC truck with Turbo-Hydra-Matic automatic transmission, without air conditioning

Interchange Number: 14
Part Number(s): 3881239
Number of blades: Four
Diameter: 18 inches
Usage: 1965–1967 C-10 to C-30 Chevrolet and 1500 to 3500 GMC truck without air conditioning or Turbo-Hydra-Matic automatic transmission

Fan Drives
Model Identification

Interchanges

Interchange Number: 1
Part Number(s): 14006729
Usage: 1973–1977 C-10 to C-30 Chevrolet and 1500 to 3500 GMC truck with 454-ci V-8, with air conditioning; 1975–1978 C-10 Chevrolet and 1500 GMC truck, Blazer, and Jimmy four-wheel drive with 400-ci V-8 and 3.73, 4.10, or 4.11 rear-axle gear ratios; early-1975 G-20 to G-30 Chevrolet and 2500 to 3500 GMC van with 400-ci V-8; 1976–1978 G-20 to G-30 Chevrolet and 2500 to 3500 GMC van with 400-ci V-8
Note(s): Stamped AT or DC

Interchange Number: 2
Part Number(s): 14006728
Usage: 1973–1976 C-10 to C-30 Chevrolet and 1500 to 3500 GMC truck, Blazer, and Jimmy with 307- or 350-ci V-8, with air conditioning; 1975–1976 C-10 Chevrolet and 1500 GMC truck, Blazer, and Jimmy four-wheel drive with 400-ci V-8 and 3.07 rear-axle ratio, without air conditioning
Note(s): Stamped AH

Interchange Number: 3
Part Number(s): 14006730
Usage: 1973–1977 Blazer and Jimmy with two-barrel V-8 and manual transmission, with air conditioning; 1973–1977 C-10 to C-30 Chevrolet and 1500 to 3500 GMC truck with 454-ci V-8, without air conditioning; 1978 C-10 to C-30 Chevrolet and 1500 to 3500 GMC truck with 305- or 350-ci V-8, with air conditioning; 1978 C-10 to C-30 Chevrolet and 1500 to 3500 GMC truck, Blazer, and Jimmy with 400-ci V-8, without air conditioning
Note(s): Stamped AM, AF, or DD

Interchange Number: 4
Part Number(s): 14006728
Usage: 1973–1977 C-10 to C-30 Chevrolet and 1500 to 3500 GMC truck with 454-ci V-8, with

air conditioning; 1975–1976 C-10 Chevrolet and 1500 GMC truck, Blazer, and Jimmy four-wheel drive with 400-ci V-8 and 3.73, 4.10, or 4.11 rear-axle gear ratios; early-1975 G-20 to G-30 Chevrolet and 2500 to 3500 GMC van with 400-ci V-8; 1976 G-20 to G-30 Chevrolet and 2500 to 3500 GMC van with 400-ci V-8; 1978 C-10 to C-30 Chevrolet and 1500 to 3500 GMC truck with 454-ci V-8, with heavy-duty cooling and manual transmission

Interchange Number: 5
Part Number(s): 14006729
Usage: 1977 C-10 to C-30 Chevrolet and 1500 to 3500 GMC truck, Blazer, and Jimmy with 400-ci V-8; 1977 G-10 to G-30 Chevrolet and 1500 to 3500 GMC van with 350-ci V-8, with air conditioning

Interchange Number: 6
Part Number(s): 14006731
Usage: 1978 C-10 Chevrolet and 1500 GMC truck with diesel engine, without air conditioning

Interchange Number: 7
Part Number(s): 14006732
Usage: 1978 C-10 Chevrolet and 1500 GMC truck with diesel engine, with air conditioning

Interchange Number: 8
Part Number(s): 476367
Usage: 1978 C-10 to C-30 Chevrolet and 1500 to 3500 GMC truck with 454-ci V-8, without air conditioning

Interchange Number: 9
Part Number(s): 14006733
Usage: 1978 C-10 to C-30 Chevrolet and 1500 to 3500 GMC truck with 400- or 454-ci V-8, with air conditioning

Interchange Number: 10
Part Number(s): 3883158
Usage: 1967–1968 C-10 to C-30 Chevrolet and 1500 to 3500 GMC truck with air conditioning and V-8 engine (except 396-ci V-8); 1967–1969 G-10 to G-20 Chevrolet and 1500 to 2500 GMC van with V-8 and air conditioning

Interchange Number: 11
Part Number(s): 3982939
Usage: 1968–1972 C-10 to C-30 Chevrolet and 1500 to 3500 GMC truck with 396/402-ci V-8, with air conditioning

Interchange Number: 12
Part Number(s): 3982940
Usage: 1969–1972 C-10 to C-30 Chevrolet and 1500 to 3500 GMC truck, Blazer, and Jimmy with 307-ci V-8 and air conditioning

Interchange Number: 13
Part Number(s): 343726
Usage: 1969–1972 C-10 to C-30 Chevrolet and 1500 to 3500 GMC truck, Blazer, and Jimmy with 350-ci V-8 and air conditioning (except with automatic transmission); 1970–1972 C-10 to C-30 Chevrolet and 1500 to 3500 GMC truck, Blazer, and Jimmy with 350-ci V-8 and automatic transmission, without air conditioning

Interchange Number: 14
Part Number(s): 343727
Usage: 1970–1972 C-10 to C-30 Chevrolet and 1500 to 3500 GMC truck, Blazer, and Jimmy with 350-ci V-8 and automatic transmission, with air conditioning

Water Pumps
Model Identification

1967	Interchange Number
283-ci V-8	1, 2, 3
327-ci V-8	1, 2, 3
1968	
307-ci V-8	2, 3
327-ci V-8	1, 2, 3
396-ci V-8	6
1969–1970	
307-ci V-8	3
350-ci V-8	3
396-ci V-8	6
1971–1972	
307-ci V-8	4
350-ci V-8	4
396-ci V-8	6
1973	
307-ci V-8	5
350-ci V-8	5
454-ci V-8	7
1974	
350-ci V-8	5
454-ci V-8	7
1975–1977	
305-ci V-8	5
350-ci V-8	5
400-ci V-8	5
454-ci V-8	7
1978	
305-ci V-8	8
350-ci V-8	8
400-ci V-8	8
454-ci V-8	7

Interchanges

Interchange Number: 1
Casting Number(s): 3757248
Usage: 1960–1968 C-10 to C-30 Chevrolet and 1500 to 3500 GMC truck with 283- or 327-ci V-8
Note(s): Has two 1/2-inch pipe outlets

Interchange Number: 2
Casting Number(s): 3839176
Usage: 1964–1967 C-10 to C-30 Chevrolet and 1500 to 3500 GMC truck with 283-ci V-8; 1967–1968 C-10 to C-30 Chevrolet and 1500 to 3500 GMC truck with 307- or 327-ci V-8
Note(s): Has one each 1/2- and 3/4-inch outlets

Interchange Number: 3
Casting Number(s): 3763493
Usage: 1960–1967 C-10 to C-30 Chevrolet and 1500 to 3500 GMC truck with 283-ci V-8; 1968–1970 C-10 to C-30 Chevrolet and 1500 to 3500 GMC truck and Blazer; 1967–1968 Camaro, Chevelle, and Nova with 307- or 350-ci V-8; 1969–1970 C-10 to C-30 Chevrolet and 1500 to 3500 GMC truck, van, Blazer, and Jimmy with 350-ci V-8
Note(s): Has one 1/2-inch outlet

Interchange Number: 4
Part Number(s): 3998206
Usage: 1971–1972 C-10 to C-30 Chevrolet and 1500 to 3500 GMC truck, Blazer, and Jimmy with 307- or 350-ci V-8
Note(s): Casting number 3782608

Interchange Number: 5
Part Number(s): 3998206
Usage: 1973–1977 C-10 to C-30 Chevrolet and 1500 to 3500 GMC truck, Blazer, and Jimmy with 307-, 250-, or 400-ci V-8; 1972–1977 Camaro, Chevelle, Impala, Monte Carlo, Nova, and Sprint with 305-, 307-, 350-, or 400-ci V-8

Interchange Number: 6
Part Number(s): 3990993
Usage: 1968–1972 C-10 to C-30 Chevrolet and 1500 to 3500 GMC truck with 396-ci V-8; 1967–1968 Camaro, Chevelle, and Impala with 396-ci/402-ci V-8; 1965–1968 Corvette and Impala with 427-ci V-8; 1968 Nova with 396-ci V-8
Note(s): Casting number is 3856284

Interchange Number: 7
Part Number(s): 6272159
Usage: 1973–1981 C-10 to C-30 Chevrolet and 1500 to 3500 GMC truck with 454-ci V-8; 1969–1972 Camaro, Chevelle, Impala, Monte Carlo, Nova, and Sprint with 396/402-ci V-8; 1973–1975 Chevelle, Impala, Monte Carlo, and Sprint with 454-ci V-8
Note(s): Casting number 369811

Interchange Number: 8
Part Number(s): 474029
Usage: 1978–1981 C-10 to C-30 Chevrolet and 1500 to 3500 GMC truck, Blazer, Jimmy, Camaro, Chevelle, Impala, and Monte Carlo with 305-, 350-, or 400-ci; 1980–1981 Camaro, Chevelle, and Monte Carlo with 229-ci (3.8-liter) V-6; 1977–1980 LeMans and Firebird 305-ci V-8; 1978–1981 Grand Prix, Cutlass, and Century with 305-ci V-8
Note(s): Casting number is 376444 or 404562

4 Exhaust Systems

Exhaust Manifolds

Exhaust manifolds are greatly interchangeable within their own family group, but certain restrictions do apply. Emissions systems—specifically the Air Injector Reactor, or AIR system—greatly influence the interchange process. Four-wheel-drive models also use a special set of manifolds, due to clearance problems with the transfer axle. Other restrictions may also apply; they will appear in the Note(s) section of each interchange entry.

Model Identification

1967   Interchange Number
283- or 327-ci V-8
  two-wheel drive without AIR, driver's side 1
  two-wheel drive without AIR, passenger's side
    without choke 3
    with choke 2
  two-wheel drive with AIR
    driver's side 7
    passenger's side 6
  four-wheel drive without AIR
    driver's side 5
    passenger's side
      without choke 4
      with choke 3
  four-wheel drive with AIR
    driver's side 10
    passenger's side
      without choke 9
      with choke 8

1968
307- or 327-ci V-8, two-wheel drive
  automatic transmission
    driver's side 1
    passenger's side 2
  manual transmission
    driver's side 7
    passenger's side 6
307- or 327-ci V-8, four-wheel drive
  automatic transmission
    driver's side 5
    passenger's side 4
  manual transmission
    driver's side 10
    passenger's side 9

396-ci V-8
  driver's side 11
  passenger's side 12

1969
307- or 350-ci V-8, two-wheel drive
  without AIR
    driver's side 13
    passenger's side 2
  with AIR
    driver's side 14
    passenger's side 6
307- or 350-ci V-8, four-wheel drive
  automatic transmission
    driver's side 4
    passenger's side 4
  manual transmission
    driver's side 9
    passenger's side 9
396-ci V-8
  driver's side 11
  passenger's side 12

1970
307- or 350-ci V-8, two-wheel drive
  driver's side 13
  passenger's side 2
307- or 350-ci V-8, four-wheel drive
  automatic transmission
    driver's side 4
    passenger's side 4
  manual transmission
    driver's side 9
    passenger's side 9
396-ci V-8
  driver's side 11
  passenger's side 12

1971
307- or 350-ci V-8
  two-wheel drive
    driver's side 13
    passenger's side 2
  four-wheel drive 4
396-ci V-8
  driver's side 15
  passenger's side 16

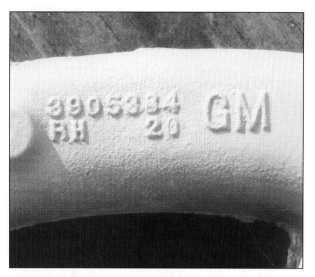

Exhaust manifolds can be identified by casting numbers.

1972
307- or 350-ci V-8, two-wheel drive
without NOX
with NOX
307- or 350-ci V-8, four-wheel drive
396-ci V-8
without NOX
with NOX

1973
307- or 350-ci V-8
without NOX
with NOX
454-ci V-8
without NOX
with NOX

1974
without NOX

with NOX
454-ci V-8
without NOX
with NOX

1975
350- or 400-ci V-8
without NOX
with NOX
454-ci V-8
without NOX
with NOX

1976
350- or 400-ci V-8
454-ci V-8
without NOX
with NOX

1977–1978
305-, 350-, or 400-ci V-8
454-ci V-8
without NOX
with NOX

Interchanges
Interchange Number: 1
Part Number(s): 3855163
Position: Driver's side
Usage: 1966–1968 C-10 to C-30 Chevrolet and
1500 to 3500 GMC truck with 283-, 307-, or
327-ci V-8 without AIR emissions—two-wheel-

drive models only

Note(s): Casting number 3855163A

Interchange Number: 2

Part Number(s): 3896956

Position: Passenger's side

Usage: 1967–1972 C-10 to C-30 Chevrolet and
1500 to 3500 GMC truck with 283-, 307-, or
327-ci V-8 without AIR emissions

Note(s): Casting number 3896956

Interchange Number: 3

Part Number(s): 3817806

Position: Passenger's side

Usage: 1964–1967 C-10 to C-30 Chevrolet and
1500 to 3500 GMC (truck four-wheel-drive
models only); 1962–1965 Impala with 283- or
327-ci V-8; 1967 G-10 to G-20 Chevrolet and
1500 to 3500 GMC van with 283-ci V-8

Note(s): Casting number 3747038Y with
choke tube

Interchange Number: 4

Part Number(s): 3989036

Position: Passenger's side

Usage: 1968 C-10 to C-30 Chevrolet and 1500 to
3500 GMC truck four-wheel-drive models
with automatic transmission only; 1968
Impala with 307- or 327-ci V-8 and automatic
transmission; 1968–1969 G-10 to G-20
Chevrolet and 1500 to 3500 GMC van with
307-ci V-8 and automatic transmission—all
without AIR emissions

Note(s): Casting number 3750556 or 3747042
without choke tube

Interchange Number: 5

Part Number(s): 3846559

Position: Driver's side

Usage: 1967–1968 C-10 to C-30 Chevrolet and
1500 to 3500 GMC truck four-wheel-drive
models (with automatic transmission only
for 1968 models); 1964–1966 C-10 to C-
30 Chevrolet, all engines, all models; 1968
Impala with 307- or 327-ci V-8 and automatic transmission; 1968–1970 G-10 to G-
20 Chevrolet and 1500 to 3500 GMC van
with 307-ci V-8 and automatic transmission—all without AIR emissions

Note(s): Casting number 3846558

Interchange Number: 6

Part Number(s): 3896956

Position: Passenger's side

Usage: 1967–1972 C-10 to C-30 Chevrolet and
1500 to 3500 GMC truck with 283-, 307-, or
327-ci V-8, with AIR emissions—two-wheel-
drive models only

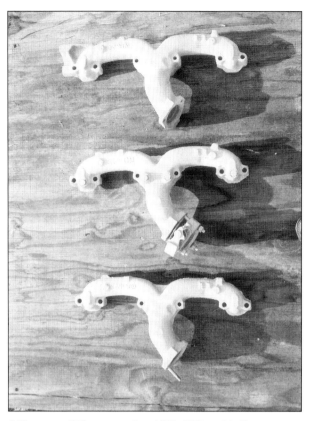

*Different manifolds were used on 1967–1972 models. The upper are
1967 models; note the platform for the alternator bracket. The middle
unit has AIR, with AIR provisions blocked off. The bottom is a later style.
All will interchange.*

Interchange Number: 7

Part Number(s): 387241

Position: Driver's side

Usage: 1967 C-10 to C-30 Chevrolet and 1500 to
3500 GMC truck with 283-, 307-, or 327-ci V-8;
1966–1967 Impala with 283- or 327-ci V-8;
1968 C-10 to C-30 Chevrolet and 1500 to
3500 GMC truck with 307- or 327-ci V-8 and
manual transmission—all are two-wheel-drive
models with AIR emissions only

Interchange Number: 8

Part Number(s): 3893604

Position: Passenger's side

Usage: 1966–1968 C-10 to C-30 Chevrolet and
1500 to 3500 GMC truck, four-wheel-drive
models only; 1968 Impala with 283- or 327-ci V-
8; 1967–1970 G-10 to G-20 Chevrolet and
1500 to 3500 GMC van with 283-ci V-8—all
models are with AIR

Note(s): With choke tube. Interchange number 9
will fit if choke is added.

Interchange Number: 9

Part Number(s): 3932461

Position: See Note(s)

Usage: 1969–1972 C-10 to C-30 Chevrolet and 1500 to 3500 GMC truck, Blazer, and Jimmy (four-wheel-drive models only) with 307- or 350-ci V-8; 1972 G-20 and 2500 van with 307-ci V-8; 1969–1974 Corvette with 350-ci V-8 (except LT-1 or L-88); 1969 Impala with 350-ci V-8 and manual transmission—all models are with AIR

Note(s): Fits either side except on these models: 1969–1971 Corvette and 1969 Impala, which is passenger's side only

Interchange Number: 10
Part Number(s): 3872765
Position: Driver's side
Usage: 1967–1968 C-10 to C-30 Chevrolet and 1500 to 3500 GMC truck four-wheel-drive models (with manual transmission only for 1968 models); 1966–1971 Corvette with 350-ci V-8 (except LT-1); 1969–1970 G-20 Chevrolet and 2500 GMC van with 307-ci V-8 and manual transmission—all models are without AIR emissions

Interchange Number: 11
Part Number(s): 3914617
Position: Driver's side
Usage: 1968–1970 C-10 to C-30 Chevrolet and 1500 to 3500 GMC truck with 396-ci V-8; Impala with 396-ci V-8; 1970 Impala with 454-ci V-8; 1968–1969 Impala with 427-ci V-8

Interchange Number: 12
Part Number(s): 3989312
Position: Passenger's side
Usage: 1968–1970 C-10 to C-30 Chevrolet and 1500 to 3500 GMC truck with 396-ci V-8; 1967–1970 Camaro and Chevelle with 396/402-ci V-8; 1968–1969 Impala and Nova with 396/402-ci or 427-ci V-8; 1970 Chevelle and Impala with 454-ci V-8; 1972 Chevelle, Impala, and Sprint with 402- or 454-ci V-8 and NOX emissions

Interchange Number: 13
Part Number(s): 3989055
Position: Driver's side
Usage: 1969–1972 C-10 to C-30 Chevrolet and 1500 to 3500 GMC truck, Blazer, and Jimmy with 307- or 350-ci V-8, without AIR emissions; 1969–1970 Impala with 350-ci V-8 and automatic transmission

Interchange Number: 14
Part Number(s): 3932469
Position: Driver's side
Usage: 1969–1972 C-10 to C-30 Chevrolet and 1500 to 3500 GMC truck, Blazer, and Jimmy with 307- or 350-ci V-8, with AIR emissions; 1969–1970 Impala with 350-ci V-8 and manual transmission

Interchange Number: 15
Part Number(s): 3994045
Position: Driver's side
Usage: 1968–1972 C-10 to C-30 Chevrolet and 1500 to 3500 GMC truck with 402-ci V-8; 1973–1981 C-10 to C-30 Chevrolet and 1500 to 3500 GMC truck with 454-ci V-8—all models are without NOX emissions

Interchange Number: 16
Part Number(s): 3994046
Position: Passenger's side
Usage: 1968–1972 C-10 to C-30 Chevrolet and 1500 to 3500 GMC truck with 402-ci V-8, without NOX emissions

Interchange Number: 17
Part Number(s): 6272280
Position: Passenger's side
Usage: 1972 C-10 to C-30 Chevrolet and 1500 to 3500 GMC truck with 402-ci V-8, with NOX emissions

Interchange Number: 18
Part Number(s): 6272279
Position: Driver's side
Usage: 1972 C-10 to C-30 Chevrolet and 1500 to 3500 GMC truck with 402-ci V-8; 1973–1981 C-10 to C-30 Chevrolet and 1500 to 3500 GMC truck with 454-ci V-8—all with NOX emissions

Interchange Number: 19
Part Number(s): 3989041
Position: Driver's side
Usage: 1973–1975 C-10 Chevrolet and 1500 GMC truck, Blazer, Camaro, Chevelle, Impala, Monte Carlo, and Nova with 307- or 350-ci V-8; 1970–1972 Camaro and Chevelle with 350-ci V-8—all with NOX/AIR emissions

Interchange Number: 20
Part Number(s): 3989043
Position: Driver's side
Usage: 1973 C-10 to C-30 Chevrolet and 1500 to 3500 GMC truck, Blazer, Camaro, Chevelle, Impala, Monte Carlo, and Nova with 307- or 350-ci V-8; 1970–1972 Camaro and Chevelle with 350-ci V-8; 1971–1972 G-10 to G-30 Chevrolet and 1500 to 3500 GMC van with 350-ci V-8; 1973 G-30 and 3500 van with 350-ci V-8; 1971–1972 Ventura II with 307-ci V-8—all without NOX/AIR emissions

Interchange Number: 21
Part Number(s): 3973432
Position: Passenger's side
Usage: 1973 C-10 to C-30 Chevrolet and 1500 to

3500 GMC truck, Blazer, Camaro, Chevelle, Impala, Monte Carlo, and Nova with 307- or 350-ci V-8; 1970–1972 Camaro and Chevelle with 350-ci V-8; 1971–1972 G-10 to G-30 Chevrolet and 1500 to 3500 GMC van with 350-ci V-8; 1973 G-30 and 3500 van with 350-ci V-8; 1971–1972 Ventura II with 307-ci V-8—all without NOX/AIR emissions

Interchange Number: 22

Part Number(s): 3959562

Position: Passenger's side

Usage: 1973–1980 C-10 to C-30 Chevrolet and 1500 to 3500 GMC truck, Blazer, and Jimmy with 305-, 350-, or 400-ci V-8 (except 1978–1980 diesel engines); 1976–1979 Camaro, Chevelle, Impala, Nova, and Sprint with 305-, 350-, or 400-ci V-8; 1977–1978 Century, Cutlass, Firebird, LeMans, Phoenix, Skylark, and Omega with 305- or 350-ci* V-8

Note(s): * Must have L engine code in VIN on non-Chevrolet and GMC models

Interchange Number: 23

Part Number(s): 333846

Position: Passenger's side

Usage: 1973–1981 C-10 to C-30 Chevrolet and 1500 to 3500 GMC truck with 454-ci V-8; 1973–1974 C-40 to C-50 Chevrolet and 4500 to 5500 GMC with 366- or 427-ci V-8—all without NOX emissions

Interchange Number: 24

Part Number(s): 353030

Position: Passenger's side

Usage: 1973–1981 C-10 to C-30 Chevrolet and 1500 to 3500 GMC truck with 454-ci V-8; 1973–1974 C-40 to C-50 Chevrolet and 4500 to 5500 GMC with 366- or 427-ci V-8—all with NOX emissions

Interchange Number: 25

Part Number(s): 336706

Position: Driver's side

Usage: 1974 C-10 to C-30 Chevrolet and 1500 to 3500 GMC truck, Blazer, and Jimmy with 350-ci V-8; 1974 G-10 to G-30 Chevrolet and 1500 to 3500 GMC van with 350-ci V-8—all without NOX emissions

Interchange Number: 26

Part Number(s): 364753

Position: Driver's side

Usage: 1976–1980 C-10 to C-30 Chevrolet and 1500 to 3500 GMC truck, Blazer, and Jimmy with 305-, 350-, or 400-ci (except 1978–1980 diesel engines); 1976–1979 Camaro, Chevelle, Impala, Nova, and Sprint with 305-, 350-, or 400-ci V-8; 1977–1978 Century, Cutlass, Firebird, LeMans, Phoenix, Skylark, and Omega with 305- or 350-ci* V-8

Note(s): * Must have L engine code in VIN on non-Chevrolet and GMC models

Mufflers
Model Identification

1967	Interchange Number
283-ci V-8	16
327-ci V-8	17
1968	
307-ci V-8	16
327-ci V-8	
except Suburban	17
Suburban	18
396-ci V-8	18
1969–1970	
307-ci V-8	20
350-ci V-8	18
396-ci V-8	21
1971–1972	
307-ci V-8	23
350-ci V-8	22
396-ci V-8	22
1973	
307- or 350-ci V-8	
C-10 to C-30	1
454-ci V-8	2
1974	
350-ci V-8	
C-10 to C-30	1
454-ci V-8	3
1975	
350-ci V-8 two-wheel drive	
117.5-inch wheelbase	
without heavy-duty chassis	6
with heavy-duty chassis	4
131.5-inch wheelbase	
without heavy-duty chassis	5
with heavy-duty chassis	4
Suburban	4
350-ci V-8 four-wheel drive	
all except Blazer	1
350-ci V-8 Blazer	
two-wheel drive	10
four-wheel drive	11
350-ci V-8 C-20 to C-30	4
400-ci V-8	
except Blazer	8
Blazer	12
454-ci V-8	9
1976	
350-ci, V-8 two-wheel drive	
117.5-inch wheelbase	
without heavy-duty chassis	6
with heavy-duty chassis	4
131.5-inch wheelbase	
without heavy-duty chassis	13
with heavy-duty chassis	4

Suburban 4
350-ci V-8 four-wheel drive
single exhaust 1
dual exhaust
driver's side 8
passenger's side .14
350-ci V-8 Blazer
two-wheel drive 10
four-wheel drive, single exhaust 1
four-wheel drive, dual exhaust
driver's side 8
passenger's side .14
350-ci V-8 C-20 to C-30 .4
400-ci V-8
dual exhaust
driver's side 8
passenger's side .14
454-ci V-8 9

1977–1978

350-ci V-8 two-wheel drive, except 1978 diesel
117.5-inch wheelbase
without heavy-duty chassis 6
with heavy-duty chassis 4
131.5-inch wheelbase
without heavy-duty chassis 13
with heavy-duty chassis 4
Suburban 4
350-ci V-8 four-wheel drive, except 1978 diesel
single exhaust 1
dual exhaust
driver's side 8
passenger's side .14
350-ci V-8 Blazer, except 1978 diesel
two-wheel drive 10
four-wheel drive, single exhaust 1
four-wheel drive, dual exhaust
driver's side 8
passenger's side .14
350-ci V-8 C-20 to C-30, except 1978 diesel 4
350-ci V-8 diesel 15
400-ci V-8
dual exhaust
driver's side 8
passenger's side .14
454-ci V-8 9

Interchanges

Interchange Number: 1
Part Number(s): 458462
Usage: 1973–1974 C-10 to C-30 Chevrolet and 1500 to 3500 GMC truck, Blazer, and Jimmy with 307- or 350-ci V-8; 1976–1978 C-10 Chevrolet and 1500 GMC truck with 307- or 350-ci V-8, four-wheel drive, with single exhaust; 1976–1978 Blazer and Jimmy with 307- or 350-ci V-8, with four-wheel drive, with single exhaust

Interchange Number: 2
Part Number(s): 344704
Usage: 1973 C-10 to C-30 Chevrolet and 1500 to 3500 GMC truck with 454-ci V-8

Interchange Number: 3
Part Number(s): 334636
Usage: 1974 C-10 to C-30 Chevrolet and 1500 to 3500 GMC truck with 454-ci V-8

Interchange Number: 4
Part Number(s): 359903
Usage: 1975–1978 C-10 to C-30 Chevrolet and 1500 to 3500 GMC truck with 350-ci V-8, with heavy-duty chassis; 1975–1978 Suburban—two-wheel-drive models only

Interchange Number: 5
Part Number(s): 359098
Usage: 1975–1978 C-10 Chevrolet and 1500 GMC truck with 350-ci V-8 and 131.5-inch wheelbase, without heavy-duty chassis—two-wheel-drive models only

Interchange Number: 6
Part Number(s): 359099
Usage: 1975 C-10 Chevrolet and 1500 GMC truck with 350-ci V-8 and 117.5-inch wheelbase, without heavy-duty chassis—two-wheel-drive models only

Interchange Number: 7
Part Number(s): 458462
Usage: 1975 C-10 to C-20 Chevrolet and 1500 to 2500 GMC truck with 350-ci V-8—four-wheel-drive models only

Interchange Number: 8
Part Number(s): 372489
Usage: 1975 C-10 to C-20 Chevrolet and 1500 to 2500 GMC truck with 400-ci V-8, four-wheel drive only; 1975 C-10 to C-20 Chevrolet and 1500 to 2500 GMC truck with 400-ci V-8 (fits either side), four-wheel drive only; 1976–1978 C-10 to C-20 Chevrolet and 1500 to 2500 GMC truck, Blazer, and Jimmy with 350- or 400-ci V-8, with four-wheel drive, with dual exhaust (left-hand side only)

Interchange Number: 9
Part Number(s): 359100
Usage: 1975–1978 C-10 to C-30 Chevrolet and 1500 to 3500 GMC truck with 454-ci V-8

Interchange Number: 10
Part Number(s): 464013
Usage: 1975–1978 Blazer and Jimmy with 350-ci V-8—two-wheel drive only

Interchange Number: 11
Part Number(s): 464015
Usage: 1975 Blazer and Jimmy with 350-ci V-8—four-wheel drive only

Interchange Number: 12
Part Number(s): 358185 (left); 358186 (right)
Usage: 1975 Blazer and Jimmy with 400-ci V-8—
four-wheel drive only

Interchange Number: 13
Part Number(s): 369178
Usage: 1976–1978 C-10 Chevrolet and 1500 GMC
truck with 350-ci V-8 and 117.5-inch wheelbase, without heavy-duty chassis—two-wheel-
drive models only

Interchange Number: 14
Part Number(s): 372498 (right)
Usage: 1976–1978 C-10 to C-20 Chevrolet and
1500 to 2500 GMC truck, Blazer, and Jimmy
with 350- or 400-ci V-8, with four-wheel drive,
with dual exhaust

Interchange Number: 15
Part Number(s): 474210 (left); 474215 (right)
Usage: 1978 C-10 Chevrolet and 1500 GMC truck
with diesel engine

Interchange Number: 16
Part Number(s): 3981946
Usage: 1967–1968 C-10 to C-30 Chevrolet and
1500 to 3500 GMC truck with six-cylinder,
283-, or 307-ci V-8 (except Suburban)
Note(s): 25 5/8-inch over all

Interchange Number: 17
Part Number(s): 3931391
Usage: 1967–1968 C-10 to C-30 Chevrolet and
1500 to 3500 GMC truck with 327-ci V-8
(except Suburban)

Interchange Number: 18
Part Number(s): 3931392
Usage: 1967–1968 Suburban with 327-ci V-8; 1968
C-10 Chevrolet and 1500 GMC truck with
396-ci V-8; 1969–1970 C-10 to C-30 Chevrolet
and 1500 to 3500 GMC truck, Blazer, and
Suburban with 350-ci V-8

Interchange Number: 19
Part Number(s): 3931392
Usage: 1967–1968 Suburban with 327-ci V-8; 1968
C-10 Chevrolet and 1500 GMC truck with
396-ci V-8

Interchange Number: 20
Part Number(s): 3931358
Usage: 1967–1968 Suburban with 283- or 307-ci V-
8; 1969–1970 C-10 to C-30 Chevrolet and
1500 to 3500 GMC truck with 307-ci V-8,
including Suburban

Interchange Number: 21
Part Number(s): 335219
Usage: 1969–1970 C-10 to C-30 Chevrolet and
1500 to 3500 GMC truck with 396-ci V-8

Interchange Number: 22
Part Number(s): 3996417
Usage: 1971–1972 C-10 to C-30 Chevrolet and
1500 to 3500 GMC truck, Blazer, and Jimmy
with 350- or 396/402-ci V-8

Interchange Number: 23
Part Number(s): 3996423
Usage: 1971–1972 C-10 to C-30 Chevrolet and
1500 to 3500 GMC truck with 307-ci V-8

Air Injection Pumps
Model Identification

1967	*Interchange Number*
283- or 327-ci V-8	1
1968–1970	
All	2
1971–1972	
All	3
1973–1974	
Except 454-ci V-8	3
454-ci V-8	4
1975–1977	
Except 454-ci V-8 or with heavy-duty chassis	3
heavy-duty chassis	4
454-ci V-8	4
1978	
All	3

Interchanges

Interchange Number: 1
Part Number(s): 5696104
Usage: 1966–1967 C-10 to C-30 Chevrolet and
1500 to 3500 GMC truck, Chevelle, Chevy II,
and Impala with 283- or 327-ci V-8, 1966–1967
Skylark, LeSabre, Delta 88, Cutlass/F-85, and
LeMans, all with V-8; 1967 Camaro with 327-ci,
two-barrel V-8

Interchange Number: 2
Part Number(s): 7806686
Usage: 1968–1970 C-10 to C-30 Chevrolet and
1500 to 3500 GMC truck, Camaro, Chevelle,
Corvette, Impala, and Nova, all powerplants
[see Note(s)]; 1969–1970 Blazer; 1970–1971
Monte Carlo; 1971 Camaro, Chevelle,
Corvette, and Monte Carlo, all powerplants
[see Note(s)]
Note(s): When interchanging to a model with a
manual transmission and six-cylinder or small-
block V-8, use red pressure-relief plug

Interchange Number: 3

Part Number(s): 7803948

Usage: 1971–1978 C-10 to C-30 Chevrolet and 1500 to 3500 GMC truck, Blazer, and Jimmy, all V-8 engines except 454-ci V-8; 1972–1978 Camaro, Chevelle, Corvette, Impala, Monte Carlo, Nova, and Sprint, all V-8 powerplants; 1973–1978 Firebird, full-size Pontiac, LeMans, Ventura II, and Grand Prix with all V-8 engines; 1975–1977 C-10 Chevrolet and 1500 GMC without heavy-duty chassis

Interchange Number: 4

Part Number(s): 7817817

Usage: 1973–1977 C-10 to C-30 Chevrolet and 1500 to 3500 GMC truck with 454-ci V-8; 1975–1977 C-10 to C-30 Chevrolet and 1500 to 3500 GMC truck with heavy-duty chassis; 1976–1977 Blazer and Jimmy

5 Transmissions and Drivelines

There are many different ways to identify a transmission. One way is by its design or type, or by the manufacture and build date codes. Although the date code will not tell what model of a truck the transmission came out of, it will tell you the assembly plant and the date the transmission was built. Note that the interchange here is for physical fit; thus more than one code may have been used.

Manual Transmissions

There were four types of manual transmissions: the three-speed manual, the three-speed manual with overdrive, the heavy-duty three-speed, and the four-speed. Note that, as with other components, the heavier duty models like the C-20 and C-30 models used a different transmission than the standard-duty C-10 models. Also, the four-wheel-drive models used a different assembly than the two-wheel-drive models; however, in some cases, a transmission from a two-wheel drive can fit a four-wheel-drive model, or vice versa, by switching the extensions.

Model Identification

A Powerglide automatic transmission cover.

Four-speed manual
   Muncie
1977–1978
Three-speed manual
   Saginaw
   Termac
Four-speed manual
   Muncie

Interchanges
THREE-SPEED MANUAL
Interchange Number: 1
   Type/Manufacturer: Without overdrive, Saginaw
   Usage: 1966–1972 C-10 to C-30 Chevrolet and
      1500 to 3500 GMC truck; 1969–1972
      Blazer; 1971–1972 Jimmy—two-wheel drive
      models only
   Note(s): Interchange Numbers 2 and 3 will fit if
      extensions are changed

Interchange Number: 2
   Type: With overdrive, Saginaw
   Usage: 1966–1972 C-10 to C-30 Chevrolet and
      1500 to 3500 GMC truck; 1969–1972
      Blazer; 1971–1972 Jimmy—two-wheel-drive
      models only
   Note(s): Interchange Numbers 1 and 3 will fit if
      extensions are changed

Interchange Number: 3
   Type: Saginaw
   Usage: 1966–1972 C-10 to C-20 Chevrolet and
      1500 to 3500 GMC truck; 1969–1972
      Blazer; 1971–1972 Jimmy—four-wheel-drive
      models only
   Note(s): Interchange Numbers 1 and 2 will fit if
      extensions are changed

Interchange Number: 4
   Type: Standard-duty Muncie
   Usage: 1964–1968 C-10 to C-30 Chevrolet and
      1500 to 3500 GMC truck—two-wheel-drive
      models only
   Note(s): Interchange Number 5 fits if extensions are
      swapped

Interchange Number: 5
   Type: Standard-duty Muncie
   Usage: 1964–1968 C-10 to C-20 Chevrolet and
      1500 to 3500 GMC truck—four-wheel-drive
      models only
   Note(s): Interchange Number 4 fits if extensions are
      swapped

Interchange Number: 6
   Type: Heavy-duty Muncie
   Usage: 1967 C-10 to C-30 Chevrolet and 1500
      to 3500 GMC truck—two-wheel-drive mod-
      els only

Interchange Number: 7
   Type: Heavy-duty Warner
   Usage: 1968 C-10 to C-30 Chevrolet and 1500
      to 3500 GMC truck—two-wheel-drive
      models only

Interchange Number: 8
   Type: Standard-duty Muncie
   Usage: 1969 C-10 to C-30 Chevrolet and 1500 to
      3500 GMC truck—two-wheel-drive models
      only, with 350- or 396-ci V-8
   Note(s): Interchange Number 9 will fit if extensions
      are swapped

Interchange Number: 9
   Type: Standard-duty Muncie
   Usage: 1970–1973 C-10 to C-30 Chevrolet and
      1500 to 3500 GMC truck—two-wheel-drive
      models only, with 350-, or 396-, or 402-ci V-8
   Note(s): Interchange Number 8 will fit if extensions
      are swapped

Interchange Number: 10

    Type: Standard-duty Muncie

    Usage: 1969–1973 C-10 to C-20 Chevrolet and 1500 to 2500 GMC truck, Blazer, and Jimmy—four-wheel-drive models only

Interchange Number: 11

    Type: Standard-duty Saginaw

    Usage: 1973–1975 C-10 to C-30 Chevrolet and 1500 to 3500 GMC truck, Blazer, and Jimmy (two-wheel-drive models only); 1968–1976 Camaro, Chevelle, Impala, and Nova; 1970–1975 Monte Carlo and Sprint

Interchange Number: 12

    Type: Standard-duty Muncie

    Usage: 1974–1975 C-10 to C-20 Chevrolet and 1500 to 2500 GMC truck, Blazer, and Jimmy—four-wheel-drive models only

Interchange Number: 13

    Type: Standard-duty Termac

    Usage: 1976–1978 C-10 to C-20 Chevrolet and 1500 to 2500 GMC truck, Blazer, and Jimmy—two-wheel-drive models only

Interchange Number: 14

    Type: Standard-duty Termac

    Usage: 1976–1978 C-10 to C-20 Chevrolet and 1500 to 2500 GMC truck, Blazer, and Jimmy—four-wheel-drive models only

Interchange Number: 15

    Type: Standard-duty Saginaw

    Usage: 1977–1981 C-10 to C-20 Chevrolet and 1500 to 2500 GMC truck, Blazer, and Jimmy—four-wheel-drive models only

FOUR-SPEED MANUAL

Interchange Number: 16

    Type: Muncie

    Usage: 1967 C-10 to C-30 Chevrolet and 1500 to 3500 GMC truck

Interchange Number: 17

    Type: New Process

    Usage: 1967–1972 C-10 to C-30 Chevrolet and 1500 to 3500 GMC truck

Interchange Number: 18

    Type: Muncie

    Usage: 1968–1980 C-10 to C-30 Chevrolet and 1500 to 3500 GMC truck; 1969–1980 Blazer; 1970–1980 Jimmy—two-wheel-drive models only

Interchange Number: 19

    Type: Muncie

    Usage: 1968–1980 C-10 to C-30 Chevrolet and 1500 to 3500 GMC truck; 1969–1980 Blazer; 1970–1980 Jimmy—four-wheel-drive models only

A Turbo-Hydra-Matic 400 transmission pan.

Automatic Transmissions

Chevrolet trucks used four types of automatic transmissions: the Powerglide (which has two forward drive speeds) and the Turbo-Hydra-Matic 350, 400, and 475, all of which had three forward drive speeds. The transmissions can be identified by their visual characteristics.

Powerglide was used up till the 1971 model year, when it was phased out. It has a flat, smooth, or rounded ridge top. A quick way to identify the transmission is to look for the word POWERGLIDE stamped into the case.

Turbo-Hydra-Matic 350 and 400 are easily identified by their two-part (converter housing/transmission housing extension) design. They can be further classified by the shape of their oil pan. The Turbo-Hydra-Matic 350 uses a square-shaped oil pan that is notched at one corner and held on with 13 bolts. The down-shift cable is

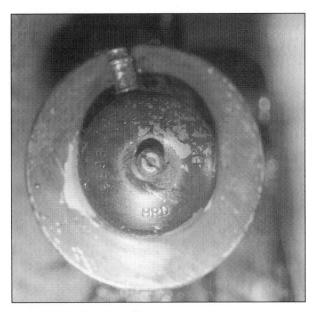
The Turbo-Hydra-Matic 400 ID number location.

located on the right-hand side of the unit. The Turbo-Hydra-Matic 400 has an oil pan that is also secured with 13 bolts, but the pan is longer on the left-hand side of the unit.

Turbo-Hydra-Matics are identified by their code letters. These codes are found stamped on the servo cover on the right-hand side of the transmission. For Turbo-Hydra-Matic 400s, the code can be found on a tag riveted to either the right-hand or left-hand side of the case, depending on model. These codes can be helpful in determining a small transmission from one used on a big-block.

Model Identification

Interchanges
POWERGLIDES
Interchange Number: 1
    Usage: 1967–1970 C-10 to C-20 Chevrolet and 1500 to 2500 GMC truck
    Note(s): Interchange Number 2 will fit if extensions are swapped; also, transmissions from the vans for these years will fit if extensions are swapped

Interchange Number: 2
    Usage: 1971 C-10 to C-20 Chevrolet and 1500 to 2500 GMC truck
    Note(s): Interchange Number 1 will fit if extensions are swapped; also, transmissions from the vans for these years will fit if extensions are swapped

Interchange Number: 3
    Usage: 1967–1970 C-10 to C-20 Chevrolet and 1500 to 2500 GMC truck
    Note(s): Interchange Number 2 will fit if extensions are swapped; also, transmissions from the vans for these years will fit if extensions are swapped

TURBO-HYDRA-MATIC 350s
Interchange Number: 3
    ID codes: B
    Usage: 1969–1972 C-10 to C-30 Chevrolet and 1500 to 3500 GMC truck, Blazer, and Jimmy (except with 396/402-ci V-8), two-wheel-drive models only; 1969–1977 Camaro, Chevelle, Impala, and Nova; 1970–1979 Monte Carlo and Nova; 1970–1977 Firebird with six-cylinder; 1973–1976 LeMans with six-cylinder

Interchange Number: 4
    Usage: 1969–1979 C-10 to C-30 Chevrolet and 1500 to 3500 GMC truck, Blazer, and Jimmy (except with 396/402-ci V-8)—four-wheel-drive models only

Interchange Number: 5
    Usage: 1973–1979 C-10 to C-30 Chevrolet and 1500 to 3500 GMC truck, Blazer, and Jimmy (except with 454-ci V-8)—two-wheel-drive models only

TURBO-HYDRA-MATIC 400s
Interchange Number: 6
    Usage: 1966–1972 C-10 to C-30 Chevrolet and 1500 to 3500 GMC truck; 1969–1972 Blazer; 1970–1972 Jimmy—all except with 396/402-ci V-8

Interchange Number: 7
Usage: 1968–1972 C-10 to C-30 Chevrolet and 1500 to 3500 GMC truck with 396/402-ci V-8; 1970–1974 Camaro and Chevelle with 396/402-ci V-8

Interchange Number: 8
Usage: 1973–1979 C-10 to C-30 Chevrolet and 1500 to 3500 GMC truck (with gasoline engines only)—two-wheel drive only

Transfer Cases

In short, the transfer case is a transmission for the front wheels in four-wheel-drive models. Factors affecting this interchange include the type of transmission; those with a Saginaw transmission used a different transfer case than those with a Muncie-built transmission. In the case of 1973 and later models, whether or not the truck was ordered with full-time or part-time four-wheel drive.

Model Identification

1967–1968	*Interchange Number*
Manual transmission	1

1969–1972
Manual transmission	3
Automatic transmission	2

1973–1975
Manual transmission	
part-time	3
full-time	5
Automatic transmission	
part-time	2
full-time	4

1976
Manual transmission	3
Automatic transmission	4

1977
Manual transmission	
early	3
late	7
Automatic transmission	
TH 350	4
TH 400	6

1978
Manual transmission	11
Automatic transmission	
TH 350	8
TH 400	
C-20	9
C-30	10

A Turbo-Hydra-Matic 350 pan design.

Interchanges

Interchange Number: 1
Part Number(s): 3928556
Usage: 1967–1968 C-10 to C-30 Chevrolet and 1500 to 3500 GMC truck with manual transmission

Interchange Number: 2
Part Number(s): 3990934
Usage: 1969–1975 C-10 to C-20 Chevrolet and 1500 to 2500 GMC truck, Blazer, and Jimmy with automatic transmission and part-time four-wheel drive

Interchange Number: 3
Part Number(s): 3990935
Usage: 1969 to early-1977 C-10 to C-20 Chevrolet and 1500 to 2500 GMC truck, Blazer, and Jimmy with manual transmission and part-time four-wheel drive
Note(s): Has 10-spline front output shaft

Interchange Number: 4
Part Number(s): 460834
Usage: 1973–1977 C-10 to C-20 Chevrolet and 1500 to 2500 GMC truck, Blazer, and Jimmy with automatic transmission and full-time four-wheel drive

Interchange Number: 5
Part Number(s): 338930
Usage: 1973–1975 C-10 to C-20 Chevrolet and 1500 to 2500 GMC truck, Blazer, and Jimmy with manual transmission and full-time four-wheel drive

Interchange Number: 6
Part Number(s): 376269
Usage: 1977 C-30 Chevrolet and 3500 GMC truck with automatic transmission

Interchange Number: 7
Part Number(s): 471711
Usage: Late-1977 C-10 to C-30 Chevrolet and 1500 to 3500 GMC truck, Blazer, and Jimmy with manual transmission
Note(s): Has 30-spline front output shaft

Interchange Number: 8
Part Number(s): 476742
Usage: 1978–1979 C-10 to C-20 Chevrolet and 1500 to 2500 GMC truck, Blazer, and Jimmy with TH 350 transmission

Interchange Number: 9
Part Number(s): 14022134
Usage: 1978–1979 C-20 Chevrolet and 2500 GMC truck with TH 400 automatic transmission

Interchange Number: 10
Part Number(s): 476741
Usage: 1978–1979 C-30 Chevrolet and 3500 GMC truck with TH 400 automatic transmission

Interchange Number: 11
Part Number(s): 474069
Usage: 1978–1979 C-10 to C-20 Chevrolet and 1500 to 2500 GMC truck; 1980–1981 C-30 Chevrolet and 3500 GMC four-door truck—all with manual transmission

Gearshifts

Gearshift interchange is based on original part numbers. In most cases it is the entire lever assembly (lower mechanism and upper lever). This interchange is for the main shifter lever. It does not include the lever for engaging the transfer case; these are listed in a separate interchange. Interchange is without the shift knob.

Model Identification

1967–1968	Interchange Number
Three-speed	.2
Four-speed	
except heavy-duty	10
heavy-duty	.9
Automatic	.2

1969–1970
Three-speed	.3
Four-speed, except heavy-duty	
two-wheel drive	10

four-wheel drive
without CST	14
with CST	12
except four-wheel drive	13
New Process	11
Automatic	.3

1971–1972
Three-speed	.4
Four-speed, except heavy-duty	
two-wheel drive	10
four-wheel drive	
without CST	14
with CST	12
except four-wheel drive	13
New Process	11
Automatic	.2

1973–1978
Three-speed	.1
Four-speed	.8
Automatic	
without tilt wheel	.5
with tilt wheel	.6

Interchanges

Interchange Number: 1
Part Number(s): 14007618
Location: Column
Usage: 1973–1979 C-10 to C-20 Chevrolet and 1500 to 2500 GMC truck, Blazer, and Jimmy with three-speed manual transmission

Interchange Number: 2
Part Number(s): 3902560
Location: Column
Usage: 1967–1968 C-10 to C-20 Chevrolet and 1500 to 2500 GMC truck with three-speed manual or automatic transmissions

Interchange Number: 3
Part Number(s): 3945084
Location: Column
Usage: 1969–1970 C-10 to C-20 Chevrolet and 1500 to 2500 GMC truck and Blazer; 1970 Jimmy—all with three-speed manual or automatic transmissions

Interchange Number: 4
Part Number(s): 3990301
Location: Column
Usage: 1971–1972 C-10 to C-20 Chevrolet and 1500 to 2500 GMC truck and Blazer; 1970 Jimmy—all with three-speed manual or automatic transmissions

Interchange Number: 5
Part Number(s): 3990498
Location: Column
Usage: 1973–1979 C-10 to C-30 Chevrolet and 1500 to 3500 GMC truck, Blazer, and Jimmy with automatic transmission, without tilt wheel

Interchange Number: 6
    Part Number(s): 6272366
    Location: Column
    Usage: 1973–1979 C-10 to C-30 Chevrolet and
        1500 to 3500 GMC truck, Blazer, and Jimmy
        with automatic transmission with tilt wheel
Interchange Number: 7
    Part Number(s): 3990498
    Location: Column
    Usage: 1973–1979 C-10 to C-30 Chevrolet and
        1500 to 3500 GMC truck, Blazer, and Jimmy
        with automatic transmission, without tilt wheel
Interchange Number: 8
    Part Number(s): 6274077
    Location: Floor
    Usage: 1973–1979 C-10 to C-30 Chevrolet and
        1500 to 3500 GMC truck, Blazer, and Jimmy
        with four-speed manual transmission
Interchange Number: 9
    Part Number(s): 3904783
    Location: Floor
    Usage: 1967–1968 C-10 to C-30 Chevrolet and
        1500 to 3500 GMC truck with four-speed
        heavy-duty manual transmission
Interchange Number: 10
    Part Number(s): 3952063
    Location: Floor
    Usage: 1967–1972 C-10 to C-30 Chevrolet and
        1500 to 3500 GMC truck, Blazer, and Jimmy
        with four-speed manual transmission (except
        heavy-duty or four-wheel-drive models)
Interchange Number: 11
    Part Number(s): 3952067
    Location: Floor
    Usage: 1969–1972 C-10 to C-30 Chevrolet and 1500
        to 3500 GMC truck, Blazer, and Jimmy with four-
        speed New Process manual transmission
Interchange Number: 12
    Part Number(s): 3963035
    Location: Floor
    Usage: 1969–1972 C-10 to C-20 Chevrolet and
        1500 to 2500 GMC truck, Blazer, and Jimmy
        four-wheel-drive models with Custom
        Sport truck option, with four-speed manual
        transmission
Interchange Number: 13
    Part Number(s): 3963040
    Location: Floor
    Usage: 1969–1972 Blazer and Jimmy two-wheel
        drive with Custom Sport truck option, with
        four-speed manual transmission
Interchange Number: 14
    Part Number(s): 3899919
    Location: Floor

    Usage: 1969–1972 C-10 to C-20 Chevrolet and
        1500 to 2500 GMC truck, Blazer, and Jimmy
        four-wheel-drive models without Custom
        Sport truck option, with four-speed manual
        transmission

Transfer Shifters
Model Identification

1967–1968	Interchange Number
All	7
1969–1970	
All	6
1971–1972	
without Cheyenne package	8
with Cheyenne package	5
1973–1978	
Manual transmission	
without Cheyenne package	1
with Cheyenne package	4
Automatic	
without Cheyenne package	2
with Cheyenne package	3

Interchanges
Interchange Number: 1
    Part Number(s): 14016393
    Usage: 1973–1978 C-10 to C-30 Chevrolet and
        1500 to 3500 GMC truck, Blazer, and Jimmy
        four-wheel drive without Cheyenne package,
        with manual transmission
    Note(s): Type 205-part-time plain finish
Interchange Number: 2
    Part Number(s): 348996
    Usage: 1973–1978 C-10 to C-30 Chevrolet and
        1500 to 3500 GMC truck, Blazer, and Jimmy
        four-wheel drive without Cheyenne package
    Note(s): Type 203-full-time
Interchange Number: 3
    Part Number(s): 348997
    Usage: 1973–1978 C-10 to C-30 Chevrolet and
        1500 to 3500 GMC truck, Blazer, and Jimmy
        four-wheel drive with automatic transmission,
        with Cheyenne package
Interchange Number: 4
    Part Number(s): 14016394
    Usage: 1973–1978 C-10 to C-30 Chevrolet and
        1500 to 3500 GMC truck, Blazer, and Jimmy
        four-wheel drive with Cheyenne package
Interchange Number: 5
    Part Number(s): 3991931
    Usage: 1971–1972 C-10 to C-20 Chevrolet and
        1500 to 2500 GMC truck, Blazer, and Jimmy
        four-wheel drive with manual or automatic
        transmission, without Cheyenne package

Interchange Number: 6
  Part Number(s): 3983531
  Usage: 1969–1970 Blazer with manual transmission
Interchange Number: 7
  Usage: 1967–1968 C-10 to C-20 Chevrolet and 1500 to 2500 GMC truck
Interchange Number: 8
  Usage: 1971–1972 C-10 to C-20 Chevrolet and 1500 to 2500 GMC truck, Blazer, and Jimmy four-wheel drive with manual or automatic transmission, with Cheyenne package

Shift Knobs
Model Identification

1967–1972	Interchange Number
Three-speed	4
Four-speed	5
Automatic	4
1973–1974	
Three-speed	1
Four-speed	2
Automatic	1
1975–1978	
Three-speed	1
Four-speed	3
Automatic	1

Interchanges
Interchange Number: 1
  Part Number(s): 14049351
  Shifter Location: Column
  Usage: 1973–1978 C-10 to C-30 Chevrolet and 1500 to 3500 GMC truck, Blazer, and Jimmy with three-speed manual or automatic transmission
Interchange Number: 2
  Part Number(s): 6274158
  Shifter Location: Floor
  Usage: 1973–1974 C-10 to C-30 Chevrolet and 1500 to 3500 GMC truck, Blazer, and Jimmy with four-speed manual transmission
Interchange Number: 3
  Part Number(s): 355435
  Shifter Location: Floor
  Usage: 1975–1978 C-10 to C-30 Chevrolet and 1500 to 3500 GMC truck, Blazer, and Jimmy with four-speed manual transmission
Interchange Number: 4
  Part Number(s): 3973042
  Shifter Location: Column
  Usage: 1967–1972 C-10 to C-20 Chevrolet and 1500 to 2500 GMC truck, Blazer, and Jimmy with three-speed manual or automatic transmission

Interchange Number: 5
  Part Number(s): 6274158
  Shifter Location: Floor
  Usage: 1968–1972 C-10 to C-30 Chevrolet and 1500 to 3500 GMC truck, Blazer, and Jimmy with four-speed manual transmission

Shift Knobs, Transfer-Case Lever
Model Identification

1967–1970	Interchange Number
All	3
1971–1972	
All	4
1973–1978	
First design	2
Second design	1

Interchanges
Interchange Number: 1
  Part Number(s): 14007661
  Usage: 1973–1974 C-10 to C-20 Chevrolet and 1500 to 2500 GMC truck, Blazer, and Jimmy with full-time four-wheel drive; 1977–1978 C-10 to C-30 Chevrolet and 1500 to 3500 GMC, Blazer, and Jimmy four-wheel drive
  Note(s): Second design has 3/8-16 thread
Interchange Number: 2
  Part Number(s): 14029120
  Usage: 1973–1978 C-10 to C-20 Chevrolet and 1500 to 2500 GMC truck, Blazer, and Jimmy
  Note(s): First design has 7/16-20 thread
Interchange Number: 3
  Part Number(s): 374993
  Usage: 1967–1970 C-10 to C-20 Chevrolet and 1500 to 2500 GMC truck, Blazer, and Jimmy
Interchange Number: 4
  Part Number(s): 3991947
  Usage: 1971–1972 C-10 to C-20 Chevrolet and 1500 to 2500 GMC truck, Blazer, and Jimmy

Shift Dials
Model Identification

1967–1970	Interchange Number
Powerglide	1
Turbo-Hydra-Matic	
without tilt wheel	2
with tilt wheel	3
1971	
Powerglide	5
Turbo-Hydra-Matic	
without tilt wheel	4
with tilt wheel	3

Interchanges

Interchange Number: 1
>
> Part Number(s): 3904747
>
> Usage: 1967–1970 C-10 to C-20 Chevrolet and 1500 to 2500 GMC truck, Blazer, and Jimmy with Powerglide automatic; 1971 G-10 to G-20 and 1500 to 2500 GMC van—all with Powerglide automatic

Interchange Number: 2
>
> Part Number(s): 3904750
>
> Usage: 1967–1970 C-10 to C-20 Chevrolet and 1500 to 2500 GMC truck, Blazer, and Jimmy with Turbo-Hydra-Matic automatic; 1971 G-10 to G-30 and 1500 to 3500 GMC van with Turbo-Hydra-Matic automatic (first design)—all without tilt wheel

Interchange Number: 3
>
> Part Number(s): 335268
>
> Usage: 1970–1972 C-10 to C-20 Chevrolet and 1500 to 2500 GMC truck, Blazer, and Jimmy with Turbo-Hydra-Matic automatic; 1971–1972 G-10 to G-30 and 1500 to 3500 GMC van with Turbo-Hydra-Matic automatic—all with tilt wheel

Interchange Number: 4
>
> Part Number(s): 335267
>
> Usage: 1971–1972 C-10 to C-20 Chevrolet and 1500 to 2500 GMC truck, Blazer, and Jimmy with Turbo-Hydra-Matic automatic; 1971–1978 G-10 to G-30 and 1500 to 3500 GMC van with Turbo-Hydra-Matic automatic (second design)—all without tilt wheel

Interchange Number: 5
>
> Part Number(s): 3978953
>
> Usage: 1971 C-10 to C-20 Chevrolet and 1500 to 2500 GMC truck, Blazer, and Jimmy with Powerglide automatic

Shift and Transfer-case Boots

Interchange here is based on reproduction or NOS (new old stock) part. Used boots should not be used. Interchange here includes the shift boot for four-speeds and the transfer case.

Model Identification
SHIFT BOOTS

Interchanges

Interchange Number: 1
>
> Part Number(s): 3904784
>
> Usage: 1968–1970 C-10 to C-20 Chevrolet and 1500 to 2500 GMC truck, Blazer, and Jimmy with four-wheel drive and four-speed transmission

Interchange Number: 2
>
> Part Number(s): 3899922
>
> Usage: 1967 C-10 to C-30 Chevrolet and 1500 to 3500 GMC truck (except four-wheel drive) with Muncie transmission

Interchange Number: 3
>
> Part Number(s): 3931297
>
> Usage: 1968–1970 C-10 to C-30 Chevrolet and 1500 to 3500 GMC truck with 396-ci V-8 and New Process transmission

Interchange Number: 4
>
> Part Number(s): 3922900
>
> Usage: 1968–1972 C-10 to C-30 Chevrolet and 1500 to 3500 GMC truck (except four-wheel drive or 396-ci V-8) with Muncie transmission

Interchange Number: 5
>
> Part Number(s): 3930237
>
> Usage: 1968–1971 C-10 to C-30 Chevrolet and 1500 to 3500 GMC truck with close ratio four-speed New Process transmission

Interchange Number: 6
>
> Part Number(s): 3936513
>
> Usage: 1968–1972 C-10 to C-30 Chevrolet and 1500 to 3500 GMC truck with 396/402-ci V-8 and Muncie wide-ratio transmission

Interchange Number: 7
>
> Part Number(s): 378340
>
> Usage: 1973–1979 C-10 to C-30 Chevrolet and 1500 to 3500 GMC truck, Blazer, and Jimmy with close ratio four-speed transmission

Interchange Number: 8
Part Number(s): 334547
Usage: 1973–1979 C-10 to C-30 Chevrolet and 1500 to 3500 GMC truck, Blazer, and Jimmy with automatic transmission
Note(s): Transfer-case boot

Interchange Number: 9
Part Number(s): 6274165
Usage: 1973–1979 C-10 to C-30 Chevrolet and 1500 to 3500 GMC truck, Blazer, and Jimmy with manual transmission
Note(s): Transfer-case boot

Interchange Number: 10
Part Number(s): 3983540
Usage: 1969–1970 C-10 to C-30 Chevrolet and 1500 to 3500 GMC truck, Blazer, and Jimmy
Note(s): Transfer-case boot

Interchange Number: 11
Part Number(s): 3991945
Usage: 1971–1972 C-10 to C-30 Chevrolet and 1500 to 3500 GMC truck, Blazer, and Jimmy
Note(s): Transfer-case boot

Interchange Number: 12
Part Number(s): 3919432
Usage: 1967–1968 C-10 to C-30 Chevrolet and 1500 to 3500 GMC truck, Blazer, and Jimmy
Note(s): Transfer-case boot

Driveshafts

Driveshaft interchange is by its physical fit, which includes the slip yoke. Driveshafts can also be identified by their length. Chevrolet driveshafts are measured from tip to tip. When available, the length is given. Four-wheel-drive models included a front from-transfer-case-to-front-axle shaft and a rear shaft. Factors that can affect the driveshaft interchange include the wheelbase, and in some cases engine size and transmission type.

Front Driveshafts
Model Identification

1967–1968	*Interchange Number*
C-10 and C-20	
four-wheel drive	6

1969
C-10 and C-20
  four-wheel drive 6
  Blazer 5

1970–1972
C-10, C-20, and Blazer
  four-wheel drive 5

1973–1976
C-10 to C-20 and Blazer
  full-time 1
  part-time 2

1977–1978
C-10, C-20, and Blazer
  automatic
    early 1
    late 3
  manual
    early 2
    late 4

Interchanges
Interchange Number: 1
Part Number(s): 326479
Usage: 1973 to early-1977 C-10 to C-20 Chevrolet and 1500 to 2500 GMC truck, Blazer, and Jimmy—all with full-time four-wheel drive

Interchange Number: 2
Part Number(s): 326487
Usage: 1973 to early-1977 C-10 to C-20 Chevrolet and 1500 to 2500 GMC truck, Blazer, and Jimmy—all with part-time four-wheel drive

Interchange Number: 3
Part Number(s): 7826670
Usage: Late-1977 to 1979 C-10 to C-20 Chevrolet and 1500 to 2500 GMC truck, Blazer, and Jimmy—all with automatic transmission and four-wheel drive

Interchange Number: 4
Part Number(s): 7826671
Usage: Late-1977 to 1979 C-10 to C-20 Chevrolet and 1500 to 2500 GMC truck, Blazer, and Jimmy—all with manual transmission and four-wheel drive

Interchange Number: 5
Part Number(s): 3966940
Usage: 1969–1972 Blazer; 1970–1972 Jimmy; 1970–1972 C-10 to C-20 Chevrolet and 1500 to 2500 GMC truck—all with four-wheel drive

Interchange Number: 6
Part Number(s): 6259684
Usage: 1967–1969 C-10 to C-20 Chevrolet and 1500 to 2500 GMC truck—all with four-wheel drive

Rear Driveshafts
Model Identification

1967–1968	*Interchange Number*
C-10 two-wheel drive	
115-inch wheelbase	
coil springs	
three-speed manual	60
four-speed manual	61
Powerglide	62
TH 400	63
leaf springs	
three-speed manual	70

Interchanges

Interchange Number: 1

Part Number(s): 7816879

Length: 59 3/8 inches

Usage: 1973–1978 C-10 Chevrolet and 1500 GMC truck with 117.5-inch wheelbase and three-speed manual transmission—two-wheel-drive models only

Interchange Number: 2

Part Number(s): 7813953

Length: 59 3/16 inches

Usage: 1973–1978 C-10 Chevrolet and 1500 GMC truck with 117.5-inch wheelbase and Turbo-Hydra-Matic 350 automatic transmission—two-wheel-drive models only

Interchange Number: 3

Part Number(s): 7815673 (front); 7815752 (rear)

Length: 25 17/32 inches (front); 23 25/32 inches (rear)

Usage: Early-1973 C-10 Chevrolet and 1500 GMC truck with 117.5-inch wheelbase; early-1973 C-10 to C-30 Chevrolet and 1500 to 2500 GMC truck with 131.5-inch wheelbase and Turbo-Hydra-Matic 400 automatic transmission—two-wheel-drive models only

Note(s): Two-piece shaft; tear shaft used in 1973–1974 models

Interchange Number: 4

Part Number(s): 6260530 (front); 0362270 (rear)

Length: 25 1/32 inches (front); 24 59/64 inches (rear)

Usage: 1975 C-10 Chevrolet and 1500 GMC truck with 117.5-inch wheelbase and Turbo-Hydra-Matic 400 automatic transmission—two-wheel-drive models only

Interchange Number: 5

Part Number(s): 6260530 (front); 7815744 (rear)

Length: 25 1/32 inches (front); 32 inches (rear)

Usage: 1976–1981 C-10 Chevrolet and 1500 GMC truck with 117.5-inch wheelbase and Turbo-Hydra-Matic 400 automatic transmission; 1979–1980 C-10 Chevrolet and 1500 GMC truck 117.5 wheelbase with four-speed manual transmission—two-wheel-drive models only

Note(s): Front shaft used in Interchange Numbers 4 and 11

Interchange Number: 6

Part Number(s): 6260936

Length: 42 27/32 inches

Usage: 1973–1979 C-10 Chevrolet and 1500 GMC truck with 117.5-inch wheelbase and full-time four-wheel drive

Interchange Number: 7

Part Number(s): 6258835

Length: 50 9/32 inches

Usage: 1973–1979 C-10 Chevrolet and 1500 GMC truck with 117.5-inch wheelbase and part-time four-wheel drive

Interchange Number: 8

Part Number(s): 7815621 (front); 7815493 (rear)

Usage: 1973–1979 C-10 Chevrolet and 1500 GMC truck with 131.5-inch wheelbase and three-

speed manual transmission—two-wheel-drive
models only

Note(s): Two-piece shaft; rear shaft also found on
1973–1980 models with TH 350 transmission

Interchange Number: 9

Part Number(s): 7815484 (front); 7819071 (rear)

Usage: 1973–1979 C-10 to C-20 Chevrolet and
1500 to 2500 GMC truck with 131.5-inch
wheelbase and four-speed manual transmission—two-wheel-drive models only

Note(s): Two-piece shaft; rear shaft also found on
1974–1978 models with TH 400 transmission
and Interchange Number 20

Interchange Number: 10

Part Number(s): 7813955

Usage: 1973–1979 C-10 Chevrolet and 1500 GMC
truck with 131.5-inch wheelbase and Turbo-Hydra-Matic 350 automatic transmission—two-wheel-drive models only

Note(s): One-piece shaft

Interchange Number: 11

Part Number(s): 6260530 (front); 7815752 (rear)

Length: 25 1/32 inches (front); 23 25/32 inches
(rear)

Usage: Late-1973–1974 C-10 Chevrolet and 1500
GMC truck with 117.5-inch wheelbase and
Turbo-Hydra-Matic 400 automatic transmission

Note(s): Front shaft used in Interchange Numbers 5
and 12

Interchange Number: 12

Part Number(s): 6260530 (front); 7819071 (rear)

Length: 25 1/32 inches (front); 37 23/64 inches
(rear)

Usage: Late-1973–1978 C-10 Chevrolet and 1500
GMC truck with 131.5-inch wheelbase and
Turbo-Hydra-Matic 400 automatic transmission

Note(s): Front shaft used in Interchange Numbers 5
and 11; early-1973 models used same rear shaft

Interchange Number: 13

Part Number(s): 6260937

Length: 57 7/8 inches

Usage: 1973–1979 C-10 Chevrolet and 1500 GMC
truck with 131.5-inch wheelbase and full-time
four-wheel drive

Interchange Number: 14

Part Number(s): 7834039 (front); 7825632 (rear)

Length: 32 13/32 inches (front); 36 9/32 inches
(rear)

Usage: 1973–1981 C-10 or 1500 Suburban two-wheel drive with four-speed manual transmission

Note(s): Rare; rear shaft same as in Interchange
Numbers 17 and 18

Interchange Number: 15

Part Number(s): 7813954

Length: 68 9/32 inches

Usage: 1973–1981 C-10 or 1500 Suburban two-wheel drive with Turbo-Hydra-Matic 350 automatic transmission

Note(s): One-piece shaft

Interchange Number: 16

Part Number(s): 7815623 (front); 7815495 (rear)

Usage: 1973–1977 C-10 and 1500 Suburban two-wheel drive with Turbo-Hydra-Matic 350 automatic transmission

Note(s): Two-piece shaft

Interchange Number: 17

Part Number(s): 359812 (front); 7825632 (rear)

Length: 24 7/16 inches (front); 36 9/32 inches (rear)

Usage: 1973–1977 C-10 or 1500 Suburban two-wheel drive with Turbo-Hydra-Matic 400 automatic transmission

Note(s): Rear shaft same as Interchange Number 18

Interchange Number: 18

Part Number(s): 6260532 (front); 7825632 (rear)

Length: 25 3/16 inches (front); 36 9/32 inches (rear)

Usage: 1973–1977 C-10 or 1500 Suburban two-wheel drive with Turbo-Hydra-Matic 400 automatic transmission

Note(s): Rear shaft same as Interchange Numbers
14 and 17

Interchange Number: 19

Part Number(s): 365301

Length: 62 3/8 inches

Usage: 1973–1977 C-10 or 1500 Suburban four-wheel drive

Interchange Number: 20

Part Number(s): 7815621 (front); 7815628 (rear)

Usage: 1973–1979 C-20 Chevrolet and 2500 GMC
two-wheel-drive truck with three-speed manual transmission

Note(s): Front shaft used in Interchange Number 9;
rear shaft used in Interchange Number 21

Interchange Number: 21

Part Number(s): 7815623 (front); 7815628 (rear)

Usage: 1973–1977 C-20 Chevrolet and 2500 GMC
two-wheel-drive truck with Turbo-Hydra-Matic
350 automatic transmission

Note(s): Front shaft used in Interchange Number
16; rear shaft used in Interchange Number 20

Interchange Number: 22

Part Number(s): 7815624

Usage: 1973–1977 C-20 Chevrolet and 2500 GMC
two-wheel-drive truck with Turbo-Hydra-Matic
350 automatic transmission

Note(s): One-piece shaft design

Interchange Number: 23
　　Usage: 1973–1977 C-20 Chevrolet and 2500 GMC two-wheel-drive truck with Turbo-Hydra-Matic 400 automatic transmission
　　Note(s): Two-piece shaft design

Interchange Number: 24
　　Part Number(s): 6258839
　　Length: 63 7/16 inches
　　Usage: 1973 C-20 Chevrolet and 2500 GMC truck with four-wheel drive

Interchange Number: 25
　　Part Number(s): 6260940
　　Length: 63 29/32 inches
　　Usage: 1974 C-20 Chevrolet and 2500 GMC truck with part-time four-wheel drive

Interchange Number: 26
　　Part Number(s): 3489928
　　Length: 56 31/32 inches
　　Usage: 1974 C-20 Chevrolet and 2500 GMC truck with full-time four-wheel drive

Interchange Number: 27
　　Part Number(s): 7838759 (front); 7819329 (rear)
　　Usage: 1973–1977 C-30 Chevrolet and 3500 GMC truck with 131.5-inch wheelbase

Interchange Number: 28
　　Usage: 1973–1977 C-30 Chevrolet and 3500 GMC truck with 131.5-inch wheelbase with dual rear wheels

Interchange Number: 29
　　Usage: 1973–1977 C-30 Chevrolet and 3500 GMC truck, except 131.5-inch wheelbase without dual rear wheels

Interchange Number: 30
　　Usage: 1973–1977 C-30 Chevrolet and 3500 GMC truck, except 131.5-inch wheelbase with dual rear wheels

Interchange Number: 31
　　Usage: 1975–1977 C-20 Chevrolet and 2500 GMC truck with 131.5-inch wheelbase and full-time four-wheel drive

Interchange Number: 32
　　Usage: 1975–1977 C-20 Chevrolet and 2500 GMC truck with 131.5-inch wheelbase and part-time four-wheel drive

Interchange Number: 33
　　Usage: 1978–1980 C-20 Chevrolet and 2500 GMC truck with 131.5-inch wheelbase and Turbo-Hydra-Matic 350 automatic transmission

Interchange Number: 34
　　Usage: 1973–1981 Blazer and Jimmy two-wheel drive with three-speed manual transmission

Interchange Number: 35
　　Usage: 1973–1980 Blazer and Jimmy two-wheel drive with four-speed manual transmission

Interchange Number: 36
　　Usage: 1973–1980 Blazer and Jimmy two-wheel drive with automatic transmission

Interchange Number: 37
　　Usage: 1973–1975 Blazer and Jimmy four-wheel drive with three-speed manual transmission and Dana transfer case

Interchange Number: 38
　　Usage: 1973–1980 Blazer and Jimmy four-wheel drive with four-speed manual transmission and New Process transfer case

Interchange Number: 39
　　Usage: 1973–1974 Blazer and Jimmy four-wheel drive with automatic transmission and New Process transfer case

Interchange Number: 40
　　Usage: 1976–1979 Blazer and Jimmy four-wheel drive with manual transmission and New Process transfer case

Interchange Number: 41
　　Usage: 1976–1979 Blazer and Jimmy four-wheel drive with automatic transmission and New Process transfer case

Interchange Number: 42
　　Usage: 1971–1972 Blazer and Jimmy two-wheel drive with V-8 and four-speed manual transmission

Interchange Number: 43
　　Usage: 1969–1970 Blazer; 1970 Jimmy two-wheel drive with V-8; 1971–1972 Blazer and Jimmy two-wheel drive with V-8, except with four-speed manual transmission

Interchange Number: 44
　　Usage: 1971–1972 Blazer and Jimmy four-wheel drive with V-8 and three-speed manual transmission

Interchange Number: 45
　　Usage: 1971–1972 Blazer and Jimmy four-wheel drive with V-8, except with three-speed manual transmission

Interchange Number: 46
　　Usage: 1969–1972 C-10 Chevrolet and 1500 GMC two-wheel-drive truck with three-speed manual transmission and coil-spring suspension (except with 402-ci V-8)
　　Note(s): Rear section of shaft in Interchange Number 47 will fit

Interchange Number: 47
　　Usage: 1968–1972 C-10 Chevrolet and 1500 GMC two-wheel-drive truck with four-speed manual transmission and coil-spring suspension (except with 396/402-ci V-8)
　　Note(s): Rear section of shaft in Interchange Number 46 will fit

The 1967–1972 rear axles with rear leaf springs used this pad to mount the springs.

Interchange Number: 48

Usage: 1970–1972 C-10 Chevrolet and 1500 GMC two-wheel-drive truck with automatic transmission and coil-spring suspension (except with 396/402-ci V-8)

Interchange Number: 49

Usage: 1971–1972 C-10 Chevrolet and 1500 GMC two-wheel-drive truck with three-speed manual transmission and leaf spring suspension (except with 396/402-ci V-8)

Interchange Number: 50

Usage: 1971–1972 C-10 Chevrolet and 1500 GMC two-wheel-drive truck with four-speed manual transmission and leaf spring suspension (except with 396/402-ci V-8)

Interchange Number: 51

Usage: 1971–1972 C-10 Chevrolet and 1500 GMC two-wheel-drive truck with automatic transmission and leaf spring suspension (except with 396/402-ci V-8)

Interchange Number: 52

Usage: 1971–1972 C-10 Chevrolet and 1500 GMC four-wheel-drive truck with three-speed manual transmission

Interchange Number: 53

Usage: 1971–1972 C-10 Chevrolet and 1500 GMC four-wheel-drive truck with four-speed manual transmission

Interchange Number: 54

Usage: 1971–1972 C-10 Chevrolet and 1500 GMC four-wheel-drive truck with automatic transmission

Interchange Number: 55

Usage: 1971–1972 C-10 Chevrolet and 1500 GMC two-wheel-drive truck with automatic transmission and 402-ci V-8

Interchange Number: 56

Usage: 1971–1972 C-10 Chevrolet and 1500 GMC two-wheel-drive truck with four-speed manual transmission and 402-ci V-8

Interchange Number: 57

Usage: 1971–1972 C-10 Chevrolet and 1500 GMC two-wheel-drive truck with three-speed manual transmission and 402-ci V-8

Interchange Number: 58

Usage: 1969–1970 Blazer and 1970 Jimmy four-wheel drive with V-8 and manual transmission

Interchange Number: 59

Usage: 1969–1970 Blazer and 1970 Jimmy four-wheel drive with V-8 and automatic transmission

Interchange Number: 60

Usage: 1967–1968 C-10 Chevrolet and 1500 GMC truck with 115-inch wheelbase, with V-8 and three-speed manual transmission (except with 396-ci V-8)

Interchange Number: 61

Usage: 1967–1968 C-10 Chevrolet and 1500 GMC truck with 115-inch wheelbase, with V-8 and four-speed manual transmission (except with 396-ci V-8)

Note(s): Coil-spring suspension

Interchange Number: 62

Usage: 1967–1968 C-10 Chevrolet and 1500 GMC truck with 115-inch wheelbase, with V-8 and Powerglide automatic transmission (except with 396-ci V-8)

Note(s): Coil-spring suspension

Interchange Number: 63

Usage: 1967–1968 C-10 Chevrolet and 1500 GMC truck with 115-inch wheelbase, with V-8 and Turbo-Hydra-Matic automatic transmission (except with 396-ci V-8)

Note(s): Coil-spring suspension

Interchange Number: 64

Usage: 1968 C-10 Chevrolet and 1500 GMC truck with 115-inch wheelbase, with 396-ci V-8 and three-speed manual transmission

Interchange Number: 65

Usage: 1968 C-10 Chevrolet and 1500 GMC truck with 115-inch wheelbase, with 396-ci V-8 and four-speed manual transmission

Interchange Number: 66

Usage: 1968 C-10 Chevrolet and 1500 GMC truck with 115-inch wheelbase, with 396-ci V-8 and automatic transmission

Interchange Number: 67

Usage: 1967–1968 C-10 Chevrolet and 1500 GMC truck with 115-inch wheelbase, with V-8 and four-speed manual transmission (except with 396-ci V-8)

Note(s): Leaf spring suspension

Interchange Number: 68

Usage: 1967–1968 C-10 Chevrolet and 1500 GMC truck with 115-inch wheelbase, with V-8 and Powerglide automatic transmission (except with 396-ci V-8)

Note(s): Leaf spring suspension

Interchange Number: 69

Usage: 1967–1968 C-10 Chevrolet and 1500 GMC truck with 115-inch wheelbase, with V-8 and Turbo-Hydra-Matic automatic transmission (except with 396-ci V-8)

Note(s): Leaf spring suspension

Interchange Number: 70

Usage: 1967–1968 C-10 Chevrolet and 1500 GMC truck with 115-inch wheelbase, with V-8 and three-speed manual transmission (except with 396-ci V-8)

Note(s): Leaf spring suspension

Interchange Number: 71

Usage: 1967–1968 C-10 Chevrolet and 1500 GMC truck with 127-inch wheelbase, with V-8 and three-speed manual transmission (except with 396-ci V-8)

Interchange Number: 72

Usage: 1967–1968 C-10 Chevrolet and 1500 GMC truck with 127-inch wheelbase, with V-8 and four-speed manual transmission (except with 396-ci V-8)

Note(s): Coil-spring suspension

Interchange Number: 73

Usage: 1967–1968 C-10 Chevrolet and 1500 GMC truck with 127-inch wheelbase, with V-8 and Powerglide automatic transmission (except with 396-ci V-8)

Note(s): Coil-spring suspension

Interchange Number: 74

Usage: 1967–1968 C-10 Chevrolet and 1500 GMC truck with 127-inch wheelbase, with V-8 and Turbo-Hydra-Matic automatic transmission (except with 396-ci V-8)

Note(s): Coil-spring suspension

Interchange Number: 75

Usage: 1968 C-10 Chevrolet and 1500 GMC truck with 127-inch wheelbase, with 396-ci V-8 and three-speed manual transmission

Interchange Number: 76

Usage: 1968 C-10 Chevrolet and 1500 GMC truck with 127-inch wheelbase, with 396-ci V-8 and four-speed manual transmission

Interchange Number: 77

Usage: 1968 C-10 Chevrolet and 1500 GMC truck with 127-inch wheelbase, with 396-ci V-8 and automatic transmission

Interchange Number: 78

Usage: 1967–1968 C-10 Chevrolet and 1500 GMC truck with 127-inch wheelbase, with V-8 and four-speed manual transmission (except with 396-ci V-8)

Note(s): Leaf spring suspension

Interchange Number: 79

Usage: 1967–1968 C-10 Chevrolet and 1500 GMC truck with 127-inch wheelbase, with V-8 and Powerglide automatic transmission (except with 396-ci V-8)

Note(s): Leaf spring suspension

Interchange Number: 80

Usage: 1967–1968 C-10 Chevrolet and 1500 GMC truck with 127-inch wheelbase, with V-8 and Turbo-Hydra-Matic automatic transmission (except with 396-ci V-8)

Note(s): Leaf spring suspension

Interchange Number: 81

Usage: 1967–1968 C-10 Chevrolet and 1500 GMC truck with 127-inch wheelbase, with V-8 and three-speed manual transmission (except with 396-ci V-8)

Note(s): Leaf spring suspension

Interchange Number: 82

Usage: 1967–1968 C-20 Chevrolet and 2500 GMC truck with 127-inch wheelbase, with V-8 and three-speed manual transmission (except with 396-ci V-8)

Interchange Number: 83

Usage: 1967–1968 C-20 Chevrolet and 2500 GMC truck with 127-inch wheelbase, with V-8 and four-speed manual transmission (except with 396-ci V-8)

Note(s): Coil-spring suspension

Interchange Number: 84

Usage: 1967–1968 C-20 Chevrolet and 2500 GMC truck with 127-inch wheelbase, with V-8 and Powerglide automatic transmission (except with 396-ci V-8)

Note(s): Coil-spring suspension

Interchange Number: 85

Usage: 1967–1968 C-20 Chevrolet and 2500 GMC truck with 127-inch wheelbase, with V-8 and Turbo-Hydra-Matic automatic transmission (except with 396-ci V-8)

Note(s): Coil-spring suspension

Interchange Number: 86

Usage: 1968 C-20 Chevrolet and 2500 GMC truck with 127-inch wheelbase, with 396-ci V-8 and three-speed manual transmission

Interchange Number: 87
   Usage: 1968 C-20 Chevrolet and 2500 GMC truck with 127-inch wheelbase, with 396-ci V-8 and four-speed manual transmission

Interchange Number: 88
   Usage: 1968 C-20 Chevrolet and 2500 GMC truck with 127-inch wheelbase, with 396-ci V-8 and automatic transmission
   Note(s): Coil springs

Interchange Number: 89
   Usage: 1967–1968 C-20 Chevrolet and 2500 GMC truck with 127-inch wheelbase, with V-8 and four-speed manual transmission (except with 396-ci V-8)
   Note(s): Leaf spring suspension

Interchange Number: 90
   Usage: 1967–1968 C-20 Chevrolet and 2500 GMC truck with 127-inch wheelbase, with V-8 and Powerglide automatic transmission (except with 396-ci V-8)
   Note(s): Leaf spring suspension

Interchange Number: 91
   Usage: 1967–1968 C-20 Chevrolet and 2500 GMC truck with 127-inch wheelbase, with V-8 and Turbo-Hydra-Matic automatic transmission (except with 396-ci V-8)
   Note(s): Leaf spring suspension

Interchange Number: 92
   Usage: 1967–1968 C-20 Chevrolet and 2500 GMC truck with 127-inch wheelbase, with V-8 and three-speed manual transmission (except with 396-ci V-8)
   Note(s): Leaf spring suspension

Interchange Number: 93
   Usage: 1967–1968 C-20 Chevrolet and 2500 GMC truck with 133-inch wheelbase, with V-8 and manual transmission (except with 396-ci V-8)

Interchange Number: 94
   Usage: 1967–1968 C-20 Chevrolet and 2500 GMC truck with 133-inch wheelbase, with V-8 and automatic transmission (except with 396-ci V-8)

Interchange Number: 95
   Usage: 1967–1968 C-30 Chevrolet and 3500 GMC truck with 133-inch wheelbase, with V-8 and manual transmission

Interchange Number: 96
   Usage: 1967–1968 C-30 Chevrolet and 3500 GMC truck with 133-inch wheelbase, with V-8 and automatic transmission

Interchange Number: 97
   Usage: 1967–1968 C-30 Chevrolet and 3500 GMC truck with 157-inch wheelbase, with V-8 and manual transmission

Interchange Number: 99
   Usage: 1967–1968 C-30 Chevrolet and 3500 GMC truck with 157-inch wheelbase, with V-8 and automatic transmission

Interchange Number: 100
   Usage: 1967–1968 C-10 Chevrolet and 1500 GMC truck with 115-inch wheelbase and four-wheel drive

Interchange Number: 101
   Usage: 1967–1968 C-10 Chevrolet and 1500 GMC truck with 127-inch wheelbase and four-wheel drive

Interchange Number: 102
   Usage: 1967–1968 C-20 Chevrolet and 2500 GMC truck with 127-inch wheelbase and four-wheel drive

Interchange Number: 103
   Usage: 1967–1968 C-20 Chevrolet and 2500 GMC truck with 133-inch wheelbase and four-wheel drive

Interchange Number: 104
   Usage: 1967–1968 C-30 Chevrolet and 3500 GMC truck with 11,000-pound axle

Interchange Number: 105
   Usage: 1969–1970 C-10 Chevrolet and 1500 GMC truck with 115-inch wheelbase, with V-8 and three-speed manual transmission (except with 396-ci V-8)

Interchange Number: 106
   Usage: 1969–1970 C-10 Chevrolet and 1500 GMC truck with 115-inch wheelbase, with V-8 and four-speed manual transmission (except with 396-ci V-8)
   Note(s): Coil-spring suspension

Interchange Number: 107
   Usage: 1969–1970 C-10 Chevrolet and 1500 GMC truck with 115-inch wheelbase, with V-8 and Powerglide automatic transmission (except with 396-ci V-8)
   Note(s): Coil-spring suspension

Interchange Number: 108
   Usage: 1969–1970 C-10 Chevrolet and 1500 GMC truck with 115-inch wheelbase, with V-8 and Turbo-Hydra-Matic automatic transmission (except with 396-ci V-8)
   Note(s): Coil-spring suspension

Interchange Number: 109
   Usage: 1969 C-10 Chevrolet and 1500 GMC truck with 115-inch wheelbase, with 396-ci V-8 and three-speed manual transmission

Interchange Number: 110
   Usage: 1969 C-10 Chevrolet and 1500 GMC truck with 115-inch wheelbase, with 396-ci V-8 and four-speed manual transmission

Interchange Number: 111
 Usage: 1969 C-10 Chevrolet and 1500 GMC truck with 115-inch wheelbase, with 396-ci V-8 and automatic transmission

Interchange Number: 112
 Usage: 1969–1970 C-10 Chevrolet and 1500 GMC truck with 115-inch wheelbase, with V-8 and four-speed manual transmission (except with 396-ci V-8)
 Note(s): Leaf spring suspension

Interchange Number: 113
 Usage: 1969–1970 C-10 Chevrolet and 1500 GMC truck with 115-inch wheelbase, with V-8 and Powerglide automatic transmission (except with 396-ci V-8)
 Note(s): Leaf spring suspension

Interchange Number: 114
 Usage: 1969–1970 C-10 Chevrolet and 1500 GMC truck with 115-inch wheelbase, with V-8 and Turbo-Hydra-Matic automatic transmission (except with 396-ci V-8)
 Note(s): Leaf spring suspension

Interchange Number: 115
 Usage: 1969–1970 C-10 Chevrolet and 1500 GMC truck with 115-inch wheelbase, with V-8 and three-speed manual transmission (except with 396-ci V-8)
 Note(s): Leaf spring suspension

Interchange Number: 116
 Usage: 1969–1970 C-10 Chevrolet and 1500 GMC truck with 127-inch wheelbase, with V-8 and three-speed manual transmission (except with 396-ci V-8)

Interchange Number: 117
 Usage: 1969–1970 C-10 Chevrolet and 1500 GMC truck with 127-inch wheelbase, with V-8 and four-speed manual transmission (except with 396-ci V-8)
 Note(s): Coil-spring suspension

Interchange Number: 118
 Usage: 1969–1970 C-10 Chevrolet and 1500 GMC truck with 127-inch wheelbase, with V-8 and Powerglide automatic transmission (except with 396-ci V-8)
 Note(s): Coil-spring suspension

Interchange Number: 119
 Usage: 1969–1970 C-10 Chevrolet and 1500 GMC truck with 127-inch wheelbase, with V-8 and Turbo-Hydra-Matic automatic transmission (except with 396-ci V-8)
 Note(s): Coil-spring suspension

Interchange Number: 120
 Usage: 1969 C-10 Chevrolet and 1500 GMC truck with 127-inch wheelbase, with 396-ci V-8 and three-speed manual transmission

Interchange Number: 121
 Usage: 1969 C-10 Chevrolet and 1500 GMC truck with 127-inch wheelbase, with 396-ci V-8 and four-speed manual transmission

Interchange Number: 122
 Usage: 1969 C-10 Chevrolet and 1500 GMC truck with 127-inch wheelbase, with 396-ci V-8 and automatic transmission

Interchange Number: 123
 Usage: 1969–1970 C-10 Chevrolet and 1500 GMC truck with 127-inch wheelbase, with V-8 and four-speed manual transmission (except with 396-ci V-8)
 Note(s): Leaf spring suspension

Interchange Number: 124
 Usage: 1969–1970 C-10 Chevrolet and 1500 GMC truck with 127-inch wheelbase, with V-8 and Powerglide automatic transmission (except with 396-ci V-8)
 Note(s): Leaf spring suspension

Interchange Number: 125
 Usage: 1969–1970 C-10 Chevrolet and 1500 GMC truck with 127-inch wheelbase, with V-8 and Turbo-Hydra-Matic automatic transmission (except with 396-ci V-8)
 Note(s): Leaf spring suspension

Interchange Number: 126
 Usage: 1967–1968 C-10 Chevrolet and 1500 GMC truck with 127-inch wheelbase, with V-8 and three-speed manual transmission (except with 396-ci V-8)
 Note(s): Leaf spring suspension

Interchange Number: 127
 Usage: 1967–1968 C-20 Chevrolet and 2500 GMC truck with 127-inch wheelbase, with V-8 and three-speed manual transmission (except with 396-ci V-8)

Interchange Number: 128
 Usage: 1969–1970 C-20 Chevrolet and 2500 GMC truck with 127-inch wheelbase, with V-8 and four-speed manual transmission (except with 396-ci V-8)
 Note(s): Coil-spring suspension

Interchange Number: 129
 Usage: 1969–1970 C-20 Chevrolet and 2500 GMC truck with 127-inch wheelbase, with V-8 and Powerglide automatic transmission (except with 396-ci V-8)
 Note(s): Coil-spring suspension

Interchange Number: 130
 Usage: 1969–1970 C-20 Chevrolet and 2500 GMC truck with 127-inch wheelbase, with V-8 and Turbo-Hydra-Matic automatic transmission (except with 396-ci V-8)
 Note(s): Coil-spring suspension

Interchange Number: 131

Usage: 1969 C-20 Chevrolet and 2500 GMC truck with 127-inch wheelbase, with 396-ci V-8 and three-speed manual transmission

Interchange Number: 132

Usage: 1969 C-20 Chevrolet and 2500 GMC truck with 127-inch wheelbase, with 396-ci V-8 and four-speed manual transmission

Interchange Number: 133

Usage: 1969 C-20 Chevrolet and 2500 GMC truck with 127-inch wheelbase, with 396-ci V-8 and automatic transmission

Note(s): Coil springs

Interchange Number: 134

Usage: 1969–1970 C-20 Chevrolet and 2500 GMC truck with 127-inch wheelbase, with V-8 and four-speed manual transmission (except with 396-ci V-8)

Note(s): Leaf spring suspension

Interchange Number: 135

Usage: 1969–1970 C-20 Chevrolet and 2500 GMC truck with 127-inch wheelbase, with V-8 and Powerglide automatic transmission (except with 396-ci V-8)

Note(s): Leaf spring suspension

Interchange Number: 136

Usage: 1969–1970 C-20 Chevrolet and 2500 GMC truck with 127-inch wheelbase, with V-8 and Turbo-Hydra-Matic automatic transmission (except with 396-ci V-8)

Note(s): Leaf spring suspension

Interchange Number: 137

Usage: 1969–1970 C-20 Chevrolet and 2500 GMC truck with 127-inch wheelbase, with V-8 and three-speed manual transmission (except with 396-ci V-8)

Note(s): Leaf spring suspension

Interchange Number: 138

Usage: 1969–1970 C-20 Chevrolet and 2500 GMC truck with 133-inch wheelbase, with V-8 and manual transmission (except with 396-ci V-8)

Interchange Number: 139

Usage: 1969–1970 C-20 Chevrolet and 2500 GMC truck with 133-inch wheelbase, with V-8 and automatic transmission (except with 396-ci V-8)

Interchange Number: 140

Usage: 1969–1970 C-30 Chevrolet and 3500 GMC truck with 133-inch wheelbase, with V-8 and manual transmission

Interchange Number: 141

Usage: 1969–1970 C-30 Chevrolet and 3500 GMC truck with 133-inch wheelbase, with V-8 and automatic transmission

Interchange Number: 142

Usage: 1969–1970 C-30 Chevrolet and 3500 GMC truck with 157-inch wheelbase, with V-8 and manual transmission

Interchange Number: 143

Usage: 1969–1970 C-30 Chevrolet and 3500 GMC truck with 157-inch wheelbase, with V-8 and automatic transmission

Interchange Number: 144

Usage: 1969–1970 C-10 Chevrolet and 1500 GMC truck with 115-inch wheelbase and four-wheel drive

Interchange Number: 145

Usage: 1969–1970 C-10 Chevrolet and 1500 GMC truck with 127-inch wheelbase and four-wheel drive, with manual transmission

Interchange Number: 146

Usage: 1969–1970 C-20 Chevrolet and 2500 GMC truck with 127-inch wheelbase and four-wheel drive, with manual transmission

Interchange Number: 147

Usage: 1969–1970 C-20 Chevrolet and 2500 GMC truck with 133-inch wheelbase and four-wheel drive, with manual transmission

Interchange Number: 148

Usage: 1969–1970 C-30 Chevrolet and 3500 GMC truck with 11,000-pound axle

Interchange Number: 149

Usage: 1969–1970 C-10 Chevrolet and 1500 GMC truck with 127-inch wheelbase and four-wheel drive, with automatic transmission

Interchange Number: 150

Usage: 1969–1970 C-20 Chevrolet and 2500 GMC truck with 127-inch wheelbase and four-wheel drive, with automatic transmission

Interchange Number: 151

Usage: 1969–1970 C-20 Chevrolet and 2500 GMC truck with 133-inch wheelbase and four-wheel drive, with automatic transmission

Interchange Number: 152

Usage: 1970 C-10 Chevrolet and 1500 GMC truck with 115-inch wheelbase, with 402-ci V-8 and manual transmission

Interchange Number: 153

Usage: 1970 C-10 Chevrolet and 1500 GMC truck with 115-inch wheelbase, with 402-ci V-8 and automatic transmission

Interchange Number: 154

Usage: 1970 C-10 Chevrolet and 1500 GMC truck with 127-inch wheelbase, with 402-ci V-8 and manual transmission

Interchange Number: 155

Usage: 1970 C-10 Chevrolet and 1500 GMC truck with 127-inch wheelbase, with 402-ci V-8 and automatic transmission

Interchange Number: 156
    Usage: 1970 C-20 Chevrolet and 2500 GMC truck with 127-inch wheelbase, with 402-ci V-8 and manual transmission
Interchange Number: 157
    Usage: 1970 C-20 Chevrolet and 2500 GMC truck with 127-inch wheelbase, with 402-ci V-8 and automatic transmission
Interchange Number: 158
    Usage: 1970 C-20 Chevrolet and 2500 GMC truck with 133-inch wheelbase, with 402-ci V-8 and manual transmission
Interchange Number: 159
    Usage: 1970 C-20 Chevrolet and 2500 GMC truck with 133-inch wheelbase, with 402-ci V-8 and automatic transmission
Interchange Number: 160
    Usage: 1971–1972 C-10 Chevrolet and 1500 GMC truck with 127-inch wheelbase and three-speed manual transmission (except with 402-ci V-8)
    Note(s): Coil springs
Interchange Number: 161
    Usage: 1971–1972 C-10 Chevrolet and 1500 GMC truck with 127-inch wheelbase and four-speed manual transmission (except with 402-ci V-8)
    Note(s): Coil springs
Interchange Number: 162
    Usage: 1971–1972 C-10 Chevrolet and 1500 GMC truck with 127-inch wheelbase and automatic transmission (except with 402-ci V-8)
    Note(s): Coil springs
Interchange Number: 163
    Usage: 1971–1972 C-10 Chevrolet and 1500 GMC truck with 127-inch wheelbase and three-speed manual transmission (except with 402-ci V-8)
    Note(s): Leaf springs
Interchange Number: 164
    Usage: 1971–1972 C-10 Chevrolet and 1500 GMC truck with 127-inch wheelbase and four-speed manual transmission (except with 402-ci V-8)
    Note(s): Leaf springs
Interchange Number: 165
    Usage: 1971–1972 C-10 Chevrolet and 1500 GMC truck with 127-inch wheelbase and automatic transmission (except with 402-ci V-8)
    Note(s): Leaf springs
Interchange Number: 166
    Usage: 1971–1972 C-10 Chevrolet and 1500 GMC truck with 127-inch wheelbase and manual transmission and four-wheel drive
Interchange Number: 167
    Usage: 1971–1972 C-10 Chevrolet and 1500 GMC truck with 127-inch wheelbase and automatic transmission and four-wheel drive

Interchange Number: 168
    Usage: 1971–1972 C-10 Chevrolet and 1500 GMC truck with 127-inch wheelbase and 402-ci V-8 and manual transmission
Interchange Number: 169
    Usage: 1971–1972 C-10 Chevrolet and 1500 GMC truck with 127-inch wheelbase and 402-ci V-8 and automatic transmission
Interchange Number: 170
    Usage: 1971–1972 C-20 Chevrolet and 2500 GMC truck with 127-inch wheelbase and three-speed manual transmission (except with 402-ci V-8)
    Note(s): Coil springs
Interchange Number: 171
    Usage: 1971–1972 C-20 Chevrolet and 2500 GMC truck with 127-inch wheelbase and four-speed manual transmission (except with 402-ci V-8)
    Note(s): Coil springs
Interchange Number: 172
    Usage: 1971–1972 C-20 Chevrolet and 2500 GMC truck with 127-inch wheelbase and automatic transmission (except with 402-ci V-8)
    Note(s): Coil springs
Interchange Number: 173
    Usage: 1971–1972 C-20 Chevrolet and 2500 GMC truck with 127-inch wheelbase and three-speed manual transmission (except with 402-ci V-8)
    Note(s): Leaf springs
Interchange Number: 174
    Usage: 1971–1972 C-20 Chevrolet and 2500 GMC truck with 127-inch wheelbase and four-speed manual transmission (except with 402-ci V-8)
    Note(s): Leaf springs
Interchange Number: 175
    Usage: 1971–1972 C-20 Chevrolet and 2500 GMC truck with 127-inch wheelbase and automatic transmission (except with 402-ci V-8)
    Note(s): Leaf springs
Interchange Number: 176
    Usage: 1971–1972 C-20 Chevrolet and 2500 GMC truck with 127-inch wheelbase and manual transmission and four-wheel drive
Interchange Number: 177
    Usage: 1971–1972 C-20 Chevrolet and 2500 GMC truck with 127-inch wheelbase and automatic transmission and four-wheel drive
Interchange Number: 178
    Usage: 1971–1972 C-20 Chevrolet and 2500 GMC truck with 127-inch wheelbase and 402-ci V-8 and manual transmission

Interchange Number: 179
> Usage: 1971–1972 C-20 Chevrolet and 2500 GMC truck with 127-inch wheelbase and 402-ci V-8 and automatic transmission

Interchange Number: 180
> Usage: 1971–1972 C-20 Chevrolet and 2500 GMC truck with 133-inch wheelbase and three-speed manual transmission (except with 402-ci V-8)

Interchange Number: 181
> Usage: 1971–1972 C-20 Chevrolet and 2500 GMC truck with 133-inch wheelbase and four-speed manual transmission (except with 402-ci V-8)

Interchange Number: 182
> Usage: 1971–1972 C-20 Chevrolet and 2500 GMC truck with 133-inch wheelbase and automatic transmission (except with 402-ci V-8)

Interchange Number: 183
> Usage: 1971–1972 C-20 Chevrolet and 2500 GMC truck with 133-inch wheelbase and manual transmission and four-wheel drive

Interchange Number: 184
> Usage: 1971–1972 C-20 Chevrolet and 2500 GMC truck with 133-inch wheelbase and automatic transmission and four-wheel drive

Interchange Number: 185
> Usage: 1971–1972 C-20 Chevrolet and 2500 GMC truck with 133-inch wheelbase and 402-ci V-8 and manual transmission

Interchange Number: 186
> Usage: 1971–1972 C-20 Chevrolet and 2500 GMC truck with 133-inch wheelbase and 402-ci V-8 and automatic transmission

Interchange Number: 187
> Usage: 1971–1972 C-30 Chevrolet and 3500 GMC truck with 133-inch wheelbase and manual transmission

Interchange Number: 188
> Usage: 1971–1972 C-30 Chevrolet and 3500 GMC truck with 133-inch wheelbase and automatic transmission

Interchange Number: 189
> Usage: 1971–1972 C-30 Chevrolet and 3500 GMC truck with 133-inch wheelbase and 11,000-pound axle

Rear Axles
Identification

Axle assemblies can be identified quickly and easily by the code that is stamped on the axle tube. Location of this code depends on the model. For C-10 models, the code is located 3 to 5 inches outboard of the carrier on the front of the right-hand axle tube. For C-20 and C-30 models, a larger, heavier duty axle was used, and the code is located 6 to 8 inches outboard of the carrier on top of the right-hand axle tube.

Breakdown is according to axle manufacturer. All but the Dana axles begin with a two- or three-letter code that represents the axle ratio. This is followed by the manufacturer code, a three-digit date code, and ends with a single number indicating the shift code.

Dana-built axles begin with the Dana part number followed by the axle-ratio code, the build-date code for the month and then the day of the month, the last digit of the model year, then the shift code, and finally the production-line code. For all of these codes the most important as it applies to interchange is the ratio code.

Rear Axle Housings
Model Identification

1967	Interchange Number
C-10	
two-wheel drive	
coil spring	1
leaf spring	11
four-wheel drive	8
C-20	
coil spring	2
leaf spring	9
four-wheel drive	3
C-30	
except dual rear wheels	4, 17
dual rear wheels	
except 11,000-pound axle	5, 6
11,000-pound axle	7
1968	
C-10 two-wheel drive	
except 396-ci V-8	
nonmoveable	23
moveable	2
leaf spring	11, 12
396-ci V-8	
except four-speed	13
four-speed	14
C-10 four-wheel drive	10
C-20	
coil spring	2
leaf spring	9
four-wheel drive	3
C-30	
except dual rear wheels	4, 17
dual rear wheels	
except 11,000-pound axle	5, 6
11,000-pound axle	7
1969	
C-10 two-wheel drive	
except 396-ci V-8	
nonmoveable	23
moveable	2
leaf spring	11, 12

This strut rod, which is used on trucks with coil springs, is the reason you cannot swap a rear with rear leaf springs to a truck with coil springs.

C-20

except four-door cab

Interchanges

Interchange Number: 1

Part Number(s): 3917864

Type: 12-bolt

Usage: 1967–1969 C-10 Chevrolet and 1500 GMC two-wheel-drive truck with coil-spring suspension only (except with 396-ci V-8 or three-speed manual or Turbo-Hydra-Matic 400)

Interchange Number: 2

Part Number(s): 6264587

Type: 10-bolt

Usage: 1963–1972 C-20 Chevrolet and 2500 GMC two-wheel-drive truck (except with leaf spring suspension)

Interchange Number: 3

Part Number(s): 3964589

Usage: 1967–1970 C-20 Chevrolet and 2500 GMC truck—four-wheel drive only

Interchange Number: 4

Part Number(s): 3909797

Usage: 1963–1970 C-30 Chevrolet and 3500 GMC truck without shocks or dual rear wheels

Interchange Number: 5

Part Number(s): 3909798

Usage: 1963–1970 C-30 Chevrolet and 3500 GMC truck with dual rear wheels, with shocks (except with 11,000-pound axle)

Interchange Number: 6

Part Number(s): 3909798

Usage: 1963–1970 C-30 Chevrolet and 3500 GMC truck with dual rear wheels, without shocks (except with 11,000-pound axle)

Note(s): Interchange Number 5 will fit; just disregard the shock brackets

Interchange Number: 7

Part Number(s): 3988439

Usage: 1968–1972 C-30 Chevrolet and 3500 GMC truck with dual rear wheels, with 11,000-pound axle

Interchange Number: 8

Part Number(s): 3917863

Usage: 1967 C-10 Chevrolet and 1500 GMC four-wheel-drive truck

Interchange Number: 9

Part Number(s): 8877647

Type: Spicer 60

Usage: 1965–1969 C-20 Chevrolet and 2500 GMC two-wheel-drive truck with rear leaf spring suspension

Interchange Number: 10

Part Number(s): 3934282

Type: GM axle

Usage: 1968 C-10 Chevrolet and 1500 GMC four-wheel-drive truck

Interchange Number: 11

Part Number(s): 3974075

Type: GM 12-bolt

Usage: 1967–1969 C-10 Chevrolet and 1500 GMC two-wheel-drive truck with rear leaf spring suspension

Interchange Number: 12

Part Number(s): 3941828

Type: Spicer

Usage: 1967–1969 C-10 Chevrolet and 1500 GMC two-wheel-drive truck with rear leaf spring suspension.

Interchange Number: 13

Part Number(s): 3953869

Usage: 1968–1969 C-10 Chevrolet and 1500 GMC two-wheel-drive truck with 396-ci V-8 (except with four-speed manual transmission)

Interchange Number: 14

Part Number(s): 3953899

Usage: 1968–1969 C-10 Chevrolet and 1500 GMC truck with 396-ci V-8 and four-speed manual transmission

Interchange Number: 15

Part Number(s): 3961499

Usage: 1969 C-10 Chevrolet and 1500 GMC truck and Blazer four-wheel drive

Interchange Number: 16

Part Number(s): 3953892

Usage: 1969–1970 C-20 Chevrolet and 2500 GMC two-wheel-drive truck with 396/402-ci V-8

Interchange Number: 17

Part Number(s): 6264588

Usage: 1967–1972 C-30 Chevrolet and 3500 GMC truck with shocks, except with dual rear wheels; 1969–1970 C-20 Chevrolet and 2500 GMC truck with 133-inch wheelbase; 1971–1972 C-20 Chevrolet and 2500 GMC truck with removable carrier and rear leaf springs—all models are two-wheel drive

Interchange Number: 18

Part Number(s): 3980820

Type: GM

Usage: 1970 C-10 Chevrolet and 1500 GMC truck, Blazer, and Jimmy two-wheel drive, except with 402-ci V-8

Interchange Number: 19
Part Number(s): 3980821
Type: GM axle
Usage: 1970–1971 C-10 Chevrolet and 1500 GMC two-wheel-drive truck with 402-ci V-8 and rear coil springs

Interchange Number: 20
Part Number(s): 3979342
Type: Spicer 60 10-bolt
Usage: 1970–1971 C-10 Chevrolet and 1500 GMC two-wheel-drive truck with rear leaf spring suspension

Interchange Number: 21
Part Number(s): 3980822
Type: GM 12-bolt
Usage: 1970–1971 C-10 Chevrolet and 1500 GMC two-wheel-drive truck with rear leaf spring suspension

Interchange Number: 22
Part Number(s): 3980823
Type: GM
Usage: 1970 C-10 Chevrolet and 1500 GMC truck, Blazer, and Jimmy four-wheel drive

Interchange Number: 23
Part Number(s): 3955300
Type: GM
Usage: 1968–1970 C-20 Chevrolet and 2500 GMC truck with rear coil springs and nonmoveable carrier

Interchange Number: 24
Part Number(s): 3990926
Type: GM
Usage: 1971 C-10 Chevrolet and 1500 GMC truck, Blazer, and Jimmy two-wheel drive with rear coil springs

Interchange Number: 25
Part Number(s): 3979691
Type: Spicer
Usage: 1971 C-10 Chevrolet two-wheel drive with rear coil springs

Interchange Number: 26
Part Number(s): 3997572
Type: GM axle
Usage: 1971 C-10 Chevrolet and 1500 GMC truck, Blazer, and Jimmy four-wheel drive with rear leaf springs

Interchange Number: 27
Part Number(s): 3979687
Type: Spicer 60
Usage: 1971 C-20 Chevrolet and 2500 GMC truck with 127-inch wheelbase, with rear leaf springs and nonremovable carrier

Interchange Number: 28
Part Number(s): 3988478
Type: GM axle
Usage: 1971 C-20 Chevrolet and 2500 GMC four-wheel-drive truck

Interchange Number: 29
Part Number(s): 6264608
Usage: 1971 C-30 Chevrolet and 3500 GMC truck with dual rear wheels (except with 11,000-pound axle)

Interchange Number: 30
Part Number(s): 6272170
Usage: 1972 C-10 Chevrolet and 1500 GMC truck, Blazer, and Jimmy two-wheel drive with rear coil springs

Interchange Number: 31
Part Number(s): 6272168
Usage: 1972 C-10 Chevrolet and 1500 GMC truck, Blazer, and Jimmy two-wheel drive with rear leaf springs

Interchange Number: 32
Part Number(s): 6272169
Type: GM axle
Usage: 1972 C-10 Chevrolet and 1500 GMC truck, Blazer, and Jimmy four-wheel drive

Interchange Number: 33
Part Number(s): 3995863
Type: GM axle
Usage: 1972 C-20 Chevrolet and 2500 GMC truck with 127-inch wheelbase, with nonremovable carrier

Interchange Number: 34
Part Number(s): 3995864
Type: GM axle
Usage: 1972 C-20 Chevrolet and 2500 GMC truck with 133-inch wheelbase, with nonremovable carrier

Interchange Number: 35
Part Number(s): 39958589
Type: GM axle
Usage: 1972 C-20 Chevrolet and 2500 GMC four-wheel-drive truck

Interchange Number: 36
Part Number(s): 62658104
Type: GM 12-bolt
Usage: 1973–1978 C-10 Chevrolet and 1500 GMC truck, Blazer, and Jimmy two-wheel drive

Interchange Number: 37
Part Number(s): 62658106
Type: GM 12-bolt
Usage: 1973–1978 C-10 Chevrolet and 1500 GMC truck, Blazer, and Jimmy four-wheel drive

Interchange Number: 38
Part Number(s): 6258344
Type: GM axle
Usage: 1973–1980 C-20 Chevrolet and 2500 GMC truck two-wheel drive (except four-door cab)

Interchange Number: 39
    Part Number(s): 6258344
    Usage: 1973–1980 C-20 Chevrolet and 2500 GMC
        four-wheel-drive truck (except four-door cab)

Interchange Number: 40
    Part Number(s): 6258344
    Type: GM axle
    Usage: 1973–1981 C-20 Chevrolet and 2500 GMC
        two-wheel drive and crew (four-door) cab
        truck; 1973–1981 C-30 Chevrolet and 3500
        GMC truck without dual rear wheels

Interchange Number: 41
    Part Number(s): 345087
    Type: 10-bolt
    Usage: 1973–1974 C-30 Chevrolet and 3500 GMC
        truck with dual rear wheels

Interchange Number: 42
    Part Number(s): 376885
    Type: 10-bolt
    Usage: 1975–1979 C-30 Chevrolet and 3500 GMC
        truck with dual rear wheels

Interchange Number: 43
    Part Number(s): 471778
    Type: 14-bolt
    Usage: 1973–1980 C-30 Chevrolet and 3500 GMC
        truck with dual rear wheels

Front Axles, Four-Wheel Drive

The interchange here is the bare front drive axle for four-wheel-drive models. A large interchange is available. Front axles are identified by the Dana part numbers.

    Note that heavier duty models like the 3/4- and 1-ton models used a different axle than those on the C-10 models.

Model Identification

Interchanges

Interchange Number: 1
    Part Number(s): 6273950
    Type: DANA 27732-X
    Usage: 1967–1972 C-10 Chevrolet and 1500 GMC
        truck; 1969–1972 Blazer; 1970–1972 Jimmy

Interchange Number: 2
    Part Number(s): 3912011
    Type: DANA 2535-1X
    Usage: 1967–1968 C-20 Chevrolet and 2500 GMC
        truck (except heavy-duty)

Interchange Number: 3
    Part Number(s): 3912012
    Type: DANA 2540-1X
    Usage: 1967–1968 C-20 Chevrolet and 2500 GMC
        truck, heavy-duty

Interchange Number: 4
    Part Number(s): 3958022
    Type: DANA 26500X
    Usage: 1969–1972 C-20 Chevrolet and 2500 GMC
        truck (except heavy-duty)

Interchange Number: 5
    Part Number(s): 3958023
    Type: DANA 26505X
    Usage: 1969–1972 C-20 Chevrolet and 2500 GMC
        truck, heavy-duty

Interchange Number: 6
    Part Number(s): 376849
    Type: DANA 27995X
    Usage: 1973–1975 C-10 to C-20 Chevrolet and
        1500 to 2500 GMC truck, Blazer, and Jimmy
    Note(s): Will fit Interchange Number 7; see note
        under that section

Interchange Number: 7
    Part Number(s): 6259018
    Type: DANA 29431X
    Usage: Early-1976 C-10 to C-20 Chevrolet and
        1500 to 2500 GMC truck, Blazer, and Jimmy
    Note(s): Interchange Number 6 will fit. Discard the
        existing inner right-hand "U" bolt and use "U"
        bolt part number 368788. Tie rod ends are off-
        set and grease fittings point towards rear of
        truck. Shock absorber bracket is approximately

4 inches from the driver's side front hub and disc assembly

Interchange Number: 8
    Part Number(s): 458473
    Type: DANA 298306
    Usage: Late-1976 to 1978 C-10 to C-20 Chevrolet and 1500 to 2500 GMC truck, Blazer, and Jimmy
    Note(s): Tie rod ends have no off-set and grease fittings point straight down; shock absorber bracket is approximately 4 inches from the carrier

Interchange Number: 9
    Part Number(s): 14050686
    Type: DANA 29731X
    Usage: 1977–1979 C-30 Chevrolet and 3500 GMC truck

Axle Shafts
Model Identification

1967   *Interchange Number*

C-10
    two-wheel drive 11
    four-wheel drive 11
C-20
    two-wheel drive
        nonremovable carrier 7
        removable carrier 6
    four-wheel drive 6
C-30
    except 11,000-pound axle 6
    11,000-pound axle 8

1968
C-10
    two-wheel drive
        10-bolt axle 10
        12-bolt axle 11
    four-wheel drive 11
C-20
    two-wheel drive, nonremovable carrier
        leaf springs 7
        coil springs 12
    two-wheel drive, removable carrier 6
    four-wheel drive 6
C-30
    except 11,000-pound axle 6
    11,000-pound axle 8

1969
C-10
    two-wheel drive
        10-bolt axle 10
        12-bolt axle 11
    four-wheel drive 11

C-20
    two-wheel drive
        nonremovable carrier 7
        removable carrier 6
    four-wheel drive 6
C-30
    except 11,000-pound axle 6
    11,000-pound axle 8

1970
C-10
    two-wheel drive
        10-bolt axle 9
        12-bolt axle 3
    four-wheel drive 3
C-20
    two-wheel drive
        nonremovable carrier 7
        removable carrier 6
    four-wheel drive 6
C-30
    except 11,000-pound axle 6
    11,000-pound axle 8

1971
C-10
    two-wheel drive 2
    four-wheel drive 3
C-20
    two-wheel drive
        nonremovable carrier 7
        removable carrier 6
    four-wheel drive 6
C-30
    except 11,000-pound axle 6
    11,000-pound axle 8

1972
C-10
    two-wheel drive 2
    four-wheel drive 3
C-20
    two-wheel drive
        nonremovable carrier 7
        removable carrier 6
    four-wheel drive 6
C-30
    except 11,000-pound axle 6
    11,000-pound axle 8

1973
C-10
    two-wheel drive 2
    four-wheel drive 3
C-20
    two-wheel drive 4
    four-wheel drive 4

C-30
    single rear wheels 4
    dual rear wheels
        10-bolt 5
        14-bolt 4

1974
C-10
    two-wheel drive 2
    four-wheel drive 3
C-20
    two-wheel drive 4
    four-wheel drive 4
C-30
    single rear wheels 4
    dual rear wheels
        10-bolt 5
        14-bolt 4

1975
C-10
    two-wheel drive 2
    four-wheel drive 3
C-20
    two-wheel drive 4
    four-wheel drive 4
C-30
    single rear wheels 4
    dual rear wheels
        10-bolt 5
        14-bolt 4

1976
C-10
    two-wheel drive 2
    four-wheel drive 3
C-20
    two-wheel drive 4
    four-wheel drive 4
C-30
    single rear wheels 4
    dual rear wheels
        10-bolt 5
        14-bolt 4

1977
C-10
    two-wheel drive 2
    four-wheel drive 3
C-20
    two-wheel drive 4
    four-wheel drive 4
C-30
    single rear wheels 4
    dual rear wheels
        10-bolt 5
        14-bolt 4

1978
C-10
    two-wheel drive
        10-bolt axle 1
        12 bolt axle 2
    four-wheel drive 3
C-20
    two-wheel drive 4
    four-wheel drive 4
C-30
    single rear wheels 4
    dual rear wheels
        10-bolt 5
        14-bolt 4

Interchanges

Interchange Number: 1
    Part Number(s): 475126
    Length: N/A
    Usage: 1978–1981 C-10 Chevrolet and 1500 GMC truck, Blazer, and Jimmy two-wheel drive only with 10-bolt rear axle

Interchange Number: 2
    Part Number(s): 326665
    Length: 31 15/32 inches (fits either side)
    Usage: 1971–1981 C-10 Chevrolet and 1500 GMC truck, Blazer, and Jimmy two-wheel drive only with 12-bolt rear axle

Interchange Number: 3
    Part Number(s): 334360
    Length: 31 11/32 inches (fits either side)
    Usage: 1970–1981 C-10 Chevrolet and 1500 GMC truck, Blazer, and Jimmy, four-wheel drive only; 1970 C-10 Chevrolet and 1500 GMC truck, Blazer, and Jimmy two-wheel drive with 12-bolt rear axle

Interchange Number: 4
    Part Number(s): 3977384 (fits either side)
    Length: N/A
    Usage: 1973–1980 C-20 Chevrolet and 2500 GMC truck, all models; 1973–1981 C-30 Chevrolet and 3500 GMC truck with single or rear dual wheels with 14-bolt rear axle

Interchange Number: 5
    Part Number(s): 6259072 (fits either side)
    Length: N/A
    Usage: 1973–1981 C-30 Chevrolet and 3500 GMC truck with dual rear wheels and 10-bolt rear axle

Interchange Number: 6
    Part Number(s): 3759849 (left); 3759850 (right)
    Length: 37 3/16 inches (left); 37 1/16 inches (right)

Usage: 1963–1972 C-20 Chevrolet and 2500 GMC truck with removable carrier; 1967–1972 C-30 Chevrolet and 3500 GMC truck with 7,200-pound axle

Note(s): Stamped T49 and T50

Interchange Number: 7

Part Number(s): 240394 (fits either side)

Length: 34 13/64 inches (fits either side)

Usage: 1965–1972 C-20 Chevrolet and 2500 GMC truck with rear leaf springs or nonremovable (Spicer) carrier

Interchange Number: 8

Part Number(s): 3762916 (fits either side)

Length: 37 7/16 inches (fits either side)

Usage: 1967–1972 C-30 Chevrolet and 3500 GMC truck with 11,000-pound axle

Interchange Number: 9

Part Number(s): 3979435 (fits either side)

Length: 30 1/16 inches (fits either side)

Usage: 1970 C-10 Chevrolet and 1500 GMC two-wheel-drive truck with 10-bolt rear axle

Interchange Number: 10

Part Number(s): 3941850 (fits either side)

Length: 30 1/16 inches (fits either side)

Usage: 1968–1969 C-10 Chevrolet and 1500 GMC two-wheel-drive truck with 10-bolt rear axle

Interchange Number: 11

Part Number(s): 3993605 (fits either side)

Length: 30 1/4 (fits either side)

Usage: 1965–1969 C-10 Chevrolet and 1500 GMC truck; 1969 Blazer with 12-bolt rear axle and rear coil-spring suspension

Interchange Number: 12

Part Number(s): 3940107 (fits either side)

Length: 34 3/4 inches (fits either side)

Usage: 1968 C-10 Chevrolet and 1500 GMC truck with nonremovable carrier and rear coil-spring suspension

6 Frame, Suspension, and Steering Systems

Frames

Frames are largely interchangeable and will cross over for several different model years. Wheelbase and rear suspension type will play an important part in the interchange, however. The longer wheelbase models like the Camper Special and Longhorn require a special frame, thus limiting the interchange possibilities. Most 1967–1972 Chevrolet trucks used rear coil springs, yet some did use rear leaf springs. Due to the way that leaf springs mount to the frame, a special frame is required. If your truck came with rear leaf springs, finding a suitable replacement frame could prove difficult.

Also, four-wheel-drive models used a different frame than their two-wheel-drive counterparts. The two cannot be interchanged.

Model Identification

1967   Interchange Number
C-10
115-inch wheelbase
two-wheel drive 1
four-wheel drive .4
127-inch wheelbase, except Suburban
two-wheel drive 2
four-wheel drive .5
127-inch wheelbase Suburban
two-wheel drive 3
four-wheel drive .6
C-20
except Suburban
two-wheel drive 7
four-wheel drive .5
Suburban
two-wheel drive 8
four-wheel drive .6
C-30
133-inch wheelbase 9

1968–1969
Blazer (1969 only) 22
C-10
115-inch wheelbase
two-wheel drive 1
four-wheel drive .4

127-inch wheelbase, except Suburban
two-wheel drive
two-wheel drive with coil springs 2
two-wheel drive with leaf springs 10
four-wheel drive .5
127-inch wheelbase Suburban
two-wheel drive 3
four-wheel drive .6
C-20, except Suburban
two-wheel drive
coil springs 7
leaf springs .11
four-wheel drive .5
133-inch wheelbase
except Longhorn 9
Longhorn 12
C-20 Suburban
two-wheel drive 8
four-wheel drive .6
C-30
133-inch wheelbase 9
Longhorn 12

1970
Blazer 22
C-10
115-inch wheelbase, two-wheel drive
coil springs 1
leaf springs .13
115-inch wheelbase, four-wheel drive 4
127-inch wheelbase, two-wheel drive,
except Suburban
coil springs 2
leaf springs .10
127-inch wheelbase, four-wheel drive 5
127-inch wheelbase Suburban
two-wheel drive 3
four-wheel drive .6
C-20, except Suburban
two-wheel drive
coil springs 7
leaf springs .11
four-wheel drive .5
133-inch wheelbase
except Longhorn 9

Steering gearboxes from 1967 to 1972. The top is a manual unit. The bottom left is a power steering unit. The bottom right is a manual unit with four-wheel drive.

C-30
  131.5-inch wheelbase
    two-wheel drive 36
    four-wheel drive 48
  135.5-inch wheelbase
    two-wheel drive
      side tank 37
      rear tank 44
    four-wheel drive 51
  159.5-inch wheelbase
    two-wheel drive 38
    four-wheel drive 61
  164.5-inch wheelbase
    two-wheel drive 34
    four-wheel drive 62

Interchanges

Interchange Number: 1
  Part Number(s): 3937967
  Wheelbase: 115 inches
  Usage: 1967–1970 C-10 Chevrolet two-wheel drive
    with coil-spring rear suspension
Interchange Number: 2
  Part Number(s): 3937965
  Wheelbase: 127 inches
  Usage: 1967–1970 C-10 Chevrolet two-wheel drive
    with coil-spring rear suspension (except Suburban
    models)
Interchange Number: 3
  Part Number(s): 6272109
  Wheelbase: 127 inches
  Usage: 1967–1972 C-10 Suburban
Interchange Number: 4
  Part Number(s): 6272109
  Wheelbase: 115 inches
  Usage: 1967–1972 C-10 Chevrolet four-wheel drive
Interchange Number: 5
  Part Number(s): 6272111
  Wheelbase: 127 inches
  Usage: 1967–1972 C-10 to C-20 Chevrolet four-
    wheel drive
Interchange Number: 6
  Part Number(s): 3977663
  Wheelbase: 127 inches
  Usage: 1967–1970 C-10 to C-20 Suburban four-
    wheel drive
  Note(s): Very rare; less than 2,000 made
Interchange Number: 7
  Part Number(s): 6272139
  Wheelbase: 127 inches
  Usage: 1967–1972 C-20 Chevrolet two-wheel drive
    with coil-spring rear suspension (except
    Suburban)

Interchange Number: 8
  Part Number(s): 3997489
  Usage: 1967–1970 C-20 Suburban two-wheel drive
Interchange Number: 9
  Part Number(s): 6272151
  Wheelbase: 133 inches
  Usage: 1967–1972 C-20 to C-30 Chevrolet two-
    wheel drive (except Longhorn)
Interchange Number: 10
  Part Number(s): 6272141
  Wheelbase: 127 inches
  Usage: 1968–1972 C-10 Chevrolet two-wheel drive
    with rear leaf springs
Interchange Number: 11
  Part Number(s): 3974229
  Wheelbase: 127 inches
  Usage: 1968–1970 C-20 Chevrolet two-wheel drive
    with rear leaf springs
Interchange Number: 12
  Part Number(s): 3977667
  Wheelbase: 133 inches
  Usage: 1968–1970 C-20 to C-30 Chevrolet with
    Longhorn camper package
Interchange Number: 13
  Part Number(s): 672143
  Wheelbase: 115 inches
  Usage: 1970–1971 C-10 Chevrolet with rear leaf
    springs
Interchange Number: 14
  Part Number(s): 3997465
  Wheelbase: 115 inches
  Usage: 1971 C-10 Chevrolet with rear coil springs
  Note(s): No other model will interchange
Interchange Number: 15
  Part Number(s): 672133
  Wheelbase: 127 inches
  Usage: 1971–1972 C-10 Chevrolet with coil springs
Interchange Number: 16
  Part Number(s): 3997499
  Usage: 1971 C-10 to C-20 Suburban four-wheel
    drive
  Note(s): Very rare
Interchange Number: 17
  Part Number(s): 6272145
  Wheelbase: 127 inches
  Usage: 1971–1972 C-20 Chevrolet two-wheel drive
    with rear leaf springs
Interchange Number: 18
  Part Number(s): 6272153
  Wheelbase: 133 inches
  Usage: 1971–1972 C-20 to C-30 Chevrolet two-
    wheel drive with Longhorn package

A 1967–1968 steering wheel.

Interchange Number: 19
Part Number(s): 622131
Wheelbase: 115 inches
Usage: 1972 C-10 Chevrolet two-wheel drive with coil springs

Interchange Number: 20
Part Number(s): 6272113
Usage: 1972 C-10 to C-20 Suburban four-wheel drive
Note(s): Very rare

Interchange Number: 21
Part Number(s): 6272137
Usage: 1972 C-20 Chevrolet two-wheel-drive Suburban
Note(s): No other model interchange

Interchange Number: 22
Part Number(s): 6272107
Usage: 1969–1972 Blazer four-wheel drive

Interchange Number: 23
Part Number(s): 325171
Usage: 1972 Blazer two-wheel drive
Note(s): Rare

Interchange Number: 24
Part Number(s): 369157
Usage: 1973–1977 Blazer and Jimmy two-wheel drive
Note(s): Rare

Interchange Number: 25
Part Number(s): 461983
Usage: 1973–1977 Blazer and Jimmy four-wheel drive

Interchange Number: 26
Part Number(s): 344492
Wheelbase: 117.5 inches
Usage: 1973–1974 C-10 and 1500 GMC two-wheel-drive truck (except Suburban)

Interchange Number: 27
Part Number(s): 471833
Wheelbase: 117.5 inches
Usage: 1973–1977 C-10 and 1500 GMC four-wheel-drive truck (except Suburban)

Interchange Number: 28
Part Number(s): 344494
Wheelbase: 131.5 inches
Usage: 1973–1974 C-10 and 1500 GMC two-wheel-drive truck (except Suburban)

Interchange Number: 29
Part Number(s): 471834
Wheelbase: 131.5 inches
Usage: 1973–1977 C-10 and 1500 GMC four-wheel-drive truck (except Suburban)

Interchange Number: 30
Part Number(s): 14016404
Usage: 1973–1980 C-10 and 1500 two-wheel-drive Suburban

Interchange Number: 31
Part Number(s): 6258097
Usage: 1973 C-10 to C-20 and 1500 to 2500 four-wheel-drive Suburban
Note(s): Interchange Number 32 will fit; interchange with fuel tank

Interchange Number: 32
Part Number(s): 370362
Usage: 1974–1975 C-10 to C-20 and 1500 to 2500 four-wheel-drive Suburban

Interchange Number: 33
Part Number(s): 14016397
Wheelbase: 131.5 inches
Usage: 1973–1978 C-20 Chevrolet and 2500 GMC two-wheel drive with side fuel tank

Interchange Number: 34
Part Number(s): 369154
Wheelbase: 164.5 inches
Usage: 1973–1976 C-20 to C-30 Chevrolet and 2500 to 3500 GMC two-wheel drive

Interchange Number: 35
Part Number(s): 461970
Wheelbase: 131.5 inches
Usage: 1973–1977 C-20 Chevrolet and 2500 GMC two-wheel-drive Suburban

Interchange Number: 36
Part Number(s): 471796
Wheelbase: 131.5 inches
Usage: 1973–1978 C-30 Chevrolet and 3500 GMC two-wheel drive

Interchange Number: 37
Part Number(s): 14002266
Wheelbase: 135.5 inches
Usage: 1973–1980 C-30 Chevrolet and 3500 GMC two-wheel drive with driver's side fuel tank

Interchange Number: 38
Part Number(s): 14002266
Wheelbase: 159.5 inches
Usage: 1973–1980 C-30 Chevrolet and 3500 GMC two-wheel drive

Interchange Number: 39
Part Number(s): 471785
Wheelbase: 117.5 inches
Usage: 1975–1977 C-10 Chevrolet and 1500 GMC two-wheel drive with heavy-duty frame

Interchange Number: 40
Part Number(s): 14002262
Wheelbase: 131.5 inches
Usage: 1975–1980 C-10 Chevrolet and 1500 GMC two-wheel drive without heavy-duty frame

Interchange Number: 41
Part Number(s): 461844
Wheelbase: 131.5 inches
Usage: 1975–1977 C-10 Chevrolet and 1500 GMC two-wheel drive with heavy-duty frame

Interchange Number: 42
Part Number(s): 370362
Usage: 1975–1976 C-10 Chevrolet GMC two-wheel-drive Suburban with 40-gallon fuel tank

Interchange Number: 43
Part Number(s): 369144
Wheelbase: 131.5 inches
Usage: 1975–1976 C-20 Chevrolet and 2500 GMC two-wheel drive with rear-mounted fuel tank

Interchange Number: 44
Part Number(s): 14002267
Wheelbase: 135.5 inches
Usage: 1975–1980 C-30 Chevrolet and 3500 GMC two-wheel drive with rear-mounted fuel tank

Interchange Number: 45
Part Number(s): 14002264
Wheelbase: 131.5 inches
Usage: 1977–1980 C-20 Chevrolet and 2500 GMC two-wheel drive with rear-mounted fuel tank

Interchange Number: 46
Part Number(s): 461991
Usage: 1977 Suburban two-wheel drive

Interchange Number: 47
Part Number(s): 461966
Wheelbase: 164.5 inches
Usage: 1977 C-20 Chevrolet and 2500 GMC two-wheel drive

Interchange Number: 48
Part Number(s): 471836
Wheelbase: 131.5 inches
Usage: 1977–1980 C-30 Chevrolet and 3500 GMC four-wheel drive

Interchange Number: 49
Part Number(s): 471838
Wheelbase: 159.5 inches

A 1971–1972 steering wheel.

Usage: 1977 C-30 Chevrolet and 3500 GMC four-wheel drive

Interchange Number: 50
Part Number(s): 461990
Wheelbase: 164.5 inches
Usage: 1977 C-30 Chevrolet and 3500 GMC four-wheel drive

Interchange Number: 51
Part Number(s): 461988
Wheelbase: 135.5 inches
Usage: 1977 C-30 Chevrolet and 3500 GMC four-wheel drive

Interchange Number: 52
Part Number(s): 14002272
Usage: 1978–1980 Blazer and Jimmy two-wheel drive

Interchange Number: 53
Part Number(s): 471855
Usage: 1978 Blazer and Jimmy two-wheel drive

Interchange Number: 54
Part Number(s): 14016395
Wheelbase: 117.5 inches
Usage: 1978–1980 C-10 Chevrolet and 1500 GMC two-wheel-drive truck (except Suburban)

Interchange Number: 55
Part Number(s): 14002274
Wheelbase: 117.5 inches
Usage: 1978–1980 C-10 Chevrolet and 1500 GMC four-wheel-drive truck (except Suburban)

Interchange Number: 56
Part Number(s): 471787
Wheelbase: 131.5 inches
Usage: 1978 C-10 Chevrolet and 1500 GMC two-wheel-drive truck with heavy-duty frame (except Suburban)

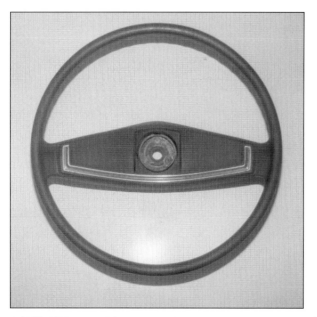

A 1973–1977 custom deluxe steering wheel.

Interchange Number: 57
    Part Number(s): 14016409
    Wheelbase: 131.5 inches
    Usage: 1978–1980 C-10 Chevrolet and 1500 GMC
        four-wheel-drive truck (except Suburban)

Interchange Number: 58
    Part Number(s): 14002276
    Wheelbase: 131.5 inches
    Usage: 1978–1980 Chevrolet GMC Suburban four-
        wheel drive

Interchange Number: 59
    Part Number(s): 14016409
    Wheelbase: 131.5 inches
    Usage: 1978–1980 C-20 Chevrolet and 2500 GMC
        four-wheel-drive truck (except Suburban)

Interchange Number: 60
    Part Number(s): 471806
    Wheelbase: 164.5 inches
    Usage: 1978 C-30 Chevrolet and 3500 GMC two-
        wheel-drive truck

Interchange Number: 61
    Part Number(s): 14002279
    Wheelbase: 159.5 inches
    Usage: 1978–1980 C-30 Chevrolet and 3500 GMC
        four-wheel-drive truck

Interchange Number: 62
    Part Number(s): 14002280
    Wheelbase: 164.5 inches
    Usage: 1978–1980 C-30 Chevrolet and 3500 GMC
        four-wheel-drive truck

Front Control Arms
Model Identification

1967–1970   *Interchange Number*

C-10
    upper 1
    lower 7

C-20
    upper 2
    lower 8

C-30
    upper 2
    lower
        without 11,000-pound axle 8
        11,000-pound axle 9

1971–1972

C-10
    upper 3
    lower 10

C-20
    upper 4
    lower 11

C-30
    upper 4
    lower
        without 11,000-pound axle 11
        11,000-pound axle 12

1973–1976

C-10
    upper 5
    lower 13

C-20
    upper 4
    lower 11

C-30
    upper 4
    lower 11

1977

C-10
    upper 5
    lower 14

C-20
    upper 4
    lower 11

C-30
    upper 4
    lower 11

1978

C-10
    upper 6
    lower 14

C-20
    upper 4
    lower 11

C-30
  upper 6
  lower 11

Interchanges

Interchange Number: 1
  Part Number(s): 3968695 (left); 3968696 (right)
  Position: Upper
  Usage: 1963–1970 C-10 Chevrolet and 1500 GMC truck; 1969–1970 Blazer; 1970 Jimmy; 1971 G-10 to G-20 Chevrolet and 1500 to 2500 GMC van

Interchange Number: 2
  Part Number(s): 3842891 (left); 3842892 (right)
  Position: Upper
  Usage: 1963–1970 C-20 to C-30 Chevrolet and 2500 to 3500 GMC truck; 1971 G-30 Chevrolet and 3500 GMC van

Interchange Number: 3
  Part Number(s): 3983839 (left); 3983840 (right)
  Position: Upper
  Usage: 1971–1972 C-10 Chevrolet and 1500 GMC truck, Blazer, and Jimmy; 1971 G-10 Chevrolet and 1500 GMC van with front disc brakes

Interchange Number: 4
  Part Number(s): 471619 (left); 471620 (right)
  Position: Upper
  Usage: 1971–1980 C-20 to C-30 Chevrolet and 2500 to 3500 GMC truck (except with heavy-duty suspension 1979–1980 models); 1971–1980 G-30 Chevrolet and 3500 GMC van

Interchange Number: 5
  Part Number(s): 471617 (left); 346892 (right)
  Position: Upper
  Usage: 1973–1977 C-10 Chevrolet and 1500 GMC truck, Blazer, and Jimmy; G-20 Chevrolet and 2500 GMC van
  Note(s): Left arm in Interchange Number 6 will fit

Interchange Number: 6
  Part Number(s): 471617 (left); 471618 (right)
  Position: Upper
  Usage: 1978–1981 C-10 Chevrolet and 1500 GMC truck, Blazer, and Jimmy; G-20 Chevrolet and 2500 GMC van
  Note(s): Left arm in Interchange Number 5 will fit

Interchange Number: 7
  Part Number(s): 3968697 (left); 14013062 (right)
  Position: Lower
  Usage: 1967–1970 C-10 Chevrolet and 1500 GMC truck; 1969–1970 Blazer; 1970 Jimmy; 1971 G-10 to G-20 Chevrolet and 1500 to 2500 GMC van

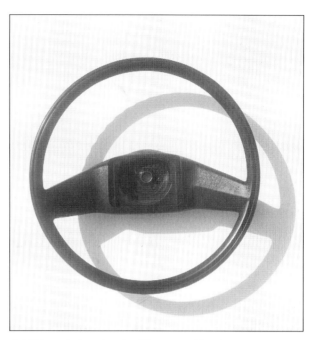

A 1978 standard steering wheel. The custom deluxe has trim.

Interchange Number: 8
  Part Number(s): 3892418 (left); 14013063 (right)
  Position: Lower
  Usage: 1967–1970 C-20 to C-30 Chevrolet and 2500 to 3500 GMC truck (except with 11,000-pound axle); 1971 G-30 Chevrolet and 3500 GMC van

Interchange Number: 9
  Part Number(s): 3906519 (left); 3906520 (right)
  Position: Lower
  Usage: 1967–1970 C-30 Chevrolet and 3500 GMC truck with 11,000-pound axle; 1971 G-30 Chevrolet and 3500 GMC van with front disc brakes

Interchange Number: 10
  Part Number(s): 343497 (left); 343498 (right)
  Position: Lower
  Usage: 1971–1972 C-10 Chevrolet and 1500 GMC truck, Blazer, and Jimmy; 1971 G-10 Chevrolet and 1500 GMC van with front disc brakes

Interchange Number: 11
  Part Number(s): 334663 (left); 14005158 (right)
  Position: Lower
  Usage: 1971–1977 C-20 to C-30 Chevrolet and 2500 to 3500 GMC truck except with 11,000-pound axle (in 1971–1973 models); 1972–1977 G-30 Chevrolet and 3500 GMC van

Interchange Number: 12
  Part Number(s): 14005165 (left); 14005166 (right)
  Position: Lower
  Usage: 1971–1973 C-30 Chevrolet and 3500 GMC truck with 11,000-pound axle

Interchange Number: 13
>Part Number(s): 344767 (left); 344768 (right)
>Position: Lower
>Usage: 1973–1976 C-10 Chevrolet and 1500 GMC truck, Blazer, and Jimmy; 1973–1974 G-20 Chevrolet and 2500 GMC van

Interchange Number: 14
>Part Number(s): 14007605 (left); 14007606 (right)
>Position: Lower
>Usage: 1977–1980 C-10 Chevrolet and 1500 GMC truck, Blazer, and Jimmy

Front Springs, Coil

Looking for a front coil spring for your Chevrolet truck? Great news: All 1963–1981 Chevrolet and GMC cab model trucks will fit the applications in this guide. Those springs from a van will not fit your pickup. Note that while all springs will fit, there were various tensions available. Heavy-duty models like the C-20 and C-30 models used higher rated springs than did a common variety C-10 model. While these heavy-duty springs will fit, they may not provide the same ride. When buying used springs, make sure they are in good condition and not broken or cut. If you see weld marks on the spring reject them. For proper handling the springs should be replaced only in pairs, and preferably from the same donor truck.

Front Springs, Leaf

Chevrolet four-wheel-drive models, including Blazer, came standard with heavy-duty suspension, which required leaf springs. Leaf springs are made up of individual stamped steel leaves. Some models used extra-heavy-duty springs, which are thicker or use an extra leaf. Unlike the front coil springs, there isn't as broad a range of interchange available with leaf springs; however, most interchanges are not limited to one model one year.

Model Identification

1967–1968	*Interchange Number*
C-10 and C-20	
standard suspension	2
heavy-duty suspension	1
1969–1971	
C-10, C-20, and Blazer	
standard suspension	3
heavy-duty suspension	4
1972	
C-10, C-20, and Blazer	
standard suspension	5
heavy-duty suspension	6

1973–1975
Blazer
standard suspension	7
heavy-duty suspension	9
soft ride	10

C-10
standard suspension	8
heavy-duty suspension	9

C-20
standard suspension	8
heavy-duty suspension	9

1976
Blazer
standard suspension	10
heavy-duty suspension	9

C-10
standard suspension	8
heavy-duty suspension	9

C-20
standard suspension	8
heavy-duty suspension	9

1977–1978
Blazer
standard suspension	10
heavy-duty suspension	9

C-10
standard suspension	11
heavy-duty suspension	9

C-20
standard suspension	8
heavy-duty suspension	9

Interchanges

Interchange Number: 1
>Part Number(s): 3916867
>Number of leaves: 3
>Usage: 1967–1968 C-10 to C-20 Chevrolet and 1500 to 2500 GMC four-wheel-drive models only with heavy-duty suspension

Interchange Number: 2
>Part Number(s): 6272499
>Number of leaves: 2
>Usage: 1967–1968 C-10 to C-20 Chevrolet and 1500 to 2500 GMC four-wheel-drive models only without heavy-duty suspension

Interchange Number: 3
>Part Number(s): 328790
>Number of leaves: 2
>Usage: 1969–1971 C-10 to C-20 Chevrolet and 1500 to 2500 GMC and Blazer; 1970–1971 Jimmy—four-wheel-drive models only without heavy-duty suspension

Interchange Number: 4
Part Number(s): 328792
Number of leaves: 2
Usage: 1969–1971 C-10 to C-20 Chevrolet and 1500 to 2500 GMC and Blazer; 1970–1971 Jimmy—four-wheel-drive models only with heavy-duty suspension

Interchange Number: 5
Part Number(s): 328795
Number of leaves: 2
Usage: 1972 C-10 to C-20 Chevrolet and 1500 to 2500 GMC, Blazer, and Jimmy four-wheel-drive models only without heavy-duty suspension

Interchange Number: 6
Part Number(s): 328796
Number of leaves: 3
Usage: 1972 C-10 to C-20 Chevrolet and 1500 to 2500 GMC, Blazer, and Jimmy four-wheel-drive models only with heavy-duty suspension

Interchange Number: 7
Part Number(s): 6260624
Number of leaves: 2
Usage: 1973–1975 Blazer and Jimmy four-wheel-drive models only without heavy-duty suspension

Interchange Number: 8
Part Number(s): 6260625
Number of leaves: 2
Usage: 1973–1976 C-10 Chevrolet and 1500 GMC truck; 1977–1981 C-20 Chevrolet and 2500 to 2500 GMC truck—four-wheel-drive models only without heavy-duty springs

Interchange Number: 9
Part Number(s): 460354
Number of leaves: 3
Usage: 1973–1981 C-10 to C-30 Chevrolet and 1500 to 3500 GMC truck, Blazer, and Jimmy four-wheel-drive models only with heavy-duty suspension

Interchange Number: 10
Part Number(s): 363915
Number of leaves: 2
Usage: 1975 Blazer and Jimmy four-wheel-drive models only, with Soft-Ride option; 1976–1981 Blazer and Jimmy four-wheel-drive models only without heavy-duty suspension

Interchange Number: 11
Part Number(s): 379304
Number of leaves: 2
Usage: 1977–1981 C-10 Chevrolet and 1500 GMC truck four-wheel-drive models only without heavy-duty suspension

Rear Springs, Coil and Leaf

Most 1967–1972 Chevrolet trucks came with rear coil springs consisting of two different sets: those for the C-10 and Blazer/Jimmy models and those for the C-20 models. Each group included two sets of springs: those with the standard-duty and heavy-duty springs. All springs, including the heavy-duty, are interchangeable. Thus, if you wanted a stiffer suspension for your C-10 to haul or tow, you could install heavy-duty springs from a C-20 model. Or if you wanted a lower profile and softer ride for your C-20, you might install standard-duty springs from a C-10 model. Whatever the case, always install springs in pairs, and never mix a standard-duty with a heavy-duty spring. In doing so you could create a dangerous handling condition.

All later and certain 1967–1972 trucks used rear leaf springs. Several different springs were used. Wheelbase and model will affect the interchange, so in some cases those from a C-20 will not necessarily fit a C-10 model. Like the front leaf springs, the rear leaf springs were made up of individual stamped pieces of steel. The more leaves, the higher the rating. Models like the Longhorn and Camper Specials used the stiffest and in turn the springs with the most leaves.

Interchanges
Interchange Number: 1
Part Number(s): 3907210
Number of leaves: 7
Usage: 1965–1968 C-10 to C-20 Chevrolet and 1500 to 2500 GMC truck with rear-leaf suspension option (except with heavy-duty springs)
Note(s): Auto wreckers say that rear springs from a 1963–1967 Ford F100 will fit

Interchange Number: 2
Part Number(s): 393124
Number of leaves: 9
Usage: 1965–1968 C-10 Chevrolet and 1500 GMC truck with rear-leaf suspension option and heavy-duty spring package
Note(s): Auto wreckers say that rear springs from a 1961–1967 Ford F100 truck will fit

Interchange Number 3
Part Number(s): 3920437
Number of leaves: 10
Usage: 1965–1968 C-20 Chevrolet and 2500 GMC truck with rear-leaf suspension option with heavy-duty springs
Note(s): Auto wreckers say that rear springs from a 1961–1967 Ford F250 truck will fit

Interchange Number 4
Part Number(s): 3888959
Number of leaves: 3

Usage: 1967–1968 C-10 to C-20 Chevrolet and 1500 to 2500 GMC four-wheel-drive truck (heavy-duty only on C-10 models)

Interchange Number 5
Part Number(s): 3888906
Number of leaves: 2
Usage: 1967–1968 C-10 Chevrolet and 1500 GMC four-wheel-drive truck (except with heavy-duty springs)

Interchange Number 6
Part Number(s): 3763005
Number of leaves: 8
Usage: 1960–1968 C-30 Chevrolet and 3500 GMC truck

Interchange Number 7
Part Number(s): 3936592
Number of leaves: 4
Usage: 1969–1972 C-10 Chevrolet and 1500 GMC truck with rear leaf springs (except with heavy-duty option)

Interchange Number 8
Part Number(s): 3941631
Number of leaves: 5
Usage: 1969–1972 C-10 Chevrolet and 1500 GMC truck with rear leaf springs with heavy-duty option; 1969–1972 C-20 Chevrolet and 2500 GMC truck with 127-inch wheelbase with standard-duty leaf springs

Interchange Number 9
Part Number(s): 3941642
Number of leaves: 6
Usage: 1969–1972 C-20 Chevrolet and 2500 GMC truck with rear leaf springs with heavy-duty option

Interchange Number 10
Part Number(s): 3987581
Number of leaves: 5
Usage: 1969–1972 C-10 to C-20 Chevrolet and 1500 to 2500 GMC four-wheel-drive truck and Blazer four-wheel drive; 1970–1972 Jimmy four-wheel drive

Interchange Number 11
Part Number(s): 3977567
Number of leaves: 6
Usage: 1969–1972 C-20 Chevrolet and 2500 GMC truck with rear leaf springs and 133-inch wheelbase; 1969–1972 C-30 Chevrolet and 3500 GMC truck (except with 11,000-pound axle)
Note(s): Some models used an auxiliary leaf in addition to the above springs

Interchange Number 12
Part Number(s): 3936592
Number of leaves: 7

Usage: 1969 C-30 Chevrolet and 3500 GMC truck with 11,000-pound axle
Note(s): Also used a five-leaf auxiliary leaf

Interchange Number 13
Part Number(s): 3981847
Number of leaves: 7
Usage: 1970–1972 C-30 Chevrolet and 3500 GMC truck with 11,000-pound axle
Note(s): Also used a five-leaf auxiliary leaf

Interchange Number 14
Number of leaves: 4
Usage: 1973–1974 C-10 Chevrolet and 1500 GMC truck, Blazer, and Jimmy—two-wheel-drive models only
Note(s): Interchange Number 15 will fit if you swap the bushings

Interchange Number 15
Number of leaves: 4
Usage: 1975–1981 C-10 Chevrolet and 1500 GMC truck, Blazer, and Jimmy—two-wheel-drive models only

Interchange Number 16
Number of leaves: 8
Usage: 1973–1977 C-10 Chevrolet and 1500 GMC truck, two-wheel-drive models only with heavy-duty suspension; 1973–1977 C-20 to C-30 with standard-duty suspension

Interchange Number 17
Number of leaves: 8
Usage: 1978 to early-1979 C-10 Chevrolet and 1500 GMC truck, two-wheel-drive models only with heavy-duty suspension; 1978 to early-1979 C-20 to C-30 with standard-duty suspension

Interchange Number 18
Number of leaves: 5
Usage: 1973–1974 C-10 Chevrolet and 1500 GMC truck with 117-inch wheelbase; 1973–1977 Blazer and Jimmy four-wheel-drive models only

Interchange Number 19
Number of leaves: 7
Usage: 1973–1977 C-20 Chevrolet and 2500 GMC four-wheel-drive truck

Interchange Number 20
Number of leaves: 9
Usage: 1973–1974 C-20 Suburban with heavy-duty suspension

Interchange Number 21
Number of leaves: 9
Usage: 1973–1981 C-20 Suburban with special heavy-duty suspension; 1973–1975 C-20 Chevrolet and 2500 GMC four-door cab truck; 1973–1981 C-30 Chevrolet and 3500 GMC truck, with heavy-duty suspension (two-door cab); 1976–1977 C-20 with extra cap rear springs

Front Sway Bars

There are two basic interchanges when it comes to front sway bars—those in the early models (1967–1972) and those of the later models (1973–1978). There are divisions in each section, partially the later models; and certain models, or packages, used a thicker diameter bar. However, a bar from a Camper Special can fit a regular run-of-the-mill C-10, provided you swap it with all of the bigger bar's mounting hardware. Advantages of a larger bar include better handling and towing capabilities.

Model Identification

1967–1972	Interchange Number
All	1

1973–1974

C-10
- two-wheel drive
  - standard 6
  - heavy-duty 5
- four-wheel drive 2

C-20
- standard 6
- heavy-duty 5
- Camper Special .4

C-30
- standard 6

1975–1978

C-10
- two-wheel drive
  - standard 6
  - heavy-duty 5
- four-wheel drive 3

C-20
- standard 6
- heavy-duty 5
- Camper Special .4

C-30
- standard 6
- heavy-duty 5
- Camper Special .7

Interchanges

Interchange Number: 1
Part Number(s): 6274060
Usage: 1965–1972 C-10 to C-30 Chevrolet and 1500 to 3500 GMC truck; 1969–1972 Blazer; 1970–1972 Jimmy with front stabilizer bar

Interchange Number: 2
Part Number(s): 328126
Usage: 1973–1974 C-10 to C-20 Chevrolet and 1500 to 3500 GMC truck, Blazer, and Jimmy—four-wheel-drive models only

Interchange Number: 3
Part Number(s): 328132
Usage: 1975–1981 C-10 to C-20 Chevrolet and 1500 to 3500 GMC truck, Blazer, and Jimmy—four-wheel-drive models only

Interchange Number: 4
Part Number(s): 328155
Usage: 1973–1981 C-20 Chevrolet and 2500 GMC truck with Camper Special package
Note(s): Heavy-duty bar

Interchange Number: 5
Part Number(s): 334583
Usage: 1973–1981 C-20 to C-30 Chevrolet and 2500 to 3500 GMC two-wheel-drive truck with heavy-duty front suspension

Interchange Number: 6
Part Number(s): 6274060
Usage: 1973–1981 C-10 to C-30 Chevrolet and 1500 to 3500 GMC truck, Blazer, and Jimmy—two-wheel-drive models only without heavy-duty suspension

Interchange Number: 7
Part Number(s): 328107
Usage: 1973–1981 C-30 Chevrolet and 3500 GMC truck with 131.5- to 164.5-inch wheelbase with camper package; 1973–1978 C-20 Chevrolet and 2500 GMC four-door cab truck with camper package
Note(s): Heavy-duty bar

Steering Gearboxes
Model Identification

1967–1969	Interchange Number
Two-wheel drive	
standard steering	1
power steering	
linkage type	1
integral	3
Four-wheel drive	2

1970–1972

Two-wheel drive
- standard steering 4
- power steering 5

Four-wheel drive
- standard 10
- power 8

1973–1976

Two-wheel drive
- standard steering 4
- power steering 6

Four-wheel drive
- standard 10
- power 8

1977–1978

Two-wheel drive
- standard steering 4
- power steering 7

Four-wheel drive

standard 10

power 9

Interchanges

Interchange Number: 1
Part Number(s):
Usage: 1967–1968 C-10 to C-30 Chevrolet and 1500 to 3500 GMC two-wheel-drive truck with standard- or linkage-type power steering

Interchange Number: 2
Part Number(s): 7801347
Usage: 1964–1968 C-10 to C-20 Chevrolet and 1500 to 2500 GMC four-wheel-drive truck

Interchange Number: 3
Part Number(s): 7802640
Usage: 1968–1969 C-10 to C-30 Chevrolet and 1500 to 3500 GMC two-wheel-drive truck with integral power steering

Interchange Number: 4
Part Number(s): 7815989
Usage: 1970–1981 C-10 to C-30 Chevrolet and 1500 to 3500 GMC truck, Blazer, and Jimmy two-wheel drive with standard steering

Interchange Number: 5
Part Number(s): 7810985
Usage: 1970–1972 C-10 to C-30 Chevrolet and 1500 to 3500 GMC truck, Blazer, and Jimmy two-wheel drive with power steering

Interchange Number: 6
Part Number(s): 7818191
Usage: 1973–1976 C-10 to C-20 Chevrolet and 1500 to 2500 GMC truck, Blazer, and Jimmy two-wheel drive with power steering

Interchange Number: 7
Part Number(s): 464157
Usage: 1977–1978 C-10 to C-30 Chevrolet and 2500 to 3500 GMC truck, Blazer, and Jimmy two-wheel drive with power steering

Interchange Number: 8
Part Number(s): 7825868
Usage: 1970–1976 C-10 to C-20 Chevrolet and 1500 to 2500 GMC truck, Blazer, and Jimmy four-wheel drive with power steering

Interchange Number: 9
Part Number(s): 464160
Usage: 1977–1978 C-10 to C-30 Chevrolet and 1500 to 3500 GMC truck, Blazer, and Jimmy four-wheel drive with power steering

Interchange Number: 10
Part Number(s): 7812914
Usage: 1970–1978 C-10 to C-30 Chevrolet and 1500 to 3500 GMC truck, Blazer, and Jimmy four-wheel drive with manual steering

Power Steering Pumps
Model Identification

Interchanges

Interchange Number: 1
Part Number(s): 5698079
Usage: 1967–1968 C-10 to C-30 Chevrolet and 1500 to 3500 GMC truck with linkage-type power steering

Interchange Number: 2
Part Number(s): 7805725
Usage: 1968–1969 C-10 to C-30 Chevrolet and 1500 to 3500 GMC truck; 1969 Blazer with integral-type power steering—all powerplants except 396-ci V-8

Interchange Number: 3
Part Number(s): 7805726
Usage: 1968–1969 C-10 to C-30 Chevrolet and 1500 to 3500 GMC truck with integral-type power steering and 396-ci V-8

Interchange Number: 4
Part Number(s): 7808576
Usage: 1970–1972 C-10 to C-30 Chevrolet and 1500 to 3500 GMC truck, Blazer, and Jimmy (except with 396/402-ci V-8)

Interchange Number: 5
Part Number(s): 7808577
Usage: 1970–1972 C-10 to C-30 Chevrolet and 1500 to 3500 GMC truck, Blazer, and Jimmy with 396-ci V-8 (402-ci)

Interchange Number: 6
Part Number(s): 7814280
Usage: 1973–1974 C-10 to C-30 Chevrolet and 1500 to 3500 GMC truck, Blazer, and Jimmy with V-8 powerplant (except with 454-ci V-8)

Interchange Number: 7
Part Number(s): 7818028
Usage: 1975–1978 C-10 to C-30 Chevrolet and 1500 to 3500 GMC truck, Blazer, and Jimmy with V-8 powerplant (except with 454-ci V-8 or Hydro boost brakes)

Interchange Number: 8
Part Number(s): 7814281
Usage: 1973–1974 C-10 to C-30 Chevrolet and 1500 to 3500 GMC truck with 454-ci V-8

Interchange Number: 9
Part Number(s): 7818029
Usage: 1975–1979 C-10 to C-30 Chevrolet and 1500 to 3500 GMC truck with 454-ci V-8, without Hydro boost brakes

Interchange Number: 10
Part Number(s): 7825105
Usage: 1976 to early-1977 C-30 Chevrolet and 3500 GMC truck with Hydro boost brakes and 350-ci V-8

Interchange Number: 11
Part Number(s): 7825358
Usage: 1976 to early-1977 C-30 Chevrolet and 3500 GMC truck with Hydro boost brakes and 454-ci V-8

Interchange Number: 12
Part Number(s): 7828420

Usage: Late-1977 to 1979 C-30 Chevrolet and 3500 GMC truck with Hydro boost brakes and 350-ci V-8

Interchange Number: 13
Part Number(s): 7828422
Usage: Late-1977–1979 C-30 Chevrolet and 3500 GMC truck with Hydro boost brakes and 454-ci V-8

Interchange Number: 14
Part Number(s): 7826091
Usage: 1976–1978 C-10 to C-20 Chevrolet and 1500 to 2500 GMC truck, Blazer, and Jimmy four-wheel drive with 350-ci V-8

Interchange Number: 15
Part Number(s): 7826563
Usage: Early-1977 C-30 Chevrolet and 3500 GMC four-wheel-drive truck with 350-ci V-8

Interchange Number: 16
Part Number(s): 7826428
Usage: Late-1977 to 1979 C-30 Chevrolet and 3500 GMC four-wheel-drive truck with 350-ci V-8

Steering Wheels

Steering-wheel interchange is based on the overall design and original replacement part number. Color-keyed steering wheels were standard items; however, no mention of color is part of this interchange. All interchanges are based on the replacement part number for a black steering wheel. You can either hunt for a wheel that matches your interior, or you can paint the wheel to match. If you decide to paint one, go for a light-color wheel, as they are the easiest to cover. All steering wheel interchanges are as a bare unit without horn cap or shroud.

Model Identification

1967–1968	Interchange Number
All 1	
1969–1972	
All 2	
1973	
Except Custom 3, 4	
Custom 5	
1974–1976	
Except Custom 3	
Custom 5	
1977	
Except Custom 3	
Custom 6	
1978	
Except Custom 7	
Custom 6	

Interchanges

Interchange Number: 1

Part Number(s): 9749393

Usage: 1967–1968 C-10 to C-30 or G-10 to G-20 Chevrolet and 1500 to 350 GMC truck or van; 1966 C-10 to C-30 Chevrolet and 1500 to 3500 GMC truck with Deluxe equipment

Interchange Number: 2

Part Number(s): 335212

Usage: 1969–1972 C-10 to C-30 or G-10 to G-30 Chevrolet and 1500 to 3500 GMC truck or van; 1969–1972 Blazer; 1970–1972 Jimmy

Interchange Number: 3

Part Number(s): 9755073

Usage: 1973–1977 C-10 to C-30 or G-10 to G-30 Chevrolet and 1500 to 3500 GMC truck and van, Blazer, and Jimmy without custom wheel

Note(s): 17.5-inch-diameter wheel with 4 27/32-inch-diameter hub; some 1973 models used Interchange Number 4

Interchange Number: 4

Part Number(s): 9762307

Usage: 1973 C-10 to C-30 or G-10 to G-30 Chevrolet and 1500 to 3500 GMC truck and van, Blazer, and Jimmy without custom wheel

Note(s): 16-inch-diameter wheel with 4 1/8-inch-diameter hub; some 1973 models used Interchange Number 3

Interchange Number: 5

Part Number(s): 9755905

Usage: 1973–1976 C-10 to C-30 or G-10 to G-30 Chevrolet and 1500 to 3500 GMC truck and van, Blazer, and Jimmy with custom wheel

Interchange Number: 6

Part Number(s): 9762307

Usage: 1977–1979 C-10 to C-30 or G-10 to G-30 Chevrolet and 1500 to 3500 GMC truck and van, Blazer, and Jimmy with custom wheel

Interchange Number: 7

Part Number(s): 9762199

Usage: 1978–1979 C-10 to C-30 or G-10 to G-30 Chevrolet and 1500 to 3500 GMC truck and van, Blazer, and Jimmy without custom wheel

Steering Columns

The steering column is usually interchanged by the model year and type of transmission and shifter. Another factor that affects the interchange is a tilt wheel, which required a special column. A column from a van will not fit a pickup.

Model Identification

1967–1969	Interchange Number
Three-speed manual	19
Automatic transmission	21
Four-speed manual	20

1970–1972

Three-speed manual	22
Automatic transmission	
without tilt wheel	24
with tilt wheel	25
Four-speed manual	23

1973–1974

Three-speed manual	2
Automatic transmission	
without tilt wheel	1
with tilt wheel	4
Four-speed manual	3

1975–1976

Three-speed manual	5
Automatic transmission	
without tilt wheel	7
with tilt wheel	8
Four-speed manual	6

1977

Three-speed manual	9
Automatic transmission	
without tilt wheel	12
with tilt wheel	13
Four-speed manual	
without tilt wheel	10
with tilt wheel	11

1978

Three-speed manual	14
Automatic transmission	
without tilt wheel	17
with tilt wheel	18
Four-speed manual	
without tilt wheel	15
with tilt wheel	16

Interchanges

Interchange Number: 1

Part Number(s): 7815201

Transmission type: Automatic

Shifter location: Column

Usage: 1973–1974 C-10 to C-30 Chevrolet, 1500 to 3500 GMC truck, Blazer, and Jimmy with automatic transmission (except with tilt wheel)

Interchange Number: 2

Part Number(s): 7815202

Transmission type: Three-speed manual

Shifter location: Column

Usage: 1973–1974 C-10 to C-20 Chevrolet, 1500 to 2500 GMC truck, Blazer, and Jimmy with three-speed manual transmission

Interchange Number: 3
    Transmission type: Four-speed manual
    Shifter location: Floor
    Usage: 1973–1974 C-10 to C-30 Chevrolet and
        1500 to 2500 GMC truck, Blazer, and Jimmy
        with four-speed manual transmission
Interchange Number: 4
    Transmission type: Automatic
    Shifter location: Column
    Usage: 1973–1974 C-10 to C-30 Chevrolet and
        1500 to 2500 GMC truck, Blazer, and Jimmy
        with automatic transmission and tilt wheel
Interchange Number: 5
    Transmission type: Three-speed manual
    Shifter location: Column
    Usage: 1975–1976 C-10 to C-20 Chevrolet and
        1500 to 2500 GMC truck, Blazer, and Jimmy
        with three-speed manual transmission
Interchange Number: 6
    Transmission type: Four-speed manual
    Shifter location: Floor
    Usage: 1975–1976 C-10 to C-20 Chevrolet and
        1500 to 2500 GMC truck, Blazer, and Jimmy
        with four-speed manual transmission
Interchange Number: 7
    Transmission type: Automatic
    Shifter location: Column
    Usage: 1975–1976 C-10 to C-30 Chevrolet and
        1500 to 3500 GMC truck, Blazer, and Jimmy
        with automatic transmission, without tilt wheel
Interchange Number: 8
    Transmission type: Automatic
    Shifter location: Column
    Usage: 1975–1976 C-10 to C-30 Chevrolet and
        1500 to 3500 GMC truck, Blazer, and Jimmy
        with automatic transmission and tilt wheel
Interchange Number: 9
    Transmission type: Three-speed manual
    Shifter location: Column
    Usage: 1977 C-10 to C-20 Chevrolet and 1500 to
        2500 GMC truck, Blazer, and Jimmy with three-
        speed manual transmission
Interchange Number: 10
    Transmission type: Four-speed manual
    Shifter location: Floor
    Usage: 1977 C-10 to C-30 Chevrolet and 1500 to
        3500 GMC truck, Blazer, and Jimmy with four-
        speed manual transmission, without tilt wheel
Interchange Number: 11
    Transmission type: Four-speed manual
    Shifter location: Floor
    Usage: 1977 C-10 to C-30 Chevrolet and 1500 to
        3500 GMC truck, Blazer, and Jimmy with four-
        speed manual transmission and tilt wheel

Interchange Number: 12
    Transmission type: Automatic
    Shifter location: Column
    Usage: 1977 C-10 to C-30 Chevrolet and 1500 to
        3500 GMC truck, Blazer, and Jimmy with auto-
        matic transmission, without tilt wheel
Interchange Number: 13
    Transmission type: Automatic
    Shifter location: Column
    Usage: 1977 C-10 to C-30 Chevrolet and 1500 to
        3500 GMC truck, Blazer, and Jimmy with auto-
        matic transmission and tilt wheel
Interchange Number: 14
    Transmission type: Three-speed manual
    Shifter location: Column
    Usage: 1978 C-10 to C-20 Chevrolet and 1500 to
        2500 GMC truck, Blazer, and Jimmy with three-
        speed manual transmission
Interchange Number: 15
    Transmission type: Four-speed manual
    Shifter location: Floor
    Usage: 1977 C-10 to C-30 Chevrolet and 1500 to
        3500 GMC truck, Blazer, and Jimmy with four-
        speed manual transmission, without tilt wheel
Interchange Number: 16
    Transmission type: Four-speed manual
    Shifter location: Floor
    Usage: 1977 C-10 to C-30 Chevrolet and 1500 to
        3500 GMC truck, Blazer, and Jimmy with four-
        speed manual transmission and tilt wheel
Interchange Number: 17
    Transmission type: Automatic
    Shifter location: Column
    Usage: 1977 C-10 to C-30 Chevrolet and 1500 to
        3500 GMC truck, Blazer, and Jimmy with auto-
        matic transmission, without tilt wheel
Interchange Number: 18
    Transmission type: Automatic
    Shifter location: Column
    Usage: 1977 C-10 to C-30 Chevrolet and 1500 to
        3500 GMC truck, Blazer, and Jimmy with auto-
        matic transmission and tilt wheel
Interchange Number: 19
    Transmission type: Three-speed manual
    Shifter location: Column
    Usage: 1967–1969 C-10 to C-20 Chevrolet and
        1500 to 2500 GMC truck; 1969 Blazer with
        three-speed manual transmission
Interchange Number: 20
    Transmission type: Four-speed manual
    Shifter location: Floor
    Usage: 1967–1969 C-10 to C-20 Chevrolet and
        1500 to 2500 GMC truck; 1969 Blazer with
        four-speed manual transmission

Interchange Number: 21
　　Transmission type: Automatic
　　Shifter location: Column
　　Usage: 1967–1969 C-10 to C-20 Chevrolet and 1500 to 2500 GMC truck; 1969 Blazer with automatic transmission

Interchange Number: 22
　　Transmission type: Three-speed manual
　　Shifter location: Column
　　Usage: 1970–1972 C-10 to C-20 Chevrolet and 1500 to 2500 GMC truck, Blazer, and Jimmy with three-speed manual transmission

Interchange Number: 23
　　Transmission type: Four-speed manual
　　Shifter location: Floor
　　Usage: 1970–1972 C-10 to C-20 Chevrolet and 1500 to 2500 GMC truck, Blazer, and Jimmy with four-speed manual transmission

Interchange Number: 24
　　Transmission type: Automatic
　　Shifter location: Column
　　Usage: 1970–1972 C-10 to C-20 Chevrolet and 1500 to 2500 GMC truck, Blazer, and Jimmy with automatic transmission, without tilt wheel

Interchange Number: 25
　　Transmission type: automatic
　　Shifter location: Column
　　Usage: 1970–1972 C-10 to C-20 Chevrolet and 1500 to 2500 GMC truck, Blazer, and Jimmy with automatic transmission and tilt wheel

Steering Knuckles
Model Identification

1967–1969	Interchange Number

C-10
　　two-wheel drive 1
　　four-wheel drive 2
C-20 and C-30
　　two-wheel drive 4
　　four-wheel drive (C-20 only) 3
1970
C-10
　　two-wheel drive
　　　　with 11x2-inch brake 1
　　　　with 11x2 3/4-inch brake 5
　　four-wheel drive 6
C-20 and C-30
　　two-wheel drive 4
　　four-wheel drive (C-20 only) 7
1971
C-10
　　two-wheel drive 8
　　four-wheel drive 9

C-20 and C-30
　　two-wheel drive 11
　　four-wheel drive (C-20 only) 12
1972
C-10
　　two-wheel drive 8
　　four-wheel drive
　　　　early 9
　　　　late 10
C-20 and C-30
　　two-wheel drive 11
　　four-wheel drive (C-20 only)
　　　　early 12
　　　　late 13
1973–1975
C-10
　　two-wheel drive 14
　　four-wheel drive 10
C-20
　　two-wheel drive 11
　　four-wheel drive 13
C-30
　　single rear wheels 11
　　dual rear wheels
　　　　nonremovable carrier 15
　　　　removable carrier 16
1976
C-10
　　two-wheel drive 14
　　four-wheel drive 10
C-20
　　two-wheel drive 11
　　four-wheel drive 13
C-30
　　single rear wheels 11
　　dual rear wheels 17
1977
C-10
　　two-wheel drive 14
　　four-wheel drive
　　　　early 10
　　　　late 18
C-20
　　two-wheel drive 11
　　four-wheel drive
　　　　early 13
　　　　late 18
C-30
　　single rear wheels 11
　　dual rear wheels 17
　　　　four-wheel drive 19

Interchanges

Interchange Number: 1
Part Number(s): 3860970
Usage: 1964–1970 C-10 Chevrolet and 1500 GMC truck; 1970 Blazer and Jimmy, two-wheel-drive models only; 1971 G-10 Chevrolet and 1500 GMC van

Interchange Number: 2
Part Number(s): 2403625
Usage: 1964–1969 C-10 Chevrolet and 1500 GMC truck; 1969 Blazer, four-wheel-drive models only; 1969–1971 Dodge W100 four-wheel drive; 1961–1965 Ford F100 four-wheel drive; 1961–1975 Ford F250 four-wheel drive with either 3,000- or 3,300-pound axle (except four-door models)

Interchange Number: 3
Part Number(s): 2403626
Usage: 1960–1969 C-20 Chevrolet and 2500 GMC four-wheel-drive truck

Interchange Number: 4
Part Number(s): 3935178
Usage: 1965–1970 C-20 to C-30 Chevrolet and 2500 to 3500 GMC two-wheel-drive truck

Interchange Number: 5
Part Number(s): 3958107
Usage: 1970 C-10 Chevrolet and 1500 GMC truck two-wheel-drive models only with 11x2 3/4-inch-diameter drums; 1971 G-20 Chevrolet and 2500 GMC van with drum brakes

Interchange Number: 6
Part Number(s): 3965127
Usage: 1970 C-10 Chevrolet and 1500 GMC truck, Blazer, and Jimmy four-wheel drive; 1966–1972 Ford Bronco

Interchange Number: 7
Part Number(s): 3979437
Usage: 1970 C-20 Chevrolet and 2500 GMC four-wheel-drive truck

Interchange Number: 8
Part Number(s): 3969445 (left); 3969446 (right)
Usage: 1971–1972 C-10 Chevrolet and 1500 GMC truck, Blazer, and Jimmy two-wheel drive

Interchange Number: 9
Part Number(s): 3979676
Usage: 1971 to early-1972 C-10 Chevrolet and 1500 GMC truck, Blazer, and Jimmy four-wheel drive

Interchange Number: 10
Part Number(s): 376853
Usage: Late-1972 to early-1977 C-10 Chevrolet and 1500 GMC truck, Blazer, and Jimmy four-wheel drive

Interchange Number: 11
Part Number(s): 3969451 (left); 3969452 (right)
Usage: 1971–1981 C-20 Chevrolet and 2500 GMC two-wheel-drive truck; 1971–1979 C-30 Chevrolet and 3500 GMC two-wheel-drive truck with single rear wheels

Interchange Number: 12
Part Number(s): 3979676
Usage: 1971 to early-1972 C-20 Chevrolet and 2500 GMC four-wheel-drive truck

Interchange Number: 13
Part Number(s): 376863
Usage: Late-1972 to early-1977 C-20 Chevrolet and 2500 GMC four-wheel-drive truck

Interchange Number: 14
Part Number(s): 6274259 (left); 6274260 (right)
Usage: 1973–1980 C-10 Chevrolet and 1500 GMC truck, Blazer, and Jimmy; G-20 Chevrolet and 2500 GMC van—two-wheel-drive models only

Interchange Number: 15
Part Number(s): 335665 (left); 335666 (right)
Usage: 1973–1975 C-30 Chevrolet and 3500 GMC truck with dual wheels and nonremovable carrier

Interchange Number: 16
Part Number(s): 331459 (left); 331460 (right)
Usage: 1973–1975 C-30 Chevrolet and 3500 GMC truck with dual wheels and removable carrier

Interchange Number: 17
Part Number(s): 363735 (left); 363736 (right)
Usage: 1976–1981 C-30 Chevrolet and 3500 GMC truck with 13x3.5-inch rear drum brakes; 1976–1981 C-30 Chevrolet service van with dual rear wheels

Interchange Number: 18
Part Number(s): 464039
Usage: Late-1977 to 1981 C-10 to C-20 Chevrolet and 1500 to 2500 GMC truck, Blazer, and Jimmy four-wheel drive

Interchange Number: 19
Part Number(s): 476075
Usage: 1977–1981 C-30 Chevrolet and 3500 GMC four-wheel-drive truck

7 Brake Systems and Parking Brakes

Master Cylinders

Interchange for master cylinders is based on the original replacement part number. This was done to give you a larger interchange field. Type of braking system is an important factor in the interchange. Two types were used—drum and front disc—and master cylinders are not interchangeable between drum and disc systems. Thus, a master cylinder designed for drum brakes cannot be used on a truck with disc brakes, and vice versa.

Note also that the lighter duty C-10 models used a different unit than the higher rated 3/4- and 1-ton models (C-20 and C-30, respectively), so be sure that you are interchanging from the proper model. Do not rely on the side fender nameplates because it is common practice to find a set of C-10 fenders on a C-20 model; always rely on the VIN/certification plate. See the introduction portion of this guide for details and location of this plate.

Model Identification

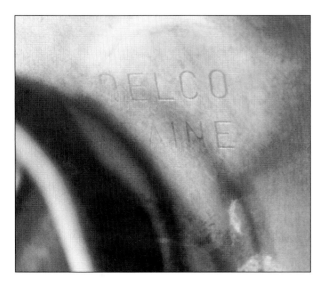
Moraine-made units are stamped with the manufacturer's name.

C-30

Interchanges

Interchange Number: 1
Part Number(s): 3912103
Usage: 1967–1970 C-10 Chevrolet and 1500 GMC truck; 1969–1979 Blazer; 1970 Jimmy
Note(s): Bendix 2226045

Interchange Number: 2
Part Number(s): 5463267
Usage: 1967–1970 C-10 Chevrolet and 1500 GMC truck; 1969–1979 Blazer; 1970 Jimmy without power brakes
Note(s): Salvage-yard owners say the master cylinder from a 1967–1969 Impala with drum brakes will fit. Moraine unit has casting code AB for trucks or AT for Impala.

Interchange Number: 3
Part Number(s): 3912128
Usage: 1967–1970 C-20 Chevrolet and 2500 GMC truck; C-30 Chevrolet and 3500 GMC truck (except with 11,000-pound axle)
Note(s): Bendix 2225835

Interchange Number: 4
Part Number(s): 3899911
Usage: 1967–1970 C-30 Chevrolet and 3500 GMC truck with 11,000 pound axle
Note(s): Wagner unit 57206-A

Interchange Number: 5
Part Number(s): 3995845
Usage: 1971–1972 C-10 Chevrolet and 1500 GMC truck without power brakes
Note(s): Bendix 2230835

Interchange Number: 6
Part Number(s): 6273936
Usage: 1971–1972 C-10 Chevrolet and 1500 GMC truck with power drum brakes
Note(s): Bendix 2231345

Interchange Number: 7
Part Number(s): 5472650
Usage: 1971–1972 C-10 Chevrolet and 1500 GMC truck, Blazer, and Jimmy; 1971–1973 G-10 to G-20 Chevrolet and 1500 to 2500 GMC van—all models with power disc brakes
Note(s): Bendix 2230835

Interchange Number: 8
Part Number(s): 2623214
Usage: 1971–1973 C-20 Chevrolet and 2500 GMC truck; C-30 Chevrolet and 3500 GMC truck, except with 11,000-pound axle; 1971–1976 G-30 Chevrolet and 3500 GMC van; 1974–1977 C-30 Chevrolet and 3500 GMC truck with 13x2-inch rear brake drums
Note(s): Vans have disc brakes

Interchange Number: 9
Part Number(s): 3996589
Usage: 1971–1972 C-30 Chevrolet and 3500 GMC truck with 11,000-pound axle

Interchange Number: 10
Part Number(s): 335075
Usage: 1973–1977 C-10 Chevrolet and 1500 GMC truck, Blazer, and Jimmy with power disc brakes
Note(s): Bendix 2231760

Interchange Number: 11
Part Number(s): 2620636
Usage: 1973–1974 C-10 Chevrolet and 1500 GMC truck, Blazer, and Jimmy; 1973 G-20 Chevrolet and 2500 GMC van; 1974 G-10 Chevrolet and 1500 GMC van; 1971–1975 Cadillac—all models with power disc brakes
Note(s): Moraine unit Stamped RA for 1973–1975; stamped RG for 1971–1972

A 1967–1972 brake pedal pad. CST and Cheyenne models have a trim plate, as shown.

Interchange Number: 12
Part Number(s): 6260961
Usage: 1974–1975 C-10 Chevrolet and 1500 GMC truck, Blazer, and Jimmy (except with power disc brakes)
Note(s): Bendix unit

Interchange Number: 13
Part Number(s): 2621568
Usage: 1974 C-10 Chevrolet and 1500 GMC truck, Blazer, and Jimmy (except with power disc brakes)
Note(s): Moraine unit

Interchange Number: 14
Part Number(s): 18000996
Usage: 1974–1976 C-10 Chevrolet and 1500 GMC truck, Blazer, and Jimmy; 1975–1976 Camaro, Nova, Firebird, Omega, Apollo, Ventura II, and Century; 1971–1976 Chevelle, Impala, Monte Carlo, Grand Prix, Sprint, full-size Buick (except 1971 LeSabre with 350-ci V-8), LeMans, Riviera, Cutlass, full-size Oldsmobile, full-size Pontiac, and Skylark
Note(s): Moraine unit with single bail

Interchange Number: 15
Part Number(s): 6260725
Usage: 1974–1975 C-30 Chevrolet and 3500 GMC truck with single or dual rear wheels and 13x2.5-inch rear brakes; 1976–1978 C-30 Chevrolet and 3500 GMC truck with nonremovable carrier and with Hydro boost
Note(s): Bendix unit

Interchange Number: 16
Part Number(s): 6269173
Usage: 1974–1976 C-30 Chevrolet and 3500 GMC truck with 15-inch rear brake drums
Note(s): Bendix unit

Interchange Number: 17
Part Number(s): 2621565
Usage: 1975 C-10 Chevrolet and 1500 GMC truck with 11 1/8x2 3/4-inch rear brake drums; 1974–1975 G-20 Chevrolet and 2500 GMC van

Interchange Number: 18
Part Number(s): 2623180
Usage: 1976 C-20 Chevrolet and 2500 GMC truck with 11-inch rear brake drum; 1976 Suburban

Interchange Number: 19
Part Number(s): 18002063
Usage: 1977–1978 C-10 Chevrolet and 1500 GMC truck, Blazer, and Jimmy; Camaro, Impala, Firebird, Nova, Omega, Ventura II, Toronado, full-size Buick (with rear brake drums), full-size Pontiac, and full-size Oldsmobile; 1977 Chevelle, Cutlass, Grand Prix, Monte Carlo, Century, LeMans, and Sprint—all with power disc brakes

Interchange Number: 20
Part Number(s): 18002456
Usage: 1977–1978 C-20 Chevrolet and 2500 GMC truck with 11-inch rear brake drums

Interchange Number: 21
Part Number(s): 18002456
Usage: 1977–1978 C-20 Chevrolet and 2500 GMC truck with 13-inch rear brake drums; 1977–1978 C-30 Chevrolet and 3500 GMC truck without Hydro boost

Power Booster Chambers

Interchange for booster chambers is based on the original replacement part number. This was done to give you a larger interchange field. Note that, as for the master cylinders, the lighter duty 1/2-ton C-10 used a different chamber than the heavier duty C-20 and C-30 models, and they cannot be interchanged, so read the interchanges very carefully.

Model Identification

1967	Interchange Number
C-10	1
C-20	2
C-30	
without 11,000-pound axle	2
with 11,000-pound axle	3, 4
1968	
C-10	1
C-20	2

Interchanges

Interchange Number: 1
   Part Number(s): 3970502
   Usage: 1967–1970 C-10 Chevrolet and 1500 GMC truck; 1969–1970 Blazer; 1970 Jimmy
   Note(s): Bendix 2508396

Interchange Number: 2
   Part Number(s): 3970503
   Usage: 1967–1970 C-20 Chevrolet and 2500 GMC truck; 1967–1970 C-30 Chevrolet and 3500 GMC truck without 11,000-pound axle
   Note(s): GMC interchange is for models with a master cylinder piston bore of 1 1/8 inches; Bendix 2506422

Interchange Number: 3
   Part Number(s): 3882288
   Usage: 1967 to early-1968 C-30 Chevrolet truck; 1967 3500 GMC truck—all with 11,000-pound axle
   Note(s): Bendix 2503151

Interchange Number: 4
   Part Number(s): 2488619
   Usage: 1967 C-30 Chevrolet and 3500 GMC truck—all with 11,000-pound axle
   Note(s): Midland unit

Interchange Number: 5
   Part Number(s): 3936566
   Usage: Late-1968–1970 C-30 Chevrolet truck; 1968–1970 3500 GMC truck—all with 11,000-pound axle

Interchange Number: 6
   Part Number(s): 3995846
   Usage: 1971–1972 C-10 Chevrolet and 1500 GMC truck, Blazer, and Jimmy
   Note(s): Bendix 2509216

Interchange Number: 7
   Part Number(s): 5472537
   Usage: 1971–1972 C-10 Chevrolet and 1500 GMC truck, Blazer, and Jimmy
   Note(s): Moraine unit has single diaphragm

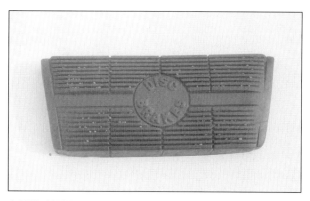
A 1973–1978 brake pedal pad with disc brakes.

Interchange Number: 8
> Part Number(s): 5472538
> Usage: 1971–1972 C-20 Chevrolet and 2500 GMC truck; 1971–1972 C-30 Chevrolet and 3500 GMC truck (except with 11,000-pound axle)

Interchange Number: 9
> Part Number(s): 331100
> Usage: 1971–1972 C-30 Chevrolet and 3500 GMC truck with 11,000-pound axle

Interchange Number: 10
> Part Number(s): 6259004
> Usage: 1973 C-10 Chevrolet and 1500 GMC truck, Blazer, and Jimmy; 1973 Suburban with two seats
> Note(s): Bendix

Interchange Number: 11
> Part Number(s): 2620594
> Usage: 1973 C-10 Chevrolet and 1500 GMC truck, Blazer, and Jimmy; 1973 Suburban with two seats
> Note(s): Moraine

Interchange Number: 12
> Part Number(s): 2620595
> Usage: 1973 C-20 to C-30 Chevrolet and 2500 to 3500 GMC truck; 1973 Suburban with three seats

Interchange Number: 13
> Part Number(s): 346401
> Usage: 1974 C-10 Chevrolet and 1500 GMC truck, Blazer, and Jimmy with 11x2-inch rear drum brakes
> Note(s): Bendix ID code XD

Interchange Number: 14
> Part Number(s): 2622044
> Usage: 1974 C-10 Chevrolet and 1500 GMC truck, Blazer, and Jimmy with 11x2-inch rear drum brakes
> Note(s): Moraine ID code NU; be careful because Interchange Number 19 uses the same ID code, but the two will not interchange

Interchange Number: 15
> Part Number(s): 2622043
> Usage: 1974 C-10 Chevrolet and 1500 GMC truck, Blazer, and Jimmy with 11 1/8x2-inch rear drum brakes; 1974 C-20 Chevrolet and 2500 GMC truck
> Note(s): ID code HF; be careful because Interchange Number 20 has the same ID code, but the two will not interchange

Interchange Number: 16
> Part Number(s): 2622042
> Usage: 1974 C-20 Chevrolet and 2500 GMC truck with 13-inch rear brake drums; 1974 C-30 Chevrolet and 3500 GMC truck without Hydro boost
> Note(s): ID code KK

Interchange Number: 17
> Part Number(s): 14034968
> Usage: 1974 C-30 Chevrolet and 3500 GMC truck with Hydro boost

Interchange Number: 18
> Part Number(s): 360808
> Usage: 1975–1977 C-10 Chevrolet and 1500 GMC truck with 11x2-inch rear brake drums; 1975 Blazer and Jimmy with 11x2-inch rear brake drums
> Note(s): Bendix unit

Interchange Number: 19
> Part Number(s): 18000020
> Usage: 1975–1978 C-10 Chevrolet and 1500 GMC truck with 11x2-inch rear brake drums; 1975 Blazer and Jimmy with 11x2-inch rear brake drums
> Note(s): Moraine unit ID code NU; be careful because Interchange Number 14 used the same ID code, but the two will not interchange

Interchange Number: 20
> Part Number(s): 180005040
> Usage: 1975–1977 C-10 Chevrolet and 1500 GMC truck with 11 1/8x2 3/4-inch rear brake drums; 1976–1977 Blazer and Jimmy; 1975 C-20 Chevrolet and 2500 GMC truck; 1975 C-30 Chevrolet and 3500 GMC truck without Hydro boost
> Note(s): ID code HF; be careful because Interchange Number 15 has the same ID code, but the two will not interchange

Interchange Number: 21
> Part Number(s): 347455
> Usage: 1975–1976 C-30 Chevrolet and 3500 GMC truck with Hydro boost

Interchange Number: 22
> Part Number(s): 2623156
> Usage: 1976–1977 C-20 Chevrolet and 2500 GMC truck with 11-inch rear brake drums

Interchange Number: 23
Part Number(s): 180005055
Usage: 1976–1977 C-20 Chevrolet and 2500 GMC truck with 13-inch rear brake drums; 1976–1977 C-30 Chevrolet and 3500 GMC truck without Hydro boost

Interchange Number: 24
Part Number(s): 476069
Usage: 1978 C-10 Chevrolet and 1500 GMC truck with diesel engine

Interchange Number: 25
Part Number(s): 18003819
Usage: 1978 C-10 Chevrolet and 1500 GMC truck with 11 1/8x2 3/4-inch rear brake drums, 1978 Blazer, and Jimmy (except with diesel engine)

Interchange Number: 26
Part Number(s): 18003820
Usage: 1978 C-20 Chevrolet and 2500 GMC truck with 11-inch rear brake drums; 1978 Suburban

Interchange Number: 27
Part Number(s): 180003826
Usage: 1978 C-20 Chevrolet and 2500 GMC truck with 13-inch rear brake drums; 1978 C-30 Chevrolet and 3500 GMC truck without Hydro boost

Interchange Number: 28
Part Number(s): 470197
Usage: 1978 C-30 Chevrolet and 3500 GMC truck; G-30 Chevrolet and 3500 GMC van—all models with Hydro boost

Brake Drums

Like other braking components in this section, interchange of brake drums relies heavily on the model selection. The lighter duty 1/2-ton C-10 used a different set of drums than the heavier duty C-20 and C-30 models, and they cannot be interchanged. Note also that four-wheel-drive models used a special set of front brake drums; those from a two-wheel-drive model will not fit, so read the interchanges very carefully.

Model Identification

1967   **Interchange Number**
C-10
  front
    except four-wheel drive 1
    four-wheel drive 2
  rear 1
C-20
  front
    except four-wheel drive 3
    four-wheel drive 4
  rear, except four-wheel drive, with coil-spring suspension
    single wheels 8
    dual rear wheels 3

A 1973–1978 parking brake cover.

    rear, except four-wheel drive, with leaf suspension . .6
    rear, four-wheel drive 12
C-30
  front
    except four-wheel drive 3
    single rear wheels .8
    dual rear wheels 9
  with 11,000-pound axle
    front 3
    rear 10

1968–1969
C-10
  11x2-inch drums, front
    except four-wheel drive 1
    four-wheel drive 2
  11x2-inch drums, rear 1
  11 1/8x2-inch drums, except four-wheel drive
    front 11
    rear 3
  11 1/8x2-inch drums, four-wheel drive
    front 2
    rear 3
C-20
  front
    except four-wheel drive 3
    four-wheel drive 4
  rear, except four-wheel drive, with coil-spring suspension
    single wheels 8
    dual rear wheels 3
  rear, except four-wheel drive,
    with leaf spring suspension 6
  rear, four-wheel drive 12
C-30
  front, except four-wheel drive 3
    single rear wheels .8
    dual rear wheels 9
  with 11,000-pound axle
    front 3
    rear 10

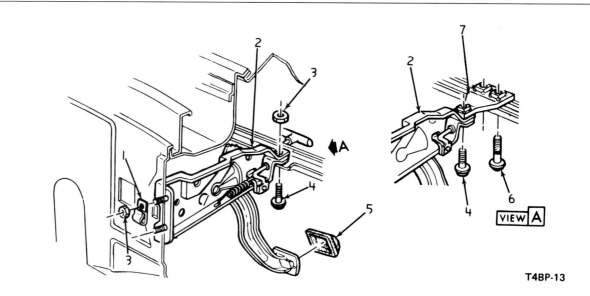

1971-72 "CK" 1,2,3 PARKING BRAKE ASSY.

1. 8.950 CLIP
2. 4.591 LEVER ASSY.
3. 8.917 NUT (5/16-18)
4. 8.913 BOLT (5/16-18 x 3/4)

5. 4.630 COVER
6. 8.977 SCREW (5/16-18 x 1)
7. 4.606 BRACKET

T4BP-13

The 1971–1972 parking brake assembly.

1970

C-10 with 11x2-inch drums
  front
    except four-wheel drive 1
    four-wheel drive 2
  rear 1
C-10 with 11 1/8x2-inch drums
  except four-wheel drive
    front 11
    rear 3
  four-wheel drive
    front 2
    rear 3
C-20 front
  except four-wheel drive 3
  four-wheel drive 13
C-20 rear
  except four-wheel drive, with coil-spring suspension
    single wheels 8
    dual rear wheels .3
  except four-wheel drive, with leaf spring suspension . .6
  four-wheel drive 12
C-30 front
  except four-wheel drive 3
    single rear wheels 8
    dual rear wheels .9

with 11,000-pound axle
  front 3
  rear 10

1971

C-10
  front disc standard
    except four-wheel drive 14
    four-wheel drive .15
C-20 rear, except four-wheel drive
  removable carrier
    nonfinned drums .16
    finned drums 18
  nonremovable carrier 17
C-20 rear, four-wheel drive 19
C-30
  without 11,000-pound axle
    single rear wheels 20
    dual rear wheels .21
  with 11,000-pound axle 10

1972

C-10
  front disc standard
    except four-wheel drive 14
    four-wheel drive .15
C-20 rear, except four-wheel drive
  removable carrier
    nonfinned drums .16
    finned drums 18
  nonremovable carrier 17

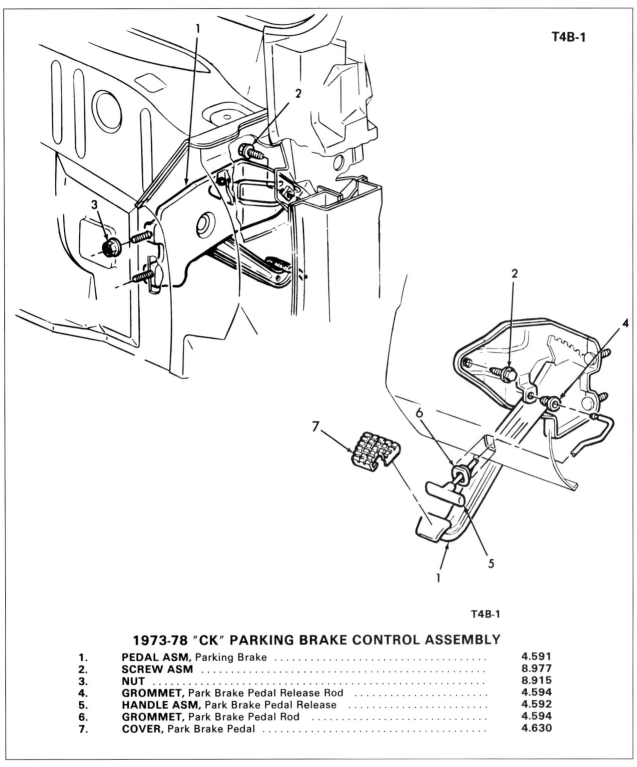

T4B-1

1973-78 "CK" PARKING BRAKE CONTROL ASSEMBLY

1.	**PEDAL ASM,** Parking Brake	4.591
2.	**SCREW ASM**	8.977
3.	**NUT**	8.915
4.	**GROMMET,** Park Brake Pedal Release Rod	4.594
5.	**HANDLE ASM,** Park Brake Pedal Release	4.592
6.	**GROMMET,** Park Brake Pedal Rod	4.594
7.	**COVER,** Park Brake Pedal	4.630

The 1973–1978 parking brake assembly.

C-20

    rear

        except Crewcab 18

        Crewcab 20

C-30

    without 11,000-pound axle

        single rear wheels 20

        dual rear wheels .22

    with 11,000-pound axle 10

1974–1978

C-10

    front disc standard

        two-wheel drive with 2-inch drums 14

        two-wheel drive with 2 3/4-inch brake 23

        four-wheel drive 24

C-20

    rear

        11-inch drum 18

        13-inch drum 25

C-30, without 11,000-pound axle

    single rear wheels

        2.5-inch drums 25

        3.5-inch drums 26

    dual rear wheels

        2.5-inch drums 22

        3.5-inch drums 27

C-30 with 11,000-pound axle 10

Interchanges

Interchange Number: 1

    Part Number(s): 3846271

    Location: Front or rear

    Usage: 1964–1970 C-10 Chevrolet and 1500 GMC truck two-wheel drive; 1969–1970 Blazer two-wheel drive; 1967–1970 C-10 Chevrolet and 1500 GMC four-wheel-drive truck rear drums only

Interchange Number: 2

    Part Number(s): 2459604

    Location: Front

    Usage: 1964–1970 C-10 Chevrolet and 1500 GMC four-wheel-drive truck; 1969–1970 Blazer four-wheel drive

Interchange Number: 3

    Part Number(s): 3846354

    Location: Front or rear

    Usage: 1964–1970 C-20 to C-30 Chevrolet and 2500 to 3500 GMC two-wheel-drive truck; 1964–1970 C-20 to C-30 Chevrolet and GMC 2500 truck with dual rear wheels and coil suspension only—rear drums only

Interchange Number: 4

    Part Number(s): 2459622

    Location: Front

    Usage: 1964–1969 C-20 Chevrolet and 2500 GMC four-wheel-drive truck

Interchange Number: 5

    Part Number(s): 3857752

    Location: Rear

    Usage: 1964–1970 C-20 Chevrolet and 2500 GMC truck (except with four-wheel drive or dual rear wheels) with coil-spring suspension only

Interchange Number: 6

    Part Number(s): 2458493

    Location: Rear

    Usage: 1965–1970 C-20 Chevrolet and 2500 GMC two-wheel-drive truck with leaf spring suspension only

Interchange Number: 7

    Part Number(s): 3857752

    Location: Front

    Usage: 1967–1970 C-20 Chevrolet and 2500 GMC four-wheel-drive truck

Interchange Number: 8

    Part Number(s): 3831784

    Location: Rear

    Usage: 1963–1973 C-30 Chevrolet and 3500 GMC truck without dual rear wheels or 11,000-pound axle

Interchange Number: 9

    Part Number(s): 3998352

    Location: Rear

    Usage: 1960–1970 C-30 Chevrolet and 3500 GMC truck with dual rear wheels, without 11,000-pound axle

Interchange Number: 10

    Part Number(s): 3996643

    Location: Rear

    Usage: 1956–1974 C-30 Chevrolet and 3500 GMC truck with 11,000-pound axle

Interchange Number: 11

    Part Number(s): 3964550

    Location: Front

    Usage: 1968–1970 C-10 Chevrolet and 1500 GMC truck with 11 1/8x2 3/4-inch brake drums; 1970–1971 G-20 Chevrolet and 2500 GMC van

Interchange Number: 12

    Part Number(s): 3754300

    Location: Rear

    Usage: 1959–1970 C-20 Chevrolet and 2500 GMC four-wheel-drive truck

Interchange Number: 13

    Part Number(s): 3982204

    Location: Front

    Usage: 1970 C-20 Chevrolet and 2500 GMC four-wheel-drive truck

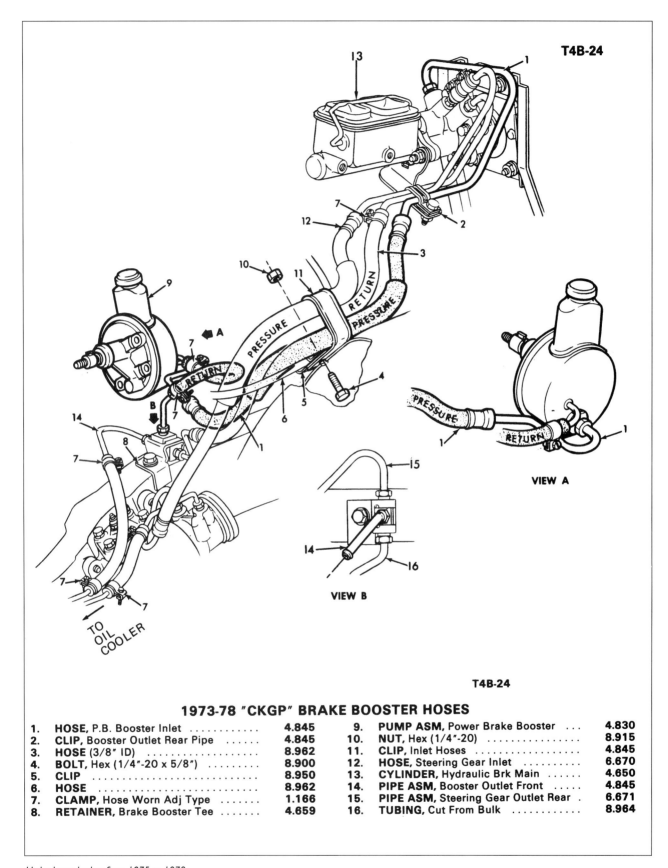

T4B-24

1973-78 "CKGP" BRAKE BOOSTER HOSES

1.	HOSE, P.B. Booster Inlet	4.845	9.	PUMP ASM, Power Brake Booster ...	4.830
2.	CLIP, Booster Outlet Rear Pipe	4.845	10.	NUT, Hex (1/4"-20)	8.915
3.	HOSE (3/8" ID)	8.962	11.	CLIP, Inlet Hoses	4.845
4.	BOLT, Hex (1/4"-20 x 5/8")	8.900	12.	HOSE, Steering Gear Inlet	6.670
5.	CLIP	8.950	13.	CYLINDER, Hydraulic Brk Main	4.650
6.	HOSE	8.962	14.	PIPE ASM, Booster Outlet Front	4.845
7.	CLAMP, Hose Worn Adj Type	1.166	15.	PIPE ASM, Steering Gear Outlet Rear .	6.671
8.	RETAINER, Brake Booster Tee	4.659	16.	TUBING, Cut From Bulk	8.964

Hydro boost brakes from 1975 to 1978.

Interchange Number: 14
Part Number(s): 3989542
Location: Rear
Usage: 1971–1974 C-10 Chevrolet and 1500 GMC truck, Blazer, and Jimmy two-wheel-drive models

Interchange Number: 15
Part Number(s): 3989543
Location: Rear
Usage: 1971–1973 C-10 Chevrolet and 1500 GMC truck, Blazer, Jimmy four-wheel drive

Interchange Number: 16
Part Number(s): 3995772
Location: Rear
Usage: 1971–1972 C-20 Chevrolet and 2500 GMC two-wheel-drive truck with removable carrier
Note(s): Nonfinned brake drums

Interchange Number: 17
Part Number(s): 39955887
Location: Rear
Usage: 1971–1972 C-20 Chevrolet and 2500 GMC two-wheel-drive truck with nonremovable carrier

Interchange Number: 18
Part Number(s): 6260829
Location: Rear
Usage: 1971–1978 C-20 Chevrolet and 2500 GMC two-wheel-drive truck with removable carrier
Note(s): Finned 11-inch brake drums

Interchange Number: 19
Part Number(s): 3996637
Location: Rear
Usage: 1971 C-20 Chevrolet and 2500 GMC four-wheel-drive truck

Interchange Number: 20
Part Number(s): 3996777
Location: Rear
Usage: 1971–1972 C-30 Chevrolet and 3500 GMC truck with single rear wheels, without 11,000-pound axle

Interchange Number: 21
Part Number(s): 3996772
Location: Rear
Usage: 1971–1972 C-30 Chevrolet and 3500 GMC truck with dual rear wheels, without 11,000-pound axle

Interchange Number: 22
Part Number(s): 6258610
Location: Rear
Usage: 1973 C-30 Chevrolet and 3500 GMC truck with dual rear wheels, without 11,000-pound axle

Interchange Number: 23
Part Number(s): 333046
Location: Rear
Usage: 1974–1980 C-10 Chevrolet and 1500 GMC truck with 11x2 3/4-inch rear brake drums; 1974–1980 G-20 Chevrolet and 2500 GMC van

Interchange Number: 24
Part Number(s): 331492
Location: Rear
Usage: 1974–1980 C-10 Chevrolet and 1500 GMC truck, Blazer, and Jimmy four-wheel drive

Interchange Number: 25
Part Number(s): 6260588
Location: Rear
Usage: 1974–1980 C-20 Chevrolet and 2500 GMC truck with 13x2.5-inch rear brake drums; 1974–1980 C-30 Chevrolet and 3500 GMC truck with single rear wheels, without 11,000-pound axle

Interchange Number: 26
Part Number(s): 620830
Location: Rear
Usage: 1974–1980 C-30 Chevrolet and 3500 GMC truck with 3.5-inch rear brake drums and single rear wheels, without 11,000-pound axle

Interchange Number: 27
Part Number(s): 6260831
Location: Rear
Usage: 1974–1980 C-30 Chevrolet and 3500 GMC truck with 3.5-inch rear brake drums and dual rear wheels, without 11,000-pound axle

Disc Brake Rotors
Model Identification

1971–1973   *Interchange Number*

C-10
  except four-wheel drive 1
  four-wheel drive 2
C-20
  except four-wheel drive 3
  four-wheel drive 4
C-30
  without 11,000-pound axle
    single rear wheels 3
    dual rear wheels 5
  with 11,000-pound axle 6

1974–1976

C-10
  except four-wheel drive 1
  four-wheel drive 2
C-20
  except four-wheel drive 3
  four-wheel drive 4

C-30
single rear wheels
1 1/4-inch-thick rotor 3
1.5-inch-thick rotor 7
dual rear wheels 8

1977
C-10
two-wheel drive 1
four-wheel drive
early 2
late 9
C-20
two-wheel drive 3
four-wheel drive
early 4
late 10
C-30
two-wheel drive
single rear wheels 7
dual rear wheels 8
four-wheel drive
single rear wheels 11
dual rear wheels 12

1978
C-10
two-wheel drive 1
four-wheel drive 9
C-20
two-wheel drive 3
four-wheel drive 10
C-30
two-wheel drive
single rear wheels 7
dual rear wheels 8
four-wheel drive
single rear wheels 13
dual rear wheels 14

Interchanges
Interchange Number: 1
Part Number(s): 6274216
Usage: 1971–1981 C-10 Chevrolet and 1500 GMC truck,
Blazer, and Jimmy two-wheel drive only; 1971–1981
G-20 Chevrolet and 2500 GMC van; 1975–1981 G-
10 Chevrolet and 1500 GMC van; 1971–1976 full-
size Buick, Chevrolet, Oldsmobile, and Pontiac
Interchange Number: 2
Part Number(s): 325068
Usage: 1971 to early-1977 C-10 Chevrolet and 1500
GMC truck, Blazer, and Jimmy four-wheel drive only
Note(s): Inner bearings stamped LM6030349 and
LM603011
Interchange Number: 3
Part Number(s): 3990928
Usage: 1971–1978 C-20 Chevrolet and 2500 GMC

two-wheel-drive truck; 1973–1976 C-30 with
single rear wheels
Note(s): Rotor thickness is 1 1/4 inches
Interchange Number: 4
Part Number(s): 3995722
Usage: 1971 to early-1977 C-20 Chevrolet and
2500 GMC four-wheel-drive truck
Note(s): Inner bearing stamped 368A and 362A
Interchange Number: 5
Part Number(s): 338301
Usage: 1971–1973 C-30 Chevrolet and 3500 GMC
truck with dual rear wheels, without 11,000-
pound axle
Interchange Number: 6
Part Number(s): 379821
Usage: 1971–1973 C-30 Chevrolet and 3500 GMC
truck with dual rear wheels, with 11,000-pound
axle
Interchange Number: 7
Part Number(s): 344016
Usage: 1974–1981 C-30 Chevrolet and 3500 GMC
truck with single rear wheels
Note(s): Rotor thickness is 1.5 inches
Interchange Number: 8
Part Number(s): 6260806
Usage: 1974–1981 C-30 Chevrolet and 3500 GMC
truck with dual rear wheels
Interchange Number: 9
Part Number(s): 14008655
Usage: Late-1977 to 1980 C-10 Chevrolet and 1500
GMC truck, Blazer, and Jimmy four-wheel drive
only
Note(s): Inner bearings stamped LM104949 and
JLM104910
Interchange Number: 10
Part Number(s): 14005706
Usage: Late-1977 to 1980 C-20 Chevrolet and 2500
GMC four-wheel-drive truck
Interchange Number: 11
Part Number(s): 462822
Usage: 1977 C-30 Chevrolet and 3500 GMC four-
wheel-drive truck with single rear wheels
Interchange Number: 12
Part Number(s): 462825
Usage: 1977 C-30 Chevrolet and 3500 GMC four-
wheel-drive truck with dual rear wheels
Interchange Number: 13
Part Number(s): 475985
Usage: 1978–1980 C-30 Chevrolet and 3500 GMC
four-wheel-drive truck with single rear wheels
Interchange Number: 14
Part Number(s): 4759896
Usage: 1978–1980 C-30 Chevrolet and 3500 GMC
four-wheel-drive truck with dual rear wheels

Brake Pedals

Transmission type weighs heavily in the interchange of brake pedals. Those with a manual transmission used a smaller pedal than those with an automatic transmission, so they cannot be interchanged. Also those models with power brakes used a different pedal than those models with manual brakes.

Model Identification

1967–1972	Interchange Number
All	
manual brakes	6
power brakes	7

1973–1974	
C-10	
manual brakes	1
power brakes	
manual transmission	2
automatic transmission	3

1975–1978	
C-10	
manual brakes	1
power brakes	
manual transmission	
without Hydro boost	2
with Hydro boost	4
automatic transmission	
without Hydro boost	3
with Hydro boost	5

Interchanges

Interchange Number: 1
Part Number(s): 358478
Usage: 1973–1978 C-10 Chevrolet and 1500 GMC truck with manual brakes

Interchange Number: 2
Part Number(s): 347459
Usage: 1973–1978 C-10 to C-30 Chevrolet and 1500 to 3500 GMC truck, Blazer, and Jimmy with manual transmission and power brakes, without Hydro boost; 1974 C-30 with Hydro boost

Interchange Number: 3
Part Number(s): 347460
Usage: 1973–1978 C-10 to C-30 Chevrolet and 1500 to 3500 GMC truck, Blazer, and Jimmy with automatic transmission and power brakes

Interchange Number: 4
Part Number(s): 347462
Usage: 1975–1978 C-30 Chevrolet and 3500 GMC truck with manual transmission and Hydro boost brakes

Interchange Number: 5
Part Number(s): 347461
Usage: 1975–1978 C-30 Chevrolet and 3500 GMC truck with automatic transmission and Hydro boost brakes

Interchange Number: 6
Part Number(s): 335358
Usage: 1967–1972 C-10 to C-30 Chevrolet and 1500 to 3500 GMC truck with manual brakes

Interchange Number: 7
Part Number(s): 3975292
Usage: 1967–1972 C-10 to C-30 Chevrolet and 1500 to 3500 GMC truck with power brakes

Brake Pedal Covers
Model Identification

1967–1972	Interchange Number
All	1

1973–1974	
Manual transmission	3
Automatic transmission	2

1975–1978	
Manual transmission	3
Automatic transmission	4

Interchanges

Interchange Number: 1
Part Number(s): 39101510
Usage: 1967–1972 C-10 to C-30 Chevrolet and 1500 to 3500 GMC truck; 1969–1972 Blazer; 1970–1972 Jimmy

Interchange Number: 2
Part Number(s): 3988288
Usage: 1973–1974 C-10 to C-30 Chevrolet and 1500 to 3500 GMC truck, Blazer, and Jimmy with automatic transmission and power brakes

Interchange Number: 3
Part Number(s): 3993614
Usage: 1973–1978 C-10 to C-30 Chevrolet and 1500 to 3500 GMC truck, Blazer, and Jimmy with manual transmission and power brakes

Interchange Number: 4
Part Number(s): 25516561
Usage: 1975–1978 C-10 to C-30 Chevrolet and 1500 to 3500 GMC truck, Blazer, and Jimmy with automatic transmission and power brakes

Calipers
Model Identification

1971–1973	Interchange Number
Except four-wheel drive	1
Four-wheel drive	2

1974–1978	
C-10 or C-20	
except four-wheel drive	1
four-wheel drive	3
C-30	
except four-wheel drive or with 1.5-inch-thick rotor	3

with 1.5-inch-thick rotor 4
four-wheel drive 4

Interchanges

Interchange Number: 1
Part Number(s): 18005036 (left); 18005037 (right)
Usage: 1971–1978 C-10 to C-30 Chevrolet and 1500 to 3500 GMC truck, Blazer, and Jimmy with front disc brakes (except four-wheel-drive models, or C-30/3500 models with 1.5-inch-thick rotors); 1971–1976 full-size Chevrolet, Buick, Oldsmobile, and Pontiac

Interchange Number: 2
Part Number(s): 5272481 (left); 5272482 (right)
Usage: 1971–1973 C-10 to C-20 Chevrolet and 1500 to 2500 GMC truck, Blazer, and Jimmy (four-wheel-drive models only); 1969–1970 full-size Pontiac
Note(s): Left-side Interchange Number 3 will fit

Interchange Number: 3
Part Number(s): 18005014 (left); 18005015 (right)
Usage: 1975–1978 C-10 to C-20 Chevrolet and 1500 to 2500 GMC truck, Blazer, and Jimmy four-wheel-drive models with front disc brakes

Interchange Number: 4
Part Number(s): 455779 (left); 455780 (right)
Usage: 1974–1978 C-30 Chevrolet and 3500 GMC truck with 1.5-inch-thick rotors and four-wheel-drive models

Parking Brakes
Model Identification

1967–1968	Interchange Number
All	3
1969–1972	
All	2
1973–1978	
All	1

Interchanges

Interchange Number: 1
Part Number(s): 362280
Usage: 1973–1978 C-10 to C-30 Chevrolet and 1500 to 3500 GMC truck, Blazer, and Jimmy

Interchange Number: 2
Part Number(s): 3907218
Usage: 1960–1968 C-10 to C-30 Chevrolet and 1500 to 3500 GMC truck

Interchange Number: 3
Part Number(s): 357560
Usage: 1969–1972 C-10 to C-30 Chevrolet and 1500 to 3500 GMC truck and Blazer; 1970–1972 Jimmy

Parking Brake Covers
Model Identification

1967–1968	Interchange Number
All	2
1969–1972	
All	1
1973	
All	3
1974	
Early	3
Late	4
1975–1978	
All	4

Interchanges

Interchange Number: 1
Part Number(s): 3948774
Usage: 1969–1972 C-10 to C-30 Chevrolet and 1500 to 3500 GMC truck and Blazer; 1970–1972 Jimmy

Interchange Number: 2
Part Number(s): 3881780
Usage: 1967–1968 C-10 to C-30 Chevrolet and 1500 to 3500 GMC truck

Interchange Number: 3
Part Number(s): 3991165
Usage: 1973 to early-1974 C-10 to C-30 Chevrolet and 1500 to 3500 GMC truck, Blazer, and Jimmy

Interchange Number: 4
Part Number(s): 3948774
Usage: Late-1974–1978 C-10 to C-30 Chevrolet and 1500 to 3500 GMC truck, Blazer, and Jimmy

8 Wheels and Wheel Covers

Wheels

There are many determining factors to consider when interchanging original-equipment-manufacture wheels. Factors affecting the interchange are the diameter and offset. (Offset is the distance the wheel is set back from the brake drum or rotor.) Offset can be measured by noting the distance from the centerline of the rim to the inner side of the wheel. Other factors include the number of mounting lugs. Heavy-duty versions of the Chevrolet truck used 8 and in some cases 10 mounting lugs. Most, however, used 5 mounting lugs.

Model Identification

1967–1970   Interchange Number
15x5.5-inch 2
16x5-inch 16
16x6-inch 20
16.5x6-inch 25

1971–1972
15x6-inch
    two-wheel drive 1
    four-wheel drive 3
16x6-inch 20
16x5.5-inch (dual rear wheels) 21
16.5x6
    single rear wheels .27
    dual rear wheels .33
16.5x6.75-inch 32
16x8.75-inch 29

1973–1974
15x6-inch
    two-wheel drive 1
    four-wheel drive
        1/8-inch offset 4
        1/2-inch offset 3
15x7-inch
    Rally wheels
        two-wheel drive 7
        four-wheel drive 14
15x8-inch
    except Rally wheels 13
    Rally wheels 11
16x5-inch 19
16x5.5-inch (dual rear wheels) 21

16x6-inch
    single rear wheels .20
    dual rear wheels .33
16x6.5-inch 22
16.5x6.75-inch 32
16.5x6-inch 27
16.5x8.25-inch 29

1975–1977
15x6-inch
    two-wheel drive 1
    four-wheel drive 3
15x7-inch
    Rally wheels
        two-wheel drive 7
        four-wheel drive 14
    steel spoke wheels 8
15x8-inch
    except Rally wheels 13
    Rally wheels 11
    steel spoke wheels
        five bolts 10
16x5-inch 19
16.5x6-inch (dual rear wheels) 33
16.5x6.74-inch 32
16.5x6-inch 27
16.5x8.25-inch 29

1978
15x6-inch
    two-wheel drive 1
    four-wheel drive 3
15x7-inch
    Rally wheels
        two-wheel drive 15
    steel spoke wheels 8
    aluminum wheels .5
15x8-inch
    Rally wheels 11
    steel spoke wheels
        five bolts 10
        six bolts 12
16x5-inch
    two-wheel drive 19
    four-wheel drive .18

Interchanges

15-INCH WHEELS

Interchange Number: 1
Size: 15x6-inch
Bolt Pattern: 5-5
Usage: 1971–1981 C-10 Chevrolet and 1500 GMC truck, Blazer, and Jimmy (two-wheel-drive models only); 1971 G-20 Chevrolet and 2500 GMC van; 1969–1976 Delta 88, Impala, and LeSabre without Rally wheels

Interchange Number: 2
Size: 15x5.5-inch
Bolt Pattern: 6-5.5
Usage: 1961–1970 C-10 Chevrolet and 1500 GMC truck; 1969–1970 Blazer; 1970 Jimmy; 1967–1970 G-20 Chevrolet and 2500 GMC van

Interchange Number: 3
Size: 15x6-inch
Bolt Pattern: 6-5.5
Usage: 1971–1981 C-10 Chevrolet and 1500 GMC truck, Blazer, and Jimmy four-wheel-drive models only
Note(s): Has 0.5-inch offset

Interchange Number: 4
Part Number(s): 333278
Size: 15x6-inch
Bolt Pattern: 6-5.5
Usage: 1973–1974 C-10 Chevrolet and 1500 GMC truck, Blazer, and Jimmy—four-wheel-drive models only
Note(s): Has 1/8-inch offset

Interchange Number: 5
Size: 15x7-inch
Bolt Pattern: 5-5
Usage: 1978–1981 C-10 Chevrolet and 1500 GMC truck, Blazer, and Jimmy—two-wheel-drive models only, with aluminum wheels

Interchange Number: 6
Part Number(s): 140005732
Size: 15x7-inch
Bolt Pattern: 5-5
Usage: 1978–1981 C-10 Chevrolet and 1500 GMC truck, Blazer, and Jimmy—two-wheel-drive models only, with Rally wheels

Interchange Number: 7
Part Number(s): 341454
Size: 15x7-inch

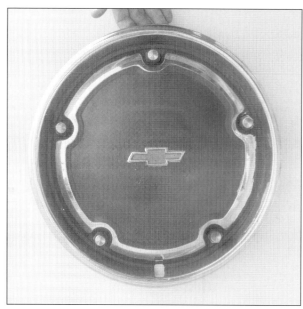

A 1969–1970–style wheel cover. Very few survived.

Bolt Pattern: 5-5
Usage: 1974–1977 C-10 Chevrolet and 1500 GMC truck, Blazer, and Jimmy—two-wheel-drive models only, with Rally wheels

Interchange Number: 8
Part Number(s): 457710
Size: 15x7-inch
Bolt Pattern: 5-5
Usage: 1977–1981 C-10 Chevrolet and 1500 GMC truck, Blazer, and Jimmy—two-wheel-drive models only, with steel spoke wheels
Note(s): Stamped CR and CU

Interchange Number: 9
Part Number(s): 140005736
Size: 15x8-inch
Bolt Pattern: 5-5
Usage: 1977–1981 C-10 Chevrolet and 1500 GMC truck, Blazer, and Jimmy—two-wheel-drive models only, with Rally wheels
Note(s): Stamped CW or DS

Interchange Number: 10
Part Number(s): 462384
Size: 15x8-inch
Bolt Pattern: 5-5
Usage: 1977–1981 C-10 Chevrolet and 1500 GMC truck, Blazer, and Jimmy—two-wheel-drive models only, with steel spoke wheels

Interchange Number: 11
Part Number(s): 14005738
Size: 15x8-inch
Bolt Pattern: 6-5.5
Usage: 1974–1981 C-10 Chevrolet and 1500 GMC truck, Blazer, and Jimmy—four-wheel-drive models only, with Rally wheels

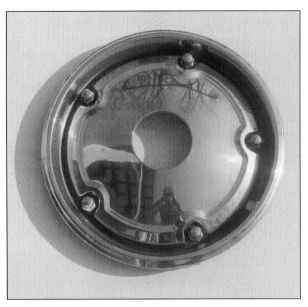

Four-wheel-drive models used a special front cover with a center opening.

Interchange Number: 12
> Part Number(s): 475967
> Size: 15x8-inch
> Bolt Pattern: 6-5.5
> Usage: 1978–1981 C-10 Chevrolet and 1500 GMC truck, Blazer, and Jimmy—two-wheel-drive models only, with steel spoke wheels

Interchange Number: 13
> Part Number(s): 341506
> Size: 15x8-inch
> Bolt Pattern: 6-5.5
> Usage: 1974–1976 C-10 Chevrolet and 1500 GMC truck, Blazer, and Jimmy—two-wheel-drive models only, without steel spoke or Rally wheels

Interchange Number: 14
> Part Number(s): 359720
> Size: 15x7-inch
> Bolt Pattern: 6-5.5
> Usage: 1974–1976 C-10 Chevrolet and 1500 GMC truck, Blazer, and Jimmy—four-wheel-drive models only, with Rally wheels
> Note(s): Stamped DS or BT

Interchange Number: 15
> Part Number(s): 140005732
> Size: 15x7-inch
> Bolt Pattern: 5-5
> Usage: 1978–1981 C-10 Chevrolet and 1500 GMC truck, Blazer, and Jimmy—two-wheel-drive models only, with Rally wheels

16-INCH WHEELS

Interchange Number: 16
> Part Number(s): 3974200
> Size: 16x5-inch
> Bolt Pattern: 6-5.5
> Usage: 1964–1970 C-10 Chevrolet and 1500 GMC truck; 1969–1970 Blazer; 1970 Jimmy

Interchange Number: 17
> Part Number(s): 341503
> Size: 16x5-inch
> Bolt Pattern: 6-5.5
> Usage: 1971–1977 C-10 Chevrolet and 1500 GMC truck, Blazer, and Jimmy—four-wheel-drive models only

Interchange Number: 18
> Part Number(s): 140054740
> Size: 16x5-inch
> Bolt Pattern: 6-5.5
> Usage: 1978–1980 C-10 Chevrolet and 1500 GMC truck, Blazer, and Jimmy—four-wheel-drive models only

Interchange Number: 19
> Part Number(s): 467154
> Size: 16x5-inch
> Bolt Pattern: 5-5
> Usage: 1971–1979 C-10 Chevrolet and 1500 GMC truck, Blazer, and Jimmy—two-wheel-drive models only

Interchange Number: 20
> Part Number(s): 335610
> Size: 16x6-inch
> Bolt Pattern: 8-6.5
> Usage: 1969–1974 C-20 to C-30 Chevrolet and 2500 to 3500 GMC truck (except with dual rear wheels)

Interchange Number: 21
> Part Number(s): 335648
> Size: 16x5.5-inch
> Bolt Pattern: 8-6.5
> Usage: 1971–1974 C-30 Chevrolet and 3500 GMC truck with dual rear wheels
> Note(s): Two-piece wheel

Interchange Number: 22
> Part Number(s): 329374
> Size: 16x6.5-inch
> Bolt Pattern: 8-6.5
> Usage: Late-1974–1977 C-20 to C-30 Chevrolet and 2500 to 3500 GMC truck (except with dual rear wheels)

Interchange Number: 23
> Part Number(s): 14005742
> Size: 16x6.5-inch
> Bolt Pattern: 8-6.5

A 1973 wheel cover.

Usage: 1978–1980 C-20 to C-30 Chevrolet and 2500 to 3500 GMC truck (except with dual rear wheels)

Interchange Number: 24
Part Number(s): 14005764
Size: 16x6-inch
Bolt Pattern: 8-6.5
Usage: 1976–1980 C-30 Chevrolet and 3500 GMC truck with dual rear wheels

16 1/2-INCH WHEELS

Interchange Number: 25
Part Number(s): 3887746
Size: 16.5x6-inch
Bolt Pattern: 6-5.5
Usage: 1967–1970 C-10 Chevrolet and 1500 GMC truck

Interchange Number: 26
Part Number(s): 3998539
Size: 16.5x8.25-inch
Bolt Pattern: 6-5.5
Usage: 1969–1974 C-10 Chevrolet and 1500 GMC truck—four-wheel-drive models only

Interchange Number: 27
Part Number(s): 359526
Size: 16.5x6-inch
Bolt Pattern: 8-6.5
Usage: 1971–1977 C-20 to C-30 Chevrolet and 2500 to 3500 GMC truck (except with dual rear wheels)

Interchange Number: 28
Part Number(s): 14005748
Size: 16.5x6-inch
Bolt Pattern: 8-6.5
Usage: 1978–1981 C-20 to C-30 Chevrolet and 2500 to 3500 GMC truck (except with dual rear wheels)

Interchange Number: 29
Part Number(s): 335616
Size: 16.5x8.25-inch
Bolt Pattern: 8-6.5
Usage: 1971–1977 C-20 to C-30 Chevrolet and 2500 to 3500 GMC truck (except with dual rear wheels)

Interchange Number: 30
Part Number(s): 14005744
Size: 16.5x8.24-inch
Bolt Pattern: 8-6.5
Usage: 1978–1979 C-20 to C-30 Chevrolet and 2500 to 3500 GMC truck (except with dual rear wheels)
Note(s): Stamped BH

Interchange Number: 31
Part Number(s): 3887746
Size: 16.5x6-inch
Bolt Pattern: 6-5.5
Usage: 1967–1970 C-10 Chevrolet and 1500 GMC truck

Interchange Number: 32
Part Number(s): 14032423
Size: 16.5x6.75-inch
Bolt Pattern: 8-6.5
Usage: 1971–1981 C-20 to C-30 Chevrolet and 2500 to 3500 GMC truck (except with dual rear wheels)

Interchange Number: 33
Part Number(s): 359402
Size: 16.5x6-inch
Bolt Pattern: 8-6.5
Usage: 1971–1977 C-30 Chevrolet and 3500 GMC truck with dual rear wheels

Interchange Number: 34
Part Number(s): 140005762
Size: 16.5x6-inch
Bolt Pattern: 8-6.5
Usage: 1978 to early-1980 C-30 Chevrolet and 3500 GMC truck with dual rear wheels

Hubcaps for Styled Wheels

The hubcaps listed in this interchange are not the standard dog-dish–style caps, which are not attractive on a show truck, nor are they a popular choice among Chevrolet truck owners today, so they are not included. Instead, the interchange information here is for the styled wheels, commonly known as "Rally" wheels.

Model Identification

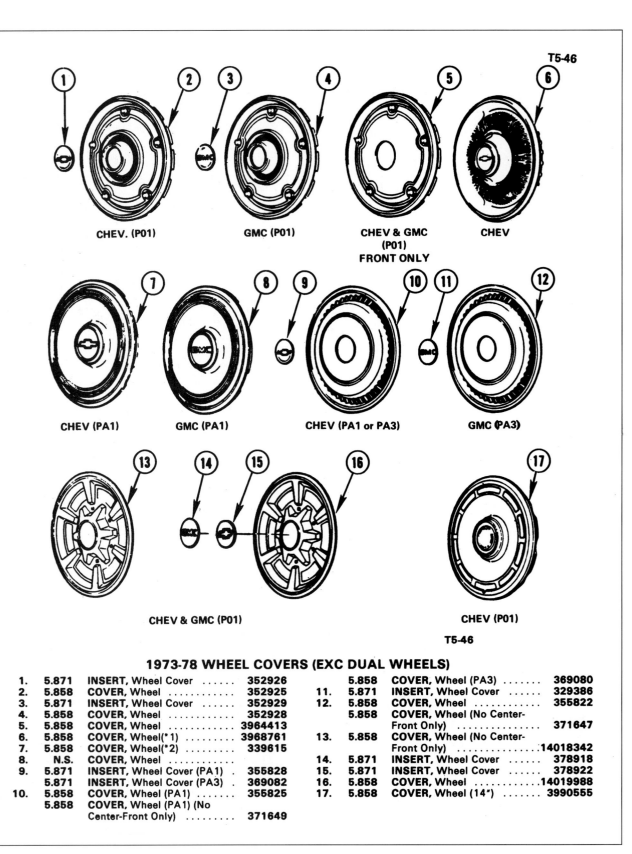

T5-46

CHEV. (P01)

GMC (P01)

CHEV & GMC
(P01)
FRONT ONLY

CHEV

CHEV (PA1)

GMC (PA1)

CHEV (PA1 or PA3)

GMC (PA3)

CHEV & GMC (P01)

CHEV (P01)

T5-46

1973-78 WHEEL COVERS (EXC DUAL WHEELS)

1.	5.871	INSERT, Wheel Cover	......	352926		5.858	COVER, Wheel (PA3)	369080
2.	5.858	COVER, Wheel	....	352925	11.	5.871	INSERT, Wheel Cover	329386
3.	5.871	INSERT, Wheel Cover	......	352929	12.	5.858	COVER, Wheel	355822
4.	5.858	COVER, Wheel	....	352928		5.858	COVER, Wheel (No Center-	
5.	5.858	COVER, Wheel	....	3964413			Front Only)	371647
6.	5.858	COVER, Wheel(*1)	....	3968761	13.	5.858	COVER, Wheel (No Center-	
7.	5.858	COVER, Wheel(*2)	....	339615			Front Only) 14018342
8.	N.S.	COVER, Wheel	....		14.	5.871	INSERT, Wheel Cover	378918
9.	5.871	INSERT, Wheel Cover (PA1)	.	355828	15.	5.871	INSERT, Wheel Cover	378922
	5.871	INSERT, Wheel Cover (PA3)	.	369082	16.	5.858	COVER, Wheel 14019988
10.	5.858	COVER, Wheel (PA1)	....	355825	17.	5.858	COVER, Wheel (14")	3990555
	5.858	COVER, Wheel (PA1) (No						
		Center-Front Only)	....	371649				

Wheel covers from 1973 to 1978.

1975–1976
Rally

    except four-wheel drive 3

    four-wheel drive

        front 5

        rear 4

1977
Rally

    except four-wheel drive

        early 3

        late 8

    four-wheel drive

        front 5

        rear 4

1978
Rally

    except four-wheel drive 8

    four-wheel drive

        front 6

        rear 7

Interchanges

Interchange Number: 1
Part Number(s): 341430

Description: Center cap for Rally wheels

Diameter: All

Usage: 1974 Chevrolet truck and G-20 Chevrolet van

Note(s): Has center insert with bow-tie symbol; GMC unit is similar but will not interchange; two-wheel-drive models only

Interchange Number: 2
Part Number(s): 341435

Description: Center cap for Rally wheels

Diameter: All

Usage: 1974 Chevrolet four-wheel-drive truck and Blazer

Note(s): Has center insert with bow-tie symbol on rear caps; GMC unit is similar but will not interchange; four-wheel-drive models only

Interchange Number: 3
Part Number(s): 359758

Description: Center cap for Rally wheels

Diameter: All

Usage: 1975 to early-1977 Chevrolet truck and G-20 Chevrolet van

Note(s): Has center insert with bow-tie symbol; GMC unit is similar but will not interchange; two-wheel-drive models only

Interchange Number: 4
Part Number(s): 371667

Description: Center cap for Rally wheels

Diameter: All

Usage: 1975–1977 Chevrolet C-10 four-wheel-drive truck and Blazer

Note(s): Has center insert with bow-tie symbol for rear wheels only; GMC unit is similar but will not interchange; four-wheel-drive models only

Interchange Number: 5
Part Number(s): 371669

Description: Center cap for Rally wheels

Diameter: All

Usage: 1975–1977 Chevrolet C-10 four-wheel-drive truck and Blazer; 1976–1977 1500 GMC four-wheel-drive Jimmy

Note(s): Has center insert with bow-tie symbol on front wheels only

Interchange Number: 6
Part Number(s): 474303

Description: Center cap for Rally wheels

Diameter: All

Usage: 1978 Chevrolet C-10 four-wheel-drive truck and Blazer; 1978 1500 GMC four-wheel drive and Jimmy

Note(s): Has center insert with bow-tie symbol on rear wheels only

Interchange Number: 7
Part Number(s): 14018276

Description: Center cap for Rally wheels

Diameter: All

Usage: Late-1977 to 1978 Chevrolet C-10 to C-20 truck—two-wheel-drive only

Note(s): Second design has three through mounting holes and is countersunk for plastic retainer attachment

Interchange Number: 8
Part Number(s): 14018276

Description: Center cap for Rally wheels

Diameter: All

Usage: Late-1977 to 1978 Chevrolet C-10 to C-20 truck—two-wheel-drive only

Interchange Number: 9
Part Number(s): N/A

Description: Center cap for Rally wheels

Diameter: All

Usage: 1970–1972 Chevrolet C-10 to C-20 truck—two-wheel drive only

Wheel Covers

Wheel covers should not be confused with hubcaps. Wheel covers are the full discs that were optional. For the most part, wheel covers were rarely ordered on Chevrolet trucks. Most trucks were built with the standard dog-dish–style hubcaps. This is due to the fact that most trucks were ordered as work vehicles. A truck that made its rounds around the farm and occasionally into town to pick up feed for the cows really did not need fancy wheel covers. Note that the diameter refers to the wheel size the cover fits, not the size of the cover.

Model Identification

Interchanges

Interchange Number: 1

Part Number(s): 352925

Description: Raised center dome with bow-tie logo insert in center, highlighted with five simulated lugs

Diameter: All

Usage: 1973–1976 C-10 to C-30 Chevrolet trucks and Blazer; 1975 G-20 Chevrolet van

Note(s): GMC cover is similar but will not correctly interchange

Interchange Number: 2

Part Number(s): 3964413

Description: Same as Interchange Number 1, but Number 2 has no center insert

Diameter: All

Usage: 1973–1976 C-10 to C-30 Chevrolet truck and Blazer—four-wheel-drive models only, and used only on front wheels of models with part-time transfer case

Interchange Number: 3

Part Number(s): 3968761

Description: Raised center dome with bow-tie logo in center, highlighted with simulated wire ribs

Diameter: All [see Note(s)]

Usage: 1974 C-10 to C-30 Chevrolet truck and Blazer; 1974 Impala

Note(s): Used on some 1974 models

Interchange Number: 4

Part Number(s): 14019988

Description: Simulated spoke wheel with simulated center spinner, with bow-tie logo [see Note(s)]

Diameter: All

Usage: 1977–1978 C-10 to C-30 Chevrolet truck and Blazer; 1500 to 3500 GMC truck and Jimmy

Note(s): GMC cover is the same and interchangeable if inserts are changed

Interchange Number: 5

Part Number(s): 140118342

Description: Simulated spoke wheel with simulated center spinner, with no insert in center [see Note(s)]

Diameter: All with Deluxe cover

Usage: 1977–1978 C-10 to C-30 Chevrolet truck and Blazer; 1500 to 3500 GMC truck and Jimmy—four-wheel-drive models with part-time transfer case only

Note(s): GMC cover is the same and interchangeable if inserts are changed; Interchange Number 4 without the insert will not fit, due to a smaller center hole

Interchange Number: 6

Part Number(s): 371680

Description: Large center dome, highlighted in the center with bow logo insert and on the outer edge by multiple ribs

Diameter: All except with Deluxe cover

Usage: 1977–1978 C-10 to C-30 Chevrolet truck and Blazer; 1500 to 3500 GMC truck and Jimmy—two-wheel-drive models only

Interchange Number: 7

Part Number(s): 371649

Description: Large center dome, highlighted in the center with opening for transfer case and on the outer edge by multiple ribs

Diameter: All except with Deluxe cover

Usage: 1977–1978 C-10 to C-30 Chevrolet truck and Blazer; 1500 to 3500 GMC truck and Jimmy—four-wheel-drive models only

Note(s): Interchange Number 6 without center insert will not fit, due to its smaller center hole

Interchange Number: 8

Part Number(s): 339615

Description: Center dome, highlighted in the center with bow with no removable bow-tie logo

Diameter: All

Usage: 1977 C-10 to C-30 Chevrolet truck and Blazer; 1500 to 3500 GMC truck and Jimmy—two-wheel-drive models only

Interchange Number: 9

Part Number(s): N/A

Description: Large center dome painted dark gray with red bow-tie symbol and five simulated lug nuts

Diameter: 15

Usage: Early-1967 C-10 to C-30 Chevrolet truck

Interchange Number: 10

Part Number(s): 3945076

Description: Large center dome painted flat black with red bow-tie symbol and five simulated lug nuts

Diameter: 15

Usage: Late-1967–1972 C-10 to C-30 Chevrolet truck; 1969–1972 Blazer

Note(s): On two-wheel-drive models, used on all four wheels; On four-wheel-drive models, used on rear wheels only

Interchange Number: 11

Part Number(s): 3964413

Description: Large center dome painted flat black with open slot in the center and five simulated lug nuts

Diameter: 15

Usage: Late-1967 to 1972 C-10 to C-30 Chevrolet truck; 1969–1972 Blazer—four-wheel-drive models only

Note(s): Fronts only

Electrical Systems

Starters
Model Identification

1967–1968   *Interchange Number*
Three-speed manual transmission 1
Four-speed manual 3
Powerglide 1
Turbo-Hydra-Matic 2

1969–1971
307-ci V-8
    manual transmission 1
    automatic transmission
        standard-duty 4
        heavy-duty 5
        Turbo-Hydra-Matic 2
350-ci V-8
    manual 1
    Powerglide 1
    Turbo-Hydra-Matic 2
    heavy-duty 3
396ci V-8 1

1972
307-ci V-8
    manual transmission 1
    automatic transmission
C-10 and C-20 4
C-30 5
350-ci V-8
    manual 1
    Turbo-Hydra-Matic 3
396ci V-8 1

1973–1978
305-ci V-8 3
350-ci V-8 3
454-ci V-8 3

Interchanges
Interchange Number: 1
    Part Number(s): 1108429
    ID Number(s): 1108429, 1108427, 1108430,
        1108480, 1108502, 1108778, 1108779,
        1108780, 1108781, 1108782, 11088784,
        1108796, 1108798, 1109036, 1107233,
        1107273, 1107274, 1107286, 1107497,
        1107664, 1107712, 1107889, 1107891,
        1108360, 1108368, 1108372, or 1108386

Usage: 1967–1972 C-10 to C-30 Chevrolet truck with V-8 engine and three-speed manual or Powerglide automatic transmission; 1960–1961 Impala with 348-ci V-8 high-performance and super-high-performance, all transmissions except Turboglide; 1961–1963 Impala with 409-ci V-8; 1962–1963 Impala with 327-ci V-8; 1968–1972 C-10 to C-30 Chevrolet and 1500 to 3500 GMC truck with 396-ci V-8; 1973–1974 C-50 Chevrolet and 5500 GMC truck with 250-ci six-cylinder or 350-ci V-8 and manual transmission; 1969–1972 C-10 to C-30 Chevrolet and 1500 to 3500 GMC with 396-ci V-8

Interchange Number: 2
    Part Number(s): 1108400
    ID Number(s): 1108400, 1108520, 1107289,
        1107342, 1107365, 1107660, 1107687,
        1107694, 1107890, 1108338, 1108382,
        1108775, 1108788, 1109059, or 1109074
    Usage: 1967–1969 C-10 to C-30 Chevrolet and 1500 to 3500 GMC with V-8 and Turbo-Hydra-Matic automatic transmission; 1970–1971 C-10 to C-30 Chevrolet truck and Blazer and 1500 to 3500 GMC truck and Jimmy with 350-ci V-8 and Turbo-Hydra-Matic automatic transmission; 1970–1974 G-10 to G-30 and 1500 to 3500 GMC van with V-8 and manual transmission, without heavy-duty starter; 1965–1968 Impala with V-8 and Turbo-Hydra-Matic automatic transmission; 1970–1972 Impala with manual transmission; 1970–1978 Camaro, Chevelle, Monte Carlo, and Nova with V-8 engine and manual transmission; 1979–1980 Camaro and Firebird with 305-ci V-8 and manual transmission; 1977–1979 Omega, Phoenix, and Ventura II with 305- or 350-ci V-8 and manual transmission
    Note(s): 1979–1980 non-Chevrolet models with 350-ci V-8 and "L" code engine only

Interchange Number: 3
    Part Number(s): 1108485
    ID Number(s): 1108485, 1108785, 1108362, 1107895, or 1107686

Usage: 1967–1970 C-10 to C-30 Chevrolet and 1500 to 3500 GMC with four- or five-speed manual transmission; 1969–1970 Blazer with 350-ci V-8 and four-speed manual transmission; 1971–1972 C-50 to C-60 Chevrolet and 5500 to 6500 GMC with manual transmission; 1969 C-10 to C-30 Chevrolet and 1500 to 3500 GMC with 350-ci V-8; 1972 C-10 to C-30 Chevrolet and 1500 to 3500 GMC with 350-ci V-8 and automatic transmission; 1973–1980 C-10 to C-30 Chevrolet and 1500 to 3500 GMC truck, Blazer, and Jimmy with 305-, 350-, or 454-ci V-8

Note(s): Interchange is 1976 and later models. It will fit earlier models, but not the other way around. Interchange Number 1 will fit if the drive housing is changed

Interchange Number: 4

Part Number(s): 1109597

ID Number(s): 1107236, 1107237, 1107247, 1107248, 1107259, 1107260, 1107374, 1107399, 1107400, 1107496, 1108366, 1108367, 1108479, 1108512, 1108774, or 1108790

Usage: 1967–1974 C-10 to C-30 Chevrolet and 1500 to 3500 GMC with 250-ci six-cylinder and Powerglide transmission; 1970–1972 C-10 to C-30 with 307-ci V-8 and automatic transmission; 1970–1974 G-10 to G-30 and 1500 to 3500 GMC van with 307-ci V-8 and automatic transmission; 1967–1969 Camaro 302-ci V-8; 1967–1974 Camaro with six-cylinder and manual transmission; 1969–1974 Camaro, Chevelle, Impala, and Nova with 307-ci V-8; 1970–1972 Blazer with 307-ci V-8 and automatic transmission; 1964–1967 Chevelle, Impala, and Nova with 283-ci V-8; 1968–1971 Skylark with six-cylinder

Interchange Number: 5

Part Number(s): 1108363

ID Number(s): 1107370 or 1108363

Usage: 1967–1970 C-10 to C-30 Chevrolet and 1500 to 3500 GMC with heavy-duty starter

Distributor

The unit described here is the bare distributor housing without cap, points, rotor, condenser (where applicable), or vacuum control. Engine size, output, and in some cases transmission and emission controls will have an effect on the distributor interchange.

Identification numbers are stamped on the distributor housing itself, and can be used to identify the assembly. The interchange is based on the replacement part number. This was done in order to provide for a larger interchange base.

Starters are stamped with their part number on the body or as a tag, as shown here.

Model Identification

	Interchange Number
1967	
283-ci V-8	
without AIR	1
with AIR	3
327-ci V-8	
two-barrel	4
four-barrel	5
1968	
307-ci	6
327-ci V-8	
two-barrel	4
four-barrel	
manual transmission	7
automatic	8
396-ci V-8	9
1969	
307-ci	6
350-ci V-8	
two-barrel	10
four-barrel and manual transmission	
early	11
late	12
four-barrel and automatic transmission	
early	13
late	14
396-ci V-8	2
1970	
307-ci	
manual transmission	6
automatic transmission	15
350-ci V-8	
manual transmission	2
automatic transmission	13
396-ci V-8	2
1971	
307-ci	
manual transmission	6
automatic transmission	15

The ID number is stamped on the distributor body. Part number 1111500 is for a 1969–1970 396-ci truck.

Alternators are stamped with two lines of information. The top line contains the part number and output. The lower line is the build date. This unit is a 1970 61-amp unit. The build date has little use in the interchange.

except Blazer, with heavy-duty chassis 39
Blazer 39
350-ci V-8 with four-barrel and manual transmission, without heavy-duty chassis without California
emissions 47
  with California emissions 48
350-ci V-8 with four-barrel and automatic transmission, without heavy-duty chassis
  C-10
    two-wheel drive 47
    four-wheel drive 46
  C-20
    without California emissions 47
    with California emissions 46
  C-30
    without California emissions 47
    with California emissions 47
350-ci V-8 with heavy-duty chassis
  without California emissions 41
  with California emissions 33
400-ci V-8
  without heavy-duty chassis
    without California emissions 43
    with California emissions 49
  with heavy-duty chassis
    without California emissions 41
    with California emissions 44
454-ci V-8
  without California emissions 37
  with California emissions 36

Interchanges

Interchange Number: 1
Part Number(s): 1111150
ID Number(s): 1111150
Usage: 1966–1967 C-10 to C-30 Chevrolet and 1500 to 3500 GMC; 1966–1967 Chevelle, Impala, and Chevy II with 283-ci V-8, without AIR emissions—all transmissions
Note(s): Interchange Number 2 will fit

Interchange Number: 2
Part Number(s): 1111500
ID Number(s): 1111500
Usage: 1969–1970 C-10 to C-30 Chevrolet and 1500 to 3500 GMC with 396-ci V-8; 1970 to early-1971 C-10 to C-30 Chevrolet and G-10 to G-30 Chevrolet and 1500 to 3500 GMC truck and van, Blazer, and Jimmy with 350-ci, four-barrel V-8 and manual transmission

Interchange Number: 3
Part Number(s): 1111114
ID Number(s): 1111114
Usage: 1967 C-10 to C-30 Chevrolet and 1500 to 3500 GMC with 283-ci V-8 and AIR emissions—all transmissions

Interchange Number: 4
Part Number(s): 1112795
ID Number(s): 1112795
Usage: 1965–1967 C-10 to C-30 Chevrolet and 1500 to 3500 GMC with 327-ci, two-barrel V-8

Interchange Number: 5
Part Number(s): 1111249
ID Number(s): 1111249
Usage: 1965–1967 C-10 to C-30 Chevrolet and 1500 to 3500 GMC, Chevelle, Chevy II, and Impala with 327-ci, four-barrel V-8, without AIR emissions; 1967 Camaro 327-ci, four-barrel V-8—all transmissions

Interchange Number: 6
Part Number(s): 1111995
ID Number(s): 1111995
Usage: 1968–1969 C-10 to C-30 Chevrolet and 1500 to 3500 GMC truck, Camaro, Chevelle, Blazer, Impala, Jimmy, and Nova with 307-ci V-8, all transmissions; 1970 C-10 to C-30 Chevrolet and 1500 to 3500 GMC truck, Blazer, Camaro, Chevelle, Jimmy, Impala, and Nova with 307-ci V-8 and manual transmission

Interchange Number: 7
Part Number(s): 1111298
ID Number(s): 1111298
Usage: 1968 C-10 to C-30 Chevrolet and 1500 to 3500 GMC truck, Chevelle, Camaro, and Nova with 327-ci, four-barrel V-8 and manual transmission

Interchange Number: 8
Part Number(s): 1111297
ID Number(s): 1111297
Usage: 1968 C-10 to C-30 Chevrolet and 1500 to 3500 GMC truck, Chevelle, Camaro, and Nova with 327-ci, four-barrel V-8 and automatic transmission

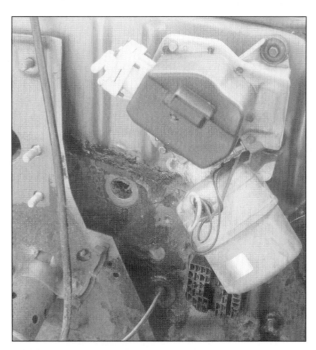
A 1973–1978 wiper motor.

Interchange Number: 9
Part Number(s): 1111147
ID Number(s): 1111109, 1111169, or 1111147
Usage: 1968 C-10 to C-30 Chevrolet and 1500 to 3500 GMC truck with 396-ci V-8; 1966–1968 Chevelle, Camaro, and Impala with 396-ci V-8 (except special-high-performance); 1968 Nova with 396-ci V-8 (except 375-horsepower version)—all transmissions

Interchange Number: 10
Part Number(s): 1111495
ID Number(s): 1111495
Usage: 1969–1970 C-10 to C-40 Chevrolet and 1500 to 4500 GMC (except tilt cabs) with 350-ci, two-barrel V-8

Interchange Number: 11
Part Number(s): 1111956
ID Number(s): 1111956
Usage: Early-1969 C-10 to C-30 Chevrolet and 1500 to 3500 GMC with 350-ci, four-barrel V-8 and manual transmission

Interchange Number: 12
Part Number(s): 1112001
ID Number(s): 1112001
Usage: Late-1969 C-10 to C-30 Chevrolet and 1500 to 3500 GMC truck and Blazer with 350-ci, four-barrel V-8 and manual transmission; 1969–1970 Camaro, Chevelle, Impala, and Nova with 350-ci, four-barrel V-8 and manual transmission

Interchange Number: 13
Part Number(s): 1111955
ID Number(s): 1111955
Usage: Early-1969 C-10 to C-30 Chevrolet and 1500 to 3500 GMC truck and Blazer with 350-ci, four-barrel V-8; 1970 C-10 to C-30 Chevrolet and 1500 to 3500 GMC truck with 350-ci, four-barrel V-8 and automatic transmission

Interchange Number: 14
Part Number(s): 1111487
ID Number(s): 1111487
Usage: Late-1969 C-10 to C-30 Chevrolet and 1500 to 3500 GMC truck and Blazer with 350-ci, four-barrel V-8 and automatic transmission; 1969 Camaro, Chevelle, Impala, and Nova with 350-ci, two-barrel V-8 and automatic transmission

Interchange Number: 15
Part Number(s): 1112005
ID Number(s): 1112005
Usage: 1970 C-10 to C-30 Chevrolet and 1500 to 3500 GMC truck, Blazer, Jimmy, Camaro, Chevelle, Impala, and Nova with 307-ci V-8 and automatic transmission; 1969 Camaro, Chevelle, Impala, and Nova with 327-ci V-8 and automatic transmission

Interchange Number: 16
Part Number(s): 1112041
ID Number(s): 1112041
Usage: 1971–1972 C-10 Chevrolet and 1500 GMC truck, Blazer, Jimmy, C-20 Suburban, G-10 to G-30 Chevrolet and 1500 to 3500 GMC van—all with 307-ci V-8 and manual transmission

Interchange Number: 17
Part Number(s): 1112040
ID Number(s): 1112040
Usage: 1971–1972 C-10 Chevrolet and 1500 GMC truck, Blazer, Jimmy, C-20 Suburban, G-10 to G-30 Chevrolet and 1500 to 3500 GMC van—all with 307-ci V-8 and automatic transmission

Interchange Number: 18
Part Number(s): 1112043
ID Number(s): 1112043
Usage: 1971–1972 C-20 to C-30 Chevrolet and 2500 to 3500 GMC truck (except Suburban)—all with 307-ci V-8, all transmissions

Interchange Number: 19
Part Number(s): 1112046
ID Number(s): 1112046
Usage: 1971–1972 C-10 to C-30 Chevrolet and 1500 to 3500 GMC truck, Blazer, Jimmy, G-10 to G-30 Chevrolet and 1500 to 3500 GMC van—all with 350-ci V-8 and manual transmission

A 1967–1972 washer jar.

Interchange Number: 20
Part Number(s): 1112047
ID Number(s): 1112047
Usage: 1971–1972 C-10 to C-30 Chevrolet and 1500 to 3500 GMC truck, Blazer, Jimmy, G-10 to G-30 Chevrolet and 1500 to 3500 GMC van—all with 350-ci V-8 and automatic transmission

Interchange Number: 21
Part Number(s): 1112064
ID Number(s): 1112064
Usage: 1971–1972 C-10 to C-30 Chevrolet and 1500 to 3500 GMC truck with 402-ci V-8—all transmissions

Interchange Number: 22
Part Number(s): 1112227
ID Number(s): 1112227
Usage: 1973 C-10 Chevrolet and 1500 GMC truck, C-20 Suburban, Blazer, Jimmy, Camaro, Chevelle, and Nova with 307-ci V-8 and manual transmission

Interchange Number: 23
Part Number(s): 1112102
ID Number(s): 1112102
Usage: 1973 C-10 Chevrolet and 1500 GMC truck, C-20 Suburban, Blazer, Jimmy, Camaro, Chevelle, and Nova with 307-ci V-8 and automatic transmission

Interchange Number: 24
Part Number(s): 1112096
ID Number(s): 1112096
Usage: 1973 C-20 to C-30 Chevrolet and 2500 to 3500 GMC truck (except Suburban) with 307-ci V-8, all transmissions

Interchange Number: 25
Part Number(s): 1112102
ID Number(s): 1112102
Usage: 1973–1974 C-10 Chevrolet and 1500 GMC truck, C-20 Suburban, Blazer, Jimmy, Chevelle, Camaro, Impala, Monte Carlo, and Nova with 350-ci four-barrel and manual transmission (except Z-28)

Interchange Number: 26
Part Number(s): 1112094
ID Number(s): 1112094
Usage: 1973–1974 C-10 Chevrolet and 1500 GMC truck, C-20 Suburban, Blazer, Jimmy, Chevelle, Camaro, Impala, Monte Carlo, and Nova with 350-ci four-barrel and automatic transmission

Interchange Number: 27
Part Number(s): 1112097
ID Number(s): 1112097
Usage: 1973–1974 C-20 to C-30 Chevrolet and 2500 to 3500 GMC truck (except C-20 Suburban) with 350-ci, four-barrel V-8 and manual transmission

Interchange Number: 28
Part Number(s): 1112504
ID Number(s): 1112504
Usage: 1973–1974 C-10 Chevrolet and 1500 GMC truck and C-20 Suburban with 454-ci V-8, all transmissions

Interchange Number: 29
Part Number(s): 1112505
ID Number(s): 1112505
Usage: 1973–1974 C-20 to C-30 Chevrolet and 2500 to 3500 GMC truck (except Suburban) with 454-ci V-8—all transmissions, with California emissions

Interchange Number: 30
Part Number(s): 1112113
ID Number(s): 1112113
Usage: 1973–1974 C-20 to C-30 Chevrolet and 2500 to 3500 GMC truck (except Suburban) with 454-ci V-8—all transmissions, without California emissions

Interchange Number: 31
Part Number(s): 1103253
ID Number(s): 1103253
Usage: 1975–1976 C-10 to C-30 Chevrolet and 1500 to 3500 GMC truck, Blazer, Camaro, Jimmy, Chevelle, Impala, Monte Carlo, Nova, and Sprint with 350-ci, four-barrel V-8—all

A 1973–1978 washer jar.

transmissions except Suburban with 454-ci V-8—with California emissions

Interchange Number: 32
  Part Number(s): 1103246
  ID Number(s): 1103246
  Usage: 1975 C-10 to C-30 Chevrolet and 1500 to 3500 GMC truck, Blazer, and Jimmy with 350-ci, two-barrel V-8; 1977 C-10 to C-30 Chevrolet and 1500 to 3500 GMC truck, Blazer, Jimmy, Camaro, Chevelle, Impala, Nova, Monte Carlo, and Sprint with 350-ci V-8 and high-altitude package, without California emissions; 1975–1977 Camaro, Chevelle, Impala, Monte Carlo, and Nova with 350-ci, two-barrel V-8; 1977 Omega, Phoenix, Skylark, Delta 88, Century, and Firebird with Chevrolet-built 350-ci V-8

Interchange Number: 33
  Part Number(s): 1103250
  ID Number(s): 1103250 or 1112884
  Usage: 1975 C-10 to C-30 Chevrolet and 1500 to 3500 GMC truck with 350-ci, four-barrel V-8 and heavy-duty chassis; 1975–1977 C-10 to C-30 Chevrolet and 1500 to 3500 GMC truck, Blazer, and Jimmy with 400-ci V-8 and California emissions; 1977–1978 C-10 to C-30 Chevrolet and 1500 to 3500 GMC with heavy-duty chassis and California emissions

Interchange Number: 34
  Part Number(s): 1124941
  ID Number(s): 1124941
  Usage: 1975–1976 C-10 to C-30 Chevrolet and 1500 to 3500 GMC truck, Blazer, and Jimmy with 400-ci V-8, without California emissions

Interchange Number: 35
  Part Number(s): 1112886
  ID Number(s): 1112886
  Usage: 1975–1976 C-10 to C-30 Chevrolet and 1500 to 3500 GMC truck with 454-ci V-8, without heavy-duty chassis; 1975 Chevelle, Monte Carlo, and Sprint with 454-ci V-8

Interchange Number: 36
  Part Number(s): 1103240
  ID Number(s): 1103240
  Usage: 1975–1978 C-10 to C-30 Chevrolet and 1500 to 3500 GMC truck with 454-ci V-8 and heavy-duty chassis and California emissions

Interchange Number: 37
  Part Number(s): 1103238
  ID Number(s): 1103238
  Usage: 1975–1978 C-10 to C-30 Chevrolet and 1500 to 3500 GMC truck with 454-ci V-8 and heavy-duty chassis, without California emissions

Interchange Number: 38
  Part Number(s): 1103252
  ID Number(s): 1103252
  Usage: 1977 C-10 to C-30 Chevrolet and 1500 to 3500 GMC truck with 305-ci V-8, without heavy-duty chassis; 1976–1977 Camaro, Chevelle, Impala, Monte Carlo, Nova, and Monza with 305-ci V-8, without California emissions

Interchange Number: 39
  Part Number(s): 1103237
  ID Number(s): 1103237
  Usage: 1977–1978 C-10 to C-30 Chevrolet and 1500 to 3500 GMC truck with 305-ci V-8 and heavy-duty chassis; 1977–1978 Blazer and Jimmy with 305-ci V-8

Interchange Number: 40
  Part Number(s): 1103254
  ID Number(s): 1103254
  Usage: 1976–1977 C-10 to C-30 Chevrolet and 1500 to 3500 GMC truck with 350-ci V-8 and California emissions, without heavy-duty chassis; 1976 Camaro, Chevelle, Impala, Monte Carlo, Nova, and Sprint with 350-ci, four-barrel V-8, with California emissions

Interchange Number: 41
  Part Number(s): 1103274
  ID Number(s): 1103274

Usage: 1977–1978 C-10 to C-30 Chevrolet and 1500 to 3500 GMC truck with 350-ci V-8 and heavy-duty chassis, without California emissions; 1977–1978 Blazer and Jimmy with 350-ci V-8; late-1975 Camaro, Chevelle, Impala, Monte Carlo, Nova, and Sprint with 350-ci, four-barrel V-8, without California emissions

Interchange Number: 42
Part Number(s): 1112940
ID Number(s): 1112940
Usage: 1976 C-10 to C-30 Chevrolet and 1500 to 3500 GMC truck with 350-ci V-8 and heavy-duty chassis; 1976 Blazer and Jimmy with 350-ci V-8

Interchange Number: 43
Part Number(s): 1103249
ID Number(s): 1103249
Usage: 1977–1978 C-10 to C-30 Chevrolet and 1500 to 3500 GMC truck, Blazer, and Jimmy with 400-ci V-8

Interchange Number: 44
Part Number(s): 1103281
ID Number(s): 1103281
Usage: 1978 C-10 to C-30 Chevrolet and 1500 to 3500 GMC truck, Blazer, and Jimmy with 305-ci V-8 and manual transmission, without heavy-duty chassis; 1978 Camaro, Chevelle, Impala, Monte Carlo, Firebird, Century, Monza, Omega, Skylark, LeMans, Sprint, Sunbird, and Starfire with 305-ci V-8 and automatic transmission or high-altitude package

Interchange Number: 45
Part Number(s): 1103338
ID Number(s): 1103338
Usage: 1978 C-10 to C-30 Chevrolet and 1500 to 3500 GMC truck with 305-ci V-8 and automatic transmission, without heavy-duty chassis

Interchange Number: 46
Part Number(s): 1103339
ID Number(s): 1103339
Usage: 1978 C-10 Chevrolet and 1500 GMC four-wheel-drive truck with 350-ci V-8 and automatic transmission and California emissions, without heavy-duty chassis; 1978 C-20 Chevrolet and 2500 GMC truck with 350-ci V-8 and automatic transmission and California emissions, without heavy-duty chassis

Interchange Number: 47
Part Number(s): 1103286
ID Number(s): 1103286
Usage: 1978 C-10 or C-30 Chevrolet and 1500 or 3500 GMC two-wheel-drive truck with automatic transmission and California emissions, without heavy-duty chassis; 1979 C-10 to C-30 Chevrolet and 1500 to 3500 GMC truck,

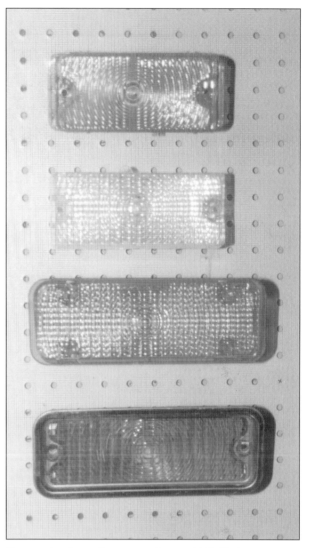

Front marker lenses from top to bottom: 1967–1968, 1969–1970, 1971–1972, and 1973–1978.

Blazer, and Jimmy with 350-ci V-8 and high-altitude package; 1978 C-10 to C-30 Chevrolet and 1500 to 3500 GMC truck with 350-ci V-8, without heavy-duty chassis or California emissions

Interchange Number: 48
Part Number(s): 1103302
ID Number(s): 1103302
Usage: 1978 C-10 to C-30 Chevrolet and 1500 to 3500 GMC truck, Blazer, and Jimmy with 350-ci V-8 and manual transmission and California emissions

Interchange Number: 49
Part Number(s): 1103301
ID Number(s): 1103301
Usage: 1978 C-10 to C-30 Chevrolet and 1500 to 3500 GMC truck with 400-ci V-8 and California emissions, without heavy-duty chassis

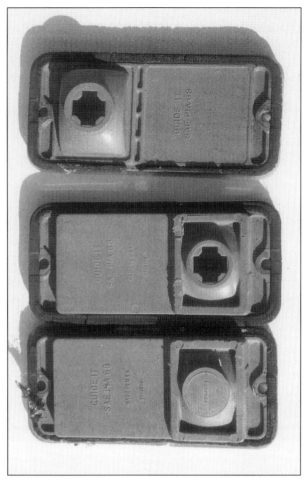

Side marker lamps from 1968 to 1972. The early style at top was prone to breakage. The second style, middle, is thicker. Not all markers included an opening for a lamp.

Ignition Coils
Model Identification

1967–1975	Interchange Number
1.8-ohm wires	1
1.3-ohm wires	2

1967–1975	
All	3

Interchanges
Interchange Number: 1
> Part Number(s): 1115202
> ID Number(s): 202-12V
> Usage: 1955–1974 C-10 to C-30 Chevrolet and 1500 to 3500 GMC, Blazer, Jimmy, and G-10 to G-30 Chevrolet and 1500 to 3500 GMC van; 1955–1974 full-size Chevrolet and Buick; 1964–1974 Chevelle, Chevy II/Nova, and Skylark; 1970–1974 Monte Carlo, Century, and Regal; 1967–1974 Camaro; 1955–1963 full-size Oldsmobile; 1955–1961 full-size Pontiac with

all powerplants and options except transistor ignition
> Note(s): Used with 1.8-ohm wires

Interchange Number: 2
> Part Number(s): 1115238
> ID Number(s): 202-12V
> Usage: 1965–1974 C-10 to C-30 Chevrolet and 1500 to 3500 GMC, Blazer, Jimmy, and G-10 to G-30 Chevrolet and 1500 to 3500 GMC van; 1964–1974 full-size Chevrolet and Buick; 1964–1974 Chevelle, Chevy II/Nova, and Skylark; 1970–1974 Monte Carlo, Century, and Regal; 1967–1974 Camaro; 1961–1963 full-size Oldsmobile; 1961–1963 full-size Pontiac with all powerplants and options except transistor ignition
> Note(s): Used with 1.3-ohm wires

Interchange Number: 3
> Part Number(s): 19855473
> Usage: 1975–1981 C-10 to C-30 Chevrolet and 1500 to 3500 GMC, Blazer, Jimmy, and G-10 to G-30 Chevrolet and 1500 to 3500 GMC van with V-8 engine; 1975–1981 Camaro, Chevelle, Impala, Nova, Monte Carlo, and Monza with V-8 engine; 1974–1977 Toronado, Delta 88, Ninety Eight, Omega, Firebird, Skylark, Skyhawk, Bonneville, LeSabre, and Regal with V-8 engine

Alternators

The alternator creates current that is used to run the truck's electrical system. Several different levels (outputs) were available. If you have added more electrical accessories to your truck than what was originally installed when it was new, then moving up to a higher rated alternator might be a wise interchange. Alternators are identified by a part number that is stamped into the housing. The interchange is based on the replacement part number, thus allowing for a larger interchange field. As a result, there may be more than one ID number in one particular interchange. Usage in the interchange lists the Chevrolet truck models that use that particular alternator. The ID number selection should be consulted when buying an alternator.

Model Identification
C-10 to C-30 Truck, Blazer, and Suburban

Year and type	Interchange Number
1967–1971 37-amp	4
1972 37-amp	5
1973–1978 37-amp	6
1967–1971 42-amp	1
1972	
without internal regulator	2
with internal regulator	3

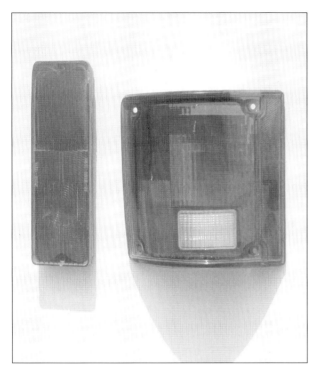

A taillamp lens for Fleetside models: left, 1967–1972, and right, 1973–1978.

Interchanges

Interchange Number: 1
Part Number(s): 1100842
ID Number(s): 1100567, 110600, 1100613, 1100615, 1100624, 1100625, 1100647, 1100659, 1100663, 1100669, 1100678, 1100680, 1100691, 1100699, 1100708, 1100727, 1100734, 1100736, 1100739, 1100744, 1100761, 1100765, 1100769, 1100795, 1100815, 1100833, 1100839, 1100841, 1100842, 1100878, 1100896, 1100908, 1100943, or 1100944
Rating: 42 amps
Usage: 1967–1970 C-10 to C-30 Chevrolet truck with 42-amp alternator

Interchange Number: 2
Part Number(s): 1102459
ID Number(s): 1102434, 1102435, 11024, 1102443, 1102458, or 1102459
Rating: 42 amps
Usage: 1972 C-10 to C-30 Chevrolet truck with 42-amp alternator

Interchange Number: 3
Part Number(s): 1102848
ID Number(s): 1100543, 1100573, 1100833, 1100859, 1100880, 1100881, 1100899, 1100900, 1100901, 1100919, 1100926, 1100940, 1100950, 1102346, 1102353, 1102382, 1102384, 1102388, 1102389, 1102394, 1102400, 1102472, 1102481, 1102485, 1102489, 1102493, 1102841, 1102848, 1102887, 1103055, or 1103075
Rating: 42 amps
Usage: 1972–1978 C-10 to C-30 Chevrolet truck with 42-amp alternator
Note(s): Has internal regulator

Interchange Number: 4
Part Number(s): 1100834
ID Number(s): 1100547, 1100558, 1100566, 1100628, 1100632, 1100668, 1100676, 1100683, 1100688, 1100689, 1100693, 1100706, 1100714, 1100729, 1100761, 1100762, 1100767, 110078, 11100794, 1100813, 1100814, 1100834, 1100836, 1100837, 1100838, 1100879, 1100888, or 1100905
Rating: 37 amps
Usage: 1967–1971 C-10 to C-30 Chevrolet truck with 37-amp alternator
Note(s): Interchange Number 1 will fit

Interchange Number: 5
Part Number(s): 1102453
ID Number(s): 1102440, 1102449, 1102452, 1102453, 1102454, or 1102456
Rating: 37 amps
Usage: 1972 C-10 to C-30 Chevrolet truck with 37-amp alternator
Note(s): Interchange Number 2 will fit

Interchange Number: 6
Part Number(s): 1102397
ID Number(s): 1100497, 1100547, 1100550, 1100588, 1100832, 1100853, 1100902, 1100919, 1100927, 1100934, 1100947, 1102349, 1102394, 1102397, 1102483, 1102491, 1102881, 1102882, or 1102887
Rating: 37 amps
Usage: 1973–1978 C-10 to C-30 Chevrolet truck with 37-amp alternator
Note(s): Interchange Number 3 will fit

Interchange Number: 7
Part Number(s): 1100849
ID Number(s): 1100548, 1100570, 1100590, 1100750, 1100796, 1100810, 1100817, 1100825, 1100843, 1100845, 1100846, 1100847, 1100849, 1100860, 1100895, 1100897, 1100907, 1100921, or 1100932
Rating: 61 amps

The 1967–1972 heater control without air conditioning.

Usage: 1967–1972 C-10 to C-30 Chevrolet truck with 61-amp alternator

Interchange Number: 8
   Part Number(s): 1100554
   ID Number(s): 1100487, 1100544, 1100575, 1100597, 1100825, 1100854, 1100884, 1100897, 1100904, 1100948, 1102347, 1102368, 1102395, 1102383, 1102391, 1102395, 1102460, 1102474, 1102480, 1102486, 1102490, 1102549, 1102843, 1102853, 1102862, 1102894, 1102901, 1102906, 1102913, 1103037, or 1103057
   Rating: 61 amps
   Usage: 1973–1978 C-10 to C-30 Chevrolet truck with 61-amp alternator

Interchange Number: 9
   Part Number(s): 11117767
   ID Number(s): 1117754, 1117756, 1117762, 1117769, or 1117782
   Rating: 62 amps
   Usage: 1967–1968 C-10 to C-30 Chevrolet truck with 62-amp alternator

Interchange Number: 10
   Part Number(s): 1102498
   ID Number(s): 1103064, 1102550, 1102842, 1102844, 1102854, 1102857, 1102879, 1102892, 1102893, 1102910, 1102908, 1102904, 1103042, 1103076, or 1103082
   Rating: 63 amps
   Usage: 1978 C-10 to C-30 Chevrolet truck with diesel engine and 63-amp alternator
   Note(s) Number in bold is original unit

Interchange Number: 11
   Part Number(s): 1117128
   ID Number(s): 1117128, 1117137, or 1117140
   Rating: 130 amps
   Usage: 1967–1972 C-10 to C-30 Chevrolet truck with 130-amp alternator
   Note(s): Usually used on Camper Special packages

Interchange Number: 12
   Part Number(s): 1117141
   ID Number(s): 1117141

Rating: 100 amps
Usage: 1970–1972 C-10 to C-30 Chevrolet truck with 100-amp alternator
Note(s): Usually used on Camper Special packages

Voltage Regulators

The type of regulator chosen as an interchange depends on the output of the alternator. The high-output alternators such as the 100- and 130-amp versions require a special regulator because a lower powered version such as for the common-variety 42-amp alternator will not withstand the higher amperages and temperatures and will quickly fail. Regulators are identified by a number stamped on them.

Model Identification

1967–1972	*Interchange Number*
Except 62-, 63-, 100-, or 130-amp alternator	
external regulator	1
internal regulator	6
62-amp	
external regulator	
except Type 250	2
Type 250 (1968 only)	3
internal regulator	6
100-amp (1970–1972)	5
130-amp (1968–1972)	3
1973–1978	
All	6

Interchanges

Interchange Number: 1
   Part Number(s): 1119515
   ID Number(s): 1119515
   Usage: 1962–1974 GM models with alternator, except 62-, 63-, 100-, or 130-amp versions; not for internal regulators

Interchange Number: 2
   Part Number(s): 1116378
   ID Number(s): 1116378
   Usage: 1963–1974 GM models with 62-amp alternator, except 1968 models with Type 250
   Note(s): Unit is transistorized

Interchange Number: 3
   Part Number(s): 9000590
   ID Number(s): 9000590
   Usage: 1968 C-10 to C-30 truck with Type 250 62-amp alternator; 1968–1972 C-10 to C-30 Chevrolet and 1500 to 3500 GMC truck and van with 130-amp alternator

Interchange Number: 4
   Part Number(s): 1116378
   ID Number(s): 1116378
   Usage: 1963–1974 GM models with 62-amp alternator, except 1968 models with Type 250

Interchange Number: 5
    Part Number(s): 1116383
    Usage: 1970–1974 C-10 to C-30 Chevrolet and
        1500 to 3500 GMC truck with 100-amp alter-
        nator
    Note(s): Internal regulator
Interchange Number: 6
    Part Number(s): 1116387
    Usage: 1970–1974 GM models with 42-, 62-, or 80-
        amp alternator
    Note(s): Internal regulator

Battery Trays
Model Identification
1967–1972	Interchange Number
All	2
1973–1978	
All	1

Interchanges
Interchange Number: 1
    Part Number(s): 6262122
    Usage: 1973–1979 C-10 to C-30 Chevrolet and
        1500 to 3500 GMC truck, Blazer, and Jimmy
Interchange Number: 2
    Part Number(s): 3886782
    Usage: 1967–1972 C-10 to C-30 Chevrolet and
        1500 to 3500 GMC truck; 1969–1972 Blazer;
        1970–1972 Jimmy; 1971–1972 G-10 to G-30
        Chevrolet and 1500 to 3500 GMC van

Windshield-Wiper Motors
Model Identification
1967–1972	Interchange Number
All	1
1973–1977	
All	2
1978	
All	3

Interchanges
Interchange Number: 1
    Part Number(s): 4911476
    Usage: 1967–1972 C-10 to C-30 Chevrolet and
        1500 to 3500 GMC truck; 1969–1972 Blazer;
        1970–1972 Jimmy; 1964–1967 Chevelle,
        Skylark, Cutlass/F-85, LeMans/Tempest, Chevy
        II, and Corvair; 1967 Camaro and Firebird—all
        have two-speed wipers
Interchange Number: 2
    Part Number(s): 4960853
    Usage: 1973–1977 C-10 to C-30 Chevrolet and
        1500 to 3500 GMC truck, Blazer, and Jimmy;
        1974–1977 G-10 to G-30 Chevrolet and 1500
        to 3500 GMC van

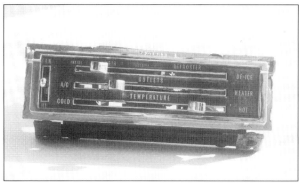

The 1967–1972 heater control with air conditioning.

Interchange Number: 3
    Part Number(s): 22020731
    Usage: 1977–1980 C-10 to C-30 Chevrolet and
        1500 to 3500 GMC truck, Blazer, and Jimmy;
        1978–1981 G-10 to G-30 Chevrolet and 1500
        to 3500 GMC van

Windshield-Wiper Arms
Model Identification
1967–1970	Interchange Number
All	3
1971–1972	
All	4
1973–1977	
All	1
1978	
All	2

Interchanges
Interchange Number: 1
    Part Number(s): 4961222
    Usage: 1973–1977 C-10 to C-30 Chevrolet and
        1500 to 3500 GMC truck, Blazer, and Jimmy
Interchange Number: 2
    Usage: 1978–1980 C-10 to C-30 Chevrolet and
        1500 to 3500 GMC truck, Blazer, and Jimmy
Interchange Number: 3
    Part Number(s): 4917171
    Usage: 1967–1970 C-10 to C-30 Chevrolet and
        1500 to 3500 GMC truck; 1969–1970 Blazer;
        1970 Jimmy
Interchange Number: 4
    Usage: 1971–1972 C-10 to C-30 Chevrolet and
        1500 to 3500 GMC truck, Blazer, and Jimmy

Windshield Washer Jars
Model Identification
1967–1972	Interchange Number
All	3
1973–1975	
All	1

Interchanges
Interchange Number: 1
Part Number(s): 6274597
Usage: 1973–1975 C-10 to C-30 Chevrolet and 1500 to 3500 GMC truck, Blazer, and Jimmy
Interchange Number: 2
Part Number(s): 399082
Usage: 1976–1979 C-10 to C-30 Chevrolet truck and 1500 to 3500 GMC truck, Blazer, and Jimmy
Interchange Number: 3
Part Number(s): 3840083
Usage: 1967–1972 C-10 to C-30 Chevrolet and 1500 to 3500 GMC truck; 1969–1972 Blazer; 1970–1972 Jimmy

Windshield Wiper Links
Model Identification

Interchanges
Interchange Number: 1
Part Number(s): 3929413
Usage: 1967–1972 C-10 to C-30 Chevrolet truck; 1969–1972 Blazer
Interchange Number: 2
Part Number(s): 4960844 (left); 49060842 (right)
Usage: 1973–1979 C-10 to C-30 Chevrolet and 1500 to 3500 GMC truck; 1969–1972 Blazer and Jimmy

Windshield-Wiper Switches
Model Identification

Interchanges
Interchange Number: 1
Part Number(s): 1993372
Usage: 1967 C-10 to C-30 Chevrolet and 1500 to 3500 GMC truck
Interchange Number: 2
Part Number(s): 1993432
Usage: 1968–1972 C-10 to C-30 Chevrolet and 1500 to 3500 GMC truck; 1969–1972 Blazer; 1970–1972 Jimmy
Interchange Number: 3
Part Number(s): 1994151
Usage: 1973–1974 C-10 to C-30 Chevrolet and 1500 to 3500 GMC truck, Blazer, Jimmy, and step van
Interchange Number: 4
Part Number(s): 1994172
Usage: 1975–1977 C-10 to C-30 Chevrolet and 1500 to 3500 GMC truck, Blazer, and Jimmy, without intermittent wipers
Interchange Number: 5
Part Number(s): 469303
Usage: 1977 C-10 to C-30 Chevrolet and 1500 to 3500 GMC truck, Blazer, and Jimmy with intermittent wipers
Interchange Number: 6
Part Number(s): 14028807
Usage: 1978 C-10 to C-30 Chevrolet and 1500 to 3500 GMC truck, Blazer, and Jimmy, without intermittent wipers
Interchange Number: 7
Part Number(s): 14028808
Usage: 1978 C-10 to C-30 Chevrolet and 1500 to 3500 GMC truck, Blazer, and Jimmy with intermittent wipers

Heater-Motor Assemblies
The biggest factor in interchanging the heater-motor assembly is whether or not the vehicle was installed with factory air conditioning. The dealer-installed air conditioning used the same motor as those models without factory air conditioning. Motors with factory air conditioning are not interchangeable with trucks without air conditioning.

Motors are identified by a number stamped into the case. This number usually matches the part number and is followed by the build date, which is represented by the month and last two digits of the year. For example 07 72 would represent July 1972. Note that there is a difference between the front and rear motors in Suburban models.

Model Identification

1968–1975

Without air conditioning .1
With air conditioning 2
Rear heater (Suburban only) 4

1977–1978

Without air conditioning .1
With air conditioning
  standard-duty motor 7
  heavy-duty motor 6
Rear heater (Suburban only) 5

Interchanges

Interchange Number: 1

Part Number(s): 3027032
Usage: 1967–1978 C-10 to C-30 Chevrolet and 1500 to 3500 GMC truck, Blazer, and Jimmy; 1967 to early-1978 Impala; 1967–1977 Chevelle; 1967–1979 Camaro and Firebird; 1971–1979 Cadillac; 1973–1978 Cutlass; 1969–1978 full-size Buick; 1964–1970 G-10 to G-20 Chevrolet and 1500 to 2500 GMC van with front heater—all above models without factory air conditioning

Interchange Number: 2

Part Number(s): 4960538
Usage: 1967 to early-1976 C-10 to C-30 Chevrolet and 1500 to 3500 GMC truck, Blazer, Jimmy, Impala; 1967–1977 Chevelle; 1967 to early-1977 Camaro and Firebird; 1971–1976 Cadillac; 1973–1977 Cutlass; 1969–1976 full-size Buick—all above models with factory air conditioning

Interchange Number: 3

Part Number(s): 5044402
Usage: 1967 Suburban with rear heater

Interchange Number: 4

Part Number(s): 4916995
Usage: 1968–1976 Suburban; 1968–1975 G-10 to G-30 and 1500 to 3500 GMC van with rear heater

Interchange Number: 5

Part Number(s): 4999707
Usage: 1977–1978 Suburban; G-10 to G-30 Chevrolet and 1500 to 3500 GMC van with rear heater

Interchange Number: 6

Part Number(s): 4999960
Usage: 1977–1978 C-10 to C-30 Chevrolet and 1500 to 3500 GMC truck, Blazer, and Jimmy with air conditioning; 1979–1981 C-10 to C-30 Chevrolet and 1500 to 3500 GMC truck with heavy-duty heater motor, without air conditioning; 1977–1979 Impala, full-size Oldsmobile, LeSabre, Camaro, and Firebird; 1978–1979 Monte Carlo, Regal, Grand Prix, Century, and

Sprint with air conditioning
Note(s): Heavy-duty motor

Interchange Number: 7

Part Number(s): 4999963
Usage: 1977–1979 C-10 to C-30 Chevrolet and 1500 to 3500 GMC truck; 1977 Omega, Nova, Skylark, and Phoenix; late-1977 Firebird and Camaro with air conditioning
Note(s): Standard-duty motor

Heater-Core Assemblies

Interchange of the heater core is determined by whether or not factory air conditioning was installed. Dealer-installed air conditioning used the same core as those units without factory air conditioning.

Model Identification

1967	*Interchange Number*

Without air conditioning
  early 1
  late 2
With air conditioning 3

1968–1972

Without air conditioning .2
With air conditioning 3

1973–1975

Without air conditioning .4
With air conditioning 5
Rear heater (Suburban only) 3

1976–1978

Without air conditioning .4
With air conditioning 5
Rear heater (Suburban only) 6

Interchanges

Interchange Number: 1

Part Number(s): 3012656
Usage: Early-1967 C-10 to C-60 Chevrolet and 1500 to 3500 GMC truck without air conditioning

Interchange Number: 2

Part Number(s): 3015169
Usage: Late-1967 to 1972 C-10 to C-30 Chevrolet and 1500 to 3500 GMC truck without air conditioning; 1971–1975 G-10 to G-30 Chevrolet and 1500 to 3500 GMC van with rear heater; 1973–1975 Suburban with rear heater

Interchange Number: 3

Part Number(s): 3025322
Usage: 1967–1972 C-10 to C-30 Chevrolet and 1500 to 3500 GMC truck with air conditioning; 1969–1972 Blazer; 1970–1972 Jimmy with air conditioning

Interchange Number: 4

Part Number(s): 3027265

Usage: 1973–1981 C-10 to C-30 Chevrolet and
1500 to 3500 GMC truck, Blazer, and Jimmy
without air conditioning

Interchange Number: 5

Part Number(s): 3027247

Usage: 1973–1981 C-10 to C-30 Chevrolet and
1500 to 3500 GMC truck, Blazer, and Jimmy
with air conditioning

Interchange Number: 6

Part Number(s): 3034749

Usage: 1976–1981 Suburban; 1976–1981 G-10 to
G-30 Chevrolet and 1500 to 3500 GMC van
with rear heater

Air Conditioning Compressors
Model Identification

1967–1970	Interchange Number
Hang-on type	1
Factory	2
1971–1978	
Factory	2

Interchanges
Interchange Number: 1

Part Number(s): 5910432

Usage: 1962–1970 C-10 to C-30 Chevrolet and
1500 to 3500 GMC truck; 1969–1970 Blazer;
1970 Jimmy; 1967–1970 Camaro; 1964–1970
Chevelle; 1962–1970 Impala; 1962–1970 Chevy
II/Nova; 1974 Vega; 1962–1963 Special six-cylinder; 1962 Tempest—all with hang-on-type air
conditioning

Interchange Number: 2

Part Number(s): 5914809

Usage: 1968–1979 C-10 to C-30 Chevrolet and
1500 to 3500 GMC truck; 1969–1979 Blazer;
1970–1979 Jimmy; 1969–1971 Camaro, Chevelle, Impala, Nova, Skylark, LeSabre, Cadillac,
Grand Prix, LeMans, Firebird, Cutlass, Delta 88,
and Toronado with factory air conditioning,
without high-temperature switch; 1976–1979
Camaro, Firebird, Nova, and Omega; 1977
Chevelle, Monte Carlo, Grand Prix, LeMans,
Cutlass, Regal, and Century with factory air
conditioning, without high-side pressure switch

Horns and Horn Relays
A total of four different horns were used. They consist-
ed of a high-note (A) part number, 18921164, and low-
note (F) part number, 1892163, and another low-note
(D) part number, 18921162. Usage is as follows:
1967–1972 models use part numbers 18921164 and
1892163. The 1973–1978 models used these same part
numbers, but a few 1976–1978 models also used part
number 18921162, along with a different high-note (C)

part number, 1892246. All horns are interchangeable
during all years.

Two different relays were used: 1967–1972 models
used part number 1116920 (this same unit can be found
in all GM models from 1959–1962) and 1973–1974
models used part number 344813; it is uncertain if this
relay will work on earlier trucks.

Turn-Signal Switches
Model Identification

1967–1972	Interchange Number
All	3
1973–1978	
Without cruise control	1
With cruise control	2

Interchanges
Interchange Number: 1

Part Number(s): 14005066

Usage: 1973–1978 C-10 to C-30 Chevrolet and
1500 to 3500 GMC truck, Blazer, and Jimmy;
1974–1978 G-10 to G-30 and 1500 to 3500
GMC van—all without cruise control

Interchange Number: 2

Part Number(s): 6465256

Usage: 1973–1978 C-10 to C-30 Chevrolet and
1500 to 3500 GMC truck, Blazer, and Jimmy;
1974–1978 G-10 to G-30 Chevrolet and 1500
to 3500 GMC van—all with cruise control

Interchange Number: 3

Part Number(s): 3909580

Usage: 1967–1972 C-10 to C-30 Chevrolet and
1500 to 3500 GMC truck; 1969–1972 Blazer;
1970–1972 Jimmy; 1971–1973 G-10 to G-30
Chevrolet and 1500 to 3500 GMC van—all
without cruise control

Turn Signal Lamps
When interchanging turn signal lenses on cars, you usually have to hunt for a salvage vehicle that matches your
car exactly—the same year, make, model, and in some
cases body style. With your truck you are much luckier,
as there is a wider array of lens and housing to select
from. This section covers the front turn/parking lamps
and side mark lamps. It does not include tail/stop lamp
assemblies. They are listed later.

Model Identification

1967	Interchange Number
Front assembly	6
1968	
Front assembly	7
Side marker lamps	
front	
except Custom Sport Truck	14
Custom Sport Truck	16

Interchanges

Interchange Number: 1

Part Number(s): 5964327 (housing)

Part/Position: Front turn lamps

Usage: 1973–1978 C-10 to C-30 Chevrolet and 1500 to 3500 GMC truck, Blazer, and Jimmy

Interchange Number: 2

Part Number(s): Lens 5964333 (left); 5964334 (right)

Part/Position: Front turn lamps

Usage: 1973–1974 C-10 to C-30 Chevrolet truck and Blazer without body side moldings or Cheyenne package; 1500 to 3500 GMC truck and Jimmy without body side moldings or Sierra package

Interchange Number: 3

Part Number(s): Lens 5965287 (left); 5965288 (right)

Part/Position: Front turn lamps

Usage: 1973–1974 C-10 to C-30 Chevrolet truck and Blazer with body side moldings or Cheyenne package; 1500 to 3500 GMC truck and Jimmy with body side moldings or Sierra package

Interchange Number: 4

Part Number(s): Lens 5947725 (left); 5947726 (right)

Part/Position: Front turn lamps

Usage: 1975–1978 C-10 to C-30 Chevrolet truck and Blazer without body side moldings; 1500 to 3500 GMC truck and Jimmy without body side moldings

Interchange Number: 5

Part Number(s): Lens 5966277 (left); 5966278 (right)

Part/Position: Front turn lamps

Usage: 1975–1978 C-10 to C-30 Chevrolet truck and Blazer with body side moldings; 1500 to 3500 GMC truck and Jimmy with body side moldings

Interchange Number: 6

Part Number(s): 911457 (left); 911458 (right)

Part/Position: Front turn lamps

Usage: 1967 C-10 to C-30 Chevrolet truck

Interchange Number: 7

Part Number(s): 916587 (left); 916588 (right)

Part/Position: Front turn lamps

Usage: 1968 C-10 to C-30 Chevrolet truck

Interchange Number: 8

Part Number(s): 911169 (left); 911170 (right)

Part/Position: Front turn lamps

Usage: 1969–1970 C-10 to C-30 Chevrolet truck

Interchange Number: 9

Part Number(s): 911531 (left); 911532 (right)

Part/Position: Front turn lamps

Usage: 1971–1972 C-10 to C-30 Chevrolet truck

Interchange Number: 10

Part Number(s): 6270433 (either side)

Part/Position: Front side marker lamps

Usage: 1973–1978 C-10 to C-30 Chevrolet and 1500 to 3500 GMC, Blazer, and Jimmy without Custom option groups

Interchange Number: 11
Part Number(s): 6270434 (either side)
Part/Position: Front side marker lamps
Usage: 1973–1978 C-10 to C-30 Chevrolet and 1500 to 3500 GMC, Blazer, and Jimmy with Custom option groups

Interchange Number: 12
Part Number(s): 329835 (either side)
Part/Position: Rear side marker lamps
Usage: 1973–1978 C-10 to C-30 Chevrolet and 1500 to 3500 GMC, Blazer, and Jimmy with Custom option groups

Interchange Number: 13
Part Number(s): 329834 (either side)
Part/Position: Rear side marker lamps
Usage: 1973–1978 C-10 to C-30 Chevrolet and 1500 to 3500 GMC, Blazer, and Jimmy without Custom option groups

Interchange Number: 14
Part Number(s): 916087 (either side)
Part/Position: Rear side marker lamps
Usage: 1968–1972 C-10 to C-30 Chevrolet and 1500 to 3500 GMC truck; 1969–1972 Blazer; 1970–1972 Jimmy without Custom Sport Truck group or Cheyenne package; 1971–1972 G-10 to G-30 Chevrolet and 1500 to 3500 GMC van (except Deluxe van models)

Interchange Number: 15
Part Number(s): 916064 (either side)
Part/Position: Front side marker lamps
Usage: 1968–1972 C-10 to C-30 Chevrolet and 1500 to 3500 GMC truck; 1969–1972 Blazer; 1970–1972 Jimmy without Custom Sport Truck group or Cheyenne package; 1971–1972 G-10 to G-30 Chevrolet and 1500 to 3500 GMC van (except Deluxe van models)

Interchange Number: 16
Part Number(s): 911310 (either side)
Part/Position: Front side marker lamps
Usage: 1968–1972 C-10 to C-30 Chevrolet and 1500 to 3500 GMC truck; 1969–1972 Blazer; 1970–1972 Jimmy with Custom Sport Truck group or Cheyenne package; 1971–1972 G-10 to G-30 Chevrolet and 1500 to 3500 GMC van, Deluxe models only

Interchange Number: 17
Part Number(s): 911311 (either side)
Part/Position: Front side marker lamps
Usage: 1968–1972 C-10 to C-30 Chevrolet and 1500 to 3500 GMC; 1969–1972 Blazer; 1970–1972 Jimmy with Custom Sport Truck group or Cheyenne package; 1971–1972 G-10 to G-30 Chevrolet and 1500 to 3500 GMC van, Deluxe models only

Roof Marker Lamps and Cargo Lamps
Model Identification

Interchanges

Interchange Number: 1
Part Number(s): 2423374
Part/Position: Roof marker lamps
Usage: 1970–1972 Blazer and Suburban with roof marker lamps
Note(s): Five required

Interchange Number: 2
Part Number(s): 684662
Part/Position: Roof marker lamps
Usage: 1970–1972 C-10 to C-30 Chevrolet and 1500 to 3500 GMC truck (except Blazer and Suburban) with roof marker lamps
Note(s): Five required

Interchange Number: 3
Part Number(s): 5962263
Part/Position: Cargo lamp
Usage: 1970–1972 C-10 to C-30 Chevrolet and 1500 to 3500 GMC truck (except Suburban, Blazer, and Jimmy models)

Interchange Number: 4
Part Number(s): 5965872 housing
Part/Position: Cargo lamp
Usage: 1973–1979 C-10 to C-30 Chevrolet and 1500 to 3500 GMC truck (except Suburban, Blazer, and Jimmy models)

Interchange Number: 5
Part Number(s): 5965876 lens
Part/Position: Cargo lamp
Usage: 1973–1976 C-10 to C-30 Chevrolet and 1500 to 3500 GMC truck (except Suburban, Blazer, and Jimmy models)
Note(s): Interchange Number 6 will fit

Interchange Number: 6
Part Number(s): 5969836 lens
Part/Position: Cargo lamp
Usage: 1977–1981 C-10 to C-30 Chevrolet and 1500 to 3500 GMC truck (except Suburban, Blazer, and Jimmy models)

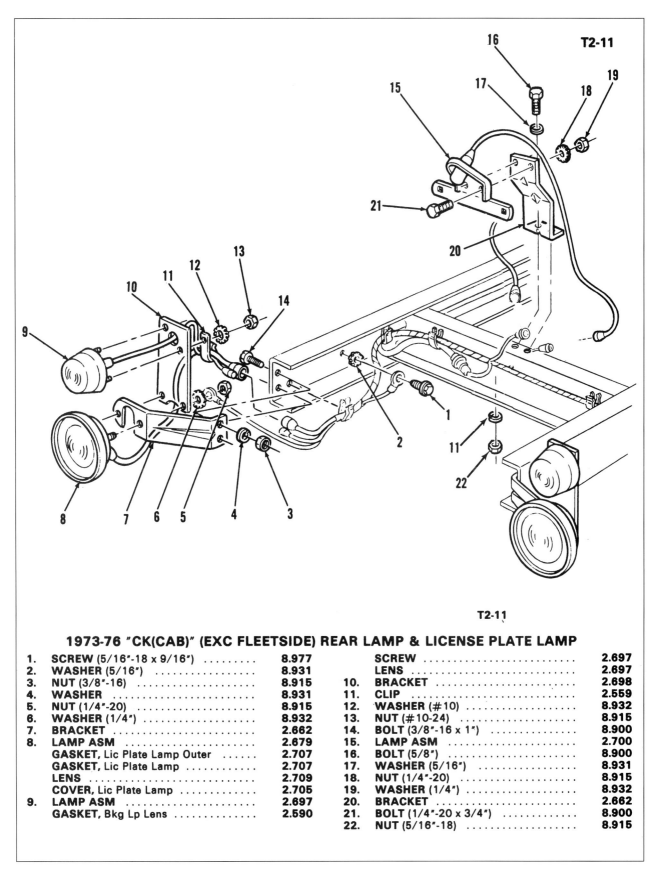

T2-11

T2-11

1973-76 "CK(CAB)" (EXC FLEETSIDE) REAR LAMP & LICENSE PLATE LAMP

No.	Part	Code	No.	Part	Code
1.	SCREW (5/16"-18 x 9/16")	8.977		SCREW	2.697
2.	WASHER (5/16")	8.931		LENS	2.697
3.	NUT (3/8"-16)	8.915	10.	BRACKET	2.698
4.	WASHER	8.931	11.	CLIP	2.559
5.	NUT (1/4"-20)	8.915	12.	WASHER (#10)	8.932
6.	WASHER (1/4")	8.932	13.	NUT (#10-24)	8.915
7.	BRACKET	2.662	14.	BOLT (3/8"-16 x 1")	8.900
8.	LAMP ASM	2.679	15.	LAMP ASM	2.700
	GASKET, Lic Plate Lamp Outer	2.707	16.	BOLT (5/8")	8.900
	GASKET, Lic Plate Lamp	2.707	17.	WASHER (5/16")	8.931
	LENS	2.709	18.	NUT (1/4"-20)	8.915
	COVER, Lic Plate Lamp	2.705	19.	WASHER (1/4")	8.932
9.	LAMP ASM	2.697	20.	BRACKET	2.662
	GASKET, Bkg Lp Lens	2.590	21.	BOLT (1/4"-20 x 3/4")	8.900
			22.	NUT (5/16"-18)	8.915

Stepside taillamps from 1967 to 1976.

Note(s): Interchange Number 5 will fit

Interchange Number: 7
Part Number(s): 985977
Part/Position: Roof marker lamp
Usage: 1973–1978 C-10 to C-30 Chevrolet and 1500 to 3500 GMC truck, including Suburban, Blazer, and Jimmy models
Note(s): Airplane type

Headlamp Switches
Model Identification

1967–1972	Interchange Number
All	1

1973–1978	
All	2

Interchanges
Interchange Number: 1
Part Number(s): 1995179
Usage: 1964–1972 C-10 to C-30 Chevrolet and 1500 to 3500 GMC truck; 1964–1972 G-10 to G-30 Chevrolet and 1500 to 3500 GMC van; 1969–1972 Blazer; 1970–1972 Jimmy; 1964–1967 full-size Chevrolet (except 1966 Caprice with bucket seats); 1964–1967 Chevy II, LeMans, Cutlass, Skylark, and LeSabre; 1964–1969 Chevelle; 1972 Chevelle; 1968–1974 Nova; 1971–1974 Ventura II; 1967 Camaro without retractable head lamps

Interchange Number: 2
Part Number(s): 1995216
Usage: 1973–1978 C-10 to C-30 Chevrolet and 1500 to 3500 GMC truck; 1964–1972 G-10 to G-30 Chevrolet and 1500 to 3500 GMC van; 1969–1972 Blazer; 1970–1972 Jimmy

Tail/Stop Lamps
Model Identification

1967–1972	Interchange Number
Housing	
except Stepside	8
Stepside	1
Lens	
except Suburban or Stepside	9
Suburban	10
Stepside	Part of unit

1973	
Housing	
except Stepside	5
Stepside	
early	1
late	2
Lens	
without body side trim or Stepside	6
with body side trim	7

Stepside	Part of unit

1974–1976	
Housing	
except Stepside	5
Stepside	2
Lens	
without body side trim or Stepside	6
with body side trim	7
Stepside	Part of unit

1977–1978	
Housing	
except Stepside or Cab only	5
Stepside	3
cab only	4
Lens	
without body side trim or Stepside	6
with body side trim	7
Stepside	Part of unit

Interchanges
Interchange Number: 1
Part Number(s): 916599
Usage: 1967 to early-1973 C-10 to C-30 Chevrolet and 1500 to 3500 GMC truck (Stepside)
Note(s): Has 21-inch lead

Interchange Number: 2
Part Number(s): 916088
Usage: Late-1973 to 1976 C-10 to C-30 Chevrolet and 1500 to 3500 GMC truck (Stepside)
Note(s): Has 10-inch lead

Interchange Number: 3
Part Number(s): 370868
Usage: 1977–1979 C-10 to C-30 Chevrolet and 1500 to 3500 GMC truck, Stepside only

Interchange Number: 4
Part Number(s): 370867 (left); 370868 (right)
Usage: 1977–1979 C-10 to C-30 Chevrolet and 1500 to 3500 GMC truck (except Fleetside or Stepside); used without pickup bed

Interchange Number: 5
Part Number(s): Housing 5965771 (left); 5965772 (right)
Usage: 1973–1979 C-10 to C-20 Chevrolet and 1500 to 2500 GMC truck, Fleetside only; 1973–1978 Blazer, Jimmy, and Suburban

Interchange Number: 6
Part Number(s): Lens 5965775 (left); 5965776 (right)
Usage: 19731979 C-10 to C-20 Chevrolet and 1500 to 2500 GMC truck, Fleetside only; 1973–1978 Blazer, Jimmy, and Suburban without body side trim

Interchange Number: 7
Part Number(s): Lens: 5968329 (left); 5968330 (right)

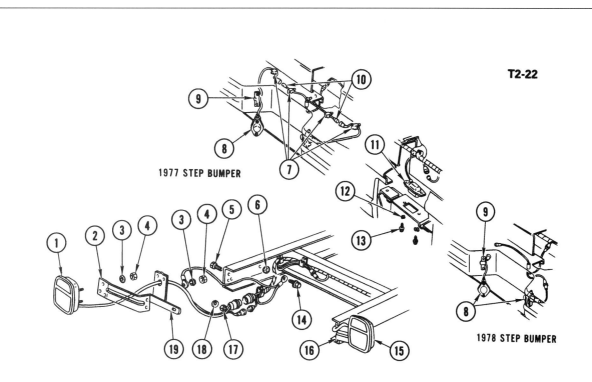

T2-22

1977 STEP BUMPER

1978 STEP BUMPER

T2-22

1977-78 "CK(CAB)" (EXC FLEETSIDE) REAR LAMP & LICENSE PLATE LAMP

1.	LAMP ASM, Tail Comb-LH	....	2.679
2.	BRACKET, Tail Comb Lp-LH	....	2.662
3.	WASHER, Lk Ext Tooth (1/4")	....	8.932
4.	NUT, Hex (1/4"-20)	....	8.915
5.	BOLT, Hex (3/8"-16 x 1")	....	8.900
6.	WASHER, Lk Ext Tooth (5/16")	....	8.932
7.	CLIP, Rr Lic Plate Lp Wire	....	2.559
8.	LAMP ASM, License (W/Step Bmpr)	....	2.700
9.	NUT, Spring	....	8.921
10.	WIRE ASM, Rr Lic Plt Lp	....	2.480
11.	LAMP ASM, License (Exc Step Bmpr)	....	2.700
12.	WASHER, Lk Ext Tooth (#10)	....	8.932
13.	SCREW, Hex Wa Hd (#10-16 x 3/4")	....	8.977
14.	SCREW, Hex Wa Hd (M8 x 1.25 x 20)	....	8.977
15.	LAMP ASM, Tail Comb-RH	....	2.679
16.	BRACKET, Tail Comb Lp-RH	....	2.662
17.	NUT, Hex (3/8"-16)	....	8.915
18.	WASHER, Lock Spring (3/8")	....	8.931
19.	BRACKET, Rr Lic Plt	....	7.800

Taillamps from 1977 to 1978.

Usage: 1973–1979 C-10 to C-20 Chevrolet and 1500 to 2500 GMC truck, Fleetside only; 1973–1979 Blazer, Jimmy, and Suburban with body side trim

Interchange Number: 8
Part Number(s): Housing 5958722 (either side)
Usage: 1967–1972 C-10 to C-20 Chevrolet and 1500 to 2500 GMC truck, Fleetside only; 1969–1972 Blazer; 1970–1972 Jimmy; 1967–1972 Suburban

Interchange Number: 9
Part Number(s): Lens 5959111 (either side)
Usage: 1967–1972 C-10 to C-20 Chevrolet and 1500 to 2500 GMC truck, Fleetside only; 1969–1972 Blazer; 1970–1972, Jimmy
Note(s): Will not fit Suburban

Interchange Number: 10
Part Number(s): Lens 5959372 (either side)
Usage: 1967–1972 Suburban

Headlamp Bezels
Model Identification

1967–1968	Interchange Number
All	1

1969–1972	
All	2

1973–1978	
All	3

Interchanges
Interchange Number: 1
Part Number(s): 3990705 (left); 3990706 (right)
Usage: 1969–1972 C-10 to C-30 Chevrolet truck and Blazer
Note(s): Aluminum, paint as required

Interchange Number: 2
Part Number(s): 3884719 (left); 3884720 (right)
Usage: 1967–1968 C-10 to C-30 Chevrolet truck

Interchange Number: 3
Part Number(s): 376627 (left); 376628 (right)
Usage: 1969–1972 C-10 to C-30 Chevrolet and 1500 to 3500 GMC truck, Blazer, and Jimmy

Heater-Control Panels and Switches
Model Identification

1967–1968	Interchange Number
Without air conditioning	1
With air conditioning	3

1969–1972	
Without air conditioning	2
With air conditioning	3

1973	
Without air conditioning	5
With air conditioning	4

1974–1978	
Without air conditioning	6
With air conditioning	8
With heavy-duty heater	7

Interchanges
Interchange Number: 1
Part Number(s): 3934832
Usage: 1967–1968 C-10 to C-30 Chevrolet and 1500 to 3500 GMC truck without air conditioning

Interchange Number: 2
Part Number(s): 3952204
Usage: 1969–1972 C-10 to C-30 Chevrolet and 1500 to 3500 GMC truck without air conditioning; 1969–1972 Blazer; 1970–1972 Jimmy without air conditioning

Interchange Number: 3
Part Number(s): 1222890
Usage: 1967–1972 C-10 to C-30 Chevrolet and 1500 to 3500 GMC truck with air conditioning; 1969–1972 Blazer; 1970–1972 Jimmy with air conditioning

Interchange Number: 4
Part Number(s): 6273304
Usage: 1973 C-10 to C-30 Chevrolet and 1500 to 3500 GMC truck, Blazer, and Jimmy with air conditioning

Interchange Number: 5
Part Number(s): 6262690
Usage: 1973 C-10 to C-30 Chevrolet and 1500 to 3500 GMC truck, Blazer, and Jimmy without air conditioning

Interchange Number: 6
Part Number(s): 14014549
Usage: 1974 C-10 to C-30 Chevrolet and 1500 to 3500 GMC truck, Blazer, and Jimmy with heavy-duty heater

Interchange Number: 7
Part Number(s): 14014540
Usage: 1974–1978 C-10 to C-30 Chevrolet and 1500 to 3500 GMC truck, Blazer, and Jimmy without air conditioning

Interchange Number: 8
Part Number(s): 14014549
Usage: 1974–1978 C-10 to C-30 Chevrolet and 1500 to 3500 GMC truck, Blazer, and Jimmy with air conditioning

Sheet Metal

Hoods

Interchange here is the bare hood, without nameplates or trim. Note that GMC hoods are listed as interchangeable, but when swapping a used GMC hood to a Chevrolet pickup, predrilled holes may have to be filled and new holes drilled to mount the Chevrolet insignias.

Model Identification

1967–1968	Interchange Number
All	1
1969–1970	
All	2
1971–1972	
All	2
1973	
All	3
1974–1978	
All	4

Interchanges

Interchange Number: 1
Part Number(s): 3882149
Usage: 1967–1968 Chevrolet C-10 to C-30 truck models; 1967–1968 GMC pickup

Interchange Number: 2
Part Number(s): 3990702
Usage: 1969–1972 Chevrolet C-10 to C-30 truck models; 1969–1972 Blazer; 1969–1972 GMC pickup and Jimmy

Interchange Number: 3
Part Number(s): 3999800
Usage: 1973 Chevrolet C-10 to C-30 truck; 1973 Blazer; 1973 GMC 1500 to 3500 truck and Jimmy

Interchange Number: 4
Part Number(s): 14013776
Usage: 1974–1978 Chevrolet C-10 to C-30 truck; 1974–1978 Blazer; 1974–1978 GMC 1500 to 3500 truck and Jimmy
Note(s): Will fit Interchange Number 3

Hood Hinges
Model Identification

1967–1972	Interchange Number
All	2
1973–1978	
All	1

Interchanges

Interchange Number: 1
Part Number(s): 6262008 (right); 6262007 (left)
Usage: 1973–1978 Chevrolet C-10 to C-30 truck models; 1973–1978 Blazer; 1973–1978 GMC pickup and Jimmy

Interchange Number: 2
Part Number(s): 3911705 (left); 3911706 (right)
Usage: 1967–1972 Chevrolet C-10 to C-30 truck models; 1967–1972 GMC pickup and Jimmy; 1969–1972 Blazer

Hood Catches and Support Assemblies
Model Identification

1967–1968	Interchange Number
Catch	7
Support	10
1969–1970	
Catch	8
Support	11
1971–1972	
Catch	9
Support	12
1973–1974	
Catch	1
Support	2

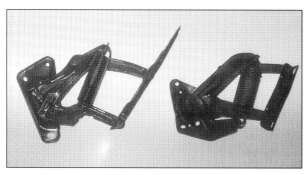

Hood hinges. The 1967–1972 style is on the right, and the 1973–1978 style is on the left.

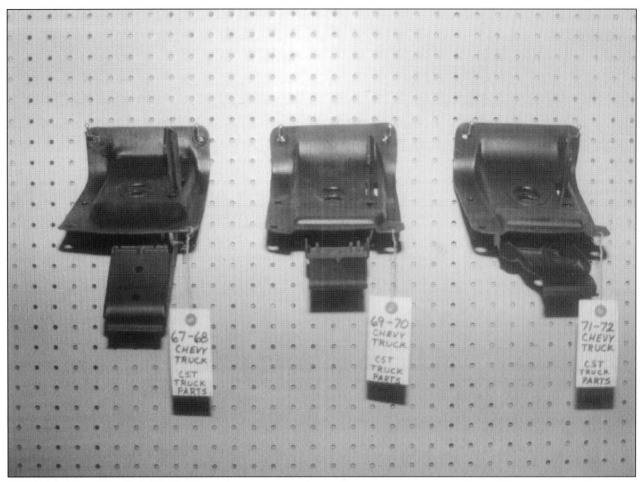

Hood catches for the 1967–1972 Chevrolet. GMC catches will not fit.

1975–1976
Catch 1
Support 3
1977
Catch 1
Support
 without inside hood release 4
 with inside hood release 5
1978
Catch 1
Support
 without inside hood release 4
 with inside hood release 6

Interchanges
Interchange Number: 1
 Part Number(s): 6271810
 Item: Catch
 Usage: 1973–1978 Chevrolet C-10 to C-30 truck, Blazer, and Suburban
 Note(s): Caution, the GMC part will not interchange

Interchange Number: 2
 Part Number(s): 349295
 Item: Catch support
 Usage: 1973–1974 Chevrolet C-10 to C-30 truck, Blazer, and Suburban; 1973–1976 1500 to 3500 GMC truck, Jimmy, and GMC Suburban
 Note(s): Caution, the 1975–1976 Chevrolet catch support will not fit

Interchange Number: 3
 Part Number(s): 347683
 Item: Catch support
 Usage: 1975–1976 Chevrolet C-10 to C-30 truck, Blazer, and Suburban
 Note(s): Caution, the GMC catch support will not fit

Interchange Number: 4
 Part Number(s): 377777
 Item: Catch support
 Usage: 1977 Chevrolet C-10 to C-30 truck, Blazer, and Suburban; 1977 1500 to 3500 GMC truck, Jimmy, and GMC Suburban with inside hood release

Interchange Number: 5
   Part Number(s): 14007507
   Item: Catch support
   Usage: 1977–1978 Chevrolet C-10 to C-30 truck, Blazer, and Suburban; 1977–1978 1500 to 3500 GMC truck, Jimmy, and GMC Suburban without inside hood release

Interchange Number: 6
   Part Number(s): 14007506
   Item: Catch support
   Usage: 1978 Chevrolet C-10 to C-30 truck, Blazer, and Suburban; 1978 1500 to 3500 GMC truck, Jimmy, and GMC Suburban with inside hood release

Interchange Number: 7
   Part Number(s): 3888570
   Item: Catch
   Usage: 1967–1968 Chevrolet C-10 to C-30 truck and Suburban
   Note(s): Caution, the GMC catch will not fit

Interchange Number: 8
   Part Number(s): 3937487
   Item: Catch
   Usage: 1969–1970 Chevrolet C-10 to C-30 truck, Suburban, and Blazer
   Note(s): Caution, the GMC catch will not fit

Interchange Number: 9
   Part Number(s): 3985103
   Item: Catch
   Usage: 1971–1972 Chevrolet C-10 to C-30 truck and Suburban
   Note(s): Caution, the GMC catch will not fit

Interchange Number: 10
   Part Number(s): 3888585
   Item: Catch support
   Usage: 1967–1968 Chevrolet C-10 to C-30 truck and Suburban
   Note(s): Caution, the GMC catch support will not fit

Door hinges for a passenger door. The upper and lower left are 1967–1972 units. The upper and lower right are 1973–1978 units.

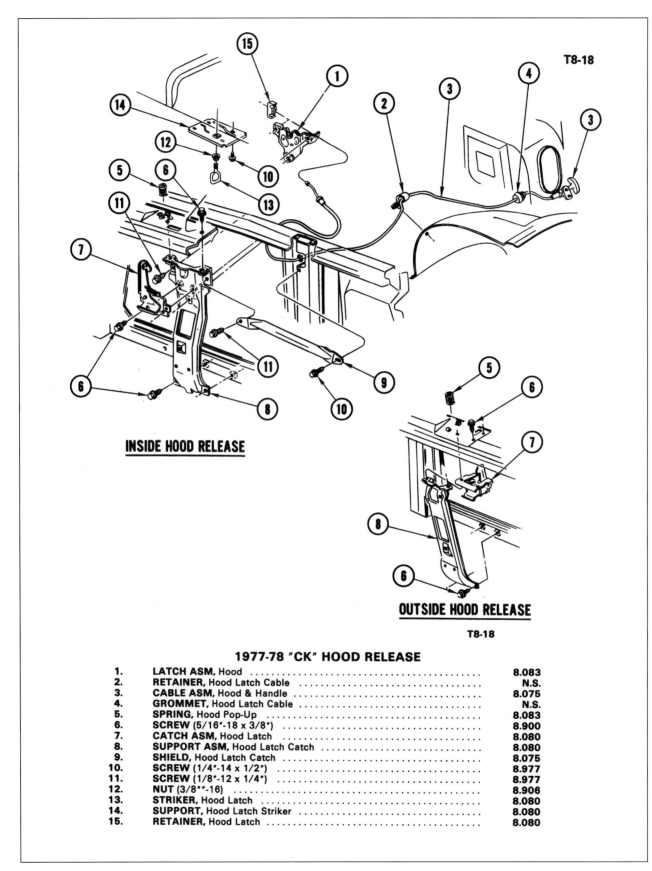

INSIDE HOOD RELEASE

OUTSIDE HOOD RELEASE

T8-18

1977-78 "CK" HOOD RELEASE

1.	LATCH ASM, Hood	8.083
2.	RETAINER, Hood Latch Cable	N.S.
3.	CABLE ASM, Hood & Handle	8.075
4.	GROMMET, Hood Latch Cable	N.S.
5.	SPRING, Hood Pop-Up	8.083
6.	SCREW (5/16"-18 x 3/8")	8.900
7.	CATCH ASM, Hood Latch	8.080
8.	SUPPORT ASM, Hood Latch Catch	8.080
9.	SHIELD, Hood Latch Catch	8.075
10.	SCREW (1/4"-14 x 1/2")	8.977
11.	SCREW (1/8"-12 x 1/4")	8.977
12.	NUT (3/8""-16)	8.906
13.	STRIKER, Hood Latch	8.080
14.	SUPPORT, Hood Latch Striker	8.080
15.	RETAINER, Hood Latch	8.080

A 1977–1978 hood catch.

Trucks with roof lights required a special roof.

Interchange Number: 11
> Part Number(s): 3936633
> Item: Catch support
> Usage: 1969–1970 Chevrolet C-10 to C-30 truck and Suburban
> Note(s): Caution, the GMC catch support will not fit

Interchange Number: 12
> Part Number(s): 3990707
> Item: Catch support
> Usage: 1971–1972 Chevrolet C-10 to C-30 truck and Suburban
> Note(s): Caution, the GMC catch support will not fit

Front Fenders

Like other Chevrolet truck parts, front fenders also have a large interchange range. The interchange is the bare unit, without nameplates or side moldings. Note that these factors will have to be weighed in when interchanging used parts, as side trim and nameplates require that holes be drilled. The predrilled holes may not match up to your existing fenders. To mount the fender, existing holes may need to be filled or new ones drilled to accommodate your specific application. This is especially true when swapping a GMC fender to a Chevrolet product. Remember, it is always easier to drill new holes than to fill existing ones, so look for a fender that matches your application or one without any trim, if possible.

Model Identification

1967	Interchange Number
All	1

1968	
All	5

1969–1972	
All	2

1973–1975	
All	3

1976–1978	
All	4

Interchanges

Interchange Number: 1
> Part Number(s): 3898859 (left); 3898860 (right)
> Usage: 1967 Chevrolet C-10 to C-30 truck; 1967 GMC pickup

Interchange Number: 2
> Part Number(s): 3936667 (left); 3936668 (right)
> Usage: 1969–1972 Chevrolet C-10 to C-30 truck; 1969–1972 Blazer

Interchange Number: 3
> Part Number(s): N/A
> Usage: 1973–1975 Chevrolet C-10 to C-30 truck; 1973–1975 Blazer; 1973–1975 GMC 1500 to 3500 truck and Jimmy
> Note(s): Interchange Number 4 will fit if you use 1976–1977 washer jar and drill holes for jack support

Interchange Number: 4
> Part Number(s): 14031989 (left); 14031990 (right)
> Usage: 1976–1978 Chevrolet C-10 to C-30 truck; 1976–1978 Blazer; 1976–1978 GMC 1500 to 3500 truck and Jimmy

Interchange Number: 5
> Part Number(s): 3936653 (left); 3936654 (right)
> Usage: 1968 Chevrolet C-10 to C-30 truck; 1968 GMC pickup

Doors, Front

Model Identification

1967–1972	Interchange Number
Except Suburban or Blazer	1
Suburban	7
Blazer	6

1973	
Except Blazer	2
Blazer	4

1974–1975	
Except Blazer	3
Blazer	4

1976–1977	
Except Blazer	3
Blazer	3

1978–1979	
All	5

Interchanges

Interchange Number: 1
> Part Number(s): 6263065 (left); 6263066 (right)
> Usage: 1967–1972 Chevrolet C-10 to C-30 truck; 1969–1972 Blazer; 1967–1972 GMC pickup; 1970–1972 Jimmy

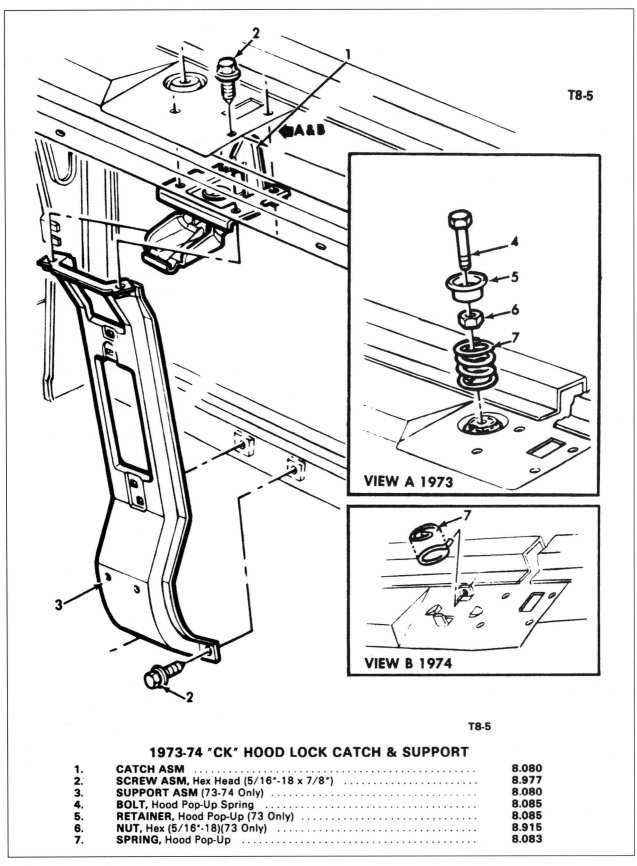

T8-5

VIEW A 1973

VIEW B 1974

T8-5

1973-74 "CK" HOOD LOCK CATCH & SUPPORT

1.	**CATCH ASM**	8.080
2.	**SCREW ASM,** Hex Head (5/16"-18 x 7/8")	8.977
3.	**SUPPORT ASM** (73-74 Only)	8.080
4.	**BOLT,** Hood Pop-Up Spring	8.085
5.	**RETAINER,** Hood Pop-Up (73 Only)	8.085
6.	**NUT,** Hex (5/16"-18)(73 Only)	8.915
7.	**SPRING,** Hood Pop-Up	8.083

A 1973–1974 hood catch.

Wheel lip moldings from 1967 and 1968. A 1968 model is shown.

Interchange Number: 2
  Part Number(s): N/A
  Usage: 1973 Chevrolet C-10 to C-30 truck; 1973 GMC 1500 to 3500 truck
  Note(s): Will not fit Blazer or Jimmy; Interchange Number 3 will fit, but regulator assembly will have to be reworked

Interchange Number: 3
  Part Number(s): 373301 (left); 373302 (right)
  Usage: 1974–1976 Chevrolet C-10 to C-30 truck; 1976 Blazer; 1974–1976 GMC 1500 to 3500 truck; 1976 Jimmy

Interchange Number: 4
  Part Number(s): 6260993 (left); 6260994 (right)
  Usage: 1973–1975 Blazer and Jimmy
  Note(s): Interchange Numbers 2 and 3 will fit if top of door frame is cut off

Interchange Number: 5
  Part Number(s): 4050350 (left); 4050351 (right)
  Usage: 1977–1981 Chevrolet C-10 to C-30 truck; 1977–1981 Blazer; 1977–1981 GMC 1500 to 3500 truck and Jimmy

Interchange Number: 6
  Part Number(s): 3981871 (left); 3981872 (right)
  Usage: 1969–1972 Blazer; 1970–1972 Jimmy

Interchange Number: 7
  Part Number(s): 6263067 (left); 6263068 (right)
  Usage: 1967–1972 Chevrolet and GMC Suburban

Front Door Hinges
Model Identification

1967–1972	Interchange Number
Upper	1
Lower	4

1973–1978	
Upper	2
Lower	3

Interchanges
Interchange Number: 1
  Part Number(s): 3962515 (left); 3962516 (right)
  Position: Upper
  Usage: 1967–1972 Chevrolet C-10 to C-60 truck; 1967–1972 GMC 1500 to 6500 truck; 1969–1972 Blazer; 1970–1972 GMC Jimmy

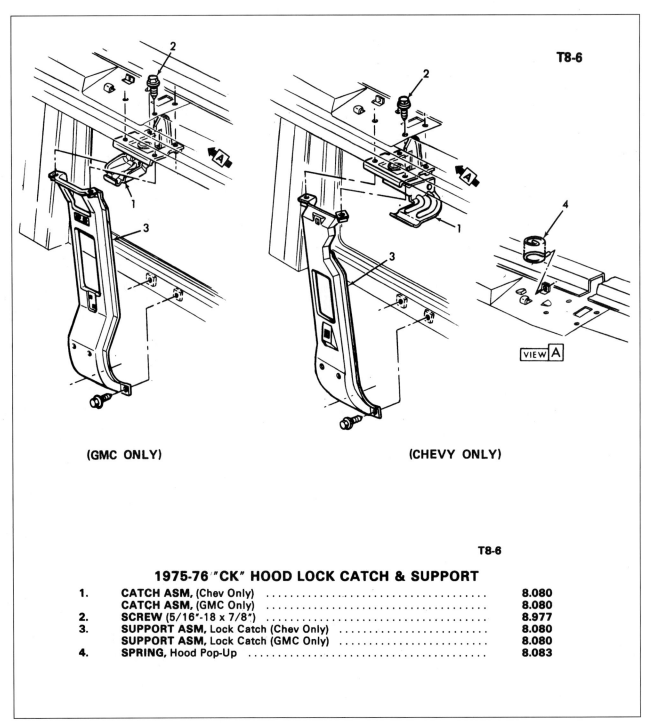

(GMC ONLY)   (CHEVY ONLY)

T8-6

1975-76 "CK" HOOD LOCK CATCH & SUPPORT

1.	CATCH ASM, (Chev Only)	8.080
	CATCH ASM, (GMC Only)	8.080
2.	SCREW (5/16"-18 x 7/8")	8.977
3.	SUPPORT ASM, Lock Catch (Chev Only)	8.080
	SUPPORT ASM, Lock Catch (GMC Only)	8.080
4.	SPRING, Hood Pop-Up	8.083

A 1975–1976 hood catch.

Interchange Number: 2
    Part Number(s): 3271981 (left); 3271982 (right)
    Position: Upper
    Usage: 1973–1981 Chevrolet C-10 to C-60 truck;
        1973–1981 Blazer; 1973–1981 GMC 1500 to
        6500 truck; 1973–1981 GMC Jimmy
Interchange Number: 3
    Part Number(s): 6271869 (left); 6271870 (right)
    Position: Lower

Usage: 1973–1981 C-10 to C-60 Chevrolet truck;
    1973–1981 GMC 1500 to 6500 truck;
    1973–1981 Blazer and Jimmy
Interchange Number: 4
    Part Number(s): 3962519 (left); 3962520 (right)
    Position: Lower
    Usage: 1967–1972 Chevrolet C-10 to C-60 truck;
        1967–1972 GMC 1500 to 6500 truck;
        1969–1972 Blazer; 1970–1972 GMC Jimmy

A body-style molding. The top is 1967–1968, the middle is 1969–1970, and the bottom is 1971–1972.

Rear Doors and Back Doors

Rear door refers to the rear passenger doors on models like the Suburban, while back doors refer to the back doors on Suburban models with rear double doors. Tailgates are not included in this interchange. Tailgates are included in their own group.

Model Identification

1967–1972	Interchange Number
Suburban	
rear	.1
back	.2
1973–1974	
Suburban	
rear	.3
back	.4
1975	
Suburban	
rear	.3
back	.6
1977	
Suburban	
rear	.5
back	.6
1978	
Suburban	
rear	.5
back, left	.7
back, right	.4

Interchanges

Interchange Number: 1
Part Number(s): 3998382
Position: Rear door
Usage: 1967–1972 Suburban and Carryall models

Interchange Number: 2
Part Number(s): 3941529 (left); 3941530 (right)
Position: Back doors
Usage: 1967–1972 Suburban and Carryall models

Interchange Number: 3
Part Number(s): 6264105 (left); 6264106 (right)
Position: Rear
Usage: 1973–1974 Suburban; 1973–1974 Chevrolet and GMC Crewcab truck

Interchange Number: 4
Part Number(s): 6264161 (left); 6264162 (right)
Position: Back
Usage: 1973–1974 Suburban with double back doors; 1978 Suburban right door only

Interchange Number: 5
Part Number(s): 363189 (left); 363190 (right)
Position: Rear
Usage: 1977–1978 Suburban and Crewcab

Interchange Number: 6
Part Number(s): 351749 (left); 351750 (right)
Position: Back
Usage: 1975–1977 Suburban with double back doors

Interchange Number: 7
Part Number(s): 14006143 (left)
Position: Back
Usage: 1978–1980 Suburban with double back doors

Outside Door Handles
Model Identification

1967–1968	Interchange Number
Front doors	.1
Rear doors, Suburban	.1
1969–1972	
Front doors	.2
Rear doors, Suburban	.2
1973–1978	
Front doors	.3
Rear doors, Suburban or Crewcab	.3

Interchanges

Interchange Number: 1
Part Number(s): 3901463 (left); 3905683 (right)
Usage: 1967–1968 Chevrolet C-10 to C-30 truck; 1967–1968 GMC pickup

Interchange Number: 2
Part Number(s): 3927895 (left); 3927899 (right)

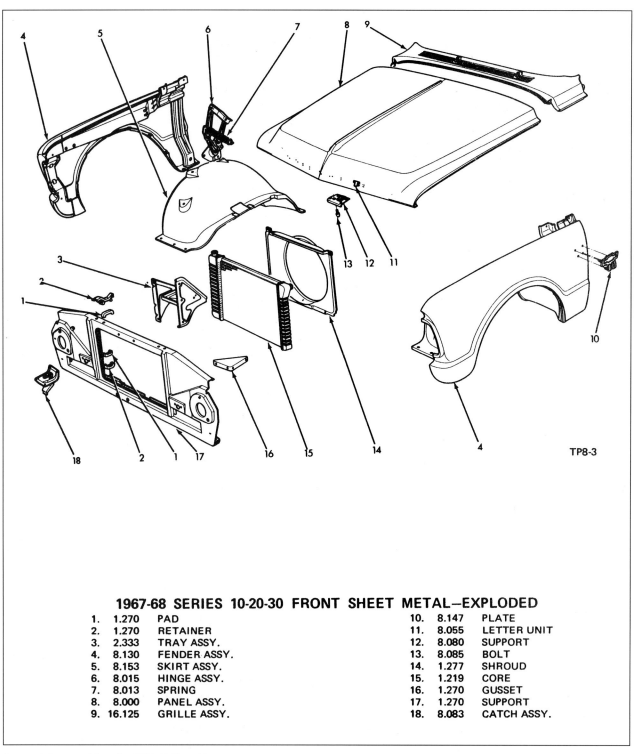

1967-68 SERIES 10-20-30 FRONT SHEET METAL—EXPLODED

1.	1.270	PAD	10.	8.147	PLATE
2.	1.270	RETAINER	11.	8.055	LETTER UNIT
3.	2.333	TRAY ASSY.	12.	8.080	SUPPORT
4.	8.130	FENDER ASSY.	13.	8.085	BOLT
5.	8.153	SKIRT ASSY.	14.	1.277	SHROUD
6.	8.015	HINGE ASSY.	15.	1.219	CORE
7.	8.013	SPRING	16.	1.270	GUSSET
8.	8.000	PANEL ASSY.	17.	1.270	SUPPORT
9.	16.125	GRILLE ASSY.	18.	8.083	CATCH ASSY.

Front end sheet metal from the 1967–1968 model year.

Usage: 1969–1972 C-10 to C-30 Chevrolet truck;
1969–1972 GMC 1500 to 3500 truck;
1969–1972 Blazer; 1970–1972 Jimmy

Interchange Number: 3
Part Number(s): 6272581 (left); 627582 (right)
Usage: 1973–1978 Chevrolet C-10–C-30 Chevrolet
truck; 1973–1978 1500 to 3500 GMC truck;
1973–1978 Blazer and Jimmy
Note(s): Paint as required

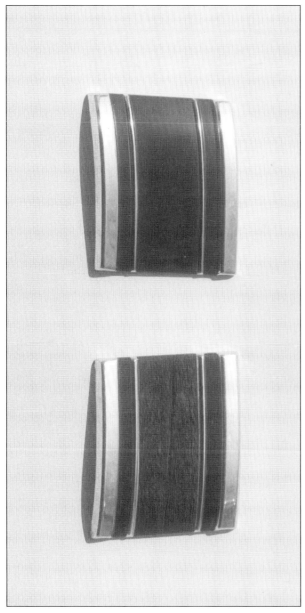

Simulated walnut trim was used in 1969–1970 as an option. The top is standard black trim, and the bottom is the optional walnut trim.

Roof Assemblies
Model Identification

Interchanges
Interchange Number: 1
    Part Number(s): 3944876
    Usage: 1967–1972 C-10 to C-50 conventional-cab truck; 1967–1972 GMC pickup
    Note(s): Some had optional roof-mounted marker lights, which will affect the interchange

Interchange Number: 2
    Part Number(s): 3999814
    Usage: 1973–1974 C-10 to C-60 Chevrolet truck with conventional cab; GMC 1500 to 6500 truck with conventional cab
    Note(s): Some had optional roof-mounted marker lights, which will affect the interchange

Interchange Number: 3
    Part Number(s): 3897908
    Usage: 1967–1972 Suburban with double back doors

Interchange Number: 4
    Part Number(s): 3936999
    Usage: 1967–1972 Suburban with tailgate

Interchange Number: 5
    Part Number(s): N/A
    Usage: 1973 Suburban with double back doors

Interchange Number: 6
    Part Number(s): N/A
    Usage: 1973 Suburban with tailgate

Interchange Number: 7
    Part Number(s): N/A
    Usage: 1974–1978 Suburban with double back doors

Interchange Number: 8
    Part Number(s): N/A
    Usage: 1974–1978 Suburban with tailgate

Interchange Number: 9
    Part Number(s): 6271846
    Usage: 1969–1972 Blazer and Jimmy

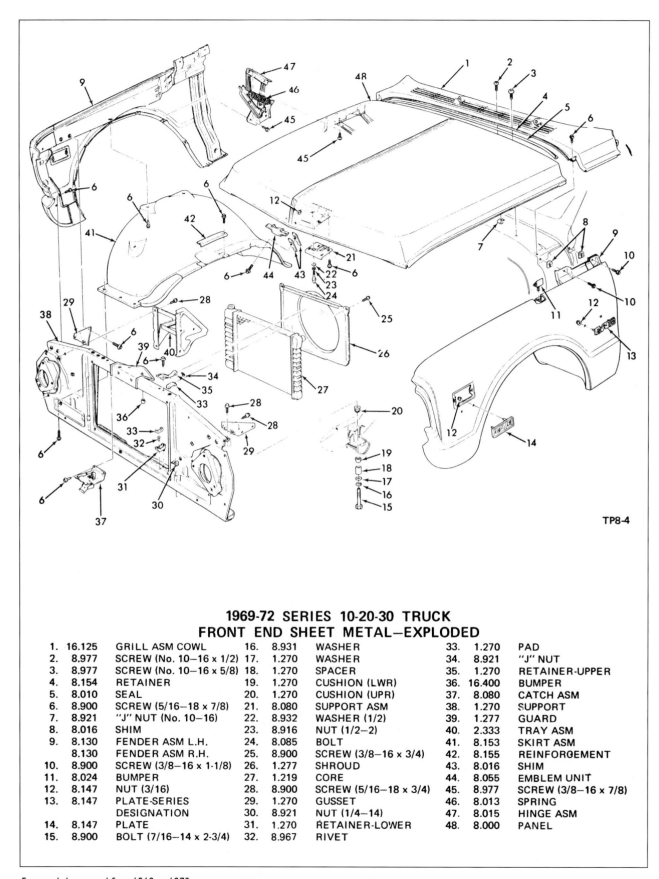

TP8-4

1969-72 SERIES 10-20-30 TRUCK
FRONT END SHEET METAL—EXPLODED

1.	16.125	GRILL ASM COWL	16.	8.931	WASHER	33.	1.270	PAD
2.	8.977	SCREW (No. 10—16 x 1/2)	17.	1.270	WASHER	34.	8.921	"J" NUT
3.	8.977	SCREW (No. 10—16 x 5/8)	18.	1.270	SPACER	35.	1.270	RETAINER-UPPER
4.	8.154	RETAINER	19.	1.270	CUSHION (LWR)	36.	16.400	BUMPER
5.	8.010	SEAL	20.	1.270	CUSHION (UPR)	37.	8.080	CATCH ASM
6.	8.900	SCREW (5/16—18 x 7/8)	21.	8.080	SUPPORT ASM	38.	1.270	SUPPORT
7.	8.921	"J" NUT (No. 10—16)	22.	8.932	WASHER (1/2)	39.	1.277	GUARD
8.	8.016	SHIM	23.	8.916	NUT (1/2—2)	40.	2.333	TRAY ASM
9.	8.130	FENDER ASM L.H.	24.	8.085	BOLT	41.	8.153	SKIRT ASM
	8.130	FENDER ASM R.H.	25.	8.900	SCREW (3/8—16 x 3/4)	42.	8.155	REINFORCEMENT
10.	8.900	SCREW (3/8—16 x 1-1/8)	26.	1.277	SHROUD	43.	8.016	SHIM
11.	8.024	BUMPER	27.	1.219	CORE	44.	8.055	EMBLEM UNIT
12.	8.147	NUT (3/16)	28.	8.900	SCREW (5/16—18 x 3/4)	45.	8.977	SCREW (3/8—16 x 7/8)
13.	8.147	PLATE-SERIES	29.	1.270	GUSSET	46.	8.013	SPRING
		DESIGNATION	30.	8.921	NUT (1/4—14)	47.	8.015	HINGE ASM
14.	8.147	PLATE	31.	1.270	RETAINER-LOWER	48.	8.000	PANEL
15.	8.900	BOLT (7/16—14 x 2-3/4)	32.	8.967	RIVET			

Front end sheet metal from 1969 to 1972.

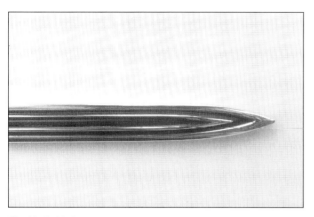

The 1967–1968 upper spear molding used on front fenders.

Interchange Number: 10
Part Number(s): 337827
Usage: 1973–1975 Blazer and Jimmy

Interchange Number: 11
Part Number(s): 355616 (front)
Usage: 1976–1980 Blazer and Jimmy

Interchange Number: 12
Part Number(s): 14014316 (rear removable hardtop)
Usage: 1976–1980 Blazer and Jimmy

Interchange Number: 13
Part Number(s): Varies (folding rear top)
Usage: 1976–1980 Blazer and Jimmy
Note(s): Available in black, white, beige, or blue

Interchange Number: 14
Usage: 1973–1978 C-20 to C-30 Crewcab and GMC 2500 to 3500 crew cab

Rear Side Panels

This interchange is the panel that extends over the rear wheels but is not the hump-shaped fenders on the dual and side-step models. The rear fenders are covered in a separate interchange.

Model Identification

Interchanges

Interchange Number: 1
Usage: 1960–1967 Chevrolet and GMC Stepside pickup

Interchange Number: 2
Part Numbers: 3884101 (left); 3884102 (right)
Usage: 1967 Chevrolet and GMC Fleetside pickup with 115-inch wheelbase

Interchange Number: 3
Part Number(s): 3931581 (left); 393582 (right)
Usage: 1967 Chevrolet and GMC Fleetside pickup with 127-inch wheelbase

Interchange Number: 4
Usage: 1968–1972 Chevrolet and GMC Stepside pickup

Interchange Number: 5
Part Number(s): 3924293 (left); 3924294 (right)

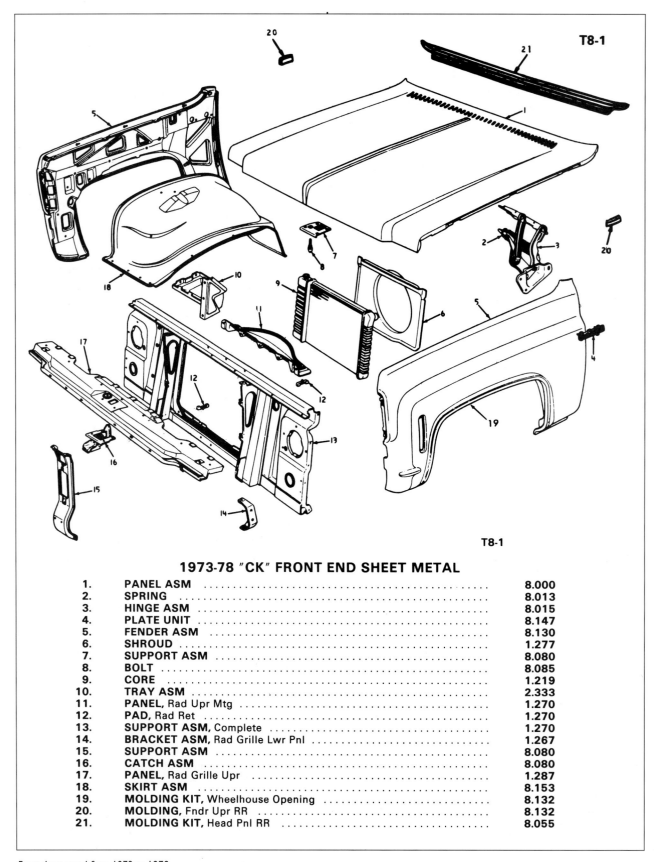

T8-1

1973-78 "CK" FRONT END SHEET METAL

1.	PANEL ASM	8.000
2.	SPRING	8.013
3.	HINGE ASM	8.015
4.	PLATE UNIT	8.147
5.	FENDER ASM	8.130
6.	SHROUD	1.277
7.	SUPPORT ASM	8.080
8.	BOLT	8.085
9.	CORE	1.219
10.	TRAY ASM	2.333
11.	PANEL, Rad Upr Mtg	1.270
12.	PAD, Rad Ret	1.270
13.	SUPPORT ASM, Complete	1.270
14.	BRACKET ASM, Rad Grille Lwr Pnl	1.267
15.	SUPPORT ASM	8.080
16.	CATCH ASM	8.080
17.	PANEL, Rad Grille Upr	1.287
18.	SKIRT ASM	8.153
19.	MOLDING KIT, Wheelhouse Opening	8.132
20.	MOLDING, Fndr Upr RR	8.132
21.	MOLDING KIT, Head Pnl RR	8.055

Front sheet metal from 1973 to 1978.

A standard 1967–1972 fixed–arm mirror.

Usage: 1968–1972 Chevrolet and GMC Fleetside pickup with 115-inch wheelbase

Interchange Number: 6
Part Number(s): 3924295 (left); 3924296 (right)
Usage: 1968–1972 Chevrolet and GMC Fleetside pickup with 127-inch wheelbase

Interchange Number: 7
Part Number(s): 3937443 (left); 3937444 (right)
Usage: 1968–1972 Chevrolet and GMC Fleetside pickup with 133-inch wheelbase

Interchange Number: 8
Part Number(s): 6272651 (left); 6272652 (right)
Usage: 1968–1972 Blazer and GMC Jimmy

Interchange Number: 9
Part Number(s): 3926691 (left); 3926692 (right)
Usage: 1968–1972 Chevrolet Suburban

Interchange Number: 10
Part Number(s): 14037297 (left); 6264102 (right)
Usage: 1973–1978 Chevrolet Suburban

Interchange Number: 11
Part Number(s): 6273513 (left); 6273514 (right)
Usage: 1973–1975 Blazer and Jimmy

Interchange Number: 13
Part Number(s): 14026209 (left); 467202 (right)
Usage: 1976–1978 Blazer and Jimmy

Interchange Number: 14
Part Number(s): 3999341 (left); 3999342 (right)
Usage: 1973 to early-1976 Chevrolet and GMC Fleetside without auxiliary tank, dual rear wheels, or toolbox
Note(s): Has hole for tailgate wedge

Interchange Number: 15
Part Number(s): 326925 (left); 3999342 (right)
Usage: 1973 to early-1976 Chevrolet and GMC Fleetside with auxiliary tank, without dual rear wheels
Note(s): Has hole for tailgate wedge; right side is the same as Interchange Number 24

Interchange Number: 16
Part Number(s): 334185 (left); 334184 (right)
Usage: 1973 to early-1976 Chevrolet and GMC Fleetside with dual rear wheels
Note(s): Has hole for tailgate wedge

Interchange Number: 17
Usage: 1973–1976 Chevrolet and GMC Stepside pickup with 117-inch wheelbase
Note(s): Interchange Number 28 will fit; see Note(s) under that section

Interchange Number: 18
Part Numbers: 14026341 (left); 14026342 (right)
Usage: 1977–1978 Chevrolet and GMC Stepside pickup with 117-inch wheelbase
Note(s): Will fit 1973–1976 models. Drill .48/.45 diameter holes for mounting rear lamps using rear bracket as template; install jack nut part number 367292 in holes and use applicable 0.250x20 screws for attachment

Interchange Number: 19
Part Numbers: 3999815 (left); 3999816 (right)
Usage: 1973 to early-1976 Chevrolet and GMC Fleetside pickup with 117-inch wheelbase, without auxiliary fuel tank

Interchange Number: 20
Part Numbers: 326929 (left); 3999816 (right)
Usage: 1973 to early-1976 Chevrolet and GMC Fleetside pickup with 117-inch wheelbase, with auxiliary fuel tank

Interchange Number: 21
Usage: 1973–1976 Chevrolet and GMC Stepside pickup with 131.5-inch wheelbase
Note(s): Interchange Number 31 will fit. See Note(s) under Interchange Number 27

Interchange Number: 22
Part Numbers: 14026319 (left); 458042 (right)
Usage: 1977–1978 Chevrolet and GMC Stepside pickup with 131.5-inch wheelbase

Interchange Number: 23
Part Numbers: 458001 (left); 458002 (right)
Usage: Late-1976 to 1978 Chevrolet and GMC Fleetside pickup with 117.5-inch wheelbase, without auxiliary fuel tank

Interchange Number: 24
Part Numbers: 458005 (left); 458002 (right)
Usage: Late-1976 to 1978 Chevrolet and GMC Fleetside pickup with 117.5-inch wheelbase and auxiliary fuel tank

Interchange Number: 25
Part Numbers: 458007 (left); 458004 (right)
Usage: Late-1976 to 1978 Chevrolet and GMC Fleetside pickup with 131.5- or 164.5-inch wheelbase and auxiliary fuel tank

The most popular style of the 1967–1972 mirror. It was standard on Cheyenne models.

Interchange Number: 26
> Part Numbers: 463377 (left); 463376 (right)
> Usage: Late-1976 to 1978 Chevrolet and GMC Fleetside pickup with dual rear wheels and auxiliary fuel tank

Interchange Number: 27
> Part Numbers: 463375 (left); 463376 (right)
> Usage: Late-1976 to 1978 Chevrolet and GMC Fleetside pickup with dual rear wheels, without auxiliary fuel tank

Interchange Number: 28
> Part Numbers: 458003 (left); 458004 (right)
> Usage: Late-1976 to 1978 Chevrolet and GMC Fleetside pickup with 131.5- or 161.5-inch wheelbase and auxiliary fuel tank

Rear Fenders
Model Identification

1969–1972	Interchange Number
Stepside	1

1968–1976

Left
  without side-mounted spare 5
  with side-mounted spare
    115-inch wheelbase .3
    127-inch wheelbase .4
Right 2

1977–1978
With single rear wheel, left
  without side-mounted spare
    without auxiliary fuel tank 13
    with auxiliary fuel tank 14
  with side-mounted spare, without auxiliary fuel tank
    117.5-inch wheelbase 15
    131.5-inch wheelbase 16
With single rear wheel, right 12
With dual rear wheels 17

Interchanges

Interchange Number: 1
> Usage: 1967 Chevrolet and GMC Stepside pickup

Interchange Number: 2
> Part Number(s): 3882660 (right)
> Usage: 1968–1972 Chevrolet and GMC Stepside pickup, all models

Interchange Number: 3
> Part Number(s): 3960563 (left)
> Usage: 1968–1972 Chevrolet and GMC Stepside pickup with side-mounted spare and 115-inch wheelbase

Interchange Number: 4
> Part Number(s): 3960565 (left)
> Usage: 1968–1972 Chevrolet and GMC Stepside pickup with side-mounted spare and 127-inch wheelbase

Interchange Number: 5
> Part Number(s): 3960559 (left)
> Usage: 1968–1972 Chevrolet and GMC Stepside pickup without side-mounted spare—all wheelbases

Interchange Number: 6
> Part Number(s): 6262084 (right)
> Usage: 1973–1976 Chevrolet C-10 to C-30, GMC 1500 to 3500—all applications
> Note(s): Interchange Number 12 will fit; see Note(s) under that section

Interchange Number: 7
> Part Number(s): 6262083 (left)
> Usage: 1973–1976 Chevrolet C-10 to C-30, GMC 1500 to 3500—all without outside spare or auxiliary fuel tank
> Note(s): Interchange Number 13 will fit; See Note(s) under that section

Interchange Number: 8
> Part Number(s): 327089 (left)
> Usage: 1973–1974 Chevrolet C-10 to C-30, GMC 1500 to 3500—all with auxiliary fuel tank, without outside spare
> Note(s): Interchange Number 14 will fit; See Note(s) under Interchange Number 12 for details

Interchange Number: 9
> Part Number(s): 6273539 (left)

Usage: 1973–1974 Chevrolet C-10 to C-30, GMC 1500 to 3500—all with outside spare, without auxiliary fuel tank

Interchange Number: 10

Part Number(s): 327967 (left)

Usage: 1973–1974 Chevrolet C-10 to C-30, GMC 1500 to 3500—all with outside spare and auxiliary fuel tank

Interchange Number: 11

Part Number(s): 3929087 (left) 3929088 (right)

Usage: 1973–1978 Chevrolet C-30, GMC 3500—all with dual rear wheels

Interchange Number: 12

Part Number(s): 375122 (right)

Usage: 1977–1978 Chevrolet C-10 to C-30, GMC 1500 to 3500—all applications

Note(s): Will fit Interchange Number 6; must use 1977–1978-style braces to mount this fender on 1973–1976 models

Interchange Number: 13

Part Number(s): 375121 (left)

Usage: 1977–1978 Chevrolet C-10 to C-30, GMC 1500 to 3500 without outside spare or auxiliary fuel tank

Note(s): Will fit Interchange Number 7. Must use 1977–1978-style braces to mount this fender on 1973–1976 models. Note also that 1977–1978 fuel filler neck and hose must also be used due to relocation of the filler neck higher up on the body.

Interchange Number: 14

Part Number(s): 375131 (left)

Usage: 1977–1978 Chevrolet C-10 to C-30, GMC 1500 to 3500—all with auxiliary fuel tank, without outside spare

Interchange Number: 15

Part Number(s): 375177 (left)

Usage: 1977–1978 Chevrolet C-10 to C-30, GMC 1500 to 3500—all with 117.5-inch wheelbase and outside spare, without auxiliary fuel tank

Note(s): Will fit Interchange Number 9

Interchange Number: 16

Part Number(s): 375113 (left)

Usage: 1977–1978 Chevrolet C-10 to C-30, GMC 1500 to 3500 with 131.5-inch wheelbase and outside spare, without auxiliary fuel tank

Interchange Number: 17

Usage: 1977–1978 Chevrolet C-10 to C-30, GMC 1500 to 3500—all with dual rear wheels

Tailgates
Model Identification

1967–1972	Interchange Number
Stepside	1
Fleetside	2

West Coast mirrors.

Blazer	
without removable hardtop	2
with removable hardtop	4
Suburban	3
1973–1976	
Stepside	9
Fleetside	7
Blazer	
without removable hardtop	7
with removable hardtop	5
Suburban	6
1977–1978	
Stepside	9
Fleetside	8
Blazer	
without removable hardtop	8
with removable hardtop	5
Suburban	6

Interchanges
Interchange Number: 1

Part Number(s): 3810424

Usage: 1954–1972 Chevrolet Stepside pickup

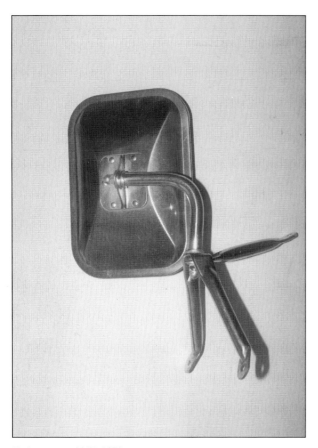

Trailer mirrors, 1967–1972.

Interchange Number: 2
    Part Number(s): 3882697
    Usage: 1967–1972 Chevrolet pickup; 1969–1972 Blazer without removable hardtop

Interchange Number: 3
    Part Number(s): 3897931 (upper); 3897937 (lower)
    Usage: 1968–1972 Suburban with end gate

Interchange Number: 4
    Part Number(s): 6263027
    Usage: 1969–1972 Blazer with removable hardtop

Interchange Number: 5
    Part Number(s): 14021333
    Usage: 1973–1978 Blazer and Jimmy with removable hardtop

Interchange Number: 6
    Part Number(s): 14057339
    Usage: 1973–1978 Suburban with end gate

Interchange Number: 7
    Part Number(s): 345806
    Usage: 1973–1976 Chevrolet Fleetside pickup; 1973–1976 Blazer without removable hardtop

Interchange Number: 8
    Part Number(s): 467206
    Usage: 1977–1978 Chevrolet Fleetside pickup; Blazer without removable top

Interchange Number: 9
    Part Number(s): 14026349
    Usage: 1973–1978 Chevrolet Stepside pickup

Hinges, Tailgate
Model Identification

1967–1972	Interchange Number
Stepside	3
Fleetside	1
Blazer	
without removable hardtop	1
with removable hardtop	11
Suburban	2, 10

1973–1975	
Stepside	3
Fleetside	4
Blazer	
without removable hardtop	4
with removable hardtop	7, 8
Suburban	6, 8

1976	
Stepside	3
Fleetside	
early	4
late	5
Blazer	
without removable hardtop	
early	4
late	5
with removable hardtop	7, 8
Suburban	6, 8

1977–1978	
Stepside	3
Fleetside	
early	4
late	5
Blazer	
without removable hardtop	5
with removable hardtop	7, 8
Suburban	6, 8

Interchanges
Interchange Number: 1
    Part Number(s): 3924245 (left); 3924246 (right)
    Usage: 1967–1972 Chevrolet and GMC Fleetside pickup, Blazer, and Jimmy

Interchange Number: 2
    Part Number(s): 3905695 (fits either side)
    Usage: 1967–1972 Suburban with end gate

Interchange Number: 3
    Part Number(s): 3810823 (left); 3810824 (right)
    Usage: 1954–1978 Chevrolet and GMC Stepside pickup

Interchange Number: 4
    Part Number(s): 3999873 (left); 3999874 (right)

Usage: 1973 to early-1976 Chevrolet and GMC
Fleetside pickup, Blazer, and Jimmy

Note(s): Has no-stud end-gate link

Interchange Number: 5

Part Number(s): 458025 (left); 458026 (right)

Usage: Late-1976 to 1978 Chevrolet and GMC
Fleetside pickup, Blazer, and Jimmy

Note(s): Has stud on end-gate link

Interchange Number: 6

Part Number(s): 7732272 (fits either side)

Usage: 1973–1978 Suburban

Note(s): Support cables

Interchange Number: 7

Part Number(s): 6274850 (fits either side)

Usage: 1973–1978 Blazer and Jimmy with removable hardtop and support cable

Interchange Number: 8

Part Number(s): 337788 (fits either side)

Usage: 1973–1978 Blazer or Jimmy with removable
hardtop

Interchange Number: 9

Part Number(s): 337787 (fits either side)

Usage: 1973–1978 Suburban with end gate

Interchange Number: 10

Part Number(s): 3919264 (gate half; fits either side);
3904415 (body half; fits either side)

Usage: 1967–1972 Suburban with end gate

Note(s): Body-half hinge same as Interchange
Number 11

Interchange Number: 11

Part Number(s): 3919264 (body half; fits either
side); 3903263 (door half; fits either side)

Usage: 1969–1972 Blazer or Jimmy with removable
hardtop

Note(s): Body-half hinge same as Interchange
Number 10

Front Bumpers
Model Identification

1967–1970	*Interchange Number*
Painted 1	
Chrome 2	
1971–1972	
Painted 3	
Chrome 4	
1973–1977	
Painted 5	
Chrome	
without impact strip 6	
with impact strip (1976–1977 only) 7	

Interchanges

Interchange Number: 1

Part Number(s): 3884700

Usage: 1967–1970 Chevrolet C-10 to C-30 truck
with painted bumper

Camper-style mirrors, 1967–1972.

Interchange Number: 2

Part Number(s): 3884701

Usage: 1967–1970 Chevrolet C-10 to C-30 truck;
1969–1970 Blazer with chrome bumper

Interchange Number: 3

Part Number(s): 3990709

Usage: 1971–1972 C-10 to C-30 Chevrolet truck,
Blazer, and Jimmy with painted bumper

Interchange Number: 4

Part Number(s): 3990710

Usage: 1971–1972 C-10 to C-30 Chevrolet truck,
Blazer, and Jimmy with chrome bumper

Interchange Number: 5

Part Number(s): 6262158

Usage: 1973–1978 C-10 to C-30 Chevrolet and
1500 to 3500 GMC truck, Blazer, and Jimmy
with painted bumper

Interchange Number: 6

Part Number(s): 6272560

Usage: 1973–1978 C-10 to C-30 Chevrolet and
1500 to 3500 GMC truck, Blazer, and Jimmy
with chrome bumper, without impact strip

Interchange Number: 7

Part Number(s): 361552

Usage: 1976–1978 C-10 to C-30 Chevrolet and
1500 to 3500 GMC truck, Blazer, and Jimmy
with chrome bumper and impact strip

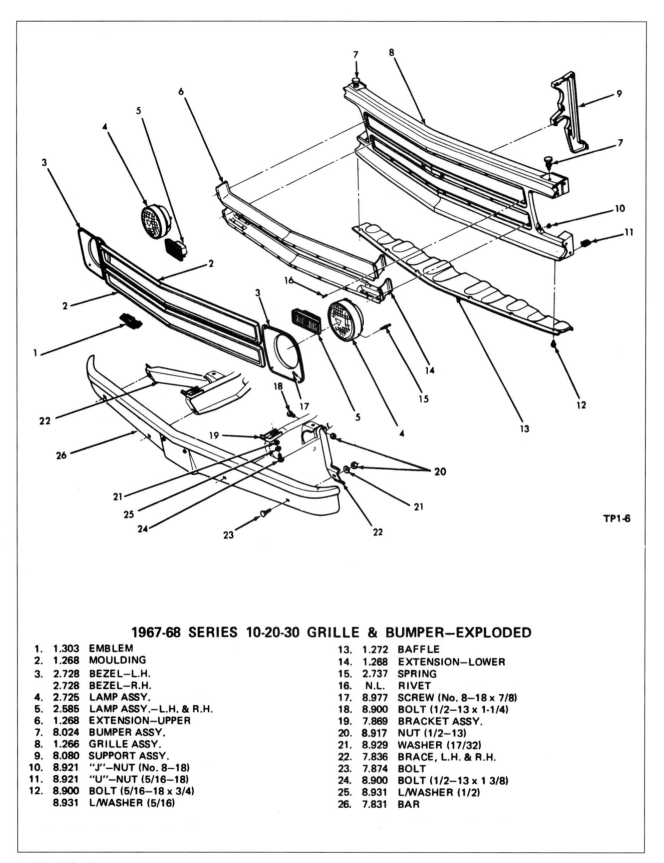

1967-68 SERIES 10-20-30 GRILLE & BUMPER—EXPLODED

1. 1.303 EMBLEM
2. 1.268 MOULDING
3. 2.728 BEZEL—L.H.
   2.728 BEZEL—R.H.
4. 2.725 LAMP ASSY.
5. 2.585 LAMP ASSY.—L.H. & R.H.
6. 1.268 EXTENSION—UPPER
7. 8.024 BUMPER ASSY.
8. 1.266 GRILLE ASSY.
9. 8.080 SUPPORT ASSY.
10. 8.921 "J"—NUT (No. 8—18)
11. 8.921 "U"—NUT (5/16—18)
12. 8.900 BOLT (5/16—18 x 3/4)
    8.931 L/WASHER (5/16)

13. 1.272 BAFFLE
14. 1.268 EXTENSION—LOWER
15. 2.737 SPRING
16. N.L. RIVET
17. 8.977 SCREW (No. 8—18 x 7/8)
18. 8.900 BOLT (1/2—13 x 1-1/4)
19. 7.869 BRACKET ASSY.
20. 8.917 NUT (1/2—13)
21. 8.929 WASHER (17/32)
22. 7.836 BRACE, L.H. & R.H.
23. 7.874 BOLT
24. 8.900 BOLT (1/2—13 x 1 3/8)
25. 8.931 L/WASHER (1/2)
26. 7.831 BAR

A 1967–1968 grille.

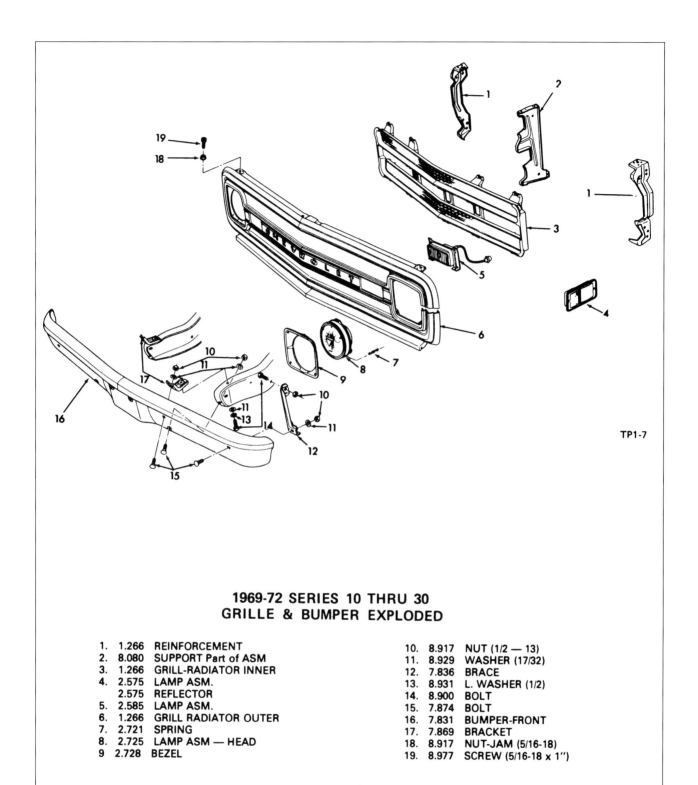

1969-72 SERIES 10 THRU 30
GRILLE & BUMPER EXPLODED

1.	1.266	REINFORCEMENT		10.	8.917	NUT (1/2 — 13)
2.	8.080	SUPPORT Part of ASM		11.	8.929	WASHER (17/32)
3.	1.266	GRILL-RADIATOR INNER		12.	7.836	BRACE
4.	2.575	LAMP ASM.		13.	8.931	L. WASHER (1/2)
	2.575	REFLECTOR		14.	8.900	BOLT
5.	2.585	LAMP ASM.		15.	7.874	BOLT
6.	1.266	GRILL RADIATOR OUTER		16.	7.831	BUMPER-FRONT
7.	2.721	SPRING		17.	7.869	BRACKET
8.	2.725	LAMP ASM — HEAD		18.	8.917	NUT-JAM (5/16-18)
9	2.728	BEZEL		19.	8.977	SCREW (5/16-18 x 1")

TP1-7

A 1969–1972 grille.

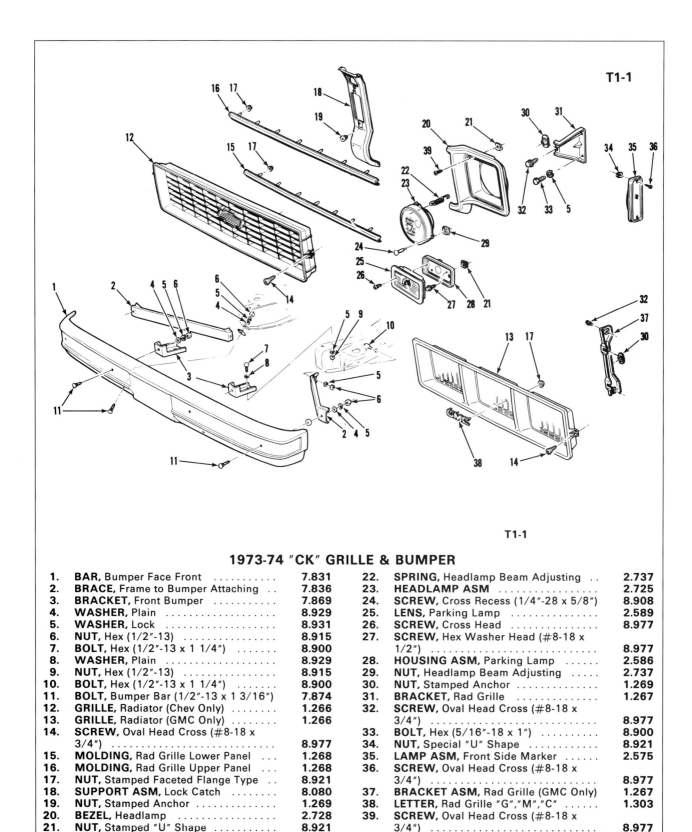

T1-1

1973-74 "CK" GRILLE & BUMPER

1.	**BAR,** Bumper Face Front	7.831	22.	**SPRING,** Headlamp Beam Adjusting		2.737
2.	**BRACE,** Frame to Bumper Attaching	7.836	23.	**HEADLAMP ASM**		2.725
3.	**BRACKET,** Front Bumper	7.869	24.	**SCREW,** Cross Recess (1/4"-28 x 5/8")		8.908
4.	**WASHER,** Plain	8.929	25.	**LENS,** Parking Lamp		2.589
5.	**WASHER,** Lock	8.931	26.	**SCREW,** Cross Head		8.977
6.	**NUT,** Hex (1/2"-13)	8.915	27.	**SCREW,** Hex Washer Head (#8-18 x 1/2")		
7.	**BOLT,** Hex (1/2"-13 x 1 1/4")	8.900				8.977
8.	**WASHER,** Plain	8.929	28.	**HOUSING ASM,** Parking Lamp		2.586
9.	**NUT,** Hex (1/2"-13)	8.915	29.	**NUT,** Headlamp Beam Adjusting		2.737
10.	**BOLT,** Hex (1/2"-13 x 1 1/4")	8.900	30.	**NUT,** Stamped Anchor		1.269
11.	**BOLT,** Bumper Bar (1/2"-13 x 1 3/16")	7.874	31.	**BRACKET,** Rad Grille		1.267
12.	**GRILLE,** Radiator (Chev Only)	1.266	32.	**SCREW,** Oval Head Cross (#8-18 x 3/4")		
13.	**GRILLE,** Radiator (GMC Only)	1.266				8.977
14.	**SCREW,** Oval Head Cross (#8-18 x 3/4")		33.	**BOLT,** Hex (5/16"-18 x 1")		8.900
		8.977	34.	**NUT,** Special "U" Shape		8.921
15.	**MOLDING,** Rad Grille Lower Panel	1.268	35.	**LAMP ASM,** Front Side Marker		2.575
16.	**MOLDING,** Rad Grille Upper Panel	1.268	36.	**SCREW,** Oval Head Cross (#8-18 x 3/4")		
17.	**NUT,** Stamped Faceted Flange Type	8.921				8.977
18.	**SUPPORT ASM,** Lock Catch	8.080	37.	**BRACKET ASM,** Rad Grille (GMC Only)		1.267
19.	**NUT,** Stamped Anchor	1.269	38.	**LETTER,** Rad Grille "G","M","C"		1.303
20.	**BEZEL,** Headlamp	2.728	39.	**SCREW,** Oval Head Cross (#8-18 x 3/4")		
21.	**NUT,** Stamped "U" Shape	8.921				8.977

A 1973–1974 grille.

Interchange Number: 8

 Part Number(s): 466978

 Usage: 1978–1981 Chevrolet C-10 to C-30 and GMC 1500 to 3500 truck with body-color and impact-strip bumper

Rear Bumpers
Model Identification

1967–1972	*Interchange Number*
Stepside	
painted	1
chrome	2
Fleetside	
painted	3
chrome	4
Stepside	5
1973–1978	
Stepside	
painted	1
chrome	2
Fleetside	
painted	6
chrome	
without impact strip	7
with impact strip (1976) only	8
body colored	9

Interchanges

Interchange Number: 1

 Part Number(s): 3884760

 Usage: 1967–1978 Chevrolet and GMC Stepside pickup with painted bumper

Interchange Number: 2

 Part Number(s): 3885643

 Usage: 1967–1978 Chevrolet and GMC Stepside pickup with chrome bumper

Interchange Number: 3

 Part Number(s): 3885614

 Usage: 1967–1972 Chevrolet and GMC Fleetside pickup; 1969–1972 Blazer and Jimmy—all with chrome bumper

Interchange Number: 4

 Part Number(s): 3885621

 Usage: 1967–1972 Chevrolet and GMC Fleetside pickup; 1969–1972 Blazer and Jimmy—all with painted bumper

Interchange Number: 5

 Part Number(s): 330367

 Usage: 1967–1972 Chevrolet C-10 to C-30 and GMC 1500 to 3500 pickup with step bumper

Interchange Number: 6

 Part Number(s): 6262166

 Usage: 1973–1978 Chevrolet C-10 to C-30 and GMC 1500 to 3500 truck with painted bumper

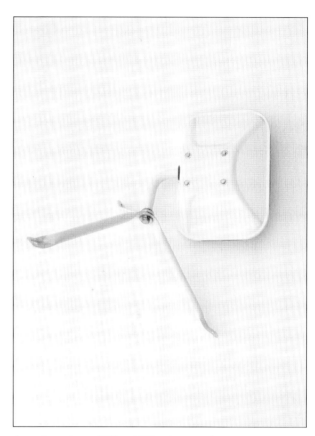

A popular option on 1973 to 1978 pickups was these mirrors.

Interchange Number: 7

 Part Number(s): 6272566

 Usage: 1973–1978 Chevrolet C-10 to C-30 and GMC 1500 to 3500 truck with chrome bumper, without impact strip

Interchange Number: 8

 Part Number(s): 359289

 Usage: 1976–1978 Chevrolet C-10 to C-30 and GMC 1500 to 3500 truck with chrome bumper and impact strip

Interchange Number: 9

 Part Number(s): 466979

 Usage: 1978–1981 Chevrolet C-10 to C-30 and GMC 1500 to 3500 truck with body-colored bumper

Grilles

Grilles for trucks, unlike those for passenger sedans, were not changed every year, so a larger interchange is available. In some cases, a newer grille can be modified to fit earlier models. If this is possible, it is listed in the Note(s) section of that particular interchange. Grilles are also one of the parts that GMC parts will not interchange to fit your Chevrolet truck.

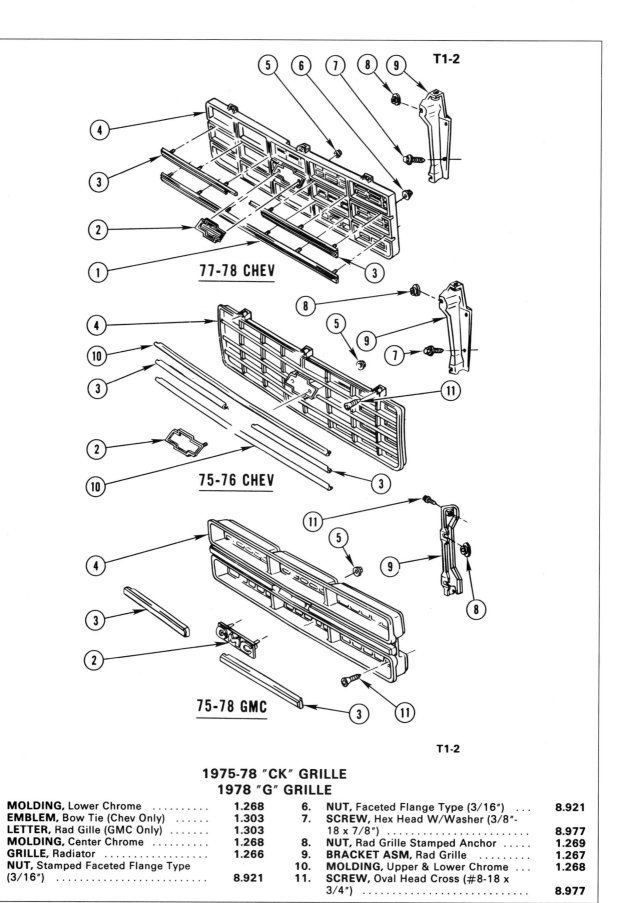

T1-2

77-78 CHEV

75-76 CHEV

75-78 GMC

T1-2

1975-78 "CK" GRILLE
1978 "G" GRILLE

1.	**MOLDING,** Lower Chrome	1.268
2.	**EMBLEM,** Bow Tie (Chev Only)	1.303
	LETTER, Rad Gille (GMC Only)	1.303
3.	**MOLDING,** Center Chrome	1.268
4.	**GRILLE,** Radiator	1.266
5.	**NUT,** Stamped Faceted Flange Type (3/16")	8.921
6.	**NUT,** Faceted Flange Type (3/16")	8.921
7.	**SCREW,** Hex Head W/Washer (3/8"-18 x 7/8")	8.977
8.	**NUT,** Rad Grille Stamped Anchor	1.269
9.	**BRACKET ASM,** Rad Grille	1.267
10.	**MOLDING,** Upper & Lower Chrome	1.268
11.	**SCREW,** Oval Head Cross (#8-18 x 3/4")	8.977

A 1975–1978 grille.

A standard 1973–1978 mirror.

Model Identification

1967–1968	Interchange Number
All	1
1969	
All	2
1970	
All	3
1971–1972	
All	4
1973–1974	
Painted	6
Chrome	5
1975–1976	
All	7
1977	
Painted	8
Chrome	9

Interchanges

Interchange Number: 1
Part Number(s): 3886762
Usage: 1967–1968 C-10 to C-30 Chevrolet truck, all body styles

Interchange Number: 2
Part Number(s): 3980036 (inner); 3980037 (outer)
Usage: 1969 C-10 to C-30 Chevrolet truck, all body styles; 1969 Blazer
Note(s): Interchange Number 3 will fit, if retainer part number 3944896 and number 10 16x3/4 screws and washers and 1 5/16-inch 16 nut are used

Interchange Number: 3
Part Number(s): 3985054 (outer); 3985056 (inner)

Usage: 1970 C-10 to C-30 Chevrolet truck, all body styles; 1970 Blazer
Note(s): Will fit Interchange Number 2; see Note(s) under that section for details

Interchange Number: 4
Part Number(s): 3990701 (outer), 3990700 (inner)
Usage: 1971–1972 C-10 to C-30 Chevrolet truck, all body styles; 1971–1972 Blazer

Interchange Number: 5
Part Number(s): 331572
Usage: 1973–1974 C-10 to C-30 and K-10 to K-30 Chevrolet truck, all body styles; 1973–1974 Blazer—all with chrome grille

Interchange Number: 6
Part Number(s): 6270858
Usage: 1973–1974 C-10 to C-30 and K-10 to K-30 Chevrolet truck, all body styles; 1973–1974 Blazer—all with painted grille

Interchange Number: 7
Part Number(s): 343981
Usage: 1975–1976 C-10 to C-30 and K-10 to K-30 Chevrolet truck, all body styles; 1975–1976 Blazer—all with painted grille
Note: If you use this replacement part number, you must use the replacement nameplates and moldings; original units will not fit. Used parts will interchange.

Interchange Number: 8
Part Number(s): 14004752
Usage: 1977 C-10 to C-30 and K-10 to K-30 Chevrolet truck, all body styles; 1977 Blazer; 1978 G-10 to G-30 Chevrolet van—all with painted grille
Note: If you use this replacement part number, you must use the replacement nameplates and moldings; original units will not fit. Holes will have to be drilled for nameplate. Used parts will interchange without modification.

Interchange Number: 9
Part Number(s): 14000078
Usage: 1978–1979 C-10 to C-30 and K-10 to K-30 Chevrolet truck (all body styles) and Blazer; 1978–1979 G-10 to G-30 Chevrolet van—all with chrome grille
Note: If you use this replacement part number, you must use the replacement nameplates and moldings; original units will not fit. Used parts will interchange without modification.

Outside Rearview Mirrors
Model Identification

1967–1970	Interchange Number
Production mirror	3
Folding-arm	2
Fixed-arm	10

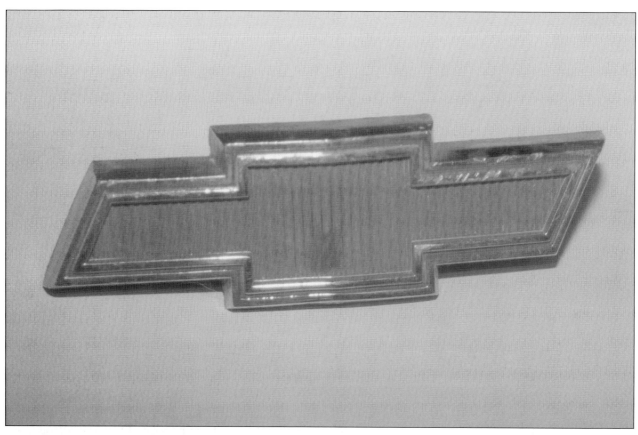

A 1967–1968 grille bow tie.

A 1970 grille bow tie.

Interchanges

Interchange Number: 1
Part Number(s): 3929463 (left); 3929464 (right)
Usage: 1967–1972 C-10 to C-50 and K-10 to K-30 Chevrolet and GMC 1500 to 5500 trucks with West Coast mirrors

Interchange Number: 2
Part Number(s): 3898376 (either side); See note(s)
Usage: 1967–1972 C-10 to C-30 Chevrolet and 1500 to 3500 GMC truck with folding-arm mirrors
Note(s): All parts are interchangeable from side to side except the reinforcement, which is unique to each side

Interchange Number: 3
Part Number(s): 3981409 (left); 3981410 (right)
Usage: 1967–1972 C-10 to C-30 and K-10 to K-30 Chevrolet truck, 1971–1978 G-10 to G-30 Chevrolet van; 1969–1972 Blazer
Note(s): Production mirrors

Interchange Number: 4
Part Number(s): See Note(s)
Usage: 1971 C-10 to C-30 and K-10 to K 30 Chevrolet truck with stainless-steel, below-eye-level mirrors
Note(s): Mirror is part number 993874. Support is part number 3980052. Arm is part number 3980053. Brace is part number 3980054.

Interchange Number: 5
Part Number(s): See Note(s)
Usage: 1972 C-10 to C-30 and K-10 to K 30 Chevrolet truck with stainless-steel, below-eye-level mirrors
Note(s): Mirror is part number 993874. Support is part number 3980052. Arm is part number 3980054. Brace is part number 3980056.

Interchange Number: 6
Part Number(s): See Note(s)

A 1973 350-ci grille ID.

Usage: 1971 C-10 to C-30 and K-10 to K-30 Chevrolet truck with white-painted, below-eye-level mirrors

Note(s): Mirror is part number 993872. Support is part number 3980048. Arm is part number 3980049. Brace is part number 3980050.

Interchange Number: 7

Part Number(s): See Note(s)

Usage: 1972 C-10 to C-30 and K-10 to K-30 Chevrolet truck with white-painted, below-eye-level mirrors

Note(s): Mirror is part number 993872. Support is part number 3980048. Arm is part number 3980053. Brace is part number 3980054.

Interchange Number: 8

Part Number(s): 993905 (pair)

Usage: 1971–1978 G-10 to G-30 Chevrolet van with white-painted, below-eye-level mirrors

Note(s): Each side is unique and will not swap sides

Interchange Number: 9

Part Number(s): 995587 (pair)

Usage: 1971–1978 G-10 to G-30 Chevrolet van with stainless-steel, below-eye-level mirrors

Note(s): Each side is unique and will not swap sides

Interchange Number: 10

Part Number(s): See Note(s)

Usage: 1967–1972 C-10 to C-30 and K-10 to K-30 Chevrolet truck with painted, fixed-arm mirrors

Note(s): Mirror is part number 3958588. Arm is part number 3893453 (left) or 3893454 (right).

Interchange Number: 11

Part Number(s): 995487 (pair)

Usage: 1967–1972 C-10 to C-30 and K-10 to K-30 Chevrolet truck and G-10 to G-30 Chevrolet van with camper-style, white-painted mirrors

Note(s): Each side is unique and will not swap sides

Interchange Number: 12

Part Number(s): 993874 (pair)

Usage: 1967–1972 C-10 to C-30 and K-10 to K-30 Chevrolet truck and G-10 to G-30 Chevrolet van with camper-style, stainless-steel mirrors

Note(s): Each side is unique and will not swap sides

Interchange Number: 13

Part Number(s): See Note(s)

Usage: 1967–1972 C-10 to C-30 Suburban without Deluxe package

Note(s): Mirror part number is 3922788. Arm part number is 3842329 (left) or 384230 (right).

Interchange Number: 14

Part Number(s): See Note(s)

Usage: 1967–1972 C-10 to C-30 Suburban with Deluxe package

Note(s): Mirror part number is 3922776. Base part number is 5946478 (fits either side).

Interchange Number: 15

Part Number(s): See Note(s)

Usage: 1969–1972 Blazer

Note(s): Mirror part number is 3960511. Arm part number is 3893453 (left) or 3893456 (right).

Interchange Number: 16

Part Number(s): N/A

Usage: 1973–1978 Chevrolet truck, all types with Sr. West Coast mirrors

Interchange Number: 17

Part Number(s): N/A

Usage: 1973–1978 C-10 to C-30 and K-10 to K-30 Chevrolet truck, all types with below-eye-level mirrors

Interchange Number: 18

Part Number(s): N/A

Usage: 1973–1978 C-10 to C-30 and K-10 to K-30 Chevrolet truck with Jr. West Coast mirrors

Interchange Number: 19

Part Number(s): N/A

Usage: 1973 C-10 to C-30 and K-10 to K-30 Chevrolet truck, all types with below-eye-level, camper-style mirrors

Interchange Number: 20

Part Number(s): N/A

Usage: 1974–1978 C-10 to C-30 and K-10 to K-30 Chevrolet truck, all types with below-eye-level, camper-style mirrors

Glass

Interchange here is "physical fit." There are two types of glass used: tinted and nontinted. Tinted glass came in two forms: either the windshield was tinted and the rest of the glass left untinted, or all the glass was tinted. Tinted glass was standard on trucks with air conditioning. The interchange does not consider tint, but you should

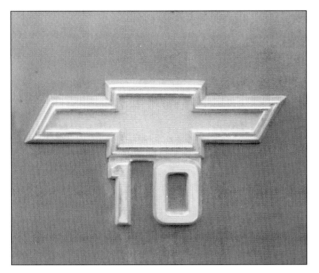
A 1967–1968 front fender nameplate for C-10 models.

match the glass to the rest of your truck. For example, if your 1972 C-10 pickup has all-tinted glass you should not replace the back glass with a nontinted type.

Windshields
Model Identification

1967–1972	Interchange Number
Cab	1
Blazer	1
Suburban	1

1973–1974
Cab
    without antenna 6
    with antenna 4
Blazer
    without antenna 6
    with antenna 4
Suburban
    without antenna 6
    with antenna 4

1975–1978
Cab
    without antenna 7
    with antenna 5
Blazer
    without antenna 7
    with antenna 5
Suburban
    without antenna 7
    with antenna 5

Interchanges

Interchange Number: 1
    Part Number(s): 3884710
    Usage: 1967–1972 C-10 to C-30 and K-10 to K-30 Chevrolet and GMC 1500 to 3500 truck, all body styles except van; 1969–1972 Blazer and Jimmy

Interchange Number: 2
    Part Number(s): 3875317
    Usage: 1967–1970 Chevrolet and GMC van

Interchange Number: 3
    Part Number(s): 363651
    Usage: 1971–1981 G-10 to G-30 Chevrolet and 1500 to 3500 GMC van

Interchange Number: 4
    Part Number(s): 14018596
    Usage: 1973–1974 C-10 to C-30 and K-5 to K-30 Chevrolet and 1500 to 3500 GMC truck, all models except van; 1973–1974 Blazer and Jimmy—all with antenna
    Note(s): Interchange 5 will fit if you use 1975–1978 weather stripping

Interchange Number: 5
    Part Number(s): 14018596
    Usage: 1975–1978 C-10 to C-30 and K-5 to K-30 Chevrolet and 1500 to 3500 GMC truck, all models except van; 1973–1974 Blazer and Jimmy—all with antenna

Interchange Number: 6
    Part Number(s): 351710
    Usage: 1973–1974 C-10 to C-30 and K-5 to K-30 Chevrolet and 1500 to 3500 GMC truck, all models except van; 1973–1974 Blazer and Jimmy—all without antenna
    Note(s): Interchange Number 7 will fit if you use 1975–1978 weather stripping

Interchange Number: 7
    Part Number(s): 351710
    Usage: 1975–1978 C-10 to C-30 and K-5 to K-30 Chevrolet and 1500 to 3500 GMC truck, all models except van; 1973–1974 Blazer and Jimmy—all without antenna

Door Glass
Model Identification

1967–1972	Interchange Number
Cab	1

Suburban
    front 2
    rear
        fixed 5
        moveable 4
Blazer 1

1973–1978
Cab 3

A 1969–1970 front fender nameplate.

Suburban

    front 3

    rear

        fixed 7

        moveable 6

Blazer 3

Interchanges

Interchange Number: 1

Usage: 1967–1972 C-10 to C-60 and K-10 to K-30 Chevrolet and GMC 1500 to 6500 truck, all models except van or Suburban; 1969–1972 Blazer and Jimmy

Interchange Number: 2

Part Number(s): 4502T

Usage: 1967–1972 Chevrolet Suburban and GMC Carryall

Interchange Number: 3

Usage: 1973–1980 C-10 to C-30 and K-5 to K-30 truck, Blazer, Jimmy, and GMC 1500 to 3500— all models except van

Interchange Number: 4

Usage: 1967–1972 Suburban with rear door and side moveable glass

Note(s): Same glass used on either side

Interchange Number: 5

Usage: 1967–1972 Suburban with fixed rear door and side glass

Note(s): Same glass used on both sides

Interchange Number: 6):

Usage: 1973–1980 Crewcab Chevrolet and GMC pickup; 1973–1980 Suburban and Carryall with moveable rear door windows

Interchange Number: 7

Usage: 1973–1980 Crewcab Chevrolet and GMC pickup; 1973–1980 Suburban and GMC Carryall with fixed rear door windows

Door-Vent Glass
Model Identification

1967–1972	Interchange Number
All 1	
1973–1978	
All 2	

Interchanges

Interchange Number: 1

Part Number(s): 3925935

Usage: 1966–1972 C-10 to C-30 Chevrolet truck and GMC 1500 to 3500 truck (except van); 1969–1972 Blazer and Jimmy

Interchange Number: 2

Part Number(s): 6271923 (left); 6271924 (right)

Usage: 1973–1979 C-10 to C-30 Chevrolet and GMC 1500 to 3500 (except van, Blazer, and Jimmy)

Quarter Glass
Model Identification

1969–1972	Interchange Number
Blazer 1	
Suburban	
fixed 5	
moveable 6	
rear side 7	
1973	
Blazer 2	
Suburban 8	

A 1967–1969 Custom Camper nameplate.

1974–1977
Blazer
    nonsliding 2
    sliding 3
Suburban
    1974 8
    1975–1977 9
1978
Blazer
    nonsliding 2
    sliding 4
Suburban 9

Interchanges
Interchange Number: 1
    Usage: 1969–1972 Blazer; 1970–1972 Jimmy
Interchange Number: 2
    Usage: 1973–1981 Blazer and Jimmy with nonsliding
       window
Interchange Number: 3
    Usage: 1974–1977 Blazer and Jimmy with sliding
       glass
Interchange Number: 4
    Usage: 1978–1980 Blazer and Jimmy with sliding
       glass
Interchange Number: 5
    Usage: 1967–1972 Suburban and Carryall with fixed
       glass
    Note: This is the same glass that is used in the right
       rear door
Interchange Number: 6
    Usage: 1967–1972 Suburban and Carryall with
       moveable glass
    Note: This is the same glass that is used in the right
       rear door

Interchange Number: 7
    Usage: 1967–1972 Suburban and Carryall rear side
       glass
Interchange Number: 8
    Usage: 1973–1974 Suburban and Carryall side glass
Interchange Number: 9
    Usage: 1975–1981 Suburban and Carryall side glass

Rear Glass
Model Identification

1967–1968	Interchange Number
Blazer 14	
Cab	
without panoramic rear window 1	
with panoramic rear window 2	
Suburban	
with doors 15	
with tailgate 12	
1969–1970	
Blazer 14	
Cab	
without sliding back glass 2	
with sliding back glass 3	
Suburban	
with doors 15	
with tailgate 12	
1971–1972	
Blazer 14	
Cab	
without sliding back glass 2	
with sliding back glass 3	
Suburban	
with doors 15	
with tailgate 13	

A 1970 Custom Camper 30.

Interchanges

Interchange Number: 1
    Part Number(s): 3884712
    Usage: 1967–1968 C-10 to C-30 Chevrolet and 1500 to 3500 GMC without panoramic rear window
    Note(s): Rare

Interchange Number: 2
    Part Number(s): 3884715
    Usage: 1967–1968 C-10 to C-30 Chevrolet and 1500 to 3500 GMC with panoramic rear window; 1969–1972 C-10 to C-30 Chevrolet and 1500 to 3500 GMC without sliding back glass

Interchange Number: 3
    Part Number(s): 3996641
    Usage: 1971–1972 C-10 to C-30 Chevrolet and 1500 to 3500 GMC with sliding back glass

    Note(s): Can be made to fit 1967–1972 cab models with the panoramic rear window

Interchange Number: 4
    Part Number(s): 6270818
    Usage: 1973–1975 C-10 to C-30 Chevrolet and 1500 to 3500 GMC without sliding back glass

Interchange Number: 5
    Part Number(s): 6262195 (left); 6262196 (right)
    Usage: 1973–1975 Suburban and GMC Carryall with back doors

Interchange Number: 6
    Part Number(s): 6327027
    Usage: 1973–1975 C-10 to C-30 Chevrolet and 1500 to 3500 GMC with sliding back glass
    Note(s): Entire assembly will fit Interchange Number 4

Interchange Number: 7
    Part Number(s): 362493 (left); 362494 (right)
    Usage: 1976–1978 Suburban and GMC Carryall with rear back doors

Interchange Number: 8
    Part Number(s): 363108
    Usage: 1976–1979 C-10 to C-30 Chevrolet and 1500 to 3500 GMC without sliding back glass

Interchange Number: 9
    Part Number(s): 327029 (left); 327030 (right)
    Usage: 1976–1979 C-10 to C-30 Chevrolet and 1500 to 3500 GMC with sliding back glass
    Note(s): Entire assembly will fit Interchange Numbers 4, 6, and 9

Interchange Number: 10
    Part Number(s): 327014
    Usage: 1973–1975 Blazer with removable hardtop
    Note(s): Tailgate window

A 1969–1970 Custom 10 front fender nameplate.

Interchange Number: 11
Part Number(s): 6264142
Usage: 1973–1979 Suburban with tailgate
Note(s): Tailgate window

Interchange Number: 12
Part Number(s): 14026489
Usage: 1976–1979 Blazer
Note(s): Tailgate window

Interchange Number: 13
Part Number(s): 3906875
Usage: 1967–1972 Suburban with tailgate
Note(s): Tailgate window

Interchange Number: 14
Part Number(s): 3964377
Usage: 1969–1972 Blazer with removable hardtop
Note(s): Tailgate window

Interchange Number: 15
Part Number(s): N/A
Usage: 1967–1972 Suburban with back door

Moldings

There are many different types of moldings used on Chevrolet trucks. Thus, to more easily help you find the molding you are looking for, different moldings have been grouped together. When interchanging a molding, it is always a good idea to interchange it with all the holding clips. Also, look for moldings that are free of deep scratches, pits, or abuse. Remove moldings carefully, as they are easily damaged.

Windshield Moldings
Model Identification

1969–1969	Interchange Number
All	
upper	3
lower	1
1970	
Upper	
early	3
late	4
Lower	
early	1
late	2
1971–1972	
Upper	4
Lower	2
1973–1978	
Base model	6
Except base models	5

Interchanges

Interchange Number: 1
Part Number(s): 3894661 (left); 3894662 (right)
Position: Lower
Usage: 1967 to early-1970 Chevrolet C-10 to C-30 truck
Note(s): Early style has retainer in center of molding

Interchange Number: 2
Part Number(s): 3985045 (left); 3985046 (right)
Position: Lower
Usage: Late-1970 to 1972 C-10 to C-30 Chevrolet truck
Note(s): Later style molding has retainer that is off center of molding

Interchange Number: 3
Part Number(s): 3894659
Position: Upper
Usage: 1967 to early-1970 Chevrolet C-10 to C-30 truck
Note(s): Early style has retainer in center of molding

Interchange Number: 4
Part Number(s): 3985043
Position: Upper
Usage: Late-1970 to 1972 C-10 to C-30 Chevrolet truck
Note(s): Later style molding has retainer that is off center of molding

Interchange Number: 5
Part Number(s): 464471 one-piece
Usage: 1973–1978 C-10 to C-30 Chevrolet truck (except base models); late-1975 to 1978 G-10 to G-30 with Beauville, Rally STX, Nomad, and Gaucho packages

Interchange Number: 6
Part Number(s): 466157 one-piece
Usage: 1973–1978 C-10 to C-30 and G-10 to G-30 Chevrolet (base models only)

Drip-Rail Moldings
Model Identification

1967–1972	Interchange Number
Cab	
except CST	1
CST	2
Suburban	3

A 1969–1970 Custom 20 front fender nameplate.

1973–1978

Interchanges

Interchange Number: 1

Part Number(s): 3885627 (left); 3885628 (right)

Usage: 1967–1972 C-10 to C-30 Chevrolet cab models only (except 1969 model with CST package)

Interchange Number: 2

Part Number(s): 3901482 (left); 3901484 (right)

Usage: 1969 C-10 with CST option

Interchange Number: 3

Part Number(s): N/A

Usage: 1967–1972 Suburban

Interchange Number: 4

Part Number(s): 342831 (left); 342832 (right)

Position: Front

Usage: 1974–1978 C-10 to C-30 Chevrolet four-door cab models only (black-painted moldings)

Interchange Number: 5

Part Number(s): 14049977 (left); 14049978 (right)

Position: Front

Usage: 1974–1978 C-10 to C-30 Chevrolet four-door cab models only (stainless-steel moldings)

Interchange Number: 6

Part Number(s): 342831 (left); 342832 (right)

Position: Rear

Usage: 1974–1978 C-10 to C-30 Chevrolet four-door cab models only (black-painted moldings)

Interchange Number: 7

Part Number(s): 14049975 (left); 14049976 (right)

Usage: 1974–1978 C-10 to C-30 Chevrolet two-door cab models only (stainless-steel moldings)

Interchange Number: 8

Part Number(s): 14028301 (left); 14028302 (right)

Usage: 1974–1978 C-10 to C-30 Chevrolet two-door cab models only (black-painted moldings)

Interchange Number: 9

Part Number(s): 355679 (left); 355680 (right)

Usage: 1976–1978 Blazer and Jimmy

A 1971–1972 Deluxe nameplate used on front fenders.

Interchange Number: 10
    Part Number(s): N/A
    Usage: 1973–1978 Suburban
Interchange Number: 11
    Part Number(s): 14049979 (either side)
    Position: Rear
    Usage: 1973–1978 C-10 to C-30 Chevrolet four-
        door cab model (stainless-steel moldings)

Wheelwell Moldings
Model Identification

1973–1976	Interchange Number
Front	1
Rear	3
1977	
Front	4
Rear	5
1978	
Front	1
Rear	3

Interchanges
Interchange Number: 1
    Part Number(s): 328843 (left); 328844 (right)
    Position: Front
    Usage: 1973–1976 C-10 to C-30 Chevrolet and
        1500 to 3500 GMC, all models (except van);
        1978 C-10 to C-30 Chevrolet and 1500 to
        3500 GMC, all models (except van); 1973–1976
        and 1978 Blazer and Jimmy
    Note(s): Will not fit 1977 models
Interchange Number: 2
    Part Number(s): 377431 (left); 377432 (right)
    Position: Front
    Usage: 1977 C-10 to C-30 Chevrolet and 1500 to
        3500 GMC, all models (except van); 1977
        Blazer and Jimmy
    Note(s): Will not fit 1973–1975 or 1978 models
Interchange Number: 3
    Part Number(s): 6273599 (left); 328820 (right)
    Position: Rear

A 1969–1972 Custom 30 front fender nameplate.

Usage: 1973–1976 C-10 to C-30 Chevrolet; 1500 to 3500 GMC, all models (except van); 1973–1976 and 1978 Blazer and Jimmy; 1978 C-10 to C-30 Chevrolet and 1500 to 3500 GMC, all models (except van)
Note(s): Will not fit 1977 models

Interchange Number: 5
Part Number(s): 377441 (left); 377442 (right)
Position: Rear
Usage: 1977 C-10 to C-30 Chevrolet and 1500 to 3500 GMC, all models (except van); 1977 Blazer and Jimmy
Note(s): Will not fit 1973–1975 or 1978 models

Body Side Moldings

Unlike passenger sedans, trucks used the same body side moldings for more than one year; thus, there is a larger interchange available. However, certain models or model packages, like the Cheyenne, used different trim than the lower-cost models, thus limiting the trim interchange. To avoid confusion, each section of trim is placed in an individual interchange that includes front fender, door, bed side, and tailgate. Body style and wheelbase have great effects on the interchange.

Body Side Moldings, Front Fender
Model Identification

Interchanges
Interchange Number: 1
Part Number(s): 3955311 (left); 3955312 (right)
Position: Lower fender, rear
Usage: 1969–1970 C-10 to C-30 Chevrolet truck and Blazer with Custom Sport Truck group; 1971–1972 C-10 to C-30 Chevrolet truck and Blazer with Cheyenne package—all Fleetside models only
Note(s): Woodgrain inserts
Interchange Number: 2
Part Number(s): 3955309 (left); 3955310 (right)
Position: Lower fender, front

A 1970 400-ci fender nameplate.

Usage: 1969–1970 C-10 to C-30 Chevrolet truck and Blazer with Custom Sport Truck group; 1971–1972 C-10 to C-30 Chevrolet truck and Blazer with Cheyenne package—all Fleetside models only

Note(s): Woodgrain inserts

Interchange Number: 3
Part Number(s): 3953887 (either side)
Position: Upper fender
Usage: 1969–1972 C-10 to C-30 Chevrolet truck with body side moldings

Interchange Number: 4
Part Number(s): 3952443 (left); 3952444 (right)
Position: Lower fender
Usage: 1969–1972 C-10 to C-30 Chevrolet truck and Blazer with black-accented body side moldings (except special wide moldings)

Interchange Number: 5
Part Number(s): 3952441 (left); 3952442 (right)
Position: Lower fender
Usage: 1969–1972 C-10 to C-30 Chevrolet truck and Blazer with special wide black-accented moldings

Interchange Number: 6
Part Number(s): 3953887 (either side)
Position: Upper fender
Usage: 1968 C-10 to C-20 Chevrolet Fleetside truck

Interchange Number: 7
Part Number(s): 3933855 (left); 3933856 (right)
Position: Front
Usage: 1968 C-10 to C-30 Chevrolet truck

Interchange Number: 8
Part Number(s): 3917729 (left); 3917730 (right)
Position: Side
Usage: 1967–1968 C-10 to C-30 Chevrolet truck

Interchange Number: 9
Part Number(s): 6260839 (left); 6260840 (right)
Position: Upper
Usage: 1973–1976 C-10 to C-30 Chevrolet and 1500 to 3500 GMC truck, Blazer, Jimmy, and Suburban; 1978 C-10 to C-30 Chevrolet and 1500 to 3500 GMC truck, Blazer, Jimmy, and Suburban
Note(s): Will not fit 1977 models

Interchange Number: 10
Part Number(s): 463339 (left); 463340 (right)
Position: Upper
Usage: 1977 C-10 to C-30 Chevrolet and 1500 to 3500 GMC truck, Blazer, Jimmy, and Suburban
Note(s): Will not fit other model years

Interchange Number: 11
Part Number(s): 6260841 (left); 6260842 (right)
Position: Lower
Usage: 1973–1976 C-10 to C-30 Chevrolet and 1500 to 3500 GMC truck, Blazer, Jimmy, and Suburban; 1978 C-10 to C-30 Chevrolet and 1500 to 3500 GMC truck, Blazer, Jimmy, and Suburban
Note(s): Will not fit 1977 models

Interchange Number: 12
Part Number(s): 463345 (left); 463346 (right)
Position: Upper
Usage: 1977 C-10 to C-30 Chevrolet and 1500 to 3500 GMC truck, Blazer, Jimmy, and Suburban
Note(s): Will not fit other model years

Body Side Moldings, Front Door
Model Identification

1967–1968	Interchange Number
Front doors	
lower	5
upper	
Rear doors, Suburban only	6
1969–1972	
Lower	
black-accented	10
woodgrain	11
Upper	
front door	
except Suburban	7
Suburban	8
Rear doors, Suburban only	9
1973–1976	
Front doors	
lower	1
upper	2
Rear doors	
lower	12
upper	14

A 1969–1972 350-ci fender nameplate.

1977
Front doors
Rear doors

1978
Front doors
Rear doors

Interchanges
Interchange Number: 1
Part Number(s): 475559 (left); 475560 (right)
Position: Lower
Usage: 1973–1976 C-10 to C-30 Chevrolet and 1500 to 3500 GMC truck, Blazer, Jimmy, and Suburban; 1978 C-10 to C-30 Chevrolet and 1500 to 3500 GMC truck, Blazer, Jimmy, and Suburban
Note(s): Will not fit 1977 models

Interchange Number: 2
Part Number(s): 463611 (left); 463612 (right)
Position: Upper
Usage: 1977 C-10 to C-30 Chevrolet and 1500 to 3500 GMC truck, Blazer, Jimmy, and Suburban
Note(s): Will not fit other model years

Interchange Number: 3
Part Number(s): 475543 (left); 475544 (right)
Position: Upper
Usage: 1973–1976 C-10 to C-30 Chevrolet and 1500 to 3500 GMC truck, Blazer, Jimmy, and Suburban; 1978 C-10 to C-30 Chevrolet and 1500 to 3500 GMC truck, Blazer, Jimmy, and Suburban
Note(s): Will not fit 1977 models

Interchange Number: 4
Part Number(s): 463607 (left); 463608 (right)
Position: Upper

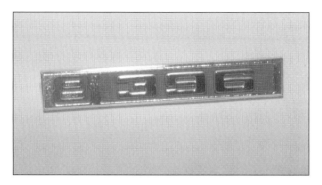

A 1969 396-ci fender nameplate.

Usage: 1977 C-10 to C-30 Chevrolet and 1500 to 3500 GMC truck, Blazer, Jimmy, and Suburban
Note(s): Will not fit other model years

Interchange Number: 5
Part Number(s): 3917731 (left); 3917732 (right)
Position: Lower
Usage: 1967–1968 C-10 to C-30 Chevrolet truck, includes Suburban

Interchange Number: 6
Part Number(s): 3904440 (right only)
Position: Lower right rear door
Usage: 1967–1968 C-10 to C-30 Chevrolet Suburban

Interchange Number: 7
Part Number(s): 3997461 (left); 399742 (right)
Position: Upper
Usage: 1969–1972 C-10 to C-30 Chevrolet Fleetside truck (except Suburban)

Interchange Number: 8
Part Number(s): 3952437 (left); 3952438 (right)
Position: Upper
Usage: 1969–1972 Suburban

Interchange Number: 9
Part Number(s): 3952468 (right side only)
Position: Upper right rear door
Usage: 1969–1972 Suburban

Interchange Number: 10
Part Number(s): 3997433 (left); 399734 (right)
Position: Lower
Usage: 1969–1972 C-10 to C-30 Chevrolet Fleetside truck, includes Suburban and Blazer, with black-accented trim

Interchange Number: 11
Part Number(s): 3997435 (left); 399736 (right)
Position: Lower
Usage: 1969–1970 C-10 to C-30 Chevrolet Fleetside truck, includes Suburban and Blazer with Custom Sport Truck package; 1971–1972 C-10 to C-30 Chevrolet Fleetside truck, includes Suburban and Blazer with Cheyenne trim

Interchange Number: 12
Part Number(s): 475571 (left); 475572 (right)
Position: Lower rear door
Usage: 1973–1976 C-10 to C-30 Chevrolet and 1500 to 3500 GMC four-door truck and Suburban; 1978 C-10 to C-30 Chevrolet and 1500 to 3500 GMC truck with four-door cab, and Suburban
Note(s): Will not fit 1977 models

Interchange Number: 13
Part Number(s): 463399 (left); 463400 (right)
Position: Lower rear door
Usage: 1977 C-10 to C-30 Chevrolet and 1500 to 3500 GMC four-door cab truck and Suburban
Note(s): Will not fit other model years

Interchange Number: 14
Part Number(s): 475551 (left); 475552 (right)
Position: Upper rear door
Usage: 1973–1976 C-10 to C-30 Chevrolet and 1500 to 3500 GMC four-door truck and Suburban; 1978 C-10 to C-30 Chevrolet and 1500 to 3500 GMC truck with four-door cab, and Suburban
Note(s): Will not fit 1977 models

Interchange Number: 15
Part Number(s): 463341 (left); 463342 (right)
Position: Upper rear door
Usage: 1977 C-10 to C-30 Chevrolet and 1500 to 3500 GMC four-door cab truck and Suburban
Note(s): Will not fit other model years

Body Side Moldings, Intermediate (Between Cab and Bed)
Model Identification

1967–1968	Interchange Number
Upper	4
Lower	3
1969–1972	
Upper	4
Lower	
black-accented	5
woodgrain	6
1973–1976	
Upper	1
Lower	1
1977	
Upper	2
Lower	2

Interchanges
Interchange Number: 1
Part Number(s): 6258145 (left); 475572 (right)
Position: Upper or lower

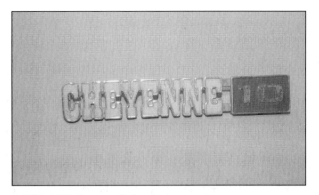

A 1971–1972 Cheyenne 10 front fender nameplate.

Usage: 1973–1976 and 1978 C-10 to C-30 Chevrolet and 1500 to 3500 GMC pickup truck

Note(s): Will not fit 1977 models

Interchange Number: 2
Part Number(s): 463609
Position: Upper or lower
Usage: 1977 C-10 to C-30 Chevrolet and 1500 to 3500 GMC pickup truck only
Note(s): Will not fit other model years

Interchange Number: 3
Part Number(s): 3917733 (left); 3917734 (right)
Position: Lower
Usage: 1967–1968 C-10 to C-30 Chevrolet pickup truck only

Interchange Number: 4
Part Number(s): 3953885 (left); 3953886 (right)
Position: Upper
Usage: 1968–1972 C-10 to C-30 Chevrolet pickup truck only

Interchange Number: 5
Part Number(s): 3952445 (left); 3952446 (right)
Position: Lower
Usage: 1969–1972 C-10 to C-30 Chevrolet pickup truck only (black-accented moldings)

Interchange Number: 6
Part Number(s): 3955307 (left); 3955308 (right)
Position: Lower
Usage: 1969–1970 C-10 to C-30 Chevrolet pickup truck only with Custom Sport Truck package; 1971–1972 C-10 to C-30 Chevrolet pickup truck only with Cheyenne package (woodgrain inserts)

Body Side Moldings, Cab (Below Rear Window)
Model Identification

1967–1972	Interchange Number
Left	7
Right	7

1973–1976
Corner

except camper	1
camper	2
Under window	4

1977
Corner

except camper	3
camper	6
Under window	5

1978
Corner

except camper	1
camper	2
Under window	4

Interchanges
Interchange Number: 1
Part Number(s): 3415124 (left); 3415125 (right)
Position: Corner of cab
Usage: 1973–1976 C-10 to C-30 Chevrolet pickup truck only, without camper package; 1978 C-10 to C-30 Chevrolet pickup truck only, without camper package

Interchange Number: 2
Part Number(s): 3415126 (left); 3415127 (right)
Position: Corner of cab
Usage: 1973–1976 C-10 to C-30 Chevrolet pickup truck only, with camper package; 1978 C-10 to C-30 Chevrolet pickup truck only, with camper package

Interchange Number: 3
Part Number(s): 463633 (left); 463634 (right)
Position: Corner of cab
Usage: 1977 C-10 to C-30 Chevrolet pickup truck only, without camper package

Interchange Number: 4
Part Number(s): 345123
Position: Below rear window
Usage: 1973–1976 C-10 to C-30 Chevrolet pickup truck only; 1978 C-10 to C-30 Chevrolet pickup truck only

Interchange Number: 5
Part Number(s): 463338
Position: Below rear window
Usage: 1977 C-10 to C-30 Chevrolet pickup truck only

Interchange Number: 6
Part Number(s): 463637 (left); 463638 (right)
Position: Corner of cab
Usage: 1977 C-10 to C-30 Chevrolet pickup truck with camper package

A 1973–1974 Custom 10 front fender nameplate.

Interchange Number: 7
    Part Number(s): 43917809 (left); 43917810 (right)
    Position: Below rear window
    Usage: 1967–1972 C-10 to C-30 Chevrolet pickup
        truck with two-tone paint only

Body Side Moldings, Bed/Quarter Panel
Model Identification

A 1973–1974 Cheyenne 10 front fender nameplate

Interchanges

Interchange Number: 1
Part Number(s): 475549 (left); 475550 (right)
Position: Upper
Usage: 1973–1976 C-10 to C-30 Chevrolet and 1500 to 3500 GMC pickup truck; 1978 C-10 to C-30 Chevrolet and 1500 to 3500 GMC pickup truck—all with 131.5-inch wheelbase

Interchange Number: 2
Part Number(s): 463617 (left); 463618 (right)
Position: Upper
Usage: 1977 C-10 to C-30 Chevrolet and 1500 to 3500 GMC pickup truck with 131.5-inch wheelbase

Interchange Number: 3
Part Number(s): 475547 (left); 475548 (right)
Position: Upper
Usage: 1973–1976 C-10 to C-30 Chevrolet and 1500 to 3500 GMC pickup truck; 1978 C-10 to C-30 Chevrolet and 1500 to 3500 GMC pickup truck—all with 117.5-inch wheelbase

Interchange Number: 4
Part Number(s): 463655 (left); 463656 (right)
Position: Upper
Usage: 1977 C-10 to C-30 Chevrolet and 1500 to 3500 GMC pickup truck with 117.5-inch wheelbase

Interchange Number: 5
Part Number(s): 475549 (left); 475550 (right)
Position: Upper
Usage: 1973–1976 C-10 to C-30 Chevrolet and 1500 to 3500 GMC pickup truck; 1978 C-10 to C-30 Chevrolet and 1500 to 3500 GMC pickup truck—all with 131.5-inch wheelbase

Interchange Number: 6
Part Number(s): 475553 (left); 475554 (right)
Position: Upper
Usage: 1973–1976 Suburban; 1978 Suburban

Interchange Number: 7
Part Number(s): 463603 (left); 463604 (right)
Position: Upper
Usage: 1977 Suburban

Interchange Number: 8
Part Number(s): 6258349 (left); 6258350 (right)
Position: Lower/front of wheel opening
Usage: 1973–1976 Suburban; 1978 Suburban

Interchange Number: 9
Part Number(s): 463349 (left); 463350 (right)

Position: Lower/front of wheel opening
Usage: 1977 Suburban

Interchange Number: 10
Part Number(s): 475563 (left); 475564 (right)
Position: Lower/front of wheel opening
Usage: 1973–1976 C-10 to C-30 Chevrolet and 1500 to 3500 GMC pickup truck; 1978 C-10 to C-30 Chevrolet and 1500 to 3500 GMC pickup truck—all with 131.5-inch wheelbase

Interchange Number: 11
Part Number(s): 463623 (left); 463624 (right)
Position: Lower/front of wheel opening
Usage: 1977 C-10 to C-30 Chevrolet and 1500 to 3500 GMC pickup truck with 131.5-inch wheelbase

Interchange Number: 12
Part Number(s): 475561 (left); 475562 (right)
Position: Lower/front of wheel opening
Usage: 1973–1976 C-10 to C-30 Chevrolet and 1500 to 3500 GMC pickup truck; 1978 C-10 to C-30 Chevrolet and 1500 to 3500 GMC pickup truck—all with 117.5-inch wheelbase

Interchange Number: 13
Part Number(s): 463351 (left); 463352 (right)
Position: Lower/front of wheel opening
Usage: 1977 C-10 to C-30 Chevrolet and 1500 to 3500 GMC pickup truck with 117.5-inch wheelbase

Interchange Number: 14
Part Number(s): 475575 (left); 475576 (right)
Position: Lower/rear of wheel opening
Usage: 1973–1976 Suburban; 1978 Suburban

Interchange Number: 15
Part Number(s): 463651 (left); 463652 (right)
Position: Lower/rear of wheel opening
Usage: 1977 Suburban

Interchange Number: 16
Part Number(s): 475565 (left); 475566 (right)

A 1973–1974 Custom 20 front fender nameplate.

Position: Lower/rear of wheel opening
Usage: 1973–1976 C-10 to C-30 Chevrolet and 1500 to 3500 GMC pickup truck; 1978 C-10 to C-30 Chevrolet and 1500 to 3500 GMC pickup truck—all with 131.5-inch wheelbase

Interchange Number: 17
Part Number(s): 463614 (left); 463615 (right)
Position: Lower/rear of wheel opening
Usage: 1977 C-10 to C-30 Chevrolet and 1500 to 3500 GMC pickup truck with 131.5-inch wheelbase

Interchange Number: 18
Part Number(s): 475581 (left); 475582 (right)
Position: Lower/rear of wheel opening
Usage: 1973–1976 C-10 to C-30 Chevrolet and 1500 to 3500 GMC pickup truck with 117.5-inch wheelbase; 1978 C-10 to C-30 Chevrolet and 1500 to 3500 GMC pickup truck with 117.5-inch wheelbase; 1973–1976 and 1978 Blazer and Jimmy

Interchange Number: 19
Part Number(s): 463621 (left); 463622 (right)
Position: Lower/rear of wheel opening
Usage: 1977 C-10 to C-30 Chevrolet and 1500 to 3500 GMC pickup truck with 117.5-inch wheelbase; 1977 Blazer and Jimmy

Interchange Number: 20
Part Number(s): 475539 (left); 475540 (right)
Position: Upper
Usage: 1973–1976 Blazer and Jimmy; 1978 Blazer and Jimmy

Interchange Number: 21
Part Number(s): 463657 (left); 463658 (right)
Position: Upper
Usage: 1977 Blazer and Jimmy

Interchange Number: 22
Part Number(s): 475587 (left); 475588 (right)
Position: Lower/front of wheel opening
Usage: 1973–1976 Blazer and Jimmy; 1978 Blazer and Jimmy

Interchange Number: 23
Part Number(s): 463653 (left); 463654 (right)
Position: Lower/front of wheel opening
Usage: 1977 Blazer and Jimmy

Interchange Number: 24
Part Number(s): 3917735 (left); 3917736 (right)
Position: Lower/front of wheel opening
Usage: 1967–1968 C-10 to C-30 Fleetside Chevrolet pickup truck with 115-inch wheelbase

Interchange Number: 25
Part Number(s): 3917745 (left); 3917746 (right)
Position: Lower/front of wheel opening
Usage: 1967–1968 C-10 to C-30 Fleetside Chevrolet pickup truck with 127-inch wheelbase

These are 1973–1974 Cheyenne Super 10 front fender nameplates.

Interchange Number: 26
Part Number(s): 3904443 (left); 3904448 (right)
Position: Lower/front of wheel opening
Usage: 1967–1968 Suburban

Interchange Number: 27
Part Number(s): 3952464 (left); 3952465 (right)
Position: Lower/front of wheel opening
Usage: 1969–1972 Suburban

Interchange Number: 28
Part Number(s): 3997437 (left); 3997438 (right)
Position: Lower/front of wheel opening
Usage: 1969–1972 C-10 to C-30 Fleetside Chevrolet pickup truck with 115-inch wheelbase (black accent)

Interchange Number: 29
Part Number(s): 3997441 (left); 3997442 (right)
Position: Lower/front of wheel opening
Usage: 1969–1972 C-10 to C-30 Fleetside Chevrolet pickup truck with 127-inch wheelbase (black accent)

Interchange Number: 30
Part Number(s): 3997445 (left); 3997446 (right)
Position: Lower/front of wheel opening
Usage: 1969–1972 C-10 to C-30 Fleetside Chevrolet pickup truck with 133-inch wheelbase (black accent; Longhorn)

Interchange Number: 31
Part Number(s): 3997455 (left); 3997456 (right)
Position: Lower/front of wheel opening
Usage: 1969–1972 Blazer (black accent)

Interchange Number: 32
Part Number(s): 3997439 (left); 3997440 (right)
Position: Lower/front of wheel opening
Usage: 1969–1970 C-10 to C-30 Fleetside Chevrolet pickup truck with Custom Sport Truck package; 1971–1972 C-10 to C-30 Chevrolet pickup truck with Cheyenne package—all with 115-inch wheelbase only and woodgrain inserts

Interchange Number: 33
Part Number(s): 3997443 (left); 3997444 (right)
Position: Lower/front of wheel opening
Usage: 1969–1970 C-10 to C-30 Fleetside Chevrolet pickup truck with Custom Sport Truck package; 1971–1972 C-10 to C-30 Chevrolet pickup truck with Cheyenne package—all with 127-inch wheelbase only and woodgrain inserts

Interchange Number: 34
Part Number(s): 3997447 (left); 3997448 (right)
Position: Lower/front of wheel opening
Usage: 1969–1970 C-10 to C-30 Fleetside Chevrolet pickup truck with Custom Sport Truck package; 1971–1972 C-10 to C-30 Chevrolet pickup truck with Cheyenne package—all with 133-inch wheelbase only and woodgrain inserts

Interchange Number: 35
Part Number(s): 3997457 (left); 3997458 (right)
Position: Lower/front of wheel opening
Usage: 1969–1970 Blazer; 1971–1972 Blazer with Cheyenne package and woodgrain inserts

Interchange Number: 36
Part Number(s): 3977554
Position: Lower/rear of toolbox door
Usage: 1969–1972 C-10 to C-30 Fleetside Chevrolet pickup truck with toolbox and black accent—all wheelbases

Interchange Number: 37
Part Number(s): 3977586
Position: Lower/toolbox door
Usage: 1969–1972 C-10 to C-30 Fleetside Chevrolet pickup truck with toolbox and black accents—all wheelbases

Interchange Number: 38
Part Number(s): 3977546
Position: Lower/front of toolbox door
Usage: 1969–1972 C-10 to C-30 Fleetside Chevrolet pickup truck with toolbox and black accents, with 127-inch wheelbase

Interchange Number: 39
Part Number(s): 3977550
Position: Lower/front of toolbox door
Usage: 1969–1972 C-10 to C-30 Fleetside Chevrolet pickup truck with toolbox and black accents, with 133-inch wheelbase

Interchange Number: 40
Part Number(s): 3977590
Position: Lower/toolbox door
Usage: 1969–1970 C-10 to C-30 Fleetside Chevrolet pickup truck with toolbox and Custom Sport Truck package; 1971–1972 C-10 to C-30 Chevrolet pickup truck with toolbox and Cheyenne package—all with woodgrain inserts

Front fender nameplates for the 1975 and 1977–1978 Custom Deluxe 10.

Interchange Number: 41
Part Number(s): 3977552
Position: Lower/rear of toolbox door
Usage: 1969–1970 C-10 to C-30 Fleetside Chevrolet pickup truck with toolbox and Custom Sport Truck package; 1971–1972 C-10 to C-30 Chevrolet pickup truck with toolbox and Cheyenne package—all with woodgrain inserts

Interchange Number: 42
Part Number(s): 3977510
Position: Lower/front of toolbox door
Usage: 1969–1970 C-10 to C-30 Fleetside Chevrolet pickup truck with toolbox and Custom Sport Truck package; 1971–1972 C-10 to C-30 Chevrolet pickup truck with toolbox and Cheyenne package—all wheelbases, with woodgrain inserts

Interchange Number: 43
Part Number(s): 3997424 (either side)
Position: Upper
Usage: 1969–1972 C-10 to C-30 Fleetside Chevrolet pickup truck with 115-inch wheelbase

Interchange Number: 44
Part Number(s): 3997425 (either side)
Position: Upper
Usage: 1969–1972 C-10 to C-30 Fleetside Chevrolet pickup truck with 127-inch wheelbase

Interchange Number: 45
Part Number(s): 3997463 (either side)
Position: Upper
Usage: 1969–1972 C-10 to C-30 Fleetside Chevrolet pickup truck with 133-inch wheelbase

Interchange Number: 46
Part Number(s): 3952439 (left); 3952440 (right)
Rear corner—3952465 (left); 3952466 (right)
Position: Upper
Usage: 1969–1972 Suburban

Interchange Number: 47
Part Number(s): 3917747 (left); 3917748 (right)
Position: Lower/rear of wheel opening
Usage: 1967–1968 C-10 to C-30 Chevrolet Fleetside with 127-inch wheelbase

Interchange Number: 48
Part Number(s): 3917739 (left); 3917740 (right)
Position: Lower/rear of wheel opening
Usage: 1967–1968 C-10 to C-30 Chevrolet Fleetside with 115-inch wheelbase

Interchange Number: 49
Part Number(s): 3904451 (left); 3904452 (right)
Position: Lower/rear of wheel opening
Usage: 1967–1968 Suburban

Interchange Number: 50
Part Number(s): 3997429 (left); 3974430 (right)
Position: Lower/rear of wheel opening
Usage: 1969–1972 Suburban

Interchange Number: 51
Part Number(s): 3997431 (left); 3997432 (right)
Position: Lower/rear of wheel opening
Usage: 1969–1972 C-10 to C-30 Chevrolet Fleetside with 115-inch wheelbase; 1969–1972 Blazer—all with black accents

Interchange Number: 52
Part Number(s): 3997451 (left); 3997452 (right)
Position: Lower/rear of wheel opening
Usage: 1969–1972 C-10 to C-30 Chevrolet Fleetside, with 127- or 133-inch wheelbase and black accents

Interchange Number: 53
Part Number(s): 3997449 (left); 3997450 (right)
Position: Lower/rear of wheel opening
Usage: 1969–1970 C-10 to C-30 Chevrolet Fleetside with 115-inch wheelbase or Blazer with Custom Sport Truck package; 1971–1972 C-10 to C-30 Chevrolet pickup truck with 115-inch wheelbase or Blazer with Cheyenne package

Interchange Number: 54
Part Number(s): 3997453 (left); 3997454 (right)
Position: Lower/rear of wheel opening
Usage: 1969–1970 C-10 to C-30 Chevrolet Fleetside with 127- or 133-inch wheelbase and Custom Sport Truck package; 1971–1972 C-10 to C-30 Chevrolet pickup truck with 127- or 133-inch wheelbase and Cheyenne package

Body Side Moldings, Tailgate
Model Identification

1968	Interchange Number
Upper	11
1969–1972	
Upper	11
Lower	12

Interchanges

Interchange Number: 1
  Part Number(s): 4745535
  Position: Upper or lower

Front fender nameplates for the 1975 and 1977–1978 Silverado 10.

  Usage: 1973–1976 C-10 to C-30 Chevrolet Fleetside pickup and 1500 to 3500 GMC Fleetside pickup, Blazer, and Jimmy; 1978 C-10 to C-30 Chevrolet Fleetside pickup and 1500 to 3500 GMC Fleetside pickup, Blazer, and Jimmy

Interchange Number: 2
  Part Number(s): 463606
  Position: Upper or lower
  Usage: 1977 C-10 to C-30 Chevrolet Fleetside pickup and 1500 to 3500 GMC Fleetside pickup, Blazer, and Jimmy

Interchange Number: 3
  Part Number(s): 475537
  Position: Upper or lower
  Usage: 1973–1976 Suburban with tailgate; 1978 Suburban with tailgate

Interchange Number: 4
  Part Number(s): 463605
  Position: Upper or lower
  Usage: 1977 Suburban with tailgate; 1978 Suburban with tailgate

Interchange Number: 5
  Part Number(s): 475555 (left); 475556 (right)
  Position: Upper
  Usage: 1973–1976 Suburban; 1978 Suburban with back doors

Interchange Number: 6
  Part Number(s): 463603 (left); 463604 (right)
  Position: Upper
  Usage: 1977 Suburban with back doors

Interchange Number: 7
  Part Number(s): 475577 (left)
  Position: Lower
  Usage: 1973–1976 Suburban; 1978 Suburban with back doors

Interchange Number: 8
  Part Number(s): N/A
  Position: Lower
  Usage: 1973 Suburban with back doors

Interchange Number: 9
  Part Number(s): 475578 (right)
  Position: Lower
  Usage: 1974–1976 Suburban; 1978 Suburban with back doors

Interchange Number: 10
  Part Number(s): 463601 (left); 463602 (right)
  Position: Lower
  Usage: 1977 Suburban with back doors

Interchange Number: 11
  Part Number(s): 3917742 (left); 3917749 (center) 3917743 (right)
  Position: Upper
  Usage: 1968–1972 C-10 to C-30 Chevrolet pickup truck

The 1976 Silverado 10 front fender nameplate has a yellow background.

Interchange Number: 12
Part Number(s): 3953877
Position: Lower
Usage: 1969–1972 C-10 to C-30 Chevrolet pickup truck

Interchange Number: 13
Part Number(s): 3955316
Position: Lower
Usage: 1969–1970 C-10 to C-30 Chevrolet pickup truck with Custom Sport Truck Package; 1971–1972 C-10 to C-30 Chevrolet pickup with Cheyenne package—all with woodgrain

Interchange Number: 14
Part Number(s): 3952469 (left); 3952470 (right)
Position: Upper
Usage: 1969–1972 Suburban with rear doors

Interchange Number: 15
Part Number(s): 3952463
Position: Upper
Usage: 1969–1972 Suburban with tailgate

Emblems, Grille
Model Identification

Interchanges

Interchange Number: 1
Part Number(s): 3893742
Style: Bow-tie
Usage: 1967–1968 C-10 to C-30 Chevrolet truck

Interchange Number: 2
Part Number(s): 3995773
Style: Bow-tie
Usage: 1971–1972 C-10 to C-30 Chevrolet truck and Blazer

Interchange Number: 3
Part Number(s): 328846
Style: 350
Usage: 1973–1974 C-10 to C-30 Chevrolet truck, all models and body styles except van
Note(s): Though the GMC model used a similar emblem, they are not interchangeable

Interchange Number: 4
Part Number(s): 328847
Style: 454
Usage: 1973–1974 C-10 to C-30 Chevrolet truck, all models and body styles except van

Interchange Number: 5
Part Number(s): 357284
Style: 350
Usage: 1975–1976 C-10 to C-30 Chevrolet truck, all models and body styles except van

Interchange Number: 6
Part Number(s): 357286
Style: 454
Usage: 1973–1974 C-10 to C-30 Chevrolet truck, all models and body styles except van

Interchange Number: 7
Part Number(s): 358266
Style: Bow-tie
Usage: 1975–1978 C-10 to C-30 Chevrolet truck, all models and body styles; G-10 to G-30 van

Interchange Number: 8
Part Number(s): 357285
Style: 400
Usage: 1975–1976 Blazer

Emblems, Hood
Model Identification

A Scottsdale 20 front fender nameplate.

Interchanges

Interchange Number: 1
    Part Number(s): 3900990
    Style: CHEVROLET
    Usage: 1967–1968 C-10 to C-30 Chevrolet truck, all models
    Note(s): Single letters

Interchange Number: 2
    Part Number(s): 3953661
    Style: Bow-tie
    Usage: 1969–1970 C-10 to C-30 Chevrolet truck, all body styles

Interchange Number: 3
    Part Number(s): 14000797
    Style: Stand up
    Usage: 1977–1978 C-10 to C-30 Chevrolet truck and Blazer

Interchange Number: 4
    Part Number(s): 14000795
    Style: Stand up
    Usage: 1978 C-10 with street coupe package

Interchange Number: 5
    Part Number(s): 715626
    Style: Bow-tie
    Usage: 1977 C-10 Stepside; 1975–1976 motor home and service van

Emblems, Front Fender
Model Identification

1967–1968	Interchange Number
10	49
20	45
30	46
Custom Camper	50
Four-wheel drive	47

1969–1970
Without CC or CST package
C-10	41
C-20	40
C-30	39

With Deluxe package
Custom 10	38
Custom 20	37
Custom 30	36

With CST package
CST 10	42

Engine callouts
350	44
396	43
400 (1970 only)	48

K/5 Blazer	34
Custom Camper	35
Four-wheel drive	47

1971–1972
Without Cheyenne package or Deluxe package
Custom 10	38
Custom 20	37
Custom 30	36

With Deluxe package	33

With Cheyenne package
Cheyenne 10	32
Cheyenne 20	31
Cheyenne 30	30

Super	29
K/5 Blazer	64
Custom Camper	35
Highlander	52

1973–1974
Without Cheyenne package or Deluxe package
Custom 10	4
Custom 20	5
Custom 30	6

With Deluxe package
Custom Deluxe 10	7
Custom Deluxe 20	8
Custom Deluxe 30	51

With Cheyenne package
Cheyenne 10	1
Cheyenne 20	2
Cheyenne 30	3
Cheyenne Super 10	9
Cheyenne Super 20	10
Cheyenne Super 30	11

K/5 Blazer	12

1975–1976
Except van
Custom Deluxe 10	13
Custom Deluxe 20	14
Custom Deluxe 30	15

With Cheyenne package
Cheyenne 10	16
Cheyenne 20	17
Cheyenne 30	18
Cheyenne Super 10	9
Cheyenne Super 20	10
Cheyenne Super 30	11

Blazer front fender nameplate.

Interchanges

Interchange Number: 1
    Part Number(s): 328854
    Style: Cheyenne-10
    Usage: 1973–1974 Chevrolet C-10 with Cheyenne package

Interchange Number: 2
    Part Number(s): 328855
    Style: Cheyenne-20
    Usage: 1973–1974 Chevrolet C-20 with Cheyenne package

Interchange Number: 3
    Part Number(s): 328856
    Style: Cheyenne-30
    Usage: 1973–1974 Chevrolet C-30 with Cheyenne package

Interchange Number: 4
    Part Number(s): 328848
    Style: Custom-10
    Usage: 1973–1974 Chevrolet C-10 Custom, without CST option package

Interchange Number: 5
    Part Number(s): 328849
    Style: Custom-20
    Usage: 1973–1974 Chevrolet C-20 Custom, without CST option package

Interchange Number: 6
    Part Number(s): 328850
    Style: Custom-30
    Usage: 1973–1974 Chevrolet C-30 Custom, without CST option package

Interchange Number: 7
    Part Number(s): 328851
    Style: Custom Deluxe-10
    Usage: 1973–1974 Chevrolet C-10 Custom with CST option package

Interchange Number: 8
    Part Number(s): 328852
    Style: Custom Deluxe-20
    Usage: 1973–1974 Chevrolet C-20 Custom with CST option package

Interchange Number: 9
    Part Number(s): 328857
    Style: Cheyenne Super-10
    Usage: 1973–1976 Chevrolet C-10 with Cheyenne Super package

Interchange Number: 10
    Part Number(s): 328858
    Style: Cheyenne Super-20
    Usage: 1973–1976 Chevrolet C-20 with Cheyenne Super package

Interchange Number: 11
    Part Number(s): 328859
    Style: Cheyenne Super-30

A 1974–1975 Blazer rear quarter panel with Cheyenne trim.

Usage: 1973–1976 Chevrolet C-30 with Cheyenne Super package

Interchange Number: 12
Part Number(s): 328860
Style: K/5 Blazer
Usage: 1973–1974 Blazer

Interchange Number: 13
Part Number(s): 14016633
Style: Custom Deluxe-10
Usage: 1975–1977 Chevrolet C-10 Custom Deluxe

Interchange Number: 14
Part Number(s): 14016634
Style: Custom Deluxe-20
Usage: 1975–1978 Chevrolet C-20 Custom Deluxe

Interchange Number: 15
Part Number(s): 14016635
Style: Custom Deluxe-30
Usage: 1975–1978 Chevrolet C-30 Custom Deluxe

Interchange Number: 16
Part Number(s): 14016636
Style: Cheyenne-10
Usage: 1975–1978 Chevrolet C-10 with Cheyenne trim option package

Interchange Number: 17
Part Number(s): 14016637
Style: Cheyenne-20
Usage: 1975–1978 Chevrolet C-30 with Cheyenne trim option package

Interchange Number: 18
Part Number(s): 14016638
Style: Cheyenne-30
Usage: 1975–1978 Chevrolet C-30 with Cheyenne trim option package

Interchange Number: 19
Part Number(s): 14016639
Style: Scottsdale-10
Usage: 1975–1978 Chevrolet C-10 with Scottsdale trim option package

Interchange Number: 20
Part Number(s): 14016640
Style: Scottsdale-20
Usage: 1975–1978 Chevrolet C-20 with Scottsdale trim option package

Interchange Number: 21
Part Number(s): 14016641
Style: Scottsdale-30
Usage: 1975–1978 Chevrolet C-30 with Scottsdale trim option package

Interchange Number: 22
Part Number(s): 14016642
Style: Silverado-10
Usage: 1975–1978 Chevrolet C-10 with Silverado trim option package

Interchange Number: 23
Part Number(s): 14016643
Style: Silverado-20
Usage: 1975–1978 Chevrolet C-20 with Silverado trim option package

Interchange Number: 24
Part Number(s): 14016644
Style: Silverado-30
Usage: 1975–1978 Chevrolet C-30 with Silverado trim option package

Interchange Number: 25
Part Number(s): 14016630
Style: K/5 Blazer
Usage: 1975–1978 Blazer

Interchange Number: 26
Part Number(s): 14016657
Style: Bonanza-10
Usage: 1976–1978 Chevrolet C-10 with Bonanza trim option package

Interchange Number: 27
Part Number(s): 14016658
Style: Bonanza-20
Usage: 1976–1978 Chevrolet C-20 with Bonanza trim option package

Interchange Number: 28
Part Number(s): 361078
Style: Bonanza-30
Usage: 1976–1978 Chevrolet C-30 with Bonanza trim option package

Interchange Number: 29
Part Number(s): 6263002
Style: Super
Usage: 1971–1972 C-10 to C-30 Chevrolet truck with CST Super package

A 1975 Suburban Estate rear quarter panel nameplate.

Interchange Number: 30
    Part Number(s): 3998218
    Style: Cheyenne-30
    Usage: 1971–1972 C-30 Chevrolet truck with CST package

Interchange Number: 31
    Part Number(s): 3998217
    Style: Cheyenne-20
    Usage: 1971–1972 C-20 Chevrolet truck with CST package

Interchange Number: 32
    Part Number(s): 3998216
    Style: Cheyenne-10
    Usage: 1971–1972 C-10 Chevrolet truck with CST package

Interchange Number: 33
    Part Number(s): 3998219
    Style: Deluxe
    Usage: 1971–1972 C-10 to C-30 Chevrolet truck with CC package

Interchange Number: 34
    Part Number(s): 3970676
    Style: K/5 Blazer
    Usage: 1969–1972 Blazer

Interchange Number: 35
    Part Number(s): 3953666
    Style: Custom Camper/20
    Usage: 1969–1972 C-20 Chevrolet truck with Camper Special package

Interchange Number: 36
    Part Number(s): 3953664
    Style: Custom-30
    Usage: 1969–1970 C-30 Chevrolet truck with CC package; 1971–1972 C-30 Chevrolet truck, without CST package

Interchange Number: 37
    Part Number(s): 3953663
    Style: Custom-20
    Usage: 1969–1970 C-20 Chevrolet truck with CC package; 1971–1972 C-20 Chevrolet truck, without CST package

Interchange Number: 38
    Part Number(s): 3953662
    Style: Custom-10
    Usage: 1969–1970 C-10 Chevrolet truck with CC package; 1971–1972 C-10 Chevrolet truck, without CST package

Interchange Number: 39
    Part Number(s): 3952402
    Style: C-30
    Usage: 1969–1970 C-30 Chevrolet truck without CC package

Interchange Number: 40
    Part Number(s): 3952401
    Style: C-20
    Usage: 1969–1970 C-20 Chevrolet truck without CC package

Interchange Number: 41
    Part Number(s): 3952400
    Style: C-10
    Usage: 1969–1970 C-10 Chevrolet truck without CC package

Interchange Number: 42
    Part Number(s): 3955313
    Style: CST/10
    Usage: 1969–1970 C-10 Chevrolet truck with CST package

Interchange Number: 43
    Part Number(s): 3955508
    Style: 396
    Usage: 1969–1970 C-10 to C-30 Chevrolet truck with 396-ci V-8

Interchange Number: 44
    Part Number(s): 3955507
    Style: 350
    Usage: 1969–1970 C-10 to C-30 Chevrolet truck with 350-ci V-8

Interchange Number: 45
    Part Number(s): 3893752
    Style: 20
    Usage: 1967–1968 C-20 Chevrolet truck

Interchange Number: 46
    Part Number(s): 3893767
    Style: 30
    Usage: 1967–1968 C-30 Chevrolet truck (except Camper Special)

Interchange Number: 47
    Part Number(s): 3930955
    Style: Four-wheel drive
    Usage: 1970 K-10 to K-20 Chevrolet truck

Interchange Number: 48
    Part Number(s): 3981887
    Style: 400
    Usage: 1970–1969 Chevrolet truck with 400-ci V-8

Interchange Number: 49
    Part Number(s): 3961365

Style: Bow-tie 10
Usage: 1967–1968 Chevrolet C-10 truck without CST package

Interchange Number: 50
Part Number(s): 3882674
Style: Custom Camper
Usage: 1967–1968 Chevrolet C-10 to C-30 truck with camper package

Interchange Number: 51
Part Number(s): 328853
Style: Custom Deluxe 30
Usage: 1973–1974 Chevrolet C-30 truck with Deluxe package

Interchange Number: 52
Part Number(s): N/A
Style: Highlander
Usage: 1971–1972 Chevrolet C-10 truck with Highlander package

Emblems, Bed Sides
Model Identification

1967–1972	Interchange Number
Longhorn (1968–1972)	2
Suburban	1
Custom Camper (1972)	4
Sierra (1971–1972)	3
1975–1978	
Camper	5
Custom Camper (single rear wheels)	7
Custom Camper (dual rear wheels)	8
Cheyenne	6
3 Plus 3	9
1975–1978	
Camper	5
Custom Camper (single rear wheels)	7
Custom Camper (dual rear wheels)	8
Cheyenne	6
Bonus cab	10
Estate	11

Interchanges

Interchange Number: 1
Part Number(s): 3894637
Style: Suburban
Usage: 1967–1972 Suburban

Interchange Number: 2
Part Number(s): 3998374
Style: Longhorn
Usage: 1968–1972 C-10 to C-30 Chevrolet with extra-long bed

Interchange Number: 3
Part Number(s): 6263003
Style: Sierra
Usage: 1971–1972 C-10 Chevrolet truck with CST package

Interchange Number: 4
Part Number(s): 328770 (Custom); 328771 (camper)
Style: Custom Camper
Usage: 1972 C-20 or C-30 Chevrolet with Custom Camper option

Interchange Number: 5
Part Number(s): 338304
Style: Camper
Usage: 1973–1978 C-10 to C-20 Chevrolet and GMC truck with Camper Special package

Interchange Number: 6
Part Number(s): 6258324
Style: Cheyenne
Usage: 1973–1978 Blazer

Interchange Number: 7
Part Number(s): 14016617
Style: Camper Special 9000 GVW
Usage: 1973–1978 C-30 Chevrolet and 3500 GMC 1-ton truck with Camper Special package, without dual rear wheels
Note(s): Also used on tailgate of these models

Interchange Number: 8
Part Number(s): 14016618
Style: Camper Special 10,000 GVW
Usage: 1973–1978 C-30 Chevrolet and 3500 GMC 1-ton truck with Camper Special package and dual rear wheels

Interchange Number: 9
Part Number(s): 14016613
Style: 3 Plus 3
Usage: 1973–1978 C-20 to C-30 Chevrolet and 3500 GMC with four-door cab

Interchange Number: 10
Part Number(s): 370365
Style: Bonus cab
Usage: 1975–1978 C-20 to C-30 Chevrolet and 3500 GMC truck

Interchange Number: 11
Part Number(s): 370364
Style: Estate
Usage: 1975–1978 Suburban

Emblems, Tailgate, and Back Door
Model Identification

1973–1978	Interchange Number
Chevrolet	1
Camper Special 8,400 GVW (1975–1978)	9
Camper Special 9,000 GVW	3
Camper Special 9,600 GVW (1975–1978)	10
Camper Special 10,000 GVW	3
Trailering Special 8,000 GVW	5
Trailering Special 9,000 GVW (1977–1978)	11
Trailering Special 10,000 GVW	6
Trailering Special 11,000 GVW (1977–1978)	12
Trailering Special 12,000 GVW (1977–1978)	13

Interchanges

Interchange Number: 1
> Part Number(s): 14016628
> Style: Chevrolet
> Usage: 1973–1978 C-10 to C-30 Chevrolet truck with side moldings (except Suburban); 1973–1978 Blazer with body side moldings

Interchange Number: 2
> Part Number(s): 14016626
> Style: Suburban
> Usage: 1975–1978 Suburban
> Note(s): GMC models use the same model name, but the plates are not interchangeable

Interchange Number: 3
> Part Number(s): 14016617
> Style: Camper Special 9000 GVW
> Usage: 1973–1978 C-30 Chevrolet and 3500 GMC 1-ton truck with Camper Special package, without dual rear wheels
> Note(s): Also used on the bed sides of these models

Interchange Number: 4
> Part Number(s): 14016618
> Style: Camper Special 10,000 GVW
> Usage: 1973–1978 C-30 Chevrolet and 3500 GMC 1-ton truck with Camper Special package with dual rear wheels
> Note(s): Also used on the bed sides of these models

Interchange Number: 5
> Part Number(s): 6260986
> Style: Trailering Special 8,000 GVW
> Usage: 1973–1978 C-10 to C-30 Chevrolet and 1500 to 3500 GMC truck, Blazer, and Jimmy with trailering special option package

Interchange Number: 6
> Part Number(s): 14016620
> Style: Trailering Special 10,000 GVW
> Usage: 1973–1978 C-10 to C-30 Chevrolet and 1500 to 3500 GMC truck, Blazer, and Jimmy with trailering special option package

Interchange Number: 7
> Part Number(s): 14016621
> Style: Trailering Special 13,000 GVW
> Usage: 1973–1978 C-10 to C-30 Chevrolet and 1500 to 3500 GMC truck with trailering special option package

Interchange Number: 8
> Part Number(s): 1406622
> Style: Trailering Special 15,000 GVW
> Usage: 1973–1978 C-20 to C-30 Chevrolet and 2500 to 3500 GMC truck with trailering special option package

Interchange Number: 9
> Part Number(s): 1406664
> Style: Camper Special 8400 GVW
> Usage: 1975–1978 C-20 Chevrolet and 2500 GMC four-wheel drive with 131.5-inch wheelbase and Camper Special option package

Interchange Number: 10
> Part Number(s): 1406669
> Style: Camper Special 9,600 GVW
> Usage: 1975–1978 C-30 Chevrolet and 3500 GMC four-door cab truck with Camper Special option package, without rear dual wheels

Interchange Number: 11
> Part Number(s): 474011
> Style: Trailering Special 9,000 GVW
> Usage: 1977–1978 C-10 to C-30 Chevrolet and 1500 to 3500 GMC truck with trailering special option package

Interchange Number: 12
> Part Number(s): 474012
> Style: Trailering Special 11,000 GVW
> Usage: 1977–1978 C-10 to C-30 Chevrolet and 1500 to 3500 GMC truck with trailering special option package

Interchange Number: 13
> Part Number(s): 474013
> Style: Trailering Special 12,000 GVW
> Usage: 1977–1978 C-10 to C-30 Chevrolet and 1500 to 3500 GMC truck with trailering special option package

Interchange Number: 14
> Part Number(s): 467276
> Style: Diesel
> Usage: 1978 C-10 to C-30 Chevrolet and 1500 to 3500 GMC truck with diesel engine

Interiors

Instrument Panels
Model Identification

1967–1970	Interchange Number
Without air conditioning	1
With air conditioning	2

1971–1972	
Without air conditioning	1
With air conditioning	2

1973–1978	
All	3

Interchanges

Interchange Number: 1
Part Number(s): N/A
Usage: 1967–1972 Chevrolet C-10 to C-30 truck and GMC 1500 to 3500 truck (except van) without air conditioning; 1969–1972 Blazer without air conditioning

Interchange Number: 2
Part Number(s): N/A
Usage: 1967–1972 Chevrolet C-10 to C-30 truck and GMC 1500 to 3500 truck (except van) with air conditioning; 1969–1972 Blazer and Jimmy with air conditioning

Interchange Number: 3
Part Number(s): 369510
Usage: 1973–1978 Chevrolet C-10 to C-30 truck and GMC 1500 to 3500 (except van) with or without air conditioning

Instrumentation
Model Identification

1967–1972	Interchange Number
Speedometer	
without speed warning	6
with speed warning	7
Tachometer	11
Fuel	
without gauges	20
with gauges	19
Oil pressure	23
Ammeter	26
Coolant	30

1973–1975	
Speedometer	
without gauges	1
with gauges	2
Tachometer	8
Fuel	
without gauges	13
with gauges (without clock)	12
with gauges (with clock)	14
Oil pressure	21
Ammeter	24
Coolant	28
Clock	31

1976	
Speedometer	
without gauges	
early	1
late	5
with gauges	
early	2
late	5
Tachometer	9
Fuel	
without gauges	
early, except Suburban or heavy-duty chassis	15
early, Suburban or heavy-duty chassis	16
late, except Suburban or heavy-duty Chassis	17
late, Suburban or heavy-duty Chassis	18
with gauges (without clock)	12
with gauges (with clock)	14
Oil pressure	21
Ammeter	25
Coolant	28
Clock	31

1977–1978	
Speedometer	5
Tachometer	9
Fuel	
without gauges	
except Suburban or heavy-duty Chassis	17
Suburban or heavy-duty Chassis	18
with gauges (without clock)	12
with gauges (with clock)	14
Oil pressure	
1977	21
1978	22

A 1967–1970 speedometer.

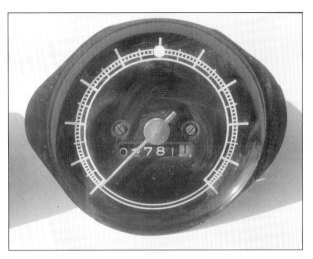

A 1971–1972 Speedometer will fit earlier models, but note the difference in shape of the high-beam indicator.

Interchanges

Interchange Number: 1
>Part Number(s): 6497570
>Usage: 1973–1975 C-10 to C-30 Chevrolet and 1500 to 3500 GMC truck (except van, Blazer, and Jimmy) without gauges
>Note(s): Speedometer

Interchange Number: 2
>Part Number(s): 64999189
>Usage: 1973–1975 C-10 to C-30 Chevrolet and 1500 to 3500 GMC truck (except van, Blazer, and Jimmy) with gauges
>Note(s): Speedometer

Interchange Number: 3
>Part Number(s): 8989524
>Usage: Early-1976 C-10 to C-30 Chevrolet and 1500 to 3500 GMC truck (except van, Blazer, and Jimmy) without gauges
>Note(s): Speedometer has none or one telltale filter at the bottom of the dial

Interchange Number: 4
>Part Number(s): 8989525
>Usage: Early-1976 C-10 to C-30 Chevrolet and 1500 to 3500 GMC truck (except van, Blazer, and Jimmy) with gauges
>Note(s): Speedometer has none or one telltale filter at the bottom of the dial

Interchange Number: 5
>Part Number(s): 25045176
>Usage: Late-1976 to 1978 C-10 to C-30 Chevrolet and 1500 to 3500 GMC truck (except van, Blazer, and Jimmy)

Note(s): Speedometer has two telltale filters at the bottom of the dial

Interchange Number: 6
>Part Number(s): 6492868
>Usage: 1967–1972 C-10 to C-30 Chevrolet and 1500 to 3500 GMC truck (except van) without speed warning
>Note(s): Speedometer

Interchange Number: 7
>Part Number(s): 6492869
>Usage: 1967–1972 C-10 to C-30 Chevrolet and 1500 to 3500 GMC truck (except van) with speed warning
>Note(s): Speedometer

Interchange Number: 8
>Part Number(s): 5659705
>Usage: 1973–1975 C-10 to C-30 Chevrolet and 1500 to 3500 GMC truck, Blazer, and Jimmy with gauges
>Note(s): Tachometer

Interchange Number: 9
>Part Number(s): 5658616
>Usage: 1976 C-10 to C-30 Chevrolet and 1500 to 3500 GMC truck, Blazer, and Jimmy with gauges
>Note(s): Tachometer

Interchange Number: 10
>Part Number(s): 5659232
>Usage: 1977–1978 C-10 to C-30 Chevrolet and 1500 to 3500 GMC truck, Blazer, and Jimmy with gauges
>Note(s): Tachometer

Interchange Number: 11
>Part Number(s): 6468228
>Usage: 1967–1972 C-10 to C-30 Chevrolet and 1500 to 3500 GMC truck, Blazer, and Jimmy with gauges and V-8 engine

Oil pressure and generator warning lamps from 1967.

Note(s): Tachometer; use 1971–1972 style of lens when swapping into a 1967–1970 truck

Interchange Number: 12
Part Number(s): 6431698
Usage: 1973–1977 C-10 to C-30 Chevrolet and 1500 to 3500 GMC truck, Blazer, and Jimmy with gauges (except clock)
Note(s): Fuel gauge

Interchange Number: 13
Part Number(s): 6431731
Usage: 1973–1975 C-10 to C-30 Chevrolet and 1500 to 3500 GMC truck, Blazer, and Jimmy without gauges
Note(s): Fuel gauge

Interchange Number: 14
Part Number(s): 6432019
Usage: 1975–1978 C-10 to C-20 Chevrolet and 1500 to 2500 GMC truck (except van), Blazer, and Jimmy with gauges and clock
Note(s): Fuel gauge

Interchange Number: 15
Part Number(s): 6432173
Usage: Early-1976 C-10 to C-30 Chevrolet and 1500 to 3500 GMC (except van) without gauges or heavy-duty chassis
Note(s): Fuel gauge

Interchange Number: 16
Part Number(s): 6432170
Usage: Early-1976 C-10 to C-30 Chevrolet and 1500 to 3500 GMC truck (except van) with heavy-duty chassis, without gauges; early-1976 C-10 to C-30 Suburban
Note(s): Fuel gauge

Interchange Number: 17
Part Number(s): 6432326
Usage: Late-1976 to 1977 C-10 to C-30 Chevrolet and 1500 to 3500 GMC truck (except van) without gauges or heavy-duty chassis; 1978 CK-10 to C-30 Chevrolet truck with California emissions
Note(s): Fuel gauge has two telltale filters

Interchange Number: 18
Part Number(s): 6432321
Usage: Late-1976 to 1977 C-10 to C-30 Chevrolet and 1500 to 3500 GMC truck (except van) with heavy-duty chassis, without gauges; 1978 C-10 to C-30 Chevrolet with California emissions; late-1976 to 1978 C-10 to C-30 Suburban
Note(s): Fuel gauge has two telltale filters

Interchange Number: 19
Part Number(s): 6457888
Usage: 1967–1972 C-10 to C-30 Chevrolet and 1500 to 3500 GMC truck (except van); 1969–1972 Blazer and Jimmy—all without gauges
Note(s): Fuel gauge

Interchange Number: 20
Part Number(s): 6457910
Usage: 1969–1972 Blazer with gauges
Note(s): Fuel gauge

Interchange Number: 21
Part Number(s): 6463341
Usage: 1973–1977 C-10 to C-30 Chevrolet and 1500 to 3500 GMC (except van), Blazer, and Jimmy
Note(s): Oil pressure gauge

Interchange Number: 22
Part Number(s): 25025164
Usage: 1978 C-10 to C-30 Chevrolet and 1500 to 3500 GMC (except van), Blazer, and Jimmy with gauges
Note(s): Oil pressure gauge

Interchange Number: 23
Part Number(s): 6460746
Usage: 1967–1972 C-10 to C-30 Chevrolet and 1500 to 3500 GMC (except van); 1970–1972 Blazer and Jimmy—all with gauges
Note(s): Oil pressure gauge

Interchange Number: 24
Part Number(s): 6474468
Usage: 1973–1975 C-10 to C-30 Chevrolet and 1500 to 3500 GMC truck (except van), Blazer, and Jimmy with gauges
Note(s): Ammeter

Interchange Number: 25
Part Number(s): 6474474
Usage: 1976–1978 C-10 to C-30 Chevrolet and

A 1967–1972 fuel gauge without the gauge package.

1500 to 3500 GMC truck (except van), Blazer, and Jimmy with gauges
Note(s): Ammeter

Interchange Number: 26
Part Number(s): 1503428
Usage: 1967–1972 C-10 to C-30 Chevrolet and 1500 to 3500 GMC truck (except van), Blazer, and Jimmy
Note(s): Ammeter

Interchange Number: 27
Part Number(s): 6490371
Usage: 1973 C-10 to C-30 Chevrolet and 1500 to 3500 GMC truck (except van), Blazer, and Jimmy
Note(s): Coolant gauge

Interchange Number: 28
Part Number(s): 6490792
Usage: 1974–1978 C-10 to C-30 Chevrolet and 1500 to 3500 GMC truck (except van), Blazer, and Jimmy
Note(s): Coolant gauge

Interchange Number: 29
Part Number(s): 8988549
Usage: 1976–1977 G-10 to G-30 Chevrolet and 1500 to 3500 GMC van without gauges
Note(s): Coolant, oil, amp, and fuel gauges

Interchange Number: 30
Part Number(s): 6489838
Usage: 1967–1972 C-10 to C-30 Chevrolet and 1500 to 3500 GMC truck (except van), Blazer, and Jimmy
Note(s): Coolant gauge

Interchange Number: 31
Part Number(s): 6499466
Usage: 1973–1978 C-10 to C-30 Chevrolet and 1500 to 3500 GMC truck (except van), Blazer, and Jimmy with gauges
Note(s): Clock

Instrument Bezels
Model Identification

1967	Interchange Number
Without tachometer	1
With tachometer	7
With speed warning	8

1968
Without tachometer	28
With tachometer	6

1969–1970
Without tachometer	5
With tachometer	4

1971–1972
Without tachometer	5
With tachometer	4
With Cheyenne package	2

Blazer
without tachometer 5
with tachometer 3

1973–1974
Without Cheyenne package
without air conditioning 9
with air conditioning 10
With Cheyenne package
without air conditioning 11
with air conditioning 13
With Super Cheyenne package
without air conditioning 12
with air conditioning 13

1975–1976
Without Cheyenne, Silverado, or Scottsdale packages
without air conditioning 27
with air conditioning 15
With Cheyenne or Silverado Package
with woodgrain panel
without air conditioning 14
with air conditioning 24
With Scottsdale Package
without woodgrain panel
without air conditioning 26
with air conditioning 25

1977
Without Silverado or Scottsdale packages
without air conditioning 27
with air conditioning 15
With Silverado package
with woodgrain panel
without air conditioning 14
with air conditioning 24
without woodgrain panel
without air conditioning 22
with air conditioning 23
With Scottsdale package
without air conditioning 26
with air conditioning 25

A 1967–1972 ammeter.

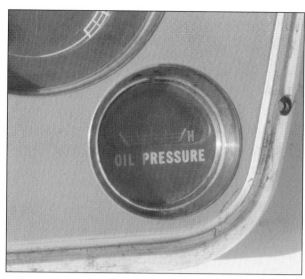

A 1967–1972 oil pressure gauge.

1978

Without Deluxe interior trim package
  without air conditioning 20
  with air conditioning 21
With Deluxe Interior trim package
  without air conditioning 16
  with air conditioning 17
With Cheyenne package
  without air conditioning 18
  with air conditioning 19

Interchanges

Interchange Number: 1
Part Number(s): 6457882
Usage: 1967 C-10 to C-30 Chevrolet truck without speed warning or tachometer

Interchange Number: 2
Part Number(s): 6497218
Usage: 1971–1972 C-10 to C-30 Chevrolet truck with Cheyenne package

Interchange Number: 3
Part Number(s): 6491403
Usage: 1970–1972 Blazer with tachometer

Interchange Number: 4
Part Number(s): 6491404
Usage: 1969–1972 C-10 to C-30 Chevrolet truck with tachometer

Interchange Number: 5
Part Number(s): 6491402
Usage: 1969–1972 C-10 to C-30 Chevrolet truck and Blazer without tachometer

Interchange Number: 6
Part Number(s): 6482927
Usage: 1968 C-10 to C-30 Chevrolet truck with tachometer and speed warning

Interchange Number: 7
Part Number(s): 6457883
Usage: 1967 C-10 to C-30 Chevrolet truck with tachometer

Interchange Number: 8
Part Number(s): 6457884
Usage: 1967 C-10 to C-30 Chevrolet truck with speed warning

Interchange Number: 9
Part Number(s): 340030
Usage: 1973–1974 C-10 to C-30 Chevrolet and 1500 to 3500 GMC truck, Blazer, and Jimmy (except with Cheyenne, Sierra, Cheyenne Super, or air conditioning, or with Custom group in 1973)

Interchange Number: 10
Part Number(s): 340026
Usage: 1973–1974 C-10 to C-30 Chevrolet and 1500 to 3500 GMC truck, Blazer, and Jimmy with air conditioning (except with Cheyenne, Sierra, or Cheyenne Super, or with Custom group in 1973)

Interchange Number: 11
Part Number(s): 340029
Usage: 1973–1974 C-10 to C-30 Chevrolet and 1500 to 3500 GMC truck, Blazer, and Jimmy with Cheyenne or Sierra packages (will not fit models with Cheyenne Super or Sierra Grande packages)—all above models without air conditioning

Interchange Number: 12
Part Number(s): 340027
Usage: 1973–1974 C-10 to C-30 Chevrolet and 1500 to 3500 GMC truck, Blazer, and Jimmy with Cheyenne Super or Sierra Grande packages—all above models without air conditioning

A 1967–1972 temperature gauge.

Interchange Number: 13
    Part Number(s): 340028
    Usage: 1973–1974 C-10 to C-30 Chevrolet and 1500 to 3500 GMC truck, Blazer, and Jimmy with Cheyenne, Super Cheyenne, Sierra, or Sierra Grande packages and air conditioning

Interchange Number: 14
    Part Number(s): 347221
    Usage: 1975–1976 C-10 to C-30 Chevrolet truck (with Silverado package) and 1500 to 3500 GMC truck (with Sierra Classic package); 1975 Blazer (with Cheyenne package) and Jimmy (with High Sierra package)—all above models without air conditioning

Interchange Number: 15
    Part Number(s): 347220
    Usage: 1975–1977 C-10 to C-30 Chevrolet truck (without Silverado package) and 1500 to 3500 GMC truck (without Sierra Classic package); 1975 Blazer (without Cheyenne package), and Jimmy (without High Sierra package)—all above models with air conditioning

Interchange Number: 16
    Part Number(s): 466706
    Usage: 1978 C-10 to C-30 Chevrolet truck and 1500 to 3500 GMC truck with Deluxe interior package, without air conditioning

Interchange Number: 17
    Part Number(s): 466705
    Usage: 1978 C-10 to C-30 Chevrolet truck and 1500 to 3500 GMC truck with Deluxe interior package and air conditioning

Interchange Number: 18
    Part Number(s): 466704
    Usage: 1978 C-10 to C-30 Chevrolet truck (with Cheyenne package) and 1500 to 3500 GMC truck (with High Sierra package), without air conditioning

Interchange Number: 19
    Part Number(s): 466703
    Usage: 1978 C-10 to C-30 Chevrolet truck (with Cheyenne package) and 1500 to 3500 GMC truck (with High Sierra package) with air conditioning

Interchange Number: 20
    Part Number(s): 466702
    Usage: 1978 C-10 to C-30 Chevrolet truck (without Cheyenne package or Deluxe interior package) and 1500 to 3500 GMC truck (without High Sierra or Deluxe interior package), without air conditioning

Interchange Number: 21
    Part Number(s): 466701
    Usage: 1978 C-10 to C-30 Chevrolet truck (without Cheyenne Package or Deluxe interior package) and 1500 to 3500 GMC truck (without High Sierra or Deluxe interior package), without air conditioning

Interchange Number: 22
    Part Number(s): 363135
    Usage: 1977 C-10 to C-30 Chevrolet truck (with Silverado package and woodgrain trim) and 1500 to 3500 GMC truck (with Sierra Classic package and woodgrain trim), without air conditioning

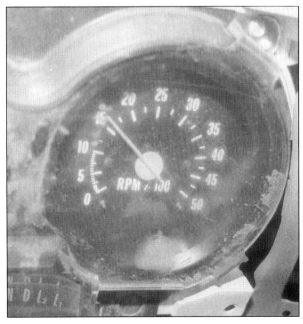

A 1973–1977 tachometer.

A 1973–1977 fuel gauge with the gauge package.

Interchange Number: 23

Part Number(s): 363136

Usage: 1977 C-10 to C-30 Chevrolet truck (with Silverado Package and woodgrain trim) and 1500 to 3500 GMC truck (with Sierra Classic package and woodgrain trim), with air conditioning

Interchange Number: 24

Part Number(s): 347222

Usage: 1975–1976 C-10 to C-30 Chevrolet truck (with Silverado Package and woodgrain trim), 1500 to 3500 GMC truck (with Sierra Classic package and woodgrain trim), Blazer (with Cheyenne package and woodgrain trim), and Jimmy (with High Sierra and woodgrain trim), all with air conditioning

Interchange Number: 25

Part Number(s): 347225

Usage: 1975–1977 C-10 to C-30 Chevrolet with Scottsdale trim package, without woodgrain panel or with air conditioning

Interchange Number: 26

Part Number(s): 347223

Usage: 1975–1977 C-10 to C-30 Chevrolet truck (with Scottsdale package without woodgrain trim) and 1500 to 3500 GMC truck (with Sierra Classic package without woodgrain trim), without air conditioning

Interchange Number: 27

Part Number(s): 347224

Usage: 1975–1977 C-10 to C-30 Chevrolet Custom Deluxe truck (without any trim packages or air conditioning) and 1500 to 3500 GMC Sierra truck (without any trim packages or air conditioning)

Interchange Number: 28

Part Number(s): 64282926

Usage: 1968 C-10 to C-30 Chevrolet without tachometer

Glovebox Compartments
Model Identification

1967–1972	Interchange Number
Without air conditioning	3
With air conditioning	4
1973–1978	
Without air conditioning	1
With air conditioning	2

Interchanges

Interchange Number: 1

Part Number(s): 343915

Usage: 1973–1982 C-10 to C-30 Chevrolet and 1500 to 3500 GMC truck without air conditioning

Interchange Number: 2

Part Number(s): 343916

Usage: 1973–1982 C-10 to C-30 Chevrolet and 1500 to 3500 GMC truck with air conditioning

Interchange Number 3

Part Number(s): 3888558

Usage: 1967–1972 C-10 to C-30 Chevrolet and 1500 to 3500 GMC truck without air conditioning

Interchange Number 4

Part Number(s): 3919291

Usage: 1967–1972 C-10 to C-30 Chevrolet and 1500 to 3500 GMC truck with air conditioning

A 1973–1977 fuel gauge without the gauge package.

An oil pressure gauge.

Glovebox Doors
Model Identification
1967–1972   **Interchange Number**
All 1
1973–1978
All 2

Interchanges
Interchange Number: 1
    Part Number(s): 3885720
    Usage: 1967–1972 C-10 to C-30 Chevrolet and 1500 to 3500 GMC truck

Interchange Number: 2
    Part Number(s): 6264131
    Usage: 1973–1982 C-10 to C-30 Chevrolet and 1500 to 3500 GMC truck

Instrument-Panel Pads
Model Identification
1967–1972   **Interchange Number**
All 2
1973–1978
All 1

Interchanges
Interchange Number: 1
    Part Number(s): 140006171
    Usage: 1973–1982 C-10 to C-30 Chevrolet and 1500 to 3500 GMC truck

Interchange Number: 2
    Part Number(s): 3968205
    Usage: 1967–1972 C-10 to C-30 Chevrolet and 1500 to 3500 GMC truck

Instrument-Panel Defrosters and Air Conditioning Outlets
Model Identification
1967–1968   **Interchange Number**
Defroster
    left 1
    right 2
Air conditioning outlets
    left 5
    center 11
    right 6
1969–1971
Defroster
    left 1
    right 2
Air conditioning outlets
    left 7
    center 11
    right 6
1972
Defroster
    left 1
    right 2
Air conditioning outlets
    left 7
    center, except Suburban 11
    center, Suburban
        without roof-mounted air conditioning 11
        with roof-mounted air conditioning 12, 14
    right 6
1973–1978
Defroster
    left 3
    right 3
Air conditioning outlets
    left 8

An ammeter.

A 1973–1977 temperature gauge without the gauge package.

Interchanges

Interchange Number: 1
Part Number(s): 341756 (left)
Location/Part: Windshield defroster outlet
Usage: 1967–1972 C-10 to C-30 Chevrolet and 1500 to 3500 GMC truck; 1969–1977 G-10 to G-30 Chevrolet and 1500 to 3500 GMC van with air conditioning (left side only), without air conditioning (both sides will fit)

Interchange Number: 2
Part Number(s): 3989620 (right)
Location/Part: Windshield defroster outlet
Usage: 1967–1972 C-10 to C-30 Chevrolet and 1500 to 3500 GMC truck

Interchange Number: 3
Part Number(s): 339839 (either side)
Location/Part: Windshield defroster outlet
Usage: 1973–1979 C-10 to C-30 Chevrolet and 1500 to 3500 GMC truck without air conditioning

Interchange Number: 4
Part Number(s): 1996506 (either side)
Location/Part: Windshield defroster outlet
Usage: 1973–1979 C-10 to C-30 Chevrolet and 1500 to 3500 GMC truck with air conditioning

Interchange Number: 5
Part Number(s): 3891271 (left)
Location/Part: Dash air conditioning outlet
Usage: 1967–1968 C-10 to C-30 Chevrolet and 1500 to 3500 GMC truck with air conditioning

Interchange Number: 6
Part Number(s): 3891272 (right)
Location/Part: Dash air conditioning outlet
Usage: 1967–1972 C-10 to C-30 Chevrolet and 1500 to 3500 GMC truck; 1969–1972 Blazer and Jimmy—all with air conditioning

Interchange Number: 7
Part Number(s): 3938491 (left)
Location/Part: Dash air conditioning outlet
Usage: 1969–1972 C-10 to C-30 Chevrolet and 1500 to 3500 GMC truck, Blazer, and Jimmy with air conditioning

Interchange Number: 8
Part Number(s): 14040873 (left); 469342 (right)
Location/Part: Dash air conditioning outlet
Usage: 1973–1978 C-10 to C-30 Chevrolet and 1500 to 3500 GMC truck, Blazer, and Jimmy with air conditioning

Interchange Number: 9
Part Number(s): 6262679
Location/Part: Dash air conditioning center outlet
Usage: 1973–1978 C-10 to C-30 Chevrolet and 1500 to 3500 GMC truck, Blazer, and Jimmy with air conditioning

Interchange Number: 10
Part Number(s): 3979751
Location/Part: Dash air conditioning center outlet (driver's side)
Usage: 1973–1978 C-10 to C-30 Chevrolet and 1500 to 3500 GMC truck, Blazer, and Jimmy with air conditioning; 1975–1979 G-10 to G-30 Chevrolet and 1500 to 3500 GMC van with air conditioning

Interchange Number: 11
Part Number(s): 3891275
Location/Part: Dash air conditioning center outlet
Usage: 1967–1972 C-10 to C-30 Chevrolet and 1500 to 3500 GMC truck; 1969–1972 Blazer and Jimmy—all with air conditioning (except Suburban with roof-mounted air conditioning)

Interchange Number: 12
Part Number(s): 3999573
Location/Part: Outlet for roof-mounted air conditioning
Usage: 1972 Chevrolet Suburban
Note(s): Overall length is 5 3/8 inches

Interchange Number: 14
Part Number(s): 3999574
Location/Part: Outlet for roof-mounted air conditioning

A 1967–1968 instrument bezel has a wiper and lights on the left-hand side.

A 1967–1968 instrument bezel has a choke opening on the right-hand side.

Usage: 1972 Chevrolet Suburban
Note(s): Overall length is 3 1/16 inches

Vent Assemblies
Model Identification
1967–1968	*Interchange Number*
Vent assembly	1
Rod control	3
Knob	4

1969–1972
Vent assembly 2
Rod control 3
Knob 5

1973–1978
Vent assembly 7
Inside baffle
    without Silverado package 8
    with Silverado package 9
Rod control 6

Interchanges
Interchange Number: 1
    Part: Vent valve assembly
    Usage: 1967–1968 C-10 to C-30 Chevrolet and 1500 to 3500 GMC truck

Interchange Number: 2
    Part Number(s): 3997091 (left); 3997092 (right)
    Part: Vent valve assembly
    Usage: 1969–1972 C-10 to C-30 Chevrolet and 1500 to 3500 GMC truck

Interchange Number: 3
    Part Number(s): 3940734 (fits either side)
    Part: Vent valve opening rod

Usage: 1967–1972 C-10 to C-30 Chevrolet and 1500 to 3500 GMC truck, G-10 to G-30 Chevrolet and 1500 to 3500 GMC van without air conditioning

Interchange Number: 4
    Part: Vent valve opening rod knob
    Usage: 1967–1968 C-10 to C-30 Chevrolet and 1500 to 3500 GMC truck

Interchange Number: 5
    Part Number(s): 3940732
    Part: Vent valve opening rod knob
    Usage: 1969–1972 C-10 to C-30 Chevrolet and 1500 to 3500 GMC truck; 1969–1977 G-10 to G-30 Chevrolet and 1500 to 3500 GMC van without air conditioning

Interchange Number: 6
    Part Number(s): 466717 (fits either side)
    Part: Vent valve opening rod
    Usage: 1973–1978 C-10 to C-30 Chevrolet and 1500 to 3500 GMC truck without air conditioning

Interchange Number: 7
    Part Number(s): 459851 (fits either side)
    Part: Vent valve
    Usage: 1973–1978 C-10 to C-30 Chevrolet and 1500 to 3500 GMC truck without air conditioning (passenger's side only with air conditioning)

Interchange Number: 8
    Part Number(s): 15590405 (left); 14025854 (right)
    Part: Vent baffle
    Usage: 1973–1978 C-10 to C-30 Chevrolet and 1500 to 3500 GMC truck without air conditioning and without Silverado or Sierra Classic trim packages

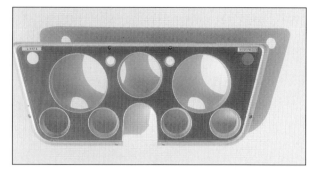

A 1969–1972 instrument bezel.

Interchange Number: 9

Part Number(s): 14032805 (fits either side)
Part: Vent baffle
Usage: 1975–1978 C-10 to C-30 Chevrolet truck with Silverado package and 1500 to 3500 GMC truck with Sierra Classic package

Seat Adjustment Rails

Seat type and seat position (in the case of bucket seats) will have the greatest effect on the interchange here. Rails are matched in pairs, so a set from a driver's side will not fit the passenger's side in most cases, nor will those from a bench seat fit bucket seats. Bucket seats were part of the CST packages in some models.

Model Identification

1967	Interchange Number
Bench seat	19

1968
Bench seat 20

1969–1970
Except Blazer or Suburban
 bench seat 4, 21
 bucket seat
  driver's side 1
  passenger's side 1
Blazer or Suburban
 bench seat 3, 4
 bucket seat
  driver's side 1
  passenger's side 1

1971–1972
Except Blazer or Suburban
 bench seat 5
 bucket seat
  driver's side 2, 12
  passenger's side 2, 12
Blazer or Suburban
 bench seat 5
 bucket seat
  driver's side 2, 12
  passenger's side 2, 12

1973–1976
Except Blazer
 bench seat
  two-door 6, 7
  four-door 10
 bucket seat 6, 7
Blazer
 1973–1974
  driver's side .13
  passenger's side 13
 1975–1976
  driver's side .14
  passenger's side 15

1977
early 1977
 bench seat, two-door, except Blazer 6, 7
 bench seat, four-door, except Blazer 10
 bucket seat, except Blazer 6, 7
late 1977
 bench seat
  two-door 8, 9
  four-door 11
 bucket seat, except Suburban or Blazer
  driver's side .18
  passenger's side 19
 bucket seat, Suburban
  driver's side .16
  passenger's side 17
 bucket seat, Blazer
  driver's side .14
  passenger's side 15

1978
Bench seat, except Blazer
 two-door 8, 9
 four-door 11

A bezel from a 2-ton truck looks similar but will not interchange due to the small steering column cut out. A 2-ton is on the left, and a 1/2- to 1-ton is on the right.

Instrument panel bezels with air conditioning from 1973 to 1978 are at top. Those without air conditioning are at bottom.

Bucket seat

Interchanges

Interchange Number: 1
Part Number(s): 3951701 (left); 3951700 (left)
Seat Type: Bucket (driver's and passenger's sides)
Usage: 1969–1970 Chevrolet C-10 to C-30 truck, Blazer, Suburban, and GMC Jimmy with bucket seats

Interchange Number: 2
Part Number(s): 6264255 (left)
Seat Type: Bucket (driver's side)
Usage: 1971–1972 Chevrolet C-10 to C-30 (except Suburban and Blazer) and 1500 to 3500 GMC truck (except Carryall and Jimmy) with bucket seats; 1972 Blazer and Jimmy with bucket seats

Interchange Number: 3
Part Number(s): 3973403 (left)
Seat Type: Bench
Usage: 1969–1970 Chevrolet Blazer, Suburban, and GMC Jimmy without bucket seats

Interchange Number: 4
Part Number(s): 3973400 (right)
Seat Type: Bench
Usage: 1969–1970 Chevrolet C-10 to C-30 (including Blazer and Suburban) and GMC 1500 to 3500 truck (including Carryall and Jimmy) without bucket seats

Interchange Number: 5
Part Number(s): 6264247 (left); 6264252 (right)
Seat Type: Bench
Usage: 1971–1972 Chevrolet C-10 to C-60 (including Blazer and Suburban) and 1500 to 6500 GMC (including Carryall and Jimmy) without bucket seats

Interchange Number: 6
Part Number(s): 3999328 (right)
Seat Type: Bench or bucket
Usage: 1973 to early-1977 Chevrolet C-10 to C-30 (except four-door cab and Suburban models) and 1500 to 3500 GMC (except four-door cab or Carryall models)
Note(s): Will not fit Blazer models

Interchange Number: 7
Part Number(s): 459871 (left)
Seat Type: Bench or bucket
Usage: 1973 to early-1977 Chevrolet C-10 to C-30 (except four-door cab and Suburban models) and 1500 to 3500 GMC (except four-door cab and Carryall models)
Note(s): Will not fit Blazer or Jimmy models

Interchange Number: 8
Part Number(s): 465502 (right)
Seat Type: Bench
Usage: Late-1977 to 1980 Chevrolet C-10 to C-30 (except four-door cab and Suburban models) and 1500 to 3500 GMC (except four-door cab and Carryall models)
Note(s): Will not fit Blazer or Jimmy models

Interchange Number: 9
Part Number(s): 465501 (left)
Seat Type: Bench
Usage: Late-1977 to 1980 Chevrolet C-10 to C-30 (except four-door cab and Suburban models)

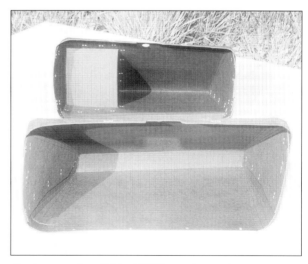

Glovebox inserts from 1967 to 1972. Those with air conditioning are at top, and those without air conditioning are at bottom.

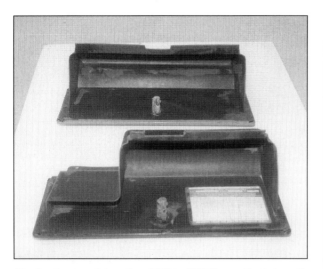

Glovebox inserts and doors from 1973 to 1978. Those without air conditioning are at top, and those with air conditioning are at bottom.

and 1500 to 3500 GMC (except four-door cab and Carryall models)

Interchange Number: 10
Part Number(s): 459873 (left); 6264174 (right)
Seat Type: Bench or bucket
Usage: 1973 to early-1977 Chevrolet C-10 to C-30 four-door cab and Suburban models, and 1500 to 3500 GMC four-door cab and Carryall models

Interchange Number: 11
Part Number(s): 465503 (left); 465504 (right)
Seat Type: Bench
Usage: Late-1977 to 1980 Chevrolet C-10 to C-30 four-door cab and Suburban models; and 1500 to 3500 GMC, four-door cab or Carryall models

Interchange Number: 12
Part Number(s): 6264256 (right)
Seat Type: Bucket (driver's side)
Usage: 1972 Chevrolet C-10 to C-30 (includes Blazer and Suburban models) and 1500 to 3500 GMC (includes Jimmy and Carryall models)

Interchange Number: 13
Part Number(s): 329061 (left); 329062 (right)
Seat Type: Bucket (driver's or passenger's side)
Usage: 1973–1974 Chevrolet Blazer and GMC Jimmy

Interchange Number: 14
Part Number(s): 340061 (left); 340062 (right)
Seat Type: Bucket (driver's side)
Usage: 1975–1980 Chevrolet Blazer and GMC Jimmy

Interchange Number: 15
Part Number(s): 340063 (left); 340064 (right)
Seat Type: Bucket (passenger's side)

Usage: 1975–1980 Chevrolet Blazer and GMC Jimmy

Interchange Number: 16
Part Number(s): 473981 (left); 473982 (right)
Seat Type: Bucket (driver's side)
Usage: Late-1977 to 1980 Chevrolet Suburban and GMC Carryall with bucket seats

Interchange Number: 17
Part Number(s): 14004721 (left); 14004722 (right)
Seat Type: Bucket (passenger's side)
Usage: Late-1977 to 1980 Chevrolet Suburban and GMC Carryall with bucket seats

Interchange Number: 18
Part Number(s): 465505 (left); 465506 (right)
Seat Type: Bucket
Usage: Late-1977 to 1980 Chevrolet C-10 to C-30 (except Suburban) and 1500 to 3500 GMC (except Carryall) with bucket seats

Interchange Number: 19
Part Number(s): 3897289 (left); 3897646 (right)
Seat Type: Bench
Usage: 1967 Chevrolet C-10 to C-30 and 1500 to 3500 GMC (except van)

Interchange Number: 20
Part Number(s): 3934351 (left); 3934352 (right)
Seat Type: Bench
Usage: 1968 Chevrolet C-10 to C-30 (except Suburban) and 1500 to 3500 GMC (except van)

Interchange Number: 21
Part Number(s): 3937393 (right)
Seat Type: Bench
Usage: 1969–1970 Chevrolet C-10 to C-30 (except Suburban and Blazer) and 1500 to 3500 GMC (except van)

Seat Frames

Even though there are certain similarities between certain seats, other factors must be weighed in when swapping seats. There is no mention of color in this interchange because this interchange is for the bare frame only, without cover or foam padding. Carefully inspect the seat for signs of repair or damage. Next, make sure the springs are tight and not broken or sagging. Note that many seats are sold with their seat adjustment rails, so you may want to cross-reference that section in this chapter.

Model Identification

1967–1972	Interchange Number
Bench seat	10
Bucket	11
Blazer	12

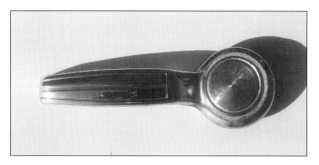

An inside door handle from 1967 to 1972.

An inside door handle from 1973 to 1978.

1973–1976
Bench seat
    two-door 1
    four-door 2
Bucket seat
    except Blazer 7
    Blazer
        1973–1974 5
        1975–1978 6

1977
Bench seat
    two-door
        early 1
        late 3
    four-door
        early 2
        late 4
Bucket seat
    except Blazer 7
    Blazer 6

1978
Bench seat
    two-door 3
    four-door 4
Bucket seat
    except Blazer or Suburban 8
    Blazer 6
    Suburban 9

Interchanges

Interchange Number: 1
    Seat Type: Bench (folding)
    Usage: 1973 to early-1977 C-10 to C-30 Chevrolet and 1500 to 3500 GMC cab-style truck (except four-door cab and Suburban models)

Interchange Number: 2
    Seat Type: Bench (fixed)
    Usage: 1973 to early-1977 C-10 to C-30 Chevrolet and 1500 to 3500 GMC four-door cab truck
    Note(s): Front seat

Interchange Number: 3
    Seat Type: Bench (folding)
    Usage: Late-1977 to 1978 C-10 to C-30 Chevrolet 1500 to 3500 GMC cab-style truck (except four-door cab and Suburban models)

Interchange Number: 4
    Seat Type: Bench (fixed)
    Usage: Late-1977 to 1978 C-10 to C-30 Chevrolet and 1500 to 3500 GMC four-door cab-style truck

Interchange Number: 5
    Seat Type: Bucket
    Usage: 1973–1974 Blazer and Jimmy

Interchange Number: 6
    Seat Type: Bucket
    Usage: 1975–1979 Blazer and Jimmy

Interchange Number: 7
    Seat Type: Bucket
    Usage: 1973–1977 C-10 to C-30 Chevrolet truck (except Blazer) and 1500 to 3500 GMC truck (except van and Jimmy)

Interchange Number: 8
    Seat Type: Bucket
    Usage: 1978–1980 C-10 to C-30 Chevrolet truck (except Blazer and Suburban) and 1500 to 3500 GMC truck (except van, Jimmy, and Carryall)

Interchange Number: 9
    Seat Type: Bucket
    Usage: 1978–1980 C-10 to C-20 Chevrolet Suburban and GMC Carryall

Interchange Number: 10
    Seat type: Bench
    Usage: 1967–1972 C-10 to C-30 Chevrolet, 1500–3500 GMC truck except Blazer or Suburban

Interchange Number: 11
    Seat type: Bucket
    Usage: 1967–1972 C-10 to C-30 Chevrolet, 1500–3500 GMC truck

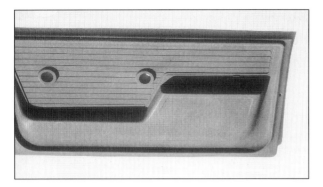

The standard 1972 door panel.

A Custom 1972 door panel.

Interchange Number: 12
Seat type: Bench
Usage: 1969–1972 Blazer, 1970–1972 Jimmy

Sun Visors
Model Identification

1967–1972	Interchange Number
Except Blazer	1
Blazer	
driver's side	3
passenger's side	2
1973–1978	
All models	
driver's side	4
passenger's side	5

Interchanges
Interchange Number: 1
Part Number(s): 3944430
Position: Fits either side
Usage: 1967–1972 C-10 to C-30 Chevrolet truck (all body styles except Blazer) and 1500 to 3500 GMC truck (all body styles except Jimmy and van)

Interchange Number: 2
Part Number(s): 3964368
Position: Passenger's side
Usage: 1969–1972 Blazer and Jimmy
Note(s): Support clip is not interchangeable between 1969–1970 and 1971–1972 models; clip will swap sides

Interchange Number: 3
Part Number(s): 3964367
Position: Driver's side
Usage: 1969–1972 Blazer and Jimmy
Note(s): Support clip is not interchangeable between 1969–1970 and 1971–1972 models; clip will swap sides

Interchange Number: 4
Part Number(s): 14013753
Position: Driver's side

Usage: 1973–1978 C-10 to C-30 Chevrolet truck (all body styles including Blazer) and 1500 to 3500 GMC truck (all body styles except van)

Interchange Number: 5
Part Number(s): 14013754
Position: Passenger's side
Usage: 1973–1978 C-10 to C-30 Chevrolet truck (all body styles including Blazer) and 1500 to 3500 GMC truck (all body styles except van)

Inside Door Panels
Model Identification

1967–1971	Interchange Number
All	10
1972	
Standard	11
Custom	12
Cheyenne	12
1973–1974	
Except Blazer	
Custom	1
Custom Deluxe	3
Super Custom	3
Blazer	
except Cheyenne or Custom	2
Custom	1
Cheyenne	4

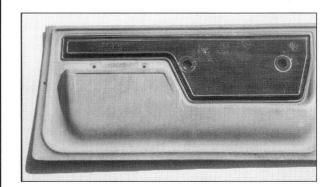

The 1972 Cheyenne door panel had a wood trim insert. A Custom door panel can be modified with this insert.

A standard 1973–1975 door panel.

1975–1976
Except Blazer
    Custom Deluxe 1
    Scottsdale 3
    Silverado 4
Blazer
    except Cheyenne or Custom 2
    Custom 1
    Cheyenne 4

1977–1978
Except Blazer
    two-door models
        Custom Deluxe 5
        Scottsdale 6
        Silverado 7
    four-door models, front door
        Custom Deluxe 5
        Scottsdale 6
        Silverado 7
    four-door models, rear door
        Custom Deluxe 8
        Scottsdale 8
        Silverado 9
Blazer
    except Cheyenne or Custom 5
    Custom 6
    Cheyenne 7

Interchanges

Interchange Number: 1
Part Number(s): 351387 (left); 351388 (right)
Usage: 1973–1974 C-10 to C-30 Chevrolet Custom and 1500 to 3500 GMC Standard Custom truck; 1973–1974 Blazer Custom and Jimmy Standard Custom; 1975–1976 C-10 to C-30 Chevrolet truck and Blazer with Custom Deluxe package, GMC 1500 to 3500 truck and Jimmy with Sierra package

Interchange Number: 2
Part Number(s): 351353 (left); 351354 (right)
Usage: 1973–1976 Blazer without Custom, Custom Deluxe, or Cheyenne package; 1973 to 1976 Jimmy without Standard Custom, Sierra, or High Sierra package

Interchange Number: 3
Part Number(s): 351363 (left); 351364 (right)
Usage: 1973–1974 C-10 to C-30 Chevrolet Custom Deluxe and Super Custom; 1973–1974 1500 to 3500 GMC truck with Custom Deluxe package; 1975–1976 C-10 to C-30 Chevrolet truck with Scottsdale package; 1976 Chevrolet C-10 with Sprint of 76 package

Interchange Number: 4
Part Number(s): 351375 (left); 351376 (right)
Usage: 1973–1976 C-10 to C-30 Chevrolet truck and Blazer with Cheyenne, Super Cheyenne, or Silverado package; 1973–1976 1500 to 3500 GMC truck and Jimmy with Sierra Grande Classic (Sierra Grande for 1973–1974) or High Sierra package

Interchange Number: 5
Part Number(s): 14014261 (left); 14014262 (right)
Usage: 1977–1978 C-10 to C-30 Chevrolet truck and Blazer without Cheyenne, Scottsdale, or Silverado package; 1977–1978 1500 to 3500 GMC truck and Jimmy without Sierra Classic, Sierra Grande, or High Sierra package

Interchange Number: 6
Part Number(s): 14014265 (left); 14014266 (right)
Usage: 1977–1978 C-10 to C-30 Chevrolet truck with Scottsdale package and 1500 to 3500 GMC truck with Sierra Grande package

Interchange Number: 7
Part Number(s): 14014255 (left); 14014256 (right)
Usage: 1977–1978 C-10 to C-30 Chevrolet truck with Silverado package, Blazer with Cheyenne package, 1500 to 3500 GMC truck with Sierra Classic package, and Jimmy with High Sierra package

Interchange Number: 8
Part Number(s): 14014277 (left); 14014278 (right)
Usage: 1977–1978 C-10 to C-30 Chevrolet four-door cab truck without Silverado package and 1500 to 3500 GMC four-door cab truck without Sierra Classic package

Interchange Number: 9
Part Number(s): 14014279 (left); 14014280 (right)
Usage: 1977–1978 C-10 to C-30 Chevrolet four-door cab truck with Silverado package and 1500 to 3500 GMC four-door cab truck with Sierra Classic package

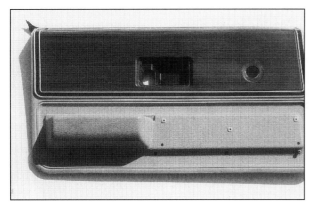

A 1973–1974 door panel with Cheyenne trim.

Interchange Number: 10
   Usage: 1967–1971 C-10 to C-30 Chevrolet truck
   Note(s): Metal units
Interchange Number: 11
   Usage: 1972 C-10 to C-30 Chevrolet truck, except
      with Cheyenne or Custom Package
Interchange Number: 12
   Usage: 1972 C-10 to C-30 Chevrolet truck with
      Custom or Cheyenne Package
   Note(s): Cheyenne Package has wood inserts

Inside Door Handles
Model Identification

1967	Interchange Number
All	4
1968–1971	
All	5
1972	
All	6
1973–1976	
All	1
1977–1978	
Two-door models	2
Four-door models	
front door	2
rear door	3

Interchanges
Interchange Number: 1
   Part Number(s): 6274561 (left); 6274562 (right)
   Usage: 1973–1976 C-10 to C-30 Chevrolet truck
      and Blazer; 1973–1976 1500 to 3500 GMC
      truck and Jimmy—all models
Interchange Number: 2
   Part Number(s): 458031 (left); 458032 (right)
   Usage: 1977–1979 C-10 to C-30 Chevrolet truck
      and Blazer; 1977–1979 1500 to 3500 GMC
      truck and Jimmy—all models
   Note(s): Front door only

Interchange Number: 3
   Part Number(s): 458033 (left); 458034 (right)
   Usage: 1977–1979 C-10 to C-30 Chevrolet four-
      door truck and Suburban; 1977–1979 1500 to
      3500 GMC four-door truck and Carryall
   Note(s): Rear door only
Interchange Number: 4
   Part Number(s): 3916981 (left); 3961982 (right)
   Usage: 1967 C-10 to C-30 Chevrolet truck and
      1500 to 3500 GMC truck (except van)
Interchange Number: 5
   Part Number(s): 3970833 (left); 3970834 (right)
   Usage: 1968–1971 C-10 to C-30 Chevrolet truck
      and 1500 to 3500 GMC truck (except van);
      1969–1971 Blazer; 1970–1971 Jimmy
Interchange Number: 6
   Part Number(s): 3993125 (left); 3993126 (right)
   Usage: 1972 C-10 to C-30 Chevrolet truck and
      1500 to 3500 GMC truck (except van)

Consoles
Model Identification

1967–1975	Interchange Number
All	1
1976	
Early	1
Late	2
1977–1978	
All	2

Interchanges
Interchange Number: 1
   Usage: 1967 to early-1976 C-10 to C-30 Chevrolet
      truck and 1500 to 3500 GMC truck with buck-
      et seats; 1969 to early-1976 Blazer; 1970 to
      early-1976 Jimmy with bucket seats
   Part Numbers: 331611 (lower); 331612 (upper);
      331613 (door)
   Note(s): Interchange Number 2 will fit if swapped as
      an entire unit. Early models have a separate
      appliqué insert; later models do not. Lower
      section and door will fit either application.
Interchange Number: 2
   Part numbers: 331611 (lower); 458089 (upper);
      331613 (door)
   Usage: Late-1976 to 1979 C-10 to C-30 Chevrolet
      truck and Blazer; late-1976 to 1979 1500 to
      3500 GMC truck and Jimmy with bucket seats
   Note(s): Interchange Number 1 will fit if swapped as
      an entire unit. Early models have a separate
      appliqué insert; later models do not. Lower
      section and door will fit either application.

Instrument Dash Plaques
Model Identification

1967–1968	Interchange Number
With CC or CST	6

1969–1972

Custom	7
CST	8
Cheyenne Super (1971–1972 only)	9

1973–1974

Custom	1

1975–1976

Cheyenne	2
Custom Deluxe	3
Silverado	4

1977–1978

Custom Deluxe	3
Silverado	4
Bonanza	5

Interchanges

Interchange Number: 1
Part Number(s): 330493
Style: Custom Chevrolet
Usage: 1973–1974 C-10 to C-30 Chevrolet truck and Blazer

Interchange Number: 2
Part Number(s): 347701
Style: Cheyenne
Usage: 1975–1978 C-10 to C-30 Chevrolet truck and Blazer

Interchange Number: 3
Part Number(s): 347707
Style: Custom Deluxe
Usage: 1975–1978 C-10 to C-30 Chevrolet truck and Blazer

Interchange Number: 4
Part Number(s): 347705
Style: Silverado
Usage: 1975–1978 C-10 to C-30 Chevrolet truck

Interchange Number: 5
Part Number(s): 363375
Style: Bonanza
Usage: 1977–1978 C-10 to C-30 Chevrolet truck

Interchange Number: 6
Part Number(s): 3886754
Style: CST
Usage: 1967–1968 C-10 to C-30 Chevrolet truck with CST package

Interchange Number: 7
Part Number(s): 3951770
Style: Custom
Usage: 1969–1972 C-10 to C-30 Chevrolet truck

Interchange Number: 8
Part Number(s): 3951772
Style: CST
Usage: 1969–1972 C-10 to C-30 Chevrolet truck

Interchange Number: 9
Part Number(s): 3999388
Style: Cheyenne Super
Usage: 1971–1972 C-10 to C-30 Chevrolet truck

Inside Rearview Mirrors
Model Identification

1967–1971	Interchange Number
All	1

1972–1978

All	2

Interchanges

Interchange Number: 1
Part Number(s): 911580
Usage: 1967–1971 C-10 to C-30 Chevrolet and 1500 to 3500 GMC truck; 1967–1971 G-10 to G-30 Chevrolet and 1500 to 3500 GMC van; 1969–1971 Blazer; 1970–1971 Jimmy

Interchange Number: 2
Part Number(s): 911582
Usage: 1972–1979 C-10 to C-30 Chevrolet and 1500 to 3500 GMC truck, G-10 to G-30 Chevrolet and 1500 to 3500 GMC van, Blazer, and Jimmy

Index